D0660745

Red Hat® Linux®
Administrator's
Handbook

Red Hat® Linux® Administrator's Handbook

Mohammed J. Kabir

M&T Books

An imprint of IDG Books Worldwide, Inc.

Foster City, CA ■ Chicago, IL ■ Indianapolis, IN ■ New York, NY

Red Hat° Linux° Administrator's Handbook
Published by
M&T Books
An imprint of IDG Books Worldwide, Inc.
919 E. Hillsdale Blvd., Suite 400
Foster City, CA 94404
www.idgbooks.com (IDG Books Worldwide Web site)

Copyright © 2000 IDG Books Worldwide, Inc. All
rights reserved. No part of this book, including interior
design, cover design, and icons, may be reproduced or
transmitted in any form, by any means (electronic,
photocopying, recording, or otherwise) without the
prior written permission of the publisher.

The image of the Linux penguin, Tux, was created by Larry
Ewing (lewing@isc.tamu.edu) using the Gimp
(http://www.gimp.org/) and was subsequently
modified for use by IDG Books Worldwide on this book's
cover by Tuomas Kuosmanen (tigert@gimp.org).
Tuomas also used the Gimp for his work with Tux.

ISBN: 0-7645-4637-6

Printed in the United States of America

10 9 8 7 6 5 4 3 2 1

1O/RR/QR/QQ/FC

Distributed in the United States by IDG Books
Worldwide, Inc.

Distributed by CDG Books Canada Inc. for Canada;
by Transworld Publishers Limited in the United
Kingdom; by IDG Norge Books for Norway; by IDG
Sweden Books for Sweden; by IDG Books Australia
Publishing Corporation Pty. Ltd. for Australia and
New Zealand; by TransQuest Publishers Pte Ltd. for
Singapore, Malaysia, Thailand, Indonesia, and Hong
Kong; by Gotop Information Inc. for Taiwan; by ICG
Muse, Inc. for Japan; by Intersoft for South Africa; by
Eyrolles for France; by International Thomson
Publishing for Germany, Austria and Switzerland; by
Distribuidora Cuspide for Argentina; by LR
International for Brazil; by Galileo Libros for Chile; by
Ediciones ZETA S.C.R. Ltda. for Peru; by WS
Computer Publishing Corporation, Inc., for the
Philippines; by Contemporanea de Ediciones for
Venezuela; by Express Computer Distributors for the
Caribbean and West Indies; by Micronesia Media
Distributor, Inc. for Micronesia; by Chips

Computadoras S.A. de C.V. for Mexico; by Editorial
Norma de Panama S.A. for Panama; by American
Bookshops for Finland.

For general information on IDG Books Worldwide's
books in the U.S., please call our Consumer Customer
Service department at 800-762-2974. For reseller
information, including discounts and premium sales,
please call our Reseller Customer Service department
at 800-434-3422.

For information on where to purchase IDG Books
Worldwide's books outside the U.S., please contact our
International Sales department at 317-596-5530 or fax
317-596-5692.

For consumer information on foreign language translations, please contact our Customer Service department
at 800-434-3422, fax 317-596-5692, or e-mail
rights@idgbooks.com.

For information on licensing foreign or domestic
rights, please phone 650-655-3109.

For sales inquiries and special prices for bulk quanti-
ties, please contact our Sales department at
650-655-3200 or write to the address above.

For information on using IDG Books Worldwide's
books in the classroom or for ordering examination
copies, please contact our Educational Sales department at 800-434-2086 or fax 317-596-5499.

For press review copies, author interviews, or other
publicity information, please contact our Public
Relations department at 650-655-3000 or fax
650-655-3299.

For authorization to photocopy items for corporate,
personal, or educational use, please contact Copyright
Clearance Center, 222 Rosewood Drive, Danvers, MA
01923, or fax 978-750-4470.

Library of Congress Cataloging-in-Publication Data
Kabir, Mohammed J., 1971-
   Red Hat Linux administrator's handbook /
Mohammed J. Kabir.
      p. cm.
   ISBN 0-7645-4637-6 (alk. paper)
   1. Linux. 2. Operating systems (Computers) I.
Title.
QA76.76.063 K313 2000
005.4'469--dc21

 is a registered trademark or trademark
under exclusive license to
IDG Books Worldwide, Inc. from
International Data Group, Inc.
in the United States and/or other countries.

 is a registered trademark of
IDG Books Worldwide, Inc.,

ABOUT IDG BOOKS WORLDWIDE

Welcome to the world of IDG Books Worldwide.

IDG Books Worldwide, Inc., is a subsidiary of International Data Group, the world's largest publisher of computer-related information and the leading global provider of information services on information technology. IDG was founded more than 30 years ago by Patrick J. McGovern and now employs more than 9,000 people worldwide. IDG publishes more than 290 computer publications in over 75 countries. More than 90 million people read one or more IDG publications each month.

Launched in 1990, IDG Books Worldwide is today the #1 publisher of best-selling computer books in the United States. We are proud to have received eight awards from the Computer Press Association in recognition of editorial excellence and three from Computer Currents' First Annual Readers' Choice Awards. Our best-selling ...For Dummies® series has more than 50 million copies in print with translations in 31 languages. IDG Books Worldwide, through a joint venture with IDG's Hi-Tech Beijing, became the first U.S. publisher to publish a computer book in the People's Republic of China. In record time, IDG Books Worldwide has become the first choice for millions of readers around the world who want to learn how to better manage their businesses.

Our mission is simple: Every one of our books is designed to bring extra value and skill-building instructions to the reader. Our books are written by experts who understand and care about our readers. The knowledge base of our editorial staff comes from years of experience in publishing, education, and journalism — experience we use to produce books to carry us into the new millennium. In short, we care about books, so we attract the best people. We devote special attention to details such as audience, interior design, use of icons, and illustrations. And because we use an efficient process of authoring, editing, and desktop publishing our books electronically, we can spend more time ensuring superior content and less time on the technicalities of making books.

You can count on our commitment to deliver high-quality books at competitive prices on topics you want to read about. At IDG Books Worldwide, we continue in the IDG tradition of delivering quality for more than 30 years. You'll find no better book on a subject than one from IDG Books Worldwide.

John Kilcullen
Chairman and CEO
IDG Books Worldwide, Inc.

Steven Berkowitz
President and Publisher
IDG Books Worldwide, Inc.

VIII
WINNER
*Eighth Annual
Computer Press
Awards ≥1992*

IX
WINNER
*Ninth Annual
Computer Press
Awards ≥1993*

WINNER

X
WINNER
*Tenth Annual
Computer Press
Awards ≥1994*

XI
WINNER
*Eleventh Annual
Computer Press
Awards ≥1995*

IDG is the world's leading IT media, research and exposition company. Founded in 1964, IDG had 1997 revenues of $2.05 billion and has more than 9,000 employees worldwide. IDG offers the widest range of media options that reach IT buyers in 75 countries representing 95% of worldwide IT spending. IDG's diverse product and services portfolio spans six key areas including print publishing, online publishing, expositions and conferences, market research, education and training, and global marketing services. More than 90 million people read one or more of IDG's 290 magazines and newspapers, including IDG's leading global brands — Computerworld, PC World, Network World, Macworld and the Channel World family of publications. IDG Books Worldwide is one of the fastest-growing computer book publishers in the world, with more than 700 titles in 36 languages. The "...For Dummies®" series alone has more than 50 million copies in print. IDG offers online users the largest network of technology-specific Web sites around the world through IDG.net (http://www.idg.net), which comprises more than 225 targeted Web sites in 55 countries worldwide. International Data Corporation (IDC) is the world's largest provider of information technology data, analysis and consulting, with research centers in over 41 countries and more than 400 research analysts worldwide. IDG World Expo is a leading producer of more than 168 globally branded conferences and expositions in 35 countries including E3 (Electronic Entertainment Expo), Macworld Expo, ComNet, Windows World Expo, ICE (Internet Commerce Expo), Agenda, DEMO, and Spotlight. IDG's training subsidiary, ExecuTrain, is the world's largest computer training company, with more than 230 locations worldwide and 785 training courses. IDG Marketing Services helps industry-leading IT companies build international brand recognition by developing global integrated marketing programs via IDG's print, online and exposition products worldwide. Further information about the company can be found at www.idg.com.   1/24/99

Credits

Acquisitions Editor
Laura Lewin

Project Editor
Eric Newman

Technical Editor
Matt Hayden

Copy Editors
Mildred Sanchez
Bill McManus

Project Coordinators
Linda Marousek
Louigene A. Santos

Quality Control Specialists
Chris Weisbart
Laura Taflinger

Graphics and Production Specialists
Mario Amador
Michael Lewis
Jude Levinson
Dina Quan
Ramses Ramirez
Victor Perez-Varela

Book Designer
Kurt Krames

Illustrator
Mary Jo Richards

Proofreading and Indexing
York Production Services

About the Author

Mohammed J. Kabir is the chief technology officer and a co-founder of Integration Logic, Inc. At work, he designed and developed FormServ, an affordable, permission-based e-messaging service for organizations of all sizes. Kabir studied computer engineering at California State University, Sacramento, and is also the author of *Red Hat Linux 6 Server*, *Apache Server Bible*, *Apache Server Administrator's Handbook*, and *CGI Primer Plus for Windows*. You can find more information about him at his public Web site, http://www.nitec.com. He can also be reached via e-mail at kabir@integrationlogic.com.

To my high school teachers in Bangladesh

Preface

Welcome to *Red Hat Linux Administrator's Handbook*. If you are a practicing Red Hat Linux administrator, you will find this book very handy.

In this book you will find practical information about how you can manage users, disk quotas, processes, and networks; how to set up a DNS server, an SMTP/POP3 e-mail server, a Web server, an FTP server, an NFS server, a Samba-based file and print server; and more. You will be able to enhance system and network security using various tools and techniques and also custom-compile the Linux kernel to fine-tune your system for higher performance.

This book is about the serious job of keeping your organization's Linux servers and workstations up and running. If you want to experience the many months or even longer of uptime that many successful Red Hat Linux administrators enjoy, start reading this book.

How This Book Is Organized

I have organized the book into three parts.

Part I: Installation and Basic Configuration

Part I will get you started with the installation of Red Hat Linux and the necessary configuration to get it up and running. You will find useful information on how to customize your Red Hat installation, how to boot up and shut down a Linux system, how to manage files and directories, and how to use the new administrative tool Linuxconf.

Part II: Advanced Configuration

The most important section of the book, Part II deals with user, process, and intranet/Internet service configuration and administration.

Chapters in this part cover:

- Managing users and groups and implementing disk quotas
- Sending signals to a running process, controlling process priority, monitoring processes using various utilities, automating process execution via the Cron facility, and logging information from processes using the Syslog facility
- TCP/IP networking, classifying IP networks, configuring your server's network interfaces, and creating sub-nets
- Configuring BIND as DNS server and performing load balancing using DNS
- Setting up DNS for SMTP mail service, configuring sendmail for SMTP mail service, enabling anti-spam measures, and setting up a Post Office Protocol 3 (POP3) mail server and clients
- Configuring wu-ftpd File Transfer Protocol (FTP) server for standard, anonymous, and guest FTP services (the in-depth coverage of this widely used FTP server will provide you with valuable configuration options that will enhance security and also provide a custom look and feel for your FTP users)
- Configuring you r Red Hat Linux server as a file and print server for the Windows computers in your LAN
- Compiling, configuring, and installing the Apache Web server for CGI scripts, Server Side Includes (SSI), virtual hosts, proxy service, and secure transactions (from experience I know that Web service is one of the primary reasons many people decide to use Red Hat Linux, and therefore a chapter has been specially prepared to provide you with all the information you need to create an elegant Web solution)
- Configuring your Red Hat Linux as an NFS server, which can provide mountable filesystems over the network, and using the rdist program, which allows you to automatically distribute and update files on other computers in your network
- Configuring the X Window System

Part III: Troubleshooting

Part III contains information on how to secure and tune Red Hat Linux using various techniques. Chapters in this part cover the use of shadow passwords, Pluggable Authentication Modules (PAM,) file/directory integrity checking tools, TCP wrapper, and COPS; the use of private IP addresses, how to masquerade IP addresses, how to use packet filtering firewalls and proxy servers, and how to use SATAN for monitoring network security holes; and how to configure, compile, and build a custom kernel.

Conventions Used in This Book

Here are a few conventions you should know about before reading this book.

- `Monospaced font` is used to indicate URLs.
- *Italic* is used for placeholders.
- Arrows are used to indicate progressive menu choices (e.g., Control ⇨ Control Panel means to select the Control menu, then select Control Panel from the submenu).
- Whenever a command-line or a script code exceeds the width of a page, a backslash character (\) is used as a line continuation symbol.

The book also uses the following icons:

Tip

Tips tell you something that is likely to save you time and effort.

Caution

Cautions indicate a potential danger.

Tell Us What You Think

Both IDG Books Worldwide and I are very interested in finding out what you think of this book. Please feel free to register this book at the IDG Books Worldwide Web site (`http://www.idgbooks.com`) and give us your feedback. If you are interested in contacting me directly, send e-mail to kabir@integrationlogic.com or visit my public Web site at `http://www.nitec.com`. I will try my best to respond promptly.

Acknowledgments

Thanks to Laura Lewin for giving me the opportunity to write this book. She has been very kind and patient with me for a long time.

Eric Newman, the book's development editor, has been very kind and friendly throughout the entire development phase of this book.

Special thanks to Matt Hayden, who greatly helped in making sure this book is technically sound. His insightful comments, suggestions, and tips did much more than just correct my technical oversights.

Overwhelming thanks to Mildred Sanchez and Bill McManus, the copy editors. They regularly reworded many of my "machine language" sentences to plain, readable English.

Sheila Kabir, my wife, tolerates my juggling act of running a promising Internet start-up company and at the same time writing about open source technologies. Her patience and great smile keep me going on a daily basis.

Finally, I would also like to thank the rest of the IDG Books team that made this book a reality. They are the people who turned a few files into a beautiful and polished book.

Contents at a Glance

Contents

Part I

Installation and Basic Configuration

Chapter 1

Getting Started

Choosing Your Platform

Red Hat Linux runs on many hardware platforms, such as *x*86 PC clones, Alpha, and Sparc. This chapter focuses on *x*86-based installation, because it is the dominant Linux platform. Installation tasks on other platforms will vary slightly; consult the Red Hat Web site for the details.

Checking Your Hardware Requirements

From the beginning, Linux has required minimum hardware to run. This has not changed yet. Red Hat Linux runs on very minimal hardware, but just being able to run Linux is different than running it to create a server-class operation. To find out whether your hardware is supported by Red Hat Linux, check the following Web site: `http://www.redhat.com/support/docs/rhl`.

Obviously, the better the hardware, the better the performance you will get out of your Red Hat Linux system. Here are some general guidelines to use to create powerful Red Hat Linux systems:

- **CPU.** The faster the better. However, buying the fastest processor available is not always necessary. For example, if you simply want to create a Web server running Apache on Red Hat Linux, consider a midrange Pentium Pro or a lower-end Pentium II processor. No need to go out and get that Pentium III running at 400+ MHz. Of course, if you plan to run CPU-intensive applications via CGI or other means on the Web server, consider a very fast CPU; for most installations, a midrange processor is the best choice.

- **RAM.** The more the merrier. This is one piece of hardware that you can go wild with and get as much as you can have. RAM is one of the most critical variables in the performance equation. That said, when deciding how much RAM is needed for a Web server, for example, first decide how many requests you want to service per second. Sometimes, determining this requests/sec figure is difficult. Perhaps you have an idea about how many requests you want to be able to service per day. Suppose that you want the Web server to be able to service 3,456,000 requests/day. You can determine the requests/sec figure as follows: 3,456,000 requests/day × 1 day/24 hours × 1 hour/3,600 seconds.

    This gives you 40 requests/sec. Now that you know how many requests/sec you will have, you also know that you need 40 Apache daemons to be able to service 40 requests simultaneously. In such a case, your memory requirements for Apache alone would be 40 × the Memory footprint of an Apache process. This could be approximately 40MB or more, depending on how you configure Apache itself. For example, if you put the Perl interpreter inside Apache (mod_perl), add FastCGI support (mod_fastcgi), or add extra modules, each Apache process might require more memory. The more you know about your memory needs, the more intelligent you can be about your memory requirements. For most typical Web server deployment tasks, I recommend 256MB of fast 100 MHz (10 nanosecond) DRAM modules for newer computers.

- **Hard disk.** How much hard disk space you need for your server is dictated by what you want to do with it. If you want the server to host numerous files for your Web site or LAN, determine the data size requirement and buy an appropriately sized hard disk. The size really isn't the big issue, given that prices of large hard disks are falling on a regular basis. Rather, what is important is the type of hard disk you choose for your server. You have two choices: IDE/EIDE or SCSI.

    If your server is going to be critical to your LAN or Internet operations, such as Web, FTP, or mail services, use multiple SCSI disks. SCSI provides much better throughput then its IDE/EIDE counterparts. I recommend use of wide SCSI hard disks that provide you approximately 20MB/sec performance. By using multiple wide-SCSI disks, you can minimize wait caused by your drive subsystem. In other words, when you use multiple SCSI disks, disk I/O-related bottlenecks can be reduced, which is a very good thing for a server. You might be tempted to get the ultrawide SCSI disks and controllers, but be aware that appropriate drivers may not be available for the blazingly fast SCSI hardware you buy. Another important point about high-performance hard disks is that such disks may get hot really fast. Be sure to include appropriate cooling equipment; for instance, extra fans that you can install in your unused drive bays are likely to help reduce the risk of a disaster.

- **Network interface card.** A good server needs a good NIC. Make sure you buy a high-performance NIC from a well-known vendor, such as 3Com or Intel. Ideally, you want to get a card that allows you to disable Plug and Play (PNP) using a switch, because PNP does not quite work on Red Hat Linux just yet.

- **Other hardware.** Other important hardware includes a reasonably fast CD-ROM drive and a floppy disk drive. Most recent motherboards come with onboard IDE controllers and offer you the capability to connect four IDE devices. Because a CD-ROM drive is not frequently used on a server, you do not need the fastest one; just get one that works in the 10–20 × speed range. Last but not least, make sure you get a server-class case and power supply for your system. You can get a case that comes with a redundant power supply and provides high wattage, 300 watts or more.

After you have your hardware ready for Red Hat Linux, you need to prepare for installation.

Preparing to Install Red Hat Linux

First, decide which Red Hat Linux you are going to use for your system. If you are interested in installing the latest version of Red Hat, check the Red Hat Web site.

You can install Red Hat Linux via FTP, NFS, or SMB services where the Red Hat CD-ROM is located in a remote computer. These methods are very error-prone and do not always work well. I highly recommend that you save time and effort by using a local CD-ROM drive and performing all installation tasks locally.

If you must install via FTP, NFS, or SMB services, make sure you have a local computer set up to provide the desired service, and the Red Hat CD-ROM mounted and exported for the intended Red Hat server computer. You could also copy the entire Red Hat CD-ROM onto the hard disk to perform speedier installations.

Also note that you can install Red Hat from a DOS partition in your local hard disk. This is recommended if you cannot have a CD-ROM on the local system even for temporary installation tasks. Assuming that you have a way of accessing a remote computer on your LAN via NFS, SMB, FTP, or other means, do the following:

1. Create a RedHat directory in a partition that will not be used for your Red Hat Linux installation. For example, if you have an MS-DOS partition that you would like to keep as is, use it for this purpose.

2. Create a subdirectory called **base** under the RedHat directory and copy the contents of the RedHat/base directory from the Red Hat CD-ROM on the remote computer.

3. Create another subdirectory called **RPMS** under the RedHat directory and copy the contents of the RedHat/RPMS directory from the Red Hat CD-ROM on the remote computer.

Because you can save a lot of trouble by doing a simple local CD-ROM-based install, the rest of the chapter is based on the assumption that you'll follow this course of action.

The next step in preparing for a Red Hat Linux installation is to determine whether you need a boot disk. If you have bought the official Red Hat CD-ROM, you'll already have a boot disk and a supplementary disk supplied by Red Hat.

If you have a newer motherboard with a BIOS that supports booting the system from a CD-ROM, you do not need to use a boot disk. In this case, you have to reconfigure your BIOS setup to boot the system from the CD-ROM. Note that you need to change this setting (that is, booting from a CD-ROM) back to hard disk after you are done with installation. Most newer BIOS versions allow you to choose a chain of devices that they will try to boot from. For example, the BIOS may allow you to choose a sequence such as CD-ROM, C, A, which means that it will try to boot the system from the CD-ROM first, then from the hard disk, and finally from the A floppy drive. Such an option allows you to keep the setting as is, because you simply need to remove any CD-ROM from the CD-ROM drive to boot from the hard disk.

Creating a boot disk under MS Windows 9x/2000

You can create the boot disk under MS Windows 9x/2000 operating systems as follows:

1. Assuming your CD-ROM drive is called D and you have the Red Hat CD-ROM mounted in the drive, run the following command from an MS-DOS shell window:

   ```
   d:/dosutils/rawrite
   ```

2. The rawrite utility will display the following prompt:

   ```
   Enter disk image source file name:
   ```
   ```
   Please insert a formatted diskette into drive A: and
   press the enter key
   ```

3. Enter **\images\boot.img** as the image source file. Now rawrite displays the following prompt:

   ```
   Enter target diskette drive:
   ```

4. Enter the appropriate drive letters. For example, if your floppy disk is in the A drive, enter **a:** as the target drive.

5. Put a blank, formatted floppy disk in the floppy drive and press Enter to continue.

6. The rawrite utility will write the boot.img image to the disk, and you are done.

Tip

If you need to use a PCMCIA-based CD-ROM to install Red Hat Linux, you also need to create a supplementary floppy disk using the technique just described. Enter only **\images\supp. img** as the image source filename in step 3.

Creating a boot disk under Linux

If you do not have an MS Windows system and thus want to use another Linux system to create the boot disk, do the following:

1. Mount your Red Hat CD-ROM as usual. These instructions assume that you have mounted it on the /mnt/cdrom directory. Change your current directory to the /mnt/cdrom/images directory where the boot image is kept.

2. Assuming your floppy drive is /dev/fd0 (the default floppy device) and you are using a 1.44MB (3.5-inch, high-density) floppy disk, run the following command:

   `dd if=boot.img  of=/dev/fd0  bs=1440K`

This should create the necessary boot disk. You can also create the supplementary floppy image disk by replacing the if=boot.img argument with if=supp.img in the preceding command. You need only the supplementary image for PCMCIA-based devices, which typically are used only on laptop/notebook computers.

After you create the boot disk, you are ready to install Red Hat Linux from the CD-ROM.

Installing Red Hat Linux

If you are booting the system from the CD-ROM, insert your Red Hat CD-ROM in the drive and restart or start your intended server computer. In case you are using a boot floppy, insert it in the bootable floppy drive and restart or start the system.

When the system is booted, you see a welcome screen from Red Hat and then this prompt:

`boot:`

You have three choices.

- Press the Enter key to start a normal installation or upgrade.

- Enter **expert** at the boot: prompt to perform the installation and upgrade in an expert user mode. In expert mode, the Red Hat installation program does not try to auto-detect your hardware, but instead allows you to select various hardware components manually. You should choose to enter expert mode only if you really are an expert or are having problems with auto-detection of certain hardware.

- Enter **rescue** at the boot: prompt. Use this option when you are trying to recover from a disaster. In such a case, you need a rescue disk along with your standard boot disk. You can create the rescue disk in the same manner as you create the boot image disk or the supplementary image disk. Just replace the image filename with rescue.img in any of the boot image creation processes described previously.

Tip

If you plan to perform an unattended installation, where user interaction is not required, you can also enter **linux ks** at the boot: prompt. This allows the installation program to use an installation mode called the Kickstart mode. This is a very advanced mode that requires that you create a custom configuration file called ks on the boot floppy disk or keep a file called *<IP address of the machine being set up>*kickstart in the bootp server.

Assuming that this is your first time Red Hat Linux installation, your only choice is to press the Enter key to start the installation process.

When the installation program starts, you see another welcome screen. Press Enter to continue with the installation.

Selecting a language, a keyboard, and an installation method

After you are past the initial greeting page, you are asked to choose the language you want to use; the default is English. Choose the appropriate language and press Enter to continue. The next screen asks you to select a keyboard type. The default is English. Press Enter or select the appropriate keyboard type and continue. Next, you are asked to choose an installation method. The available options are Local CD-ROM, NFS Image, hard drive, FTP, and SMB image. Because you are going to do a CD-ROM installation, press the Enter key to start the actual installation process.

Deciding whether to do a new installation or an upgrade

The next screen asks you to choose between a new installation or an upgrade.

If you are installing Red Hat Linux for the first time, choose the Install option; conversely, if you plan to upgrade an existing Red Hat system, choose the Upgrade option. The difference is that the upgrade process will upgrade only your existing kernel and software packages and will not allow you to add new packages. This discussion assumes that you are installing for the first time; hence, choose the Install option to continue.

Choosing an installation class

The installation program offers you three installation class options:

- **Workstation.** Choose this option if you plan to use the Red Hat Linux system as a personal workstation computer. This option allows the installation program to remove all of your existing Linux partitions and use the entire unpartitioned disk space to create a preconfigured system. The Workstation class system typically has a small swap partition (32MB) and a 16MB /boot partition for kernel and related files. The rest of the unpartitioned disk space is used to create a single / (root) partition. Typically, you should have at least 600MB of disk space for a Workstation class installation.

- **Server.** Choose this option to create a server system. It uses a 64MB swap partition, a 16MB /boot partition for kernel and related files, a 256MB / (root) partition, a 512MB (or more) /usr partition for storing commonly used applications and utilities, a 512MB (or more) /home partition for user home directories, and a 256MB /var partition for system logs and queues. You should have approximately 1.6GB of disk space for such a system.

- **Custom.** Allows you to choose whatever partitioning you want using partitioning tools and therefore is the most flexible.

For this discussion, choose the Custom class option. The installation program then automatically probes the system for an existing SCSI adapter. If the installer is able to detect a SCSI adapter, it displays a message stating the brand name of the adapter.

However, if auto-probing for a SCSI adapter fails, the installation program displays a status screen telling you that it could not detect your SCSI adapter card.

This means that you either don't have a SCSI adapter or have one that couldn't be detected in auto-probe mode. In the latter case, choose Yes to select a SCSI adapter manually from a list of known adapters. If you do not have a SCSI adapter, you can simply choose No to continue to the next step.

Partitioning your disks

Partitioning your disks is a very important step, because you cannot safely change disk partitions without losing data. So, be very careful in this step. The installation program displays a screen that asks you to choose a disk partitioning tool.

You have two choices—Disk Druid or the fdisk program. The Disk Druid partitioning utility is more user-friendly than the fdisk program, so it is recommended for beginning users. After you select this tool, your current disk partitions are displayed.

If you have partitions from your previous OS, such as MS Windows 9*x*/NT, you can either delete these partitions here or use unused partitions to create a dual-boot Red Hat Linux system.

Red Hat Linux allows you to partition each disk, where each partition is labeled using the hd[a–z][N] scheme for IDE hard disks and the sd[a–z][N] scheme for SCSI disks. Here, N is the partition number. For example, hda1 is partition 1 on the first IDE disk—hda, and similarly, sda1 is the first partition of the first SCSI disk. You have to decide how you want to partition your disk(s.) Here are some pointers.

1. You need a / (root) partition to store your kernel and related files. This partition need not be very large. In fact, you can make it as small as 256MB according to the Red Hat Server class specification, discussed earlier. Make sure that you choose Linux native as the partition type for the root partition.

2. After you decide the size of the / (root) partition, decide the size of the /usr partition. This is where all of your applications will reside, so make sure this partition is fairly large. Your /usr partition should occupy at least 512MB. Make sure to choose Linux native as the partition type for the /usr partition.

3. Next, create a /home partition for user home directories. If you have a lot of users, decide how much space you want to allow per user, multiply it by the total number of users you expect to have, and create a suitable partition. Note that you can enforce a user's disk usage by adding disk quota support later. Unlike with / or /usr, you can choose to name your user home partition anything you want. For example, if you are creating a Web server on which you want to have a partition called /www for all user Web sites, you can also put user home directories under the same partition. In other words, you are not restricted to naming the partition /home. If you use a different name than /home as your user home partition, make sure you update the necessary configuration files for the useradd, userdel, usermod, and related programs. Be sure to choose Linux native as the partition type for the home directory partition.

4. Next, create a swap partition (partition type Linux swap) such that the partition size does not exceed twice the size of your physical RAM or 128MB, whichever is less. For example, if you have 32MB of RAM, you can create a 64MB swap partition.

5. If you have disks or disk space left, feel free to add extra partitions.

6. After you create the partitions and mount-point assignments, select the OK button to continue with the next step.

If you have chosen fdisk over Disk Druid, you see a screen showing all the available hard disks on your system. Here, you can choose the hard disk that you want to partition using the fdisk program.

The fdisk program works with one disk at a time, and even though it provides a simple, inelegant user interface, it actually provides quite a bit more flexibility than the Disk Druid tool.

fdisk has a simple, command-prompt-oriented interface. It is also the default partitioning tool available after you have already installed Red Hat Linux. You can run fdisk from the command line by using the following syntax:

```
fdisk hard disk device
```

For example,

```
fdisk /dev/sda
```

tells fdisk that you want to work on the first SCSI disk's partitions. After you enter such a command, fdisk displays its command prompt, Command (m for help):, to which you can enter **m** to get a help screen such as the following:

```
Command action
   a   toggle a bootable flag
   b   edit bsd disklabel
   c   toggle the dos compatibility flag
   d   delete a partition
   l   list known partition types
   m   print this menu
   n   add a new partition
   o   create a new empty DOS partition table
   p   print the partition table
   q   quit without saving changes
   t   change a partition's system id
   u   change display/entry units
   v   verify the partition table
   w   write table to disk and exit
   x   extra functionality (experts only)
```

To view your existing partitions in the selected disk, enter **p**, which causes all of your current partitions to be displayed in a table format, such as the following:

```
Disk /dev/sda: 33 heads, 63 sectors, 1014 cylinders
Units = cylinders of 2079 * 512 bytes
```

Device Boot	Start	End	Blocks	Id	System
/dev/sda1	1	505	524916	83	Linux native
/dev/sda2	506	1014	529105+	5	Extended
/dev/sda5	506	886	396018	83	Linux native
/dev/sda6	887	1011	129906	82	Linux swap

As shown here, the /dev/sda disk has been divided into four partitions, where the first partition is /dev/sda1, which starts at block 1 and ends at block 505. Each block is 1,024 bytes, or 1K, so the first partition consists of 524,916 blocks, or 524,916K, or approximately 512MB.

To remove all existing partitions one by one, use the d command and enter the partition number you want to remove. After you remove one or more partitions, you can create new partitions as follows.

First, enter **n** to add a new partition:

```
Command (m for help): n
Command action
  e   extended
  p   primary partition (1-4)
```

As indicated, you get two choices: create either an extended partition or a primary partition. You need extended partitions only if you want to create more than four partitions. Because you only need /, /usr, /home, and a swap partition to get things going under Linux, you really don't need to create extended partitions. So, create a primary partition by entering **p** at the prompt. The next prompt asks you to select a partition number:

```
Partition number (1-4): 1
```

Enter **1** for the first partition, **2** for the second, and so on. The next prompt asks you to select the starting block number. The range shown in the parentheses is the total blocks available for partitioning. If this is the first partition, you can choose 1 as the starting block:

```
First cylinder (1-1014): 1
```

To create a 512MB partition, you can enter the size in bytes, kilobytes, or megabytes. Because a value in megabytes is easy to deal with, this example uses +512MB for the last cylinder:

```
Last cylinder or +size or +sizeM or +sizeK ([1]-1014): +512M
```

To see whether the partition has been created as requested, use the p command to see the partition information:

```
Disk /dev/sda: 33 heads, 63 sectors, 1014 cylinders
Units = cylinders of 2079 * 512 bytes
```

```
Device Boot    Start    End   Blocks   Id  System
/dev/sda1              1    505   524916   83  Linux native
```

As the last two lines show, the first partition has been created as requested, and the default partition type is Linux native; if you want to change this, use the t command to toggle a partition's system ID flag. For example, to toggle a partition's system ID flag to Linux swap, use the following commands:

```
Command (m for help): t
Partition number (1-4): 1
Hex code (type L to list codes): 82
Changed system type of partition 1 to 82 (Linux swap)

Command (m for help): p

Disk /dev/sda: 33 heads, 63 sectors, 1014 cylinders
Units = cylinders of 2079 * 512 bytes

  Device Boot    Start    End   Blocks   Id  System
/dev/sda1              1    505   524916   82  Linux
swap
```

First, the t command is entered to toggle the system ID of a partition. Then, the partition is selected and 82 is entered as the swap partition type. The L command can be used to list all the available partition types.

Note that if you use fdisk to create partitions, you must make a Linux native partition bootable. For example, to turn on /dev/sda1 as a bootable partition, the boot flag needs to be toggled, by entering the following:

```
Command (m for help): a
Partition number (1-6): 1
```

Using the p command displays the existing partition table:

```
Disk /dev/sda: 33 heads, 63 sectors, 1014 cylinders
Units = cylinders of 2079 * 512 bytes
```

Device	Boot	Start	End	Blocks	Id	System
/dev/sda1	*	1	505	524916	83	Linux native
/dev/sda2		506	1014	529105+	5	Extended
/dev/sda5		506	886	396018	83	Linux native
/dev/sda6		887	1011	129906	82	Linux swap

/dev/sda1 has "*" in the Boot column, showing that this partition is bootable.

Activating your swap partition

In the previous step, using Disk Druid or fdisk, you created a swap partition, which you now need to activate so that installation can continue.

The next screen asks you to choose the swap partition; this might seem a bit silly if you have only a single swap partition. It isn't silly, however, because the swap partition will be formatted and all data will be lost in this partition. No installation program should ever format something without first asking for permission. If you want the installation program to detect bad blocks, select the option using the spacebar. After you select the swap partition, it will be formatted and activated for the rest of the installation.

Formatting your partitions

Next, you are asked to format any available partitions other than the swap partition.

Remember that each partition that you submit for formatting will lose all existing data, so you must be very careful in making selections here. If you want to find out whether your hard disk has bad sectors, select the Check for bad blocks during format option to check for bad sectors, and then continue by clicking the OK button.

Depending on your hard disk size, this step may take a lot of time. So, if you have a very large hard disk, such as 8 to 10GB, you may want to take a coffee break at this point.

Selecting software to install

After your hard disk partitions have been formatted, the installation program asks you to choose packages.

I recommend installing only the components that you need to run on a server or workstation. However, you can always add or remove components later using the rpm command or the X Window-based glint tool.

 Tip

A server doesn't need to run the X Window System, so you shouldn't install any X Window software unless you simply are curious and want to see how it looks or works. In this example installation process, I assume you won't install X Window.

If you want to select individual packages within a component category, select the Select individual packages option.

To select packages within a component, such as Networking/Daemons, do the following:

1. Select the component category and click the Edit button, which brings up the Select Packages dialog box.

2. Select the appropriate components.

3. After you select all the packages you want and deselect the packages you don't want, continue by clicking OK.

The next screen tells you that a complete installation log will be created in the /tmp/install.log file. Click OK to continue installation. The installation program displays a status screen.

If you want to see what exactly the installation program is doing, use the Alt+F1 to Alt+F4 keys to switch to and from the virtual console. After all the packages are installed, the installation program probes your system for a mouse.

Selecting a mouse

If the installer automatically detects a mouse on your system, it displays a dialog box showing the port information for the detected mouse; on the other hand, if the installer fails to find a mouse, it displays a dialog box asking you to select the mouse.

If you choose the X Window packages, you are asked to configure the X Window System at this point. The steps needed to configure it aren't presented here.

Configuring the TCP/IP network

The network configuration is really the basic TCP/IP configuration.

Because you are doing a server installation, select Yes and continue. You are asked to choose the way you want to configure the IP address for the server.

The BOOTP option or the DHCP option should be selected for a workstation installation that gets its IP from a BOOTP or DHCP server on the LAN. For a server, the Static IP address option is really the only option, so select this option and continue to the next screen.

You need to enter the IP address of the server, along with the netmask, the default gateway, and the primary name server. If you are setting up a server for your own LAN, you should know the necessary information; if you are setting up a co-located server in an ISP network, ask your ISP for the IP addresses needed to complete this step.

The default gateway is typically the router that connects your network to the Internet. The default gateway IP must belong to the same network. In other words, if your server IP is 206.171.50.50, the default gateway has to be 206.171.50.*x*, where *x* can be any appropriate number. The primary name server can be anywhere, but ideally it should also be close to the server in terms of networking. Technically, you can use any name server on the Internet to do your DNS service, but it isn't polite (and probably not legal either) to use a DNS server for which you don't have permission. If you plan to run your own DNS server on the machine being set up, you can supply the same IP address here.

After you enter the IP addresses and continued to the next screen, you are asked to enter the domain name, host name, secondary name server IP (optional), and tertiary name server IP (optional).

The domain name is the Internet domain name for your network. If you are setting up a server on a private LAN that is not connected to the Internet, you can use any domain name you want. Typically, you should choose your organization's name as the domain name. For example, if your organization is called Form Track, you can call your domain name formtrack.com. However, if you plan to use the system on the Internet, make sure you choose a valid domain name. The host name can be anything you want as long as it hasn't been given to another host on the same network. The IP addresses for the secondary and tertiary name servers are not required, but having them provides better DNS support for the server.

Configuring the clock

Next, you are asked to configure the clock.

If your (CMOS) hardware clock is set to Greenwich Mean Time (GMT), select the Hardware clock set to GMT option. Then, choose the appropriate time zone the server will reside in.

Configuring services or daemons to run

The next screen enables you to select the services or daemons that you want to run automatically.

You should try to choose only the needed services or daemons.

Configuring printers

The next dialog box asks you to configure a printer. If you don't have any, simply select No and you will be able to skip this step of installation. However, if you plan to use your server as a print server, or if you want to use a remote printer on this system, you have to configure it here.

After you choose to configure a printer, you are asked to choose whether you want to configure a local printer or a remote printer.

Select the appropriate connection type. This discussion assumes that you want to configure a local printer. Next, you have to enter the print queue and spool directory information. The default values should be fine for a local printer.

Next, you are asked to select the printer type from a list of supported printers. Choose the most appropriate printer make/model from the list and continue to the next dialog box.

If you chose a PostScript printer, you are asked to provide additional information — paper size, resolution, and so forth.

Next, you are given a chance to see all the information you have selected for the printer.

If you have made any mistakes, you can use the Back button to go back and correct the problem. Otherwise, confirm that the printer information is correct.

Setting a root password

The root account is the default superuser account on a Red Hat Linux system. You use this account to log in to your new system.

Choose a password for this account. You have to enter this password twice, and it isn't displayed on the screen, for security reasons. Choose a good password. Don't ever use dictionary words in a password; always use one or more punctuation characters and numbers in the password. Also, make sure you use a long password. Typically, anywhere from five to eight characters are acceptable.

Creating a custom boot disk

You are asked whether or not you want to create a custom boot disk.

Creating a boot disk should be mandatory, because a custom boot disk is a must-have. It allows you to boot your system even if the boot loader program (such as LILO) fails to boot your system. Thus, you should create this disk. Select Yes, and you are asked to enter a floppy in /dev/fd0.

Use a brand-new blank floppy disk to create the boot disk. This boot disk can be used in conjunction with the rescue disk that you can create using the rescue.img image. If you don't create the custom boot disk at this point simply because you don't have a floppy handy, make sure you create it later, using the mkbootdisk program.

Selecting LILO installation options

You can install the Red Hat Linux boot loader either in the master boot record or in the first sector of the boot partition. If you don't have any other OSs installed, choose the master boot record. Conversely, if you already have an OS installed and want to keep it running, you have to choose the first sector of the boot partition.

Remember that placing LILO in the master boot record gives LILO control over the boot process of your entire system. If you want to keep the system in a dual-boot setup with another OS, chances are the other OS has already installed its boot loader in the master boot record. So, be careful about what you select here.

Next, you are asked to pass any additional information to the kernel at boot.

In most cases, you do not need to provide any additional information here. Next, you need to select bootable partitions that you want LILO to manage. A dialog box displays all the partitions on your system (except for the swap) that can be used to boot OSs, including Linux and others.

The default bootable Red Hat Linux partition is marked with an * character. This partition is given a default boot label called *linux*. In other words, when LILO starts during the boot process, it allows you to type **linux** at the boot: prompt to boot Red Hat Linux. If you have another OS coexisting on this system, you can select the partition it resides on and create a boot label for it. Select the partition involved, and choose to edit the entry.

Enter the appropriate boot label name to easily identify the OS. After you edit the boot labels, click OK to continue. The installation will complete.

Now, you are ready to reboot the system for the first time. Remove the CD-ROM and any floppy disk you have from the drives, and then click OK to reboot.

Starting Red Hat Linux for the First Time

The system reboots and displays the boot: prompt. You can either type **linux** or press Enter to start Red Hat Linux for the first time. Of course, if you forget to do either, LILO will time out shortly and start the default OS.

After the Linux kernel starts booting, you see a dialog box full of information. Do not despair if the information you see passes by too fast. You will have access to all of this information soon. Be patient and let the system display a login prompt on the console.

When the login prompt is displayed, log in as the user **root**, using the password you entered earlier in the installation process. You now should be logged in to the system as root. You just became the superuser of your very own Red Hat Linux server. Your Linux system awaits your command.

If you want to see what went flying by during the bootup process, then run the dmesg command to see the bootup messages. If the screen scrolls too much, use dmesg | more to see a page at a time.

Tip

Linux has a feature not found in Microsoft-based systems: the capability to scroll back into the console's history. Pressing Shift+PgUp shows what just flashed by on your screen. But, when you shift to a different virtual console, this history is lost. The fact that the login screen does a "clear screen" that destroys the last lines of the bootstrap display is frustrating. For this reason, you can modify /etc/inittab to refrain from running getty on virtual console 1.

This is a good time to make sure that your hardware is detected properly by the kernel. Read the output of the dmesg program to find out.

Chapter 2

Boot Up and Shutdown Configuration

Configuring the Very First Process: init

A Red Hat Linux kernel (that is, the core operating system) is typically stored in a compressed file. When the kernel is started by a boot loader program, such as LILO, it uncompresses itself, initializes the display device, and starts checking other hardware attached to your computer. As it finds your hard disks, floppy drives, network cards, and so forth, it loads the appropriate device driver modules. During this process, it displays text messages on your console screen.

 Tip

If you are at the console when booting your system, you can press Shift+PgUp to scroll back the display to view boot messages. You can also view the boot messages at any time by running the dmesg program. The /var/log/messages files will also have many of the boot messages.

At this point, the kernel mounts the root file system (/) as read-only and performs checks on the file system. If the kernel finds that everything is okay, it mounts the root file system as read/write. If a problem arises and the kernel fails to mount the root partition, the kernel panics and the system halts. If the disk somehow was corrupt, the kernel might provide an option to run a file system checker program, such as fsck.ext2, from a restricted shell. In such a case, run fsck.ext2 on the root partition or any other partition that failed during boot. For example, if your system's root partition resides on /dev/sda1 (an SCSI disk partition) and it fails, run

```
fsck.ext2 /dev/sda1
```

Once the repair process is complete, exit the shell by typing **exit** and the system will attempt to boot again. Hopefully, it will succeed this time around.

After the root file system is mounted, the kernel starts a program called init. This program starts all other programs. After init starts up all the necessary programs, the system is up and running and the boot process is complete.

What init runs as part of the bootup process is highly customizable. The following sections discuss init in detail.

The init program comes in two flavors—UNIX System V init and BSD init. The Red Hat distribution comes with the UNIX System V init program. The difference between the two flavors is that System V init uses run levels (discussed later in this section), and BSD init does not. Because the Red Hat distribution uses UNIX System V init, this *Administrator's Handbook* limits discussion of init to that flavor.

Because init is the first program run by the kernel, its process ID (PID) is 1. When init starts, it reads a configuration file called /etc/inittab. The /etc/inittab file in a typical Red Hat Linux system is shown in Listing 2-1.

Listing 2-1 *A Typical /etc/inittab File*

```
#
# inittab - This file describes how the init
# process should set up the system in a
# certain run level.
#
# Author: Miquel van Smoorenburg,
#         <miquels@drinkel.nl.mugnet.org>
#
# Modified for RHS Linux by Marc Ewing and Donnie Barnes
#
```

```
# Default runlevel. The runlevels used by RHS are:
#   0 - halt (Do NOT set initdefault to this)
#   1 - Single-user mode
#   2 - Multiuser, without NFS (The same as 3, if you
#                          do not have networking)
#   3 - Full multiuser mode
#   4 - unused
#   5 - X11
#   6 - reboot (Do NOT set initdefault to this)
#
id:3:initdefault:

# System initialization.
si::sysinit:/etc/rc.d/rc.sysinit

l0:0:wait:/etc/rc.d/rc 0
l1:1:wait:/etc/rc.d/rc 1
l2:2:wait:/etc/rc.d/rc 2
l3:3:wait:/etc/rc.d/rc 3
l4:4:wait:/etc/rc.d/rc 4
l5:5:wait:/etc/rc.d/rc 5
l6:6:wait:/etc/rc.d/rc 6

# Things to run in every runlevel.
ud::once:/sbin/update

# Trap Ctrl+Alt+Delete
ca::ctrlaltdel:/sbin/shutdown -t3 -r now

# When our UPS tells us power has failed, assume we have
# a few minutes of power left. Schedule a shutdown for
# 2 minutes from now.
#
```

Continued

Listing 2-1 *Continued*

```
# This does, of course, assume you have powerd installed
and your
# UPS connected and working correctly.
#
pf::powerfail:/sbin/shutdown -f -h +2 "Power Failure; \
System Shutting Down"

# If power was restored before the shutdown kicked in,
cancel it.
pr:12345:powerokwait:/sbin/shutdown -c "Power Restored; \
Shutdown Cancelled"

# Run gettys in standard runlevels
1:12345:respawn:/sbin/mingetty tty1
2:2345:respawn:/sbin/mingetty tty2
3:2345:respawn:/sbin/mingetty tty3
4:2345:respawn:/sbin/mingetty tty4
5:2345:respawn:/sbin/mingetty tty5
6:2345:respawn:/sbin/mingetty tty6

# Run xdm in runlevel 5
x:5:respawn:/usr/bin/X11/xdm -nodaemon
```

This file defines how init behaves during server startup or shutdown events. The following discussion takes a closer look at this file.

The init program ignores all the blank and comment lines (that is, lines that start with a # sign) in the /etc/inittab file. The lines with colon-delimited fields are the init configuration lines. The syntax for such a line is as follows:

id:runlevels:action:process arguments

The first field is a unique label field to identify an entry in the file. An *id* can be 2 to 4 characters long. The second field, *runlevels*, defines which run levels this line applies to. The third field defines what action needs to be taken. The last field (*process*) defines which process needs to be run.

Optionally, you can also specify command-line arguments for the process in the fourth field.

As mentioned before, a run level specifies a state of the system. The nine run levels are described in Table 2-1.

Table 2-1 *The Run Levels for init*

Run Level	Description
0	Halt – used to halt the system
1	Single-user – used to set the system in a minimal configuration suitable for a single user
2	Not used
3	Multiuser – used to set the system in a configuration that supports multiple users
4	Not used
5	Used to start X Window System and the xdm program
6	Reboot – used to reboot the system
S or s	Used internally by scripts that run in run level 1
a, b, c	On-demand run levels; typically not used

Note that you can specify multiple run levels in a single init configuration line. For example, if you want init to run a process for both single- and multiuser modes, you can specify a line such as the following:

```
id:13:action:process arguments
```

Table 2-2 shows the possible values for actions.

Table 2-2 *Possible Actions for a Specific Run Level*

Action	Description
respawn	The process is restarted whenever it terminates.
wait	The process is run once, and init waits until it terminates.
once	The process is run once.
boot	The process is run during system boot, and init ignores the run level field.
bootwait	The process is run during system boot, and init waits for the process to terminate.

Continued

Table 2-2 *Continued*

Action	Description
off	No action is taken. This can be used to disable a configuration line without removing it. However, you can simply comment out the line by using a leading # character, instead.
ondemand	Useful only when the run level is a, b, or c. The process is run whenever init is called with any of the three ondemand run levels. Typically not used.
initdefault	Sets the default run level for the system. The process field is ignored.
sysinit	The process is run once during system boot. A sysinit action takes precedence over boot or bootwait actions.
powerwait	The process is run when init receives a SIGPWR signal. Typically, UPS monitoring software detects a power problem and issues such a signal to init. In such a case, init waits until the process terminates.
powerfail	Same as powerwait, but init does not wait for the process to complete.
powerokwait	The process is run when init receives a SIGPWR signal and a text file called /etc/powerstatus contains an "OK" string. Typically, a UPS monitoring program creates this file and sends the SIGPWR signal to init to indicate that the power problem has been fixed.
ctrlaltdel	The process is run when init receives a SIGINT signal.
kbrequest	The process is run when init receives a KeyboardSignal from the keyboard handler.

The System V flavor of init, which is what Red Hat Linux init is, uses the following directory structure:

```
/etc
 +--rc.d
    +--init.d (dir)
    +--rc0.d  (dir)
    +--rc1.d  (dir)
    +--rc2.d  (dir)
    +--rc3.d  (dir)
    +--rc4.d  (dir)
    +--rc5.d  (dir)
    +--rc6.d  (dir)
    +--rc.sysinit  (script)
    +--rc.local    (optional script, supplied with Red
Hat Linux)
    +--rc.serial   (optional script)
    +--rc (script)
```

The /etc/rc.d/rc.sysinit script

As you already know, when a Red Hat Linux system boots, the kernel runs init, which in turn runs the /etc/rc.d/rc.sysinit script before processing any other scripts for the desired run level. The following line in the /etc/inittab file causes init to run this script before running anything else:

```
si::sysinit:/etc/rc.d/rc.sysinit
```

Notice that the run level field is empty, because init recognizes sysinit as a system initialization action. The rc.sysinit script does many things, including setting the host name, enabling the swap partition, checking the file systems, loading kernel modules, and more. Typically, you do not need to modify this script.

The /etc/rc.d/init.d directory

The init.d subdirectory is used to store all the scripts needed for all the run levels. Keeping all the scripts in one location makes managing them easier. Each script is used to start/stop a particular service—Domain Name Service (DNS), Web service, or another such service. All of these scripts follow a special command-line argument syntax. For example, to start NFS (Network File System) service, you can run the following script:

```
/etc/rc.d/init.d/nfs start
```

To stop the same service, you can run the same script as follows:

```
/etc/rc.d/init.d/nfs stop
```

The nfs script takes start and stop as arguments. This is true for all the scripts in this directory, which are symbolically linked to the rc0.d through rc6.d directories, as needed.

The /etc/rc.d/rc script

When init is told to change the run level to one of the seven possible run levels, it runs a script specified in one of the following lines in the /etc/inittab file:

```
l0:0:wait:/etc/rc.d/rc 0
l1:1:wait:/etc/rc.d/rc 1
```

```
12:2:wait:/etc/rc.d/rc 2
13:3:wait:/etc/rc.d/rc 3
14:4:wait:/etc/rc.d/rc 4
15:5:wait:/etc/rc.d/rc 5
16:6:wait:/etc/rc.d/rc 6
```

As you can see, for each run level (0 through 6), a script called /etc/rc.d/rc is run, with the run level as the argument to the script. This script is responsible for starting and stopping all the services for the desired run level. For example, suppose that init is told to change the run level to 3. It will run the /etc/rc.d/rc script with an argument of 3 in a command line similar to this:

```
/etc/rc.d/rc 3
```

The /etc/rc.d/rc script is shown in Listing 2-2.

Listing 2-2 *The Script /etc/rc.d/rc*

```
#!/bin/bash
#
# rc This file is responsible for starting/stopping
#      services when the runlevel changes. It is also
#      responsible for the very first setup of basic
#      things, such as setting the hostname.
#
# Original Author:  Miquel van Smoorenburg,
#                        <miquels@drinkel.nl.mugnet.org>
#

# Source function library.
. /etc/rc.d/init.d/functions

# Now find out what the current and what the previous
# runlevel are.
argv1="$1"
set `/sbin/runlevel`
runlevel=$2
```

```
previous=$1
export runlevel previous


# Get first argument. Set new runlevel to this argument.
[ "$1" != "" ] && runlevel="$argv1"


# Tell linuxconf what runlevel we are in
[ -d /var/run ] && echo "/etc/rc.d/rc$runlevel.d" >
/var/run/runlevel.dir


# Is there an rc directory for this new runlevel?
if [ -d /etc/rc.d/rc$runlevel.d ]; then
    # First, run the KILL scripts.
    for i in /etc/rc.d/rc$runlevel.d/K*; do
        # Check if the script is there.
        [ ! -f $i ] && continue


        # Don't run [KS]??foo.{rpmsave,rpmorig} scripts
        [ "${1%.rpmsave}" != "${1}" ] && continue
        [ "${1%.rpmorig}" != "${1}" ] && continue


        # Check if the subsystem is already up.
        subsys=${i#/etc/rc.d/rc$runlevel.d/K??}
        [ ! -f /var/lock/subsys/$subsys ] && \
        [ ! -f /var/lock/subsys/${subsys}.init ] && continue


        # Bring the subsystem down.
        $i stop


    done


    # Now run the START scripts.
    for i in /etc/rc.d/rc$runlevel.d/S*; do
```

Continued

Listing 2-2 *Continued*

```
     # Check if the script is there.
     [ ! -f $i ] && continue

     # Don't run [KS]??foo.{rpmsave,rpmorig} scripts
     [ "${1%.rpmsave}" != "${1}" ] && continue
     [ "${1%.rpmorig}" != "${1}" ] && continue

     # Check if the subsystem is already up.
     subsys=${i#/etc/rc.d/rc$runlevel.d/S??}
     [ -f /var/lock/subsys/$subsys ] || \
     [ -f /var/lock/subsys/${subsys}.init ] && continue

     # Bring the subsystem up.
     $i start

done
fi
```

This script primarily does the following:

1. Checks whether a subdirectory exists for the run level specified in the argument. In other words, if the script is run with an argument of 3, it checks to see whether or not the /etc/rc.d/rc3.d/ directory exists. If it exists, the script continues to the next step.

2. Determines whether any of the programs (often called services) that are supposed to run in the new run level are already running. If a service is already running, the script kills the service so that it can restart it in the next step. To kill a running service, the script runs the necessary "K" script with the stop argument.

3. Runs all the "S" scripts with the start argument.

The /etc/rc.d/rc0.d through rc6.d directories

The rc0.d to rc6.d subdirectories are used for run levels 0 to 6. These directories contain symbolic links to scripts in the /etc/rc.d/init.d directory.

Take a look at the rc3.d directory in an example Red Hat Linux 6.1 system. This directory lists the symbolic links shown in Listing 2-3.

Listing 2-3 *A Directory Listing of /etc/rc.d/rc3.d*

```
lrwxrwxrwx root root 14 K05innd -> ../init.d/innd
lrwxrwxrwx root root 15 K10xntpd -> ../init.d/xntpd
lrwxrwxrwx root root 13 K15gpm -> ../init.d/gpm
lrwxrwxrwx root root 15 K15httpd -> ../init.d/httpd
lrwxrwxrwx root root 20 K15postgresql ->
../init.d/postgresql
lrwxrwxrwx root root 20 K20bootparamd ->
../init.d/bootparamd
lrwxrwxrwx root root 17 K20rusersd -> ../init.d/rusersd
lrwxrwxrwx root root 16 K20rwalld -> ../init.d/rwalld
lrwxrwxrwx root root 15 K20rwhod -> ../init.d/rwhod
lrwxrwxrwx root root 15 K25squid -> ../init.d/squid
lrwxrwxrwx root root 19 K34yppasswdd ->
../init.d/yppasswdd
lrwxrwxrwx root root 15 K35dhcpd -> ../init.d/dhcpd
lrwxrwxrwx root root 16 K35ypserv -> ../init.d/ypserv
lrwxrwxrwx root root 18 K45arpwatch -> ../init.d/arpwatch
lrwxrwxrwx root root 15 K50snmpd -> ../init.d/snmpd
lrwxrwxrwx root root 16 K55routed -> ../init.d/routed
lrwxrwxrwx root root 15 K75gated -> ../init.d/gated
lrwxrwxrwx root root 16 K87ypbind -> ../init.d/ypbind
lrwxrwxrwx root root 16 K96pcmcia -> ../init.d/pcmcia

lrwxrwxrwx root root 17 S01kerneld -> ../init.d/kerneld
lrwxrwxrwx root root 17 S10network -> ../init.d/network
lrwxrwxrwx root root 17 S11portmap -> ../init.d/portmap
lrwxrwxrwx root root 15 S15nfsfs -> ../init.d/nfsfs
lrwxrwxrwx root root 16 S20random -> ../init.d/random
lrwxrwxrwx root root 16 S30syslog -> ../init.d/syslog
lrwxrwxrwx root root 13 S40atd -> ../init.d/atd
```

Continued

Listing 2-3 *Continued*

```
lrwxrwxrwx root root 15 S40crond -> ../init.d/crond
lrwxrwxrwx root root 14 S50inet -> ../init.d/inet
lrwxrwxrwx root root 15 S55named -> ../init.d/named
lrwxrwxrwx root root 13 S60lpd -> ../init.d/lpd
lrwxrwxrwx root root 13 S60nfs -> ../init.d/nfs
lrwxrwxrwx root root 18 S75keytable -> ../init.d/keytable
lrwxrwxrwx root root 18 S80sendmail -> ../init.d/sendmail
lrwxrwxrwx root root 13 S91smb -> ../init.d/smb
lrwxrwxrwx root root 19 S99linuxconf ->
../init.d/linuxconf
lrwxrwxrwx root root 11 S99local -> ../rc.local
```

Notice that scripts from the /etc/rc.d/init.d directory are linked in two different ways. Some scripts are linked as follows:

```
K{two-digit number}{script name}
```

Other scripts are linked as shown here:

```
S{two-digit number}{script name}
```

All the scripts that are prefixed with *K* are run with the stop argument, and all the scripts that are prefixed with *S* are run with the start argument. The two-digit number is used to set the execution order. Thus, a script called S01foo will be run before S10bar. These *S* and *K* scripts are run by /etc/rc.d/rc script.

After the rc script is finished, the processing done by init also finishes, and the system becomes available in the new run level.

The /etc/rc.d/rc.local script

The rc.local script typically is run once at the end of run levels 2, 3, and 5. You can add anything that needs to be run once per boot in this file.

The /etc/rc.d/rc.serial script

The rc.serial script typically is run once at the end of run level 1 or 3 to initialize serial ports.

Booting Up Your System

During the bootup process, init first runs the rc.sysinit script and then runs the script for the default run level. The default run level is set in /etc/ inittab, using a line such as the following:

```
id:3:initdefault:
```

Here, the default run level is set to 3. This means that init will run the script needed to put the system in multiuser mode.

Looking back at Listing 2-1, the following line specifies what needs to be run for run level 3:

```
l3:3:wait:/etc/rc.d/rc 3.
```

The rc script is run with an argument of 3. As previously mentioned, this script runs all the scripts whose names start with *S* in the /etc/rc.d/rc3.d directory. It also supplies start as an argument to each of the *S*-prefixed scripts. After all the *S* scripts are run, the rc script finishes and the system becomes available in the default run level.

 Tip

It is possible to override the default run level at the LILO prompt. For example, if you want to boot the system in single-user mode, you can specify **linux single** to boot in single-user mode. If you use a label other than "linux" to boot Linux, you have to specify *yourlabel* **single**, instead, where *yourlabel* is the name of the appropriate label.

Shutting Down Your System

You can run init manually and tell it to change the system run level, by providing the desired run level in the command line. For example,

```
init 1
```

tells init to change the current run level to 1. In other words, this halts the system. If you are running in multiuser mode (run level 3), the preceding command is less than ideal, because it does not inform the users on the system that the system is going to halt.

Typically, the shutdown command is used to shut down a system. It broadcasts a warning message to all logged-in users that the system is changing the run level. It also provides you with an option to schedule the shutdown event.

The shutdown command works by telling init to change the current run level of the system to either halt (0) or reboot (6). For example,

```
shutdown -h now
```

signals init to change the run level to 0 (halt) immediately.

Canceling a shutdown

The shutdown command allows you to schedule a shutdown event at a later time. For example,

```
shutdown +10
```

schedules a shutdown exactly ten minutes after the command is entered at the shell prompt. Suppose a need arises to cancel the shutdown event; in such a case, you can issue another shutdown command, with a −c option. For example,

```
shutdown -c
```

cancels any scheduled shutdown event.

Rebooting your server

You can also run init manually to reboot your server. For example,

```
init 6
```

If you are running in multiuser mode (run level 3), this command is not the best approach, because it does not inform the users on the system that the system is going to reboot. Instead, you can use the shutdown command to reboot the server. For example,

```
shutdown -r +10
```

reboots the server in ten minutes. All the users receive a message saying that the system is going to reboot shortly, enabling them to finish up and save their work.

Tip

When you use a delayed shutdown command, such as the one just described, users who are logged in see the warning message it broadcasts, but the shutdown does not prevent anyone from logging in during the shutdown countdown period. To disallow new logins, you can create a text file called /etc/nologin with an appropriate message stating that a shutdown already has been scheduled and that users should try to log in at a later time. Do not forget to rename or delete the file after you reboot.

Caution

If you are remotely rebooting a server, be absolutely sure to remove or rename this file prior to the actual shutdown. No normal user accounts are allowed to log in when this file is present. In fact, you might want to add rm −f /etc/nologin at the end of the /etc/rc.local script and make sure that it is run by init at the end of run level 3.

To reboot immediately, you can run the following command as the superuser:

```
shutdown -r  now
```

Rebooting using Ctrl+Alt+Delete

If you are on the system console, you can use the traditional Ctrl+Alt+Delete key combination to reboot your server. The following line in /etc/inittab makes this possible:

```
ca::ctrlaltdel:/sbin/shutdown -t3 -r now
```

This line allows init to trap the Ctrl+Alt+Delete key combination and call the shutdown script to reboot immediately.

Caution

Anyone who has physical access to your system console can shut down the system by pressing the Ctrl+Alt+Delete key combination. To protect yourself from such a shutdown, you can create a file called /etc/shutdown.allow that will contain a list of users (one username per line) who are allowed to shut down the system. The root account does not need to be listed in this file.

Automatic shutdown on power failure

If you use an uninterruptible power supply (UPS) to provide backup power for your system, you can use init to shut down the system gracefully when your UPS power is nearly drained. The default /etc/inittab includes the following line:

```
pf::powerfail:/sbin/shutdown -f -h +2 "Power Failure; \
System Shutting Down"
```

This line tells init to run shut down in case of a power failure. The powerfailaction is activated when a UPS program or powerd (a power monitoring daemon) sends the SIGPWR signal to init. The default setting allows the system to run on UPS power for two minutes before it halts. If your UPS is capable of sustaining power for a greater or lesser length of time, you should modify this value.

Because it is quite possible for power to come back before your UPS power is reasonably drained, init can be called to cancel a previously scheduled shutdown event. This is done using the following line in /etc/inittab:

```
pr:12345:powerokwait:/sbin/shutdown -c "Power Restored; \
Shutdown Cancelled"
```

When init receives a SIGPWR signal, and a file called /etc/powerstatus contains an OK string, the powerokwait action is activated.

Managing init Files

As you already know, System V init uses a lot of files, symbolic links, and directories. To simplify management of init files, a few tools are available. This section discusses two such commonly used tools.

Using chkconfig to manage run levels

The chkconfig utility enables you to maintain the various symbolic links necessary for starting and stopping services in a run level. This utility can manage run level configuration for all the scripts in the /etc/rc.d/init.d directory. Its uses are described next.

Listing manageable services

To view what services will start or stop in what run levels, run the following command:

```
chkconfig --list
```

This command lists all the chkconfig-manageable services and tells you what services are going to be started (on) or stopped (off) for each run level. You can also check to see the run level configuration for a particular service by specifying the service name (that is, the script name in /etc/rc.d/init.d) in the command line. For example,

```
chkconfig --list httpd
```

shows the following output in an example Red Hat Linux server:

```
httpd 0:off 1:off 2:off 3:on 4:on 5:on 6:off
```

The httpd service is on for run levels 2, 3, 4, and 5 and is off for levels 0, 1, and 6.

Adding a new service

If you just added a new script in the /etc/rc.d/init.d directory and want to make the service it offers available for a particular run level, you can run the chkconfig command as follows:

```
chkconfig --add service_name [--level runlevel]
```

For example,

```
chkconfig --add named
```

adds a service called named to the current run level. In other words, it creates a symbolic link, which will have an S{*two-digit number*} prefix, in the current run level directory that points to the /etc/rc.d/init.d/named script. If you want to add the service to a different run level than the current one, you can specify the run level with --level option. For example,

```
chkconfig --level 4 --add named
```

adds the named service to run level 4.

Deleting an existing service

To remove an existing service from a run level, use the following command:

```
chkconfig --del service_name [--level runlevel]
```

For example,

```
chkconfig --del named
```

removes the named service from the current run level. To remove the service from a different run level than the current one, use the --level option. For example,

```
chkconfig --del named --level 5
```

removes the named service from run level 5.

Using ntsysv to manage run levels

The ntsysv utility enables you to turn on and off various services in any run levels, using a simple menu interface. When you run the command without any argument, it displays a screen similar to the one shown in Figure 2-1.

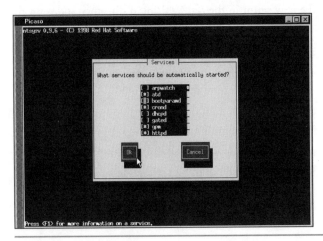

Figure 2-1 The ntsysv screen

The scrollable screen shows the state of all the services in the current run level. To turn on a service, you need to select it; to turn off a service, you simply deselect it. After you make all the changes, you can save the changes by clicking the OK button, or you can abort your changes by clicking the Cancel button. If you want to work on a different run level configuration, simply supply the run level with the --level option. For example,

```
ntsysv --level 1
```

enables you to work on the run level 1 configuration.

Using linuxconf to manage run levels

You can also use the linuxconf tool to configure run levels. Follow these instructions:

1. Select Control ⇨ Control Panel ⇨ Control Service.
2. Enable or disable one or more services.
3. Accept the changes.
4. Activate the changes before you quit linuxconf.

Creating a new service for a run level

If you install server software packages from well-known vendors, most likely they will provide you with a nice RPM package that also includes the necessary service script to go in /etc/rc.d/init.d. Sometimes, however, you will find useful software that does not come with all the bells and whistles, and you will end up customizing it, or at least modifying how it works on your system. In such a case, you might need to create a service script for your new software. This section shows how you can easily create a new service script that goes in the /etc/rc.d/init.d directory.

First, take a look at Listing 2-4, which shows the httpd script, an existing service script from the /etc/rc.d/init.d directory. This script is used to start and stop the Apache Web server.

Listing 2-4 */etc/rc.d/init.d/httpd*

```
#!/bin/sh
#
# Startup script for the Apache Web Server
#
# chkconfig: 345 85 15
# description: Apache is a World Wide Web server. \
#              It is used to serve HTML files and CGI.
# processname: httpd
# pidfile: /var/run/httpd.pid
# config: /etc/httpd/conf/access.conf
# config: /etc/httpd/conf/httpd.conf
# config: /etc/httpd/conf/srm.conf

# Source function library.
. /etc/rc.d/init.d/functions

# See how we were called.
case "$1" in
  start)
      echo -n "Starting httpd: "
      daemon httpd
      echo
      touch /var/lock/subsys/httpd
      ;;
  stop)
      echo -n "Shutting down http: "
      [ -f /var/run/httpd.pid ] && {
         kill `cat /var/run/httpd.pid`
         echo -n httpd
      }
      echo
      rm -f /var/lock/subsys/httpd
      rm -f /var/run/httpd.pid
      ;;
```

```
status)
    status httpd
    ;;
restart)
    $0 stop
    $0 start
    ;;
reload)
    echo -n "Reloading httpd: "
    [ -f /var/run/httpd.pid ] && {
        kill -HUP `cat /var/run/httpd.pid`
        echo -n httpd
    }
    echo
    ;;
*)
    echo "Usage: $0 {start|stop|restart|reload|status}"
    exit 1
esac

exit 0
```

This sh script is really a simple case (conditional) statement. You now
are going to see an example of how you can create a new service script from
an existing service script. Assume that your new service is called webmonitor and the executable is stored in /usr/sbin/webmonitor.

Tip

It is a convention to use the same name for both the script and
the executable program.

Here is how you can create the /etc/rc.d/init.d/webmonitor script:

1. Copy an existing script from /etc/rc.d/init.d as /etc/rc.d/init.d/
webmonitor. For simplicity and ease of understanding, this example
assumes that you copied the /etc/rc.d/init.d/httpd script shown in
Listing 2-4.

2. Using your favorite text editor (such as vi), search and replace all instances of "httpd" with the string "webmonitor."

3. If you keep the executable in any directories other than /sbin, /usr/sbin, /bin, or /usr/bin, you have to change the daemon webmonitor line to reflect the path of the webmonitor executable. For example, if you keep the executable in the /usr/local/web/bin directory, you have to change the daemon webmonitor line to daemon /usr/local/web/bin/webmonitor.

4. If /usr/sbin/webmonitor does not create a PID file (/var/run/webmonitor.pid), then you have to replace the kill `cat /var/run/webmonitor.pid` line with killproc webmonitor and remove the rm -f /var/run/webmonitor.pid line.

5. Run chmod 750 /etc/rc.d/init.d/webmonitor to change the file permissions so that the root user can read, write, and execute the script.

That's all you need to do to create the new webmonitor service. You can now use the chkconf, ntsysv, or linuxconf utility to add this new service to a desired run level.

Chapter 3

File Permissions

Understanding File/Directory Permissions

As do all other UNIX and UNIX-like operating systems, Linux associates a file or directory with a user and a group. Consider an example:

```
-rw-rw-r--  1 sheila  intranet  512 Feb 6 21:11
milkyweb.txt
```

The preceding line is produced by the ls –1 milkyweb.txt command on my Red Hat Linux system. You might already know that the ls program lists files and directories. The –1 option shows the complete listing for the milkyweb.txt file. Table 3-1 shows the same information in a tabular format.

Table 3-1 *Output of an Example ls –1 Command*

Information Type	ls Output
File access permission	-rw-rw-r--
Number of links	1
User (file owner)	sheila
Group	intranet
File size (in bytes)	512
Last modification date	Feb 6

Continued

45

Table 3-1 *Continued*

Information Type	ls Output
Last modification time	21:11
Filename	Milkyweb.txt

Here, the milkyweb.txt file is owned by a user called sheila. She is the only regular user who can change the access permissions of this file. The only other user who can change the permissions is the superuser. The group for this file is intranet. Any user who belongs to the intranet group can access (read, write, or execute) the file based on what current group permission is set (by the owner).

To become a file owner, a user must create the file. Under Red Hat Linux, when a user creates a file or directory, its group is also set as the default group of the user, which happens to be the private group with the same name as the user. To make this a bit clearer, suppose that I've logged into a Red Hat Linux system as kabir and am using a text editor such as vi to create a file called todo.txt. If I use the ls –l todo.txt command, the following output appears:

```
-rw-rw-r--  1 kabir   kabir    4848 Feb 6 21:37 todo.txt
```

The file owner and the group name are the same, because under Red Hat Linux, user kabir's default (private) group is also called kabir. This might be a bit confusing, but it is done to save you some worries; and, of course, you can change this behavior quite easily. However, the point here is that when a new file is created, the file owner is the file creator, and the group is the owner's default group. Next, see how you can change ownership of files.

As a regular user, you cannot reassign a file's or directory's ownership to someone else. For example, I cannot create a file as user kabir and reassign its ownership to a user called sheila. The reason is security, of course. If a regular user were allowed to reassign file ownership to others, someone could create a nasty program that deleted files, changed the program's ownership to the superuser, and wiped out the entire file system. Only the superuser can reassign file or directory ownership.

Changing ownership of a file/directory using chown

As a superuser, you can change the file/directory ownership by using the chown command. To change the ownership of a file or directory, run the command as follows:

```
chown  newuser file or directory
```

For example, the following makes user sheila the new owner of the file kabirs_plans.txt:

```
chown  sheila kabirs_plans.txt
```

If the superuser also wants to change the group for a file or directory, she can use the chown command as follows:

```
chown  newuser.newgroup file or directory
```

For example, the following not only makes sheila the new owner, but also resets the group of the file to be admin:

```
chown  sheila.admin kabirs_plans.txt
```

If the superuser wants to change the user and/or group ownership of all the files or directories under a given directory, she can use the −R option to run the chown command in recursive mode. For example, the following changes the user and group ownership of the /home/kabir/plans directory and all the files and subdirectories within it:

```
chown  -R sheila.admin /home/kabir/plans/
```

Although you have to be the superuser to change the ownership of a file, you can still change a file's or directory's group as a regular user, by using the chgrp command.

Changing group ownership of a file/directory using chgrp

The chgrp command lets you change a file's or directory's group ownership as long as you are also part of the new group. In other words, you can change groups only if you belong to both the old and new groups or as usual, if you are a superuser. For example, if you run the following command to change the group for all the HTML files in a directory, you must also be part of the httpd group:

```
chgrp httpd *.html
```

You can find out what groups you are in by using the groups command without any argument. Like the chown command, chgrp also uses –R to recursively change group names of one or more files or directories.

Setting file/directory permissions using octal numbers

Although using octal numbers is my favorite method for setting file/directory permissions, I must warn you that it involves bits. If you feel you are mathematically challenged, skip to the next section, which explains the same permissions using a much simpler access string.

Because an infrequently used numbering system (the *octal number system*) is used to explain access permissions, here is a small memory refresher on octal numbers. The octal number system uses eight digits as opposed to the commonly used ten digits of the decimal system. The octal digits are 0 through 7, and each digit can be represented by three bits (in binary system). Table 3-2 shows the binary equivalent for each octal digit.

Table 3-2 *Octal to Binary Conversion*

Octal	Binary
0	000
1	001
2	010
3	011
4	100
5	101
6	110
7	111

This table will become useful in understanding file/directory permissions. Figure 3-1 shows how you can visualize the permissions as four octal digits. Here, the first octal digit is the leftmost or most significant one.

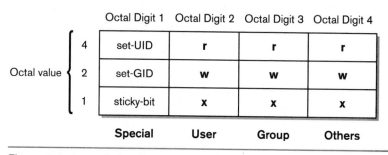

Figure 3-1 *A permission diagram using four octal digits*

As Figure 3-1 demonstrates, the first octal digit is used for setting special permissions, the second digit is used for setting permissions for the file owner, the third digit is used for setting permissions for the group, and the fourth digit is used for setting permissions for everyone else. When any of these digits is omitted, it is considered to be a 0. Table 3-3 shows a few example permission values.

Table 3-3 *Example Permission Values*

Permission Value	Explanation
0400	Only read (r) permission for the file owner. This is equivalent to 400, where the missing octal digit is treated as a leading 0.
0440	Read (r) permission for both the file owner and the users in the group. This is equivalent to 440.
0444	Read (r) permission for everyone. This is equivalent to 444.
0644	Read (r) and write (w) permissions for the file owner. Everyone else has read-only access to the file. This is equivalent to 644; the number 6 is derived by adding 4 (r) and 2 (w).
0755	Read (r), write (w), and execute (x) permissions for the file owner, and read (r) and execute (x) permissions for everyone else. This is equivalent to 755; the number 7 is derived by adding 4 (r) + 2 (w) + 1 (x).

Continued

Table 3-3 *Continued*

Permission Value	Explanation
4755	Same as 755 in the last example, except that this file is set-UID. When an executable file with set-UID permission is run, the process runs as the file owner. In other words, if a file is set-UID and owned be the user gunchy, any time it is run, the running program enjoys the privileges of the user gunchy. So, if a file is owned by root, and is also set to be set-UID, anyone who can run the file essentially has the privileges of the superuser. If a set-UID root file can be altered by anyone but root, it is a major security hole. Be very careful when setting the set-UID bit.
2755	Similar to 755, but also sets the set-GID bit. When such a file is executed, it essentially has all the privileges of the group of the file.
1755	Similar to 755, but also sets the sticky bit, formally known as the save text mode. This is an infrequently used feature that tells the OS to keep an executable program's image in memory even after it exits. This is an external attempt to reduce the startup time of a large program. Instead of setting the sticky bit, you should try to recode the application for better performance, when possible.

To come up with a suitable permission setting, you need to determine what type of access the user, the group, and everyone else should have, and consider whether the set-UID, set-GID, or sticky bit is necessary. After you determine the need, to construct each octal digit, use 4 (read), 2 (write), and 1 (execute), or use a custom value, by adding any of these three values. Although the octal-number-based permissions may seem a bit hard at the beginning, with practice, their use can become second nature.

Setting file/directory permissions using access strings

Setting permissions by using the access string method is (supposedly) simpler than the numeric method discussed in the preceding section. Figure 3-2 shows the access-string version of the permissions diagram.

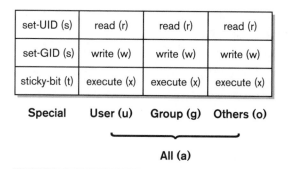

set-UID (s)	read (r)	read (r)	read (r)
set-GID (s)	write (w)	write (w)	write (w)
sticky-bit (t)	execute (x)	execute (x)	execute (x)
Special	**User (u)**	**Group (g)**	**Others (o)**

All (a)

Figure 3-2 *The permissions diagram using access strings*

Each type of permission is represented with a single character (in parentheses). To create a permission string, you need to specify the following:

- **Who it affects.** Your choices are u (user), g (group), o (others), or a (all).

- **The type of permission that needs to be set.** Your choices are r (read), w (write), x (execute), s (set-UID or set-GID), or t (sticky bit).

- **The action type.** Indicate whether you're setting the permission or removing it. When setting the permissions, you need to specify + to specify an addition, and – to specify a removal.

For example, to allow the file owner read access to the file, you need to specify a permission string such as u+r. To allow everyone to read and execute a file, you need a permission string such as a+rx. Similarly, to make a file set-UID, you need u+s; to set it as set-GID, you need g+s.

Changing file/directory permission modes using chmod

The chmod utility allows you to **ch**ange permission **mod**es, and hence is called chmod. You can use either the octal or the string method with this nifty utility. For example,

```
chmod 755 *.pl
```

changes permissions for files ending with extension .pl. Each of the PL files is set as read, write, and execute (7 = 4 [read] + 2 [write] + 1 [execute]) by the owner. The files are also set to be readable and executable (5 = 4 [read] + 1 [execute]) by the group and others.

You can accomplish the same result by using the string method as follows:

```
chmod a+rx,u+w *.pl
```

Here a+rx is used to allow read (r) and execute (x) permissions for all (a), and u+w is used to allow the file owner (u) to write (w) to the file. Note that when multiple access strings need to be used, each pair of strings needs to be separated by a comma. Also note that no space is allowed between the permission strings.

If you want to change permissions for all the files and subdirectories within a directory, you can use the –R option to perform a recursive permission operation. For example,

```
chmod -R 750 /www/mysite
```

applies the 750 octal permission to all the files and subdirectories of the /ww/mysite directory.

Caution

Be very careful when using the –R option with chmod. You could change permissions for sub-directories that could create potential security problems.

Special notes on directory permissions

The permission settings for a directory are similar to those for regular files, but not identical. Here are some special notes on directory permissions:

- Read-only access to a directory doesn't allow you to cd into that directory; to do that, you need execute permission.

- Execute-only permission allows you to access the files inside a directory as long as you know their names and have permission to read the files.

- To list the contents of a directory by using a program such as ls, or to cd into a directory, you need both read and execute permissions.

- If you have write permission for a directory, you can create, delete, or modify any files or subdirectories within that directory, even when the file or subdirectory is owned by someone else.

Managing Permissions for Links

Apart from the regular files and directories, you will quite frequently encounter another type of file — *links.*

Links are pointer files that point to other files. A link allows you to create multiple names for a single file or directory. The two types of links are hard and soft (symbolic) links. This section discusses the special permission issues that arise from the use of links.

Changing permissions or ownership of a hard link

If you change the permission or the ownership of a hard link, you also change the permission of the original file. For example, take a look at the following ls −l output:

```
-rw-r--r--   1 root          21 Feb  7 11:41
todo.txt
```

Now, if the root user creates a hard link (using the command line ln todo.txt plan) called plan for todo.txt, the ls −l output looks as follows:

```
-rw-r--r--   2 root          21 Feb  7 11:41 plan
-rw-r--r--   2 root          21 Feb  7 11:41
todo.txt
```

As you can see, the hard link, plan, and the original file, todo.txt, have the same file size (shown in the fourth column) and also share the same permission and ownership settings. Now, if the root user runs

```
chown  Sheila plan
```

to give the ownership of the hard link to a user called sheila, will it work as usual? Take a look at the ls −l output after the preceding command:

```
-rw-r--r--   2 Sheila   root      21 Feb  7 11:41 plan
-rw-r--r--   2 Sheila   root      21 Feb  7 11:41
todo.txt
```

The chown command changed the ownership of plan, but the ownership of todo.txt (the original file) has also changed. So, when you change the ownership or permissions of a hard link, the effect also applies to the original file.

Changing permissions or ownership of a soft link

Changing the ownership of a soft link, or *symbolic* link, does not work the same way as it does for a hard link. For example, take a look at the following ls –l output:

```
lrwxrwxrwx   1 sheila   root       8 Feb  7 11:49 plan ->
todo.txt
-rw-r--r--   1 sheila   root      21 Feb  7 11:41 todo.txt
```

The plan file is a symbolic link for todo.txt. Now, suppose the root user changes the ownership of the symbolic link as follows:

```
chown kabir plan
```

The ls –l output shows:

```
lrwxrwxrwx   1 kabir    root       8 Feb  7 11:49 plan ->
todo.txt
-rw-r--r--   1 sheila   root      21 Feb  7 11:41 todo.txt
```

The question now is whether user kabir can write to todo.txt using the symbolic link (plan). The answer is no, unless the directory where these files are stored is owned by kabir. So, changing a soft link's ownership does not work in the same way as with hard links. However, if you change the permission settings of a soft link, the file it points to gets the new settings. For example,

```
chmod 666 plan
```

changes the todo.txt file's permission, as shown in the ls −l listing:

```
-rw-rw-rw-   1 kabir    kabir      25 Feb  7 11:52 plan
-rw-r--r--   1 sheila   root       21 Feb  7 11:41
todo.txt
```

So, be cautious with links, because the permission and ownership settings on these special files are a bit nonintuitive.

Creating a Permission Policy for a Multiuser Server

Most user problems on UNIX and UNIX-like systems are related to file permissions. If something that was working fine yesterday suddenly stops working, you should first suspect a permission problem. One of the most common causes of permission problems is the root account. Many inexperienced system administrators often access files and programs via a superuser (root) account. When a program is run using the root user account, the files that such a program creates often can be set with root ownership. This section discusses a few permission policies that you might want to implement, especially if you have many users on a single system.

Setting users' configuration file permissions

Each user's home directory houses some semihidden files that start with a period (or dot). These files often are used to execute commands at user login. For example, all the shells (csh, tcsh, bash, and so on) available to a user read their settings from a dot file, such as those with the extension .cshrc or .bashrc. If a user is not careful to keep file permissions set properly, another not-so-friendly user can cause problems for the naive user. For example, if one user's .cshrc file is writable by a second user, the latter can play a silly trick, such as putting a logout command at the beginning of the .cshrc file so that the first user will be logged out as soon as she logs in. Of course, the silly trick could develop into other tricks that will violate a user's file privacy in the system. Therefore, you might want to watch for such situations on a multiuser system. You can run the COPS program to detect many permission problems. If you have only a handful of users, you can also quickly perform simple checks, such as the following:

```
find /home -type f -name ".*rc" -exec ls -l {} \;
```

This command displays permissions for all the dot files (ending in "rc" to list only .cshrc, .bashrc, and so on) in the /home directory hierarchy. If your users' home directories are kept in /home, this quickly shows you which users might have a permission problem.

Setting default file permissions for users

As a system administrator, you can define the default permission settings for all the user files that get on your system. To set the default permissions for new files, you can use the umask command, as follows:

```
umask mask
```

To understand how umask works, consider an example. Suppose that umask is set to 022. When a new file is created, typically, a permission setting of 0666 is requested by the file creation function — open. However, in such a case, the final permission settings for the file are derived by the system, as shown in Figure 3-3.

As Figure 3-3 shows, the requested permission, 0666, is ANDed with the complement of the current mask (that is, 022 becomes 755) so that the result is 0644, which allows the file owner read and write access, but gives everyone else only read access.

To create a default mask for file permissions, you can embed the umask command in a global shell resource file in /etc so that when a user logs in and runs a shell, the global resource file for that shell is executed. This in turn executes the umask command and provides a default mask for the user session. For example, if your users use the /bin/csh or /bin/tcsh shell, you can put a desirable umask command in the /etc/csh.cshrc file for this purpose.

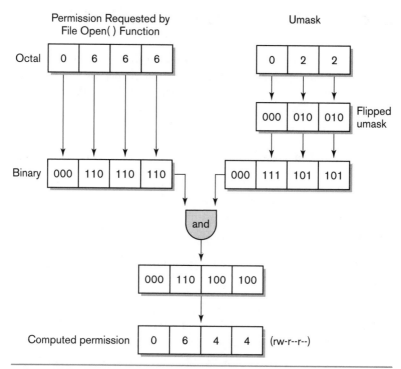

Figure 3-3 *How umask is used by the system*

Setting executable file permissions

Program files that can be run by regular users should never have write permission set for anyone but the owner. For example, the program files in /usr/bin should have permission settings such that only root can read, write, and execute, and everyone else can only read and execute these files. Allowing others to write into a program file can create serious security holes. For example, if someone other than the root is allowed to write to a program such as /usr/bin/zip, a malicious user can replace the real Zip program with a Trojan-horse program that compromises system security and does damage to files and directories as it pleases. So, always check to make sure that the program files on your systems have proper permissions. You should run COPS frequently to detect permission-related problems.

Setting default file permissions for FTP

If many of your users FTP their files on the server, you can control the default umask setting for the FTP server such that one user's file is not accessible by another. For example, if you want to set permissions such that only the user and her group can read a file uploaded on a Web server via FTP, you can modify the in.ftpd line in the /etc/inetd.conf file. This line by default looks as follows:

```
ftp  stream tcp nowait root  /usr/sbin/tcpd  in.ftpd -l -a
```

To set a default umask for all files uploaded via FTP, you need to add a −u argument with the appropriate umask value. For example, to set 640 (rw-r-----) permission for each file uploaded, you can set the umask to 026. So, change the preceding line as follows:

```
ftp  stream tcp nowait root  /usr/sbin/tcpd  in.ftpd -l -
a -u026
```

Restart the inetd server (killall −HUP inetd) and FTP a file via a user account to see whether the permissions are set as expected.

This could be very handy for systems that act as Web servers for many different clients. If you do not want one client to see another client's files, you can use this option along with a special ownership setting. For example, suppose that you keep all of your Web client files in the /www partition or directory, where each client site has a directory of its own (for example, /www/myclient1, /www/myclient2, and so on). You probably already gave each client an FTP account to upload files in these directories. To stop a client from seeing another client's files, use umask, as described, with the FTP server and also reset the ownership of each client site as follows:

```
chown -R client.Web server user   /www/client dir
```

For example, if you run your Web server as httpd and have a client user called myclient, then the preceding command will look like this:

```
chown -R myclient.httpd /www/myclient
```

This changes the ownership of the /www/myclient directory along with all of its subdirectories and files to myclient (user) and httpd (group). This is done to allow the client user to own, modify, and delete her files and to allow the Web server to read the files in the directory. However, to disallow everyone else, you must change the permissions as follows:

```
chmod -R 2770    /www/client dir
```

For the current example, the actual command is as follows:

```
chmod -R 2770    /www/myclient
```

This sets all the files and subdirectory permissions for /www/myclient to 2770, which allows the files and directories to be readable, writable, and executable by the owner (myclient) and the Web server user (httpd) and also makes sure that when new files are created, they have their permissions set to allow the Web server to read the file. This is done using the set-GID (2) digit.

Using Common File/Directory Utilities

This section shows you how to work with a few commonly used file and directory utility programs that are readily available on your Red Hat Linux system.

Viewing files and directories

The ls program probably is the most widely used program on any UNIX or UNIX-like platform. The most widely used options for ls are –l (long listing), –a (all files including filenames starting with a period), –1 (single-column, filenames-only listing), and –R (recursive listing).

Navigating your way into directories

You likely already know the cd command, which is really a built-in shell command. If you don't provide a directory name as an argument, the cd command returns you to the home directory of the user account you are currently using. Any time you are in doubt about where you are in the file system, you can use the pwd command, which displays your current directory name.

Determining file type

Unlike Microsoft Windows operating systems, Linux does not rely on file extensions to determine file types. You can use the file utility to determine a file's type. For example,

```
file /usr/bin/file
```

shows what type of file /usr/bin/file (itself) is. Here is an example of its output:

```
/usr/bin/file: ELF 32-bit LSB executable, Intel 80386, \
version 1, dynamically linked, not stripped
```

Viewing the access statistics of a file or directory

You can use the stat program to get statistics on a file or directory. For example,

```
stat /tmp
```

shows statistics on the /tmp directory. Here is an example of its output:

```
File: "/tmp"
  Size: 2048          Filetype: Directory
  Mode: (1777/drwxrwxrwt)        Uid: (    0/    root)
Gid: (    0/    root)
Device: 3,0    Inode: 16321    Links: 22
Access: Sun Feb  7 02:00:35 1999(00000.00:01:11)
Modify: Sun Feb  7 02:01:01 1999(00000.00:00:45)
Change: Sun Feb  7 02:01:01 1999(00000.00:00:45)
```

Copying files and directories

Use the cp command to copy files from one location to another. For example,

```
cp  /some/important.txt   /new/place/
```

copies a file called important.txt from the /some directory to the /new/place directory. You can specify a new destination filename, as well. Commonly used options for cp include –f, which allows you to force a file to be copied to a location where another file exists with the same name. For example,

```
cp  -f /some/important.txt /new/place/
```

copies the important.txt file even if a file by that name is already in the /new/place directory.

To copy a directory along with all of its files and subdirectories, use the following:

```
cp -r source-directory destination-directory
```

For example,

```
cp -r /tmp/foo   /zoo/foo
```

Moving files and directories

To move files or directories, use the mv command. For example, the following moves /file1 to /tmp/file2:

```
mv  /file1   /tmp/file2
```

Similarly, you can move a directory along with all of its contents. Note that mv does not move directories across different file systems. To do this, use cp with the –r option to copy the directory to the new file system, and then remove the directory (see the text that follows) from the current location.

Deleting files and directories

To delete a file or directory, use the rm command. For example, the following removes the file:

```
rm filename
```

If you are using the /bin/tcsh shell, you may have an alias called rm set as follows:

```
alias rm   rm -i
```

In such a case, the –i prompt tells the command to prompt you before actually deleting anything. If you prefer to be prompted, you can explicitly use the –i option. On the other hand, you can use the –f option to force a removal.

To remove a directory, you need to specify the –r option. For example,

```
rm -rf directory
```

removes all the files and subdirectories within the specified directory.

Finding files

To locate a file, you can use various commands. To locate the exact path of a program, you can use the which command. For example,

```
which  httpd
```

shows you the fully qualified path name of the httpd program if it is available in a directory that is included in the $PATH environment variable. Some shells have a built-in which command, and others use /usr/sbin/which instead.

You can locate a file or directory by a partial or full name using the locate program. For example, the following queries the updatedb filename database and returns all occurrences of the netpr.pl file:

```
locate  netpr.pl
```

For locate to work properly, you must make sure that you have a cron job set up to run updatedb on a daily or weekly basis. Red Hat default installation actually sets up such a job automatically.

Tip

You can use the find program to locate files or directories. For example, to locate all the HTML files in the current directory and all of its subdirectories, run find as follows:

```
find . -type f -name "*.html"
```

Overriding the default file permission mask

The system administrator can set a default permission mask in a global resource file for the shell you are using. For example, if you are using the /bin/tcsh shell, the system administrator can set default file permissions for you in the /etc/csh.cshrc file by using the umask command. If you want to override the default permission mask, however, you can run umask from the command line to change the default mask. For example,

```
umask 222
```

sets the default permission mask to be read, read, and read for everyone. In other words, it turns off the write permission for user, group, and others. This also overrides whatever the system default was for your shell. However, this change is temporary; when you log out and log back in, the system default will be effective again. If you basically dislike the system's permission mask, put the appropriate umask command in your shell's resource file. For example, if you prefer the mask to be 222 all the time and use /bin/tcsh as a shell, you can put this command in your ~/.cshrc file so that every time you log in, the umask command overrides the system's default.

Using ext2 File System-Specific Permissions

The ext2 file system used for Red Hat Linux provides some unique features. One of these features allows a file to be immutable for even the root user. For example,

```
chattr +i filename
```

sets the i attribute of a file in an ext2 file system. When this attribute is set, the file cannot be modified, deleted, or renamed by anyone. No links can be added to point to this file, either. This attribute can be set or cleared only by the root user. So, you can use this attribute to protect against accidents involving files. When you need to clear the attribute, you can run the following:

```
chattr -i filename
```

A few other interesting features of the ext2 system, such as the undelete attribute, are not yet implemented, but will become available in a future ext2 file system version. If you start using the chattr command, you will notice that you sometimes can't modify or delete a file even though you have permission to do so. This happens when you forget that you had previously set the immutable attribute of the file using chattr; because this attribute does not show up in ls output, it can be confusing. To see which files have what ext2 attributes, run the lsattr program with the filename as the argument.

Chapter 4

Using Linuxconf

Is Linuxconf for You?

Linuxconf is a system administration tool that provides a core set of functionality that is accessible via multiple interfaces, such as a Web browser, a text-based menu-oriented interface, or an X Window System-based interface. Linuxconf comes with a core set of modules; each module provides a set of administrative functions for a certain system service or task. For example, the Apache Web server management is implemented in the Apache module. Modules are stored in the /usr/lib/linuxconf/module directory. Currently, many modules are distributed with the RPM package version of Linuxconf. For example, Table 4-1 shows all the modules shipped with Linuxconf version 1.1.6.

Table 4-1 *Modules Shipped with Linuxconf Version 1.1.6*

Module	Description
apache	The Apache Web server configuration module
dhcpd	The Dynamic Host Configuration Protocol server configuration module
dialout	The outgoing PPP connection configuration module; this is not required if you use the red-hatppp module
dnscnf	The DNS configuration module for BIND 4 and 8 versions of the name server
inittab	The /etc/inittab file configuration module
firewall	The firewall configuration module, which allows you packet filtering at the kernel level, IP masquerading, port redirections, and IP accounting

Continued

Table 4-1 *Continued*

Module	Description
mailconf	The sendmail SMTP server configuration module
motd	The message of the day file (/etc/motd) configuration module
mrtg	The Multirouter Traffic Grapher configuration module
netadm	The network configuration module
pppdialin	The PPP-related configuration module
rarp	The Linux kernel's RARP table configuration module
redhatppp	The dial-up services (PPP/SLIP/PLIP) configuration module for Red Hat Linux
samba	The Samba configuration module
squid	The Squid proxy configuration module
status	The system status module
treemenu	An internal module for Linuxconf
userinfo	An extra user info configuration module
usermenu	An internal module for Linuxconf
uucp	The UUCP configuration module
wuftpd	The wu-ftpd FTP server configuration module
xterminals	The X-terminal configuration module

You can find many other modules at `www.solucorp.qc.ca/ linuxconf/`.

Although the idea behind Linuxconf is very impressive, I'm not quite sold on the current state of the application. I found a number of annoying problems that are likely to be fixed in future versions. For example, many of the important help pages are missing or not done yet, and the error messages generated by Linuxconf itself are a bit cryptic in nature. Apart from these annoyances, it functions as expected. In short, I recommend that you consider Linuxconf as an ongoing development project that is very close to being mature.

Installing Linuxconf

Installing Linuxconf is quite simple. If you did not install Linuxconf during your Red Hat Linux installation, you can install it at any time from the

RPM package shipped with the official Red Hat CD-ROM. Also, you can download the RPM package from the official Linuxconf FTP site at `ftp://ftp.solucorp.qc.ca/pub/linuxconf/devel/`.

Make sure you download the right RPM package for your version of Red Hat Linux. After you download the RPM package, you can install it by running the **rpm –ivh** *package* command, where *package* is the actual package name.

Configuring Linuxconf

Linuxconf can be used in multiple ways. It automatically chooses between the text mode (for console or remote shell) or graphics mode (for X Windows). For example, if you log in to your system console and run **/bin/linuxconf** from the command line, you will see a screen similar to the one shown in Figure 4-1.

Figure 4-1 *The text interface for Linuxconf*

The Linuxconf interface uses a tree-style menu structure. Figure 4-1 shows the two top-level menu entries — Config and Control. Here is how the navigation works in text mode.

To expand a particular branch of the menu, select it using the arrow keys and then press Enter. For example, to expand the Config menu, select Config and press Enter. The result is shown in Figure 4-2.

Figure 4-2 *Expanding the Config menu in Linuxconf*

As you can see, Config has multiple branches (Networking, Users accounts, File systems, and boot mode). To close a branch, select it and press Enter. To quit the application, use the Tab key to select the Quit button and press Enter. Linuxconf will probe the running servers and configuration and determine whether anything needs to be activated. If something needs to be activated, because you made some changes to something, you will see a screen with the choices shown in Figure 4-3.

Figure 4-3 *Linuxconf choices on quit*

In such a case, if you want to see what Linuxconf would do to synchronize the running system with the current configuration, select the Preview what has to be done option and press Enter. Another screen appears with a Things to-do list, as shown in Figure 4-4.

Figure 4-4 *Linuxconf's Things to do list*

If you decide to let Linuxconf activate the listed changes, then quit the preview screen, select the Activate the changes option, and press Enter. Linuxconf will activate whatever is necessary and then exit.

If you want to use Linuxconf's GUI from X Windows, run **/usr/bin/ gnome-linuxconf** or **/bin/linuxconf** from an X-terminal window or via your Window manager. The tree menu appears much nicer in the GUI version, as shown in Figure 4-5.

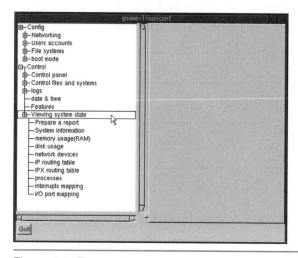

Figure 4-5 *The graphical user interface for Linuxconf*

Any branch that can be further expanded displays a + sign in front of the branch name, and an already expanded branch shows a − sign. For example, in Figure 4-5, the Control branch is completely expanded and everything else is further expandable. Double-clicking the + or − sign expands or closes a branch.

A very interesting feature of the Linuxconf GUI is that each item you select from the tree menu appears on the right side of the screen as a separate tab. While working on one item, you can decide to work on another. In such a case, you have multiple tabs on the right side. Figure 4-6 shows one such scenario, in which tabs appear on the right side of the interface for both the Features and the Workstation date and time settings. More tabs can be added by clicking other items on the tree on the left side of the interface. This is a very flexible way of working on multiple items simultaneously.

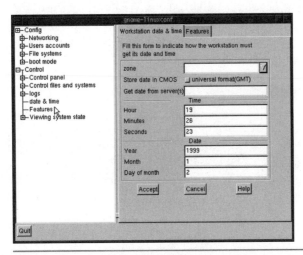

Figure 4-6 *Tab windows in the Linuxconf GUI*

As with the text-based interface, when you decide to quit the GUI, Linuxconf asks you to activate any changes you made. You also can preview or quit without activating the current configuration.

Unfortunately, the Web-based Linuxconf interface is the worst looking one among the three interfaces, although it could have been the jazziest one. Because my favorite interface is the GUI, it is used throughout the chapter for Linuxconf-related discussions.

By default, you can access the Web-based Linuxconf interface only from the localhost. In other words, you need to run your Web browser on the same machine on which you are running Linuxconf. Figure 4-7 shows the main Linuxconf page for this interface.

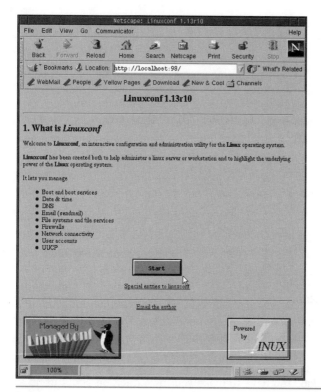

Figure 4-7 *Linuxconf's top Web page*

Notice the URL (http://localhost:98/). Here, "localhost" is required, because remote administrative access via the Web is not enabled, by default, for security reasons. The following section shows you how to enable it.

Setting up Web-based remote access for Linuxconf

The advantages of being able to administer via a Web browser from any platform at any time are limitless. This is especially helpful for those who manage a large number of Linux systems in an organization. If you allow your Linux system to be managed from anywhere, however, you create a big security risk — anyone can now try to break into your system via the

Web-accessible Linuxconf interface. This is why you must restrict Web-based Linuxconf access only to your trusted network.

The Web-based Linuxconf is an inetd-run service. When you install the Linuxconf RPM package, a line such as the following gets added to your /etc/inetd.conf file:

```
linuxconf stream tcp wait root /bin/linuxconf \
  linuxconf --http
```

Another line such as the next one gets added to your /etc/services file:

```
linuxconf  98/tcp
```

This allows inetd to run Linuxconf in HTTP mode when a request for connection is made on TCP/IP port 98. In other words, when you use a browser on your Linux system to access `http://localhost:98/`, the inetd daemon starts /bin/linuxconf using the –http option.

Caution

Linuxconf runs as a setuid root process. Therefore, if a security hole is discovered in Linuxconf, it is likely to allow root privileges to anyone. Linuxconf is over 80,000 lines of C++ code. Frankly, I don't feel too comfortable running a large setuid program via the Web. You have to make your own decision about using it over the Web.

As previously mentioned, by default, Linuxconf allows Web-based access only from the localhost. If you want to enable remote administrative access to Linuxconf via the Web, follow these steps:

1. Run **linuxconf** from your console or X Windows.

2. Select the Config menu option and expand its branches either by pressing Enter for text mode or by double-clicking it for GUI mode. Expand the Misc menu and select Linuxconf network access; you should see a tab on the right similar to the one shown in Figure 4-8.

3. Select the Enable network access check box.

4. Select the Log access in /var/log/htmlaccess.log check box to allow logging of Linuxconf access requests via the network.

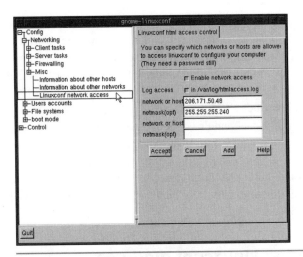

Figure 4-8 *Configuring network access for Linuxconf*

5. In the network or host text box, enter the name of the host that you want to permit for Linuxconf access via the Web. You can also enter the IP or network address here. If you want to allow any host on your LAN to be able to manage this system remotely, you can use the network address here. In Figure 4-8, a network address of 206.171.50.48 is used. To enable all the machines in this network, the netmask 255.255.255.240 is specified in the optional netmask text box. The netmask is optional because Linuxconf can compute the netmask from your network address. If you plan to add multiple hosts but not your entire network, you can just add their IP addresses. By default, the screen allows you to enter two IP addresses and two optional netmasks. If you need more space, click the Add button to get extra entry boxes for additional hosts.

6. After you enter the host names or IP addresses or the network/netmask pairs, click the Activate button.

7. Click the Quit button to exit Linuxconf, and activate the current configuration when prompted.

This should allow the named hosts (or IP addresses) to access Linuxconf via the Web.

As previously mentioned, Linuxconf uses both internal code functions and external modules to perform the actual configuration. Currently, the Linuxconf RPM package ships with virtually all the available modules. This is likely to change, because Linuxconf modules ideally should be shipped with individual packages. For example, the Apache package for Red Hat should include a Linuxconf module. If you do not use the Apache Web server, the Apache module is not needed in your Linuxconf configuration. The more modules you have, the more cluttered the Linuxconf interface looks. If application developers shipped modules themselves, then you would have only what you need. Hopefully, that's the way Linuxconf will go soon. Until this happens, you can manually configure which modules are needed.

Configuring Linuxconf modules

You can add new modules or deactivate existing modules. Modules are kept in the /usr/lib/linuxconf/modules directory. To add a new module, download the necessary RPM package from a Linuxconf FTP site. The list of FTP sites carrying Linuxconf files is available at http://dns. solucorp.qc.ca/linuxconf/available.html.

After you download the new Linuxconf module, use the **rpm −ivh** **module_package** command to install it. Once installed, the module automatically appears in the module list in Linuxconf. It is also automatically activated.

To deactivate a module, do the following:

1. Run **linuxconf** from your console or X Windows.

2. Select Control ⇨ Control files and systems ⇨ Configure Linuxconf modules from the left side of the Linuxconf screen. You will see a screen similar to that shown in Figure 4-9.

3. Scroll down the module list and locate the module you want to deactivate. Toggle the This module is active check box so that the module becomes inactive.

4. Click the Accept button.

5. If you have nothing else to do in Linuxconf, click the Quit button. You are prompted to activate the changes. Click Activate the changes to complete the process.

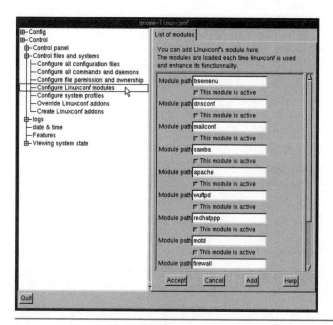

Figure 4-9 *Configuring Linuxconf modules*

The next time you run Linuxconf, it will display the message box shown in Figure 4-10.

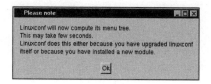

Figure 4-10 *The reconfiguring Linuxconf message box*

This message means that Linuxconf is removing the menu items related to the inactive module. Linuxconf also allows you to create privileged user accounts that can be used to administer a certain aspect of your Linux system. This feature should be a great help if you have coadministrators in your organization. Perhaps you want to offload some of the simpler administrative tasks to junior administrators. In such a case, you can create normal user accounts with restricted sets of privileges. This is discussed in the following section.

Defining user privileges

Linuxconf allows you to associate certain administrative privileges with normal users. Consider this example. Suppose that you have a normal user account called pikeb and want to assign some administrative privileges to this account. Do the following:

1. Run **linuxconf** from your root account.

2. Select Config ⇨ Users accounts ⇨ Normal ⇨ User accounts from the left side of the Linuxconf screen. A list of all normal users on your system appears.

3. Locate the target user (pikeb in this example) and double-click the line of the user's record. You will see a screen similar to the one shown in Figure 4-11.

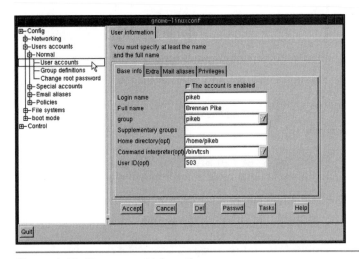

Figure 4-11 *User account information*

4. As Figure 4-11 shows, the Base Info tab is displayed first. Click the Privileges tab to configure available privilege options, as shown in Figure 4-12.

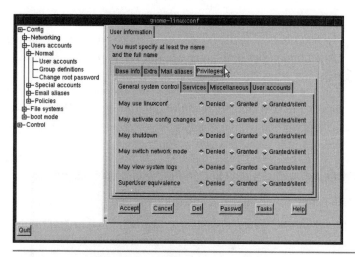

Figure 4-12 *User privilege options*

5. As Figure 4-12 shows, the Privileges tab has four of its own tabs. The first one is the General system control tab, which provides the options shown in Table 4-2.

Table 4-2 *General System Control Options*

Privilege Option	Explanation
May use linuxconf	Grant this privilege if you want the user to be able to run Linuxconf.
May activate config changes	Grant this privilege if you want the user to be able to activate any changes to the current system configuration.
May shutdown	Grant this privilege if you want the user to be able to shut down the system.
May switch network mode	Grant this privilege if you want the user to be able to enable/disable network connectivity.
May view system logs	Grant this privilege if you want the user to be able to see system log files.
SuperUser equivalence	Grant this privilege only to user(s) who need to have superuser (root) access.

To grant any of the privileges shown in Table 4-2, you need to click the appropriate Granted or Granted/silent option, the difference being that the latter doesn't require the user to authenticate using a password. I recommend not using the silent mode for anything.

If you want the user to administer one or more services, click the Services tab to view the service options. The services available to your system will vary depending on what you have installed. Figure 4-13 shows the services available on an example system.

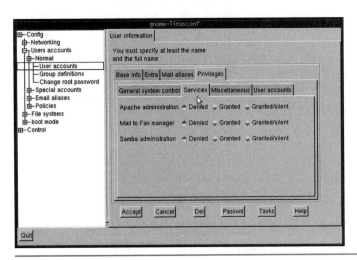

Figure 4-13 *Available Linuxconf-manageable services*

If you want the user to become an account manager for POP/PPP/UCCP users, click the User accounts tab and grant appropriate privileges. You can also click the Miscellaneous tab and grant miscellaneous privileges to the user.

To activate any changes that you made to the user's privileges, click the Accept button and then exit Linuxconf by clicking the Quit button.

After you exit Linuxconf, log in to your system as the user and run Linuxconf. Test your new privileges. Make sure they are what you want them to be. If you are sure that the user in question has all the right privileges, then you are done. Give the lucky (hopefully) user the good news.

Using multisystem configuration profiles

By default, Linuxconf offers two system profiles: Office and Home. You can find the list of available system profiles in Linuxconf. Select Control ⇨ Control files and systems ⇨ Configure system profiles from the left side of the Linuxconf screen. You will see the list of available configurations in the Configuration versioning tab, as shown in Figure 4-14.

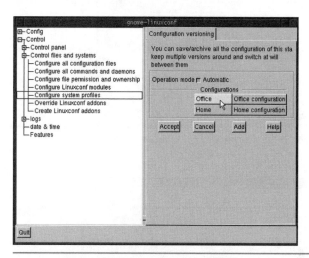

Figure 4-14 *Available (default) system profiles*

To determine which system profile is currently being used by Linuxconf, select Control ⇨ Control panel ⇨ Switch system profile from the left side of the Linuxconf screen. You will see the list of available configurations in the Pick a version tab, as shown in Figure 4-15.

You can also create your own system profiles, as follows:

1. Select Control ⇨ Control files and systems ⇨ Configure system profiles from the left side of the Linuxconf screen. You will see a window similar to the one previously shown in Figure 4-14.

2. Click the Add button to add a new system profile. You will be asked to enter a name for the new system profile, as shown in Figure 4-16. The name must be a single word and cannot have any space characters in it. Enter a name of your choice and click Accept.

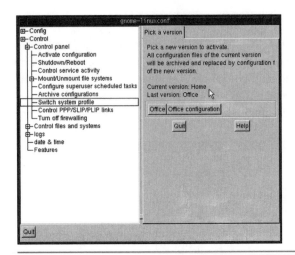

Figure 4-15 *Determining the current system profile*

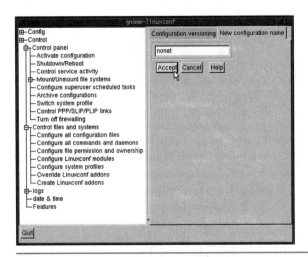

Figure 4-16 *Adding a name for the new system profile*

3. You now are asked to enter a title for your new profile. This can be anything you want; it is used only to help you distinguish the profile from the others. Enter something meaningful in terms of your needs.

4. You need to provide the archiving family names (that is, /etc/linux-conf/archive/*subsystem-family-name*) for various subsystems, such as crond, PPP/SLIP/PLIP, DNS server, firewalling rules, wu-ftpd server, gated, inet, httpd, lpd, and so on. You can also provide a default archiving family name, to be used when you don't explicitly define an archiving family name for a certain subsystem. If you neither set a default family name nor provide an explicit family name, the subsystem's data is stored in the /etc/conf.linuxconf file. If you want to use an existing subsystem from another profile, you can enter the existing family name for that profile. Note that if a subsystem is shared between multiple archives, any changes to the subsystem's configuration files will be effective in all system profiles using that subsystem.

5. After you specify all the archiving family names, click the Accept button. Your new profile will be added to the list of available profiles. Click Accept again.

6. To use your newly created profile, select Control ⇨ Control panel ⇨ Switch system profile from the left side of the Linuxconf screen. Click your profile to switch to it. After you switch to your new profile, it is automatically archived when you switch back to another profile. If you want to archive it manually, select Control ⇨ Control panel ⇨ Archive configurations from the left side of the Linuxconf screen.

As you can see, Linuxconf provides a very powerful means for you to experiment with various configurations without the fear of losing your existing configuration.

Using Linuxconf at system startup

When you install Linuxconf, it modifies the /etc/rc.d/rc.sysinit file by inserting a line such as this one:

```
/sbin/askrunlevel
```

Because /etc/rc.d/rc.sysinit is run by init (which is run by the kernel as the first user process) before anything, the askrunlevel program runs even before init can switch the system to the default run level. The askrunlevel program displays a menu screen on the system console; a similar menu (in GUI mode) is shown in Figure 4-17.

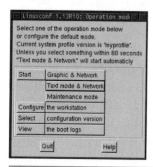

Figure 4-17 *The Linuxconf boot menu*

This menu enables you to select an operation mode from three prebuilt configurations:

- **Graphics & Network.** Suitable for an X Windows workstation connected to the network.
- **Text mode & Network.** Suitable for a server.
- **Maintenance mode.** Suitable for doing maintenance work, such as running the file-system scanner (fsck) or troubleshooting some problem.

If no option is selected before a set timeout period, a default operation mode is selected.

You can also choose to start the system by using one of your system configuration profiles. To start the system by using an existing system profile, select either the Select option or the configuration version option. You are asked to enter the root password. After you successfully authenticate yourself as the root user, you are allowed to select a system configuration to start. You can also view the boot logs to detect boot errors.

It is also possible to bypass this menu or change the default operation mode or timeout value by using Linuxconf. Here is how:

1. Run **linuxconf**.

2. From the Config menu, select the boot mode and then select the default boot mode option.

3. If you want to disable the boot menu, deselect the Boot time menu enabled check box.

4. To change the default operation mode, select either the Graphic & Network option or the Text mode & Network option.

5. To change the prompt timeout or activation delay, enter an appropriate time in seconds in the Prompt timeout or Delay to activate entry box, respectively.

6. After you make all the changes, click the Accept button and activate the changes before you exit Linuxconf.

Part II

Advanced Configuration

Chapter 5

User Administration

Creating Multiple Superuser Accounts

Many novice system administrators think that the user root is the only superuser. This is not true at all. The username "root" is not what makes an account into a superuser. Take a look at the following lines from an example /etc/passwd file:

```
root:dcw12Y6bSUfyo:0:0:root:/root:/bin/tcsh
bin:*:1:1:bin:/bin:
daemon:*:2:2:daemon:/sbin:
kabir:.HoiviYBP4/8U:0:0:Mohammed
sheila:gTwD/qLMFM9M.:501:501::/home/sheila:/bin/tcsh
apache:!!:502:502::/usr/local/apache:/bin/false
```

This password file has two superuser accounts: root and kabir. To understand why, you have to remember that that the /etc/passwd file has the following format:

username: *password*: *UID*: *GID*: *fullname*: *home-dir*: *shell*

Notice the UID (user ID) and GID (group ID) fields of the root account. They are both set to 0. And, if you look back at the line for the ordinary-looking user kabir, you see that his UID and GID are also set to 0. This is what turns a user into a superuser. In other words, any user with a UID and GID of 0 is equivalent to what is called root.

As you can see, you can turn any ordinary user account into a superuser account. In most situations, you do not want to do that, because having multiple superuser accounts could mean additional security risks. But, multiple superuser accounts sometimes are used in organizations that have multiple system administrators working on the same systems. This is done to ensure a little more accountability in a multiadministrator environment. For example, if the kabir and root accounts in the password file just described are for two different system administrators, then it will be a bit easier to tell who did what as the superuser by looking at various log files than if the two system administrators were to share the default root account.

Multiple superuser accounts can be used in one other, not-so-desirable situation — when a system has been hacked by someone. In such a case, the hacker creates an ordinary-looking superuser account by setting the UID and GID values to 0. This allows the hacker to log back in and become a superuser without knowing the root user's password. This trick works on systems where the system administrator is a novice or just too busy to keep an eye open for such things.

Realistically, no system administrator has the time (in the context of a real for-profit organization) to monitor for hackers on a daily basis, so you might want to employ some scripts as your helpers in such a case. For example,

```
/bin/grep '0:0' /etc/passwd | awk 'BEGIN {FS=":"}
{print $1}' | mail -s "`date +"%D %T"`" root
```

This is a really small script that uses a few standard commands to check the /etc/passwd file for users with UID and GID values set to 0. It can mail the root user a list of such accounts. If this script is run via cron by placing it in a file in /etc/cron.daily, you will get an e-mail message from it every day that will show you the list of superusers. You can then quickly check the e-mail every day to know which accounts have superuser privileges. Of course, a smart hacker can find out about this and will be able to change the script to feed you fake information. But, my personal experience shows that most hacking is done by thrill seekers who hardly spend the time to investigate things for themselves. In my experience, most so-called hackers just find an exploitable program on the Internet, compile it, and run it to get access; they often lack the skills to go through the checks that a careful system administrator might have put in place.

Now that you know that any user account can be turned into a superuser account, you might think that any such user can log in to a Red Hat Linux system quite easily. Not so. The Red Hat Linux system, by default, uses the Pluggable Authentication Module (PAM) for login authentication, which requires that superuser access be allowed only from terminals that are considered secured. By default, the PAM configuration file for login, /etc/pam.d/login, contains a line such as the following:

```
auth        required      /lib/security/pam_securetty.so
```

This line states that the security restrictions enforced by the pam_securetty.so module need to be satisfied before a login can be permitted. This particular module considers a superuser login attempt satisfactory only if the login is being attempted from a TTY listed in the /etc/securetty file. So, if you decide to turn an ordinary user into a superuser and attempt to log in via Telnet (which will use a pseudo-TTY device), you will not be able to log in. But, this can be easily changed by adding the pseudo-TTY devices (typically, ttyp1 to ttyp12) in the /etc/securetty file. This is not recommended, however, because it creates a security risk. Instead, if you must use multiple superuser accounts because of some real administrative and accountability reasons, you should do the following:

1. Create multiple superuser accounts.

2. Create one ordinary user account per superuser.

3. Instruct each superuser to log in to the system as an ordinary user and change to the superuser account by using the su command.

The su command can be used to substitute UIDs and GIDs. For example, you can log in as an ordinary user and change to the root account by running su without any argument. You will be prompted for the root password; if you know the root password, su will start a new shell, and you will be logged in as the root user.

Remember that superusers (UID = 0, GID = 0) have full access to everything, and thus these are very sensitive accounts.

Assigning Privileges to Ordinary Users

Using the sudo command, you can allow ordinary users to execute commands that are typically run by a superuser. Suppose that you are the chief system administrator for your organization and have just been blessed with two new assistant system administrators, to whom you want to distribute some of your routine administrative tasks. Should you create two superuser accounts with UIDs and GIDs set to 0, so that these two administrators can have full access to everything, as you do? That depends on how confident you are in their ability to be as careful as you are when working as the ultimate user. Because confidence is something that requires a certain amount of time to build, you probably want to allow them access only to what they need to have access to, and you thus need to configure sudo to allow these individuals to run privileged commands as regular users. Here is how.

The sudo command allows users specified in the /etc/sudoers file to run superuser commands. For example, an ordinary user who is permitted to run superuser commands via sudo can run the following:

```
sudo vi /etc/passwd
```

This allows this user to modify the /etc/passwd file. The sudo program is very configurable, so you can custom-tailor what an ordinary user who is listed in /etc/sudoers can or cannot do. The /etc/sudoers files have the following types of lines:

- **Blank and comment lines (starting with # characters).** Ignored lines.

- **Optional host alias lines.** Used to create short names for the list of hosts. A host alias line must start with the Host_Alias keyword, and the hosts in the list must be separated by commas. For example, in the following line:

```
Host_Alias REDHAT=wormhole,blackhole
```

wormhole and blackhole are two hosts that can be called REDHAT.

■ **Optional user alias lines.** Used to create short names for the list of users. A user alias line must start with the User_Alias keyword, and the users in the list must be separated by commas. For example,

```
User_Alias ASSISTANTS=mike,brian
```

■ **Optional command alias lines.** Used to create short names for the list of commands. A command alias must start with the following:

```
Cmnd_Alias CMDS=/bin/rm,/bin/chmod,/bin/chown
```

■ **Optional run-as alias lines.** Used to create short names for the list of users. Such an alias can be used to tell sudo to run commands as one of the aliased users. For example,

```
Runas_Alias OP=root,operator
```

■ **Required user access specification lines.** The syntax for the user access specification is as follows:

```
user  host=[run as user]  command list
```

You can specify a real username as user or use the User_Alias to specify a list. Similarly, you can use a real host name or a Host_Alias for host. By default, all commands executed via sudo are run as root. If you want to run a command using a different user, you can specify the username (or a Runas_Alias). You also can specify a command (or a Cmnd_Alias); for example,

```
kabir  wormhole= /sbin/shutdown
```

allows the user kabir to run the /sbin/shutdown command on a host called wormhole. Note that you can insert a ! in front of a command or a command alias to deny the command or command alias, as permitted.

It is possible to define multiple aliases in a single line; for example,

```
UserAlias ASSISTANTS=mike,brian:INTERNS=joe,robert,steve
```

defines two aliases (ASSISTANTS and INTERNS) in a single line, where the alias definitions are separated by a colon character. This same syntax also applies to the other alias types.

Two special keywords exist: ALL and NOPASSWD. ALL is used to mean "everything," and NOPASSWD is used to state that no password should be required. Listing 5-1 shows an example /etc/sudoers file.

Listing 5-1 *An Example /etc/sudoers File*

```
# sudoers file.
#
# This file MUST be edited with the 'visudo'
# command as root.
#
# See the man page for the details on how to
# write a sudoers file.
#

# Host alias specification

# User alias specification
User_Alias    SENIORADMIN=kabir
User_Alias    ASSISTANTS=mike,john
# User privilege specification

SENIORADMIN ALL=ALL
ASSISTANTS  ALL=ALL
```

This /etc/sudoers file defines two user aliases, SENIORADMIN and ASSISTANTS, where the former has only one user (kabir), and the latter has two users (mike and john). The user privilege specification states the following:

- The users listed in user alias SENIORADMIN can run sudo on all hosts as root (default), and can also run all commands. Because user kabir is the only one in this group, this effectively states that kabir can run all commands via sudo. In other words, the user kabir can do anything the user root can do.

- The second user specification states that users listed in the user alias ASSISTANTS are allowed the exact same access privileges as those in the first specification.

Returning to the first example scenario, where you have two assistants who don't yet need full superuser access, suppose that you (user ID = yourid) want these two users (sysad1, sysad2) to have privileges to run only the shutdown command. In such a case, your /etc/sudoers file might look like this:

```
# User alias specification
User_Alias  SENIORADMIN=yourid
User_Alias  ASSISTANTS=sysad1,sysad2


# User privilege specification
SENIORADMIN ALL=ALL
ASSISTANTS  ALL=/sbin/shutdown
```

Suppose that after a while, you become confident that these two users can handle other superuser privileges in a responsible manner, so you want to give them full access except for the privilege to run the su command. The /etc/sudoers file now looks as follows:

```
# User alias specification
User_Alias  SENIORADMIN=yourid
User_Alias  ASSISTANTS=sysad1,sysad2


# User privilege specification
SENIORADMIN ALL=ALL
ASSISTANTS  ALL=ALL,!/bin/su
```

As you can see from the user specifications for the ASSISTANTS, they are allowed to run ALL commands via sudo except for the /bin/su command.

Managing Users with Command-Line Tools

This section shows you the traditional way of doing user administration using various command-line tools.

Creating a new user account

Creating a new user account is quite easy. To create a user account from your command line, you can run the useradd command. For example, to create a user called newuser, you can run this command as follows:

```
useradd newuser
```

This adds a new entry in /etc/passwd (and in /etc/shadow if you use shadow passwords) using system defaults. For example, when I run the preceding command on my Red Hat system, /etc/passwd shows a new line such as the following:

```
newuser:!!:506:506::/home/newuser:/bin/bash
```

If you remember the /etc/passwd fields from the earlier discussion, you will see that the password field (the second field) is set to !!. This means that this password is not set and newuser cannot log in yet. So, you need to create a password for this user by running the passwd command as follows:

```
passwd newuser
```

You are asked to enter the password twice, and after your password is accepted, it is encrypted and added to the user's entry in the /etc/passwd file.

The UID and the GID values will be selected automatically by useradd. Basically, it just increments the last UID in /etc/passwd by 1 and the last GID in /etc/group by 1 to create the UID and GID, respectively, for the new user. You also can set manually the UID and group using command line switches −u and −g respectively. The home directory is created in the default top-level home directory. Similarly, the login shell is selected from a system default. Setting these defaults is explained in a later section. If you want to override a system default, you can specify a command-line option. To override the default home directory, use the −d *newdirectory* option (where *newdirectory* is the name of your directory). For example,

```
useradd newuser -d /www/newuser
```

The new user (newuser) will be created, and her home directory will be set to /www/newuser. Note that useradd will create only the final directory, not the entire path. For example, if you specify −d /some/new/dir/myuser as the option, useradd will create myuser only if /some/new/dir/ already exists.

When the new home directory is created, files contained in the /etc/skel directory are copied to the new home directory. These files are typically the dot configuration files for the default shell. For example, if the default shell is /bin/bash, you should have default versions of .bashrc, .bash_profile, and .bash_login in the /etc/skel directory so that the new user's home directory can be automatically set up with these files.

The useradd that comes with Red Hat Linux creates a private group for the user with the same name as the username. For example, if you run useradd kabir, then a new user named kabir will be created in the /etc/passwd file, and a new group called kabir will be created in the /etc/group file. This method allows the new user to be totally isolated from the rest of the users, and therefore ensures greater privacy for the user. Whenever the new user creates a new file, by virtue of this private group, the file is accessible only by the new user. The user has to change the file permissions explicitly to allow someone else to see the file.

However, if your user account philosophy clashes with this kind of private group idea, you can override it by using the −g *group* option (where *group* is the name of your group). For example,

```
useradd mjkabir -g users
```

makes useradd create the new user (mjkabir) with the default group set to the users.

 Tip

You can use the groups *username* command to find out which user belongs to what group.

If you want to make the new user a member of additional groups on your system, you can use the –G *comma-separated list of groups* option. For example,

```
useradd mjkabir -G wheel,admins
```

adds the new user (mjkabir) to the wheel and admins groups in the /etc/group file.

Creating a new group

To create a new group, use the groupadd command. For example, the following adds a new group called mygroup in the /etc/group and in the /etc/gshadow file (if you are using shadow passwords):

```
groupadd mygroup
```

By default, the groupadd program creates the group with a GID above 499, because 0 through 499 are (sort of) reserved for system-level accounts such as root, bin, and mail. So if your /etc/group file has the last group GID set to 511, the new group you create with this program will have a GID of 512, and so on. If you want to set the GID of your new group specifically, use the –g *GID* option. Also, if you want to create a group with a GID in the 0 to 499 range, use the –r option with the –g *GID* option to force groupadd to create the new group as a system group. Note that if the group or GID you are trying to use with the program is already in use in /etc/group, you will get an error message.

Modifying an existing user account

Dealing with forgotten user passwords is the most common task a system administrator performs. This section explains how to change various details of a user account.

Changing a password

To change or set a user's password, use the passwd command. For example, the following enables you to change user kabir's password:

```
passwd kabir
```

You are asked to enter the password twice to confirm it. Choose good passwords for your users. Do not use simple-to-remember passwords that use common dictionary words. Note that the passwd program can also be run by a user to change her own password. When an ordinary user runs the passwd program, no username argument is required, because it allows her to change only her own password.

Changing the shell

If the default shell is not appropriate for a user, you may change it to any shell you list in /etc/shells. Use the chsh command to change a user's shell. For example, the following enables you to change user brian's current shell:

```
chsh brian
```

If you specify any shell or program name that is not in /etc/shells, the user will not be able to log in. Note that a user can change her own shell using this command. An ordinary user does not need to specify the username as an argument, because the only shell she can change is her own.

You can also use the usermod command to modify the shell information, as follows:

```
usermod -s new shell path username
```

where *new shell path* and *username* are the correct values.

Changing the home directory

To change the home directory of an existing user, run the usermod command as follows:

```
usermod -d new home directory username
```

where *new home directory* and *username* are the correct values.

For example, if a user called keller has /home/keller as her home directory, and you want to move it to /home2/keller, you can run the usermod command as follows:

```
usermod -d /home2/keller keller
```

This sets the new directory as her home directory. However, if you want to move the contents of her home directory to the new location, use the —m option as follows:

```
usermod -d -m /home2/keller keller
```

Changing a UID

To change the UID of a user, use the usermod command as follows:

```
usermod -u UID username
```

where *UID* and *username* are the correct values.

For example, the following changes the UID for user mrfrog to 500:

```
usermod -g 500 mrfrog
```

All the files and directories that are owned by the user within her home directory will automatically reflect the UID change. However, if the user owns files outside her own home directory, you will have to manually change the ownership using the chown command.

Changing a default group

To change the default group for a user, use the usermod command as follows:

```
usermod -g group name or GID username
```

where *group name or GID* and *username* are the correct values.

For example, the following changes the default group for user mrfrog to 777:

```
usermod -g 777 myfrog
```

Changing an account expiration date

If you are using shadow passwords, you can change the expiration date of a user account using the usermod command as follows:

```
usermod -e MM/DD/YY username
```

where *MM/DD/YY* and *username* are the correct values.

For example, the following resets the account expiration date for user kabir to 12/31/99:

```
usermod -e 12/31/99 kabir
```

Changing finger information

If you allow your users to use the finger program to locate each other or run a finger daemon for people outside to finger your user accounts, you can also change the finger information, such as the full name and phone numbers. Run the chfn command to change a user's finger information. For example, the following allows you to change user jennifer's finger information, which is stored in the /etc/passwd file:

```
chfn jennifer
```

A user can change her own finger information by using this program, as well. A user can also create a .plan file in her home directory that will get appended to the information shown by the finger program.

Modifying an existing group

To modify an existing group name or GID, use the groupmod command. To rename a group to a new name, use the following syntax:

```
groupmod -n new group  current group
```

For example, the following renames the existing novices group to experts:

```
groupmod -n experts novices
```

To change the GID, use the −g *new GID* option. For example, the following changes the current GID of the troublemakers group to 666:

```
groupmod -g 666 troublemakers
```

Deleting or disabling a user account

To delete an existing user, use the userdel command. For example, the following deletes the user called snake:

```
userdel snake
```

If you want to remove the user's home directory and all of its contents, use the −r option. Note that userdel will not delete the user if the user is currently logged in. Ask the user to log out by sending her a write message (write *username*), and if asking isn't an option, use the killall command to terminate all processes associated with the user, and then run the userdel command.

If you want to temporarily disable a user account, you can do one of the following:

- Use the usermod −s *new shell username* command to change the shell to /bin/false (make sure the new shell is listed in the /etc/shells file). This disallows the user from logging in to the system.

- If you are using the shadow passwords, use the usermod −e *MM/DD/YY username* command to cause the user account to expire.

If you want to disable all user account access temporarily, you can create a file called /etc/nologin with a message explaining why you are not allowing access. The login program will not allow any nonroot account to log in as long as this file is in place.

 Caution

If you administer the server via Telnet or any other means, such as secure shell (ssh) access, do not create /etc/nologin, because you will not be able to log in to your system. This is because, by default, root or superuser accounts are not allowed to log in directly from a nonsecured TTY (that is, any TTY not specified in /etc/securetty), so you can't log in as an ordinary user first and then su to a privileged user account.

Creating default user settings

The default settings for creating new users using useradd come from /etc/default/useradd. An example of this file is shown in Listing 5-2.

Listing 5-2 *An Example /etc/default/useradd File*
```
# useradd defaults file
GROUP=100
HOME=/home
INACTIVE=-1
EXPIRE=
SHELL=/bin/bash
SKEL=/etc/skel
```

The following are explanations of the entries in this file:

- **GROUP=100.** Specifies that the default GID is 100. This value is used only when you disable (using the −n option) the default private group (the group with the same name as the new user). You can specify a group name instead of the numeric value, as well. The value you specify in this line must exist in /etc/group. You can change this value as follows:

  ```
  useradd -D -g newsgroup name or GID
  ```

  where *newsgroup name* and *GID* are the proper values.

- **HOME=/home.** Specifies the default top-level home directory for new users. For example, when you create a new user called joe, the default home directory is /home/joe. You can change this to fit your needs. Make sure that the directory already exists. You can change this value as follows:

  ```
  useradd -D -d directory
  ```

- **INACTIVE=−1.** Specifies when (in days) the account will become inactive after the password expires. This is useful only if you are using shadow passwords. The default value of −1 states that accounts are never inactive. You can change this value as follows:

  ```
  useradd -D -f number of days
  ```

- **EXPIRE=.** Specifies when a account should be disabled. This is useful only if you are using shadow passwords. By default, accounts never become disabled. You can change this value as follows:

  ```
  useradd -D -e  MM/DD/YY
  ```

  The defaults used in creating new users come from the /etc/login. def file. Listing 5-3 shows an example of this file.

- **SHELL=/bin/bash.** Specifies the default login shell path. You can change this value as follows:

  ```
  useradd -D -s /bin/tcsh
  ```

  Note that the useradd program does not check whether the path you specify is a valid shell, or even whether it exists. So, make sure that the path you specify is a valid shell and listed in /etc/shells file.

- **SKEL=/etc/skel.** Specifies the directory where various user configuration files are kept, such as dot files for shells, X Windows, and so forth. The files in this directory are copied to the new home directory of a new user account. Normally, you do not want to change this path to some other directory. On the other hand, if you do want to change it, you have to modify the /etc/default/useradd file by using an editor, or simply create a symbolic link /etc/skel that points to the desired directory.

If you are using the shadow passwords, another default configuration file called /etc/login.defs is used in creating user accounts. Listing 5-3 shows an example of this file.

Listing 5-3 *An Example /etc/login.defs File*

```
# *REQUIRED*
#   Directory where mailboxes reside, _or_ name
#   of file, relative to the home directory.
#   If you _do_ define both, MAIL_DIR takes precedence.
#   QMAIL_DIR is for Qmail
#
#QMAIL_DIR   Maildir
MAIL_DIR   /var/spool/mail

#MAIL_FILE   .mail
# Password aging controls:
```

```
#
#  PASS_MAX_DAYS  Maximum number of days a
#                 password may be used.
#
#  PASS_MIN_DAYS  Minimum number of days allowed
#                 between password changes.
#
#  PASS_MIN_LEN   Minimum acceptable password length.
#
#  PASS_WARN_AGE  Number of days warning given before
#                 a password expires.
#
PASS_MAX_DAYS  99999
PASS_MIN_DAYS  0
PASS_MIN_LEN   5
PASS_WARN_AGE  7

#
# Min/max values for automatic uid
# selection in useradd
#
UID_MIN   500
UID_MAX   60000

#
# Min/max values for automatic gid
# selection in groupadd
#
GID_MIN   500
GID_MAX   60000

#
# Require password before chfn/chsh can make
# any changes.
```

Continued

Listing 5-3 *Continued*

```
#
CHFN_AUTH   yes


#
# Don't allow users to change their "real name"
# using chfn.
#
CHFN_RESTRICT   yes


#
# If defined, this command is run when removing a user.
# It should remove any at/cron/print jobs etc. owned by
# the user to be removed (passed as the first argument).
#
#USERDEL_CMD   /usr/sbin/userdel_local


#
# If useradd should create home directories for
# users by default on RH systems, we do. This option is
# ORed with the -m flag on useradd command line.
#
CREATE_HOME   yes
```

Because the comments in this file are sufficient to explain the configuration details, they are not discuss any further here.

Managing Users with linuxconf

The linuxconf command can be used to perform all the user administration tasks. This section uses the X Windows-based interface for linuxconf.

Adding a new user account

To access the user administrative interface in linuxconf, select Config ⇨ Users accounts ⇨ Normal ⇨ User accounts from the left side of the linuxconf window.

To add a new user, follow these steps:

1. Click the Add button on the right side of the window. A new window with multiple tabs appears.

2. In the Base Info tab, enter the Login name (username), Full name, group , Supplementary groups (optional), Home directory (optional), Command interpreter (optional), and User ID (optional). You can also choose to create this account but not yet enable it, by deselecting the This account is enabled check box.

   You can use the other tabs (Extra, Mail aliases, and Privileges) to set up additional information about this account. The privilege options found in the Privileges tab are applicable only to linuxconf. In other words, if you assign privileges to an ordinary account, the privilege is applicable only if the user is able to run linuxconf. For example, if you want this user to be able to run linuxconf, you can choose to allow that in the Privileges tab.

3. After you select the appropriate privileges (if any), click Accept to add the user. Note that the user is not added until you either tell linuxconf to activate the configuration via the Control ⇨ Control Panel ⇨ Activate configuration option or allow it to activate the configuration before you quit the application.

Modifying an existing user account

To modify a user account in linuxconf, do the following:

1. Select Config ⇨ User accounts ⇨ Normal ⇨ User accounts from the left side of the linuxconf window.

2. Click the account name on the right side, and you see a tab that has all the user account information preloaded. Modify anything that you want, and then either use the Control ⇨ Control Panel ⇨ Activate configuration option to activate the changes immediately or activate them when you quit the application.

Deleting or disabling an existing user account

To delete or disable a user account, do the following:

1. Select Config ➪ User accounts ➪ Normal ➪ User accounts from the left side of the linuxconf window.

2. Click the account name on the right side, and you see a tab that has all the account information preloaded. To delete this account, click the Del button. To disable it, deselect the This account is enabled check box.

Adding, modifying, and deleting groups

To add, modify, or delete groups, do the following:

- Select Config ➪ User accounts ➪ Normal ➪ Group definitions from the left side of the linuxconf screen.

- To add a new group, click Add. This opens a new window. Enter the name and optionally the GID, members, and so on. Click Accept. The new group will be effective when you activate the changes you make in linuxconf.

- To modify an existing group, click an existing group name. A new tab appears with the selected group's information preloaded. Make necessary changes and click Accept. The modified group will be effective when you activate the changes you make in linuxconf.

- To delete an existing group, click an existing group name. A new tab appears with the selected group's information preloaded. Click Delete. The deletion will be effective when you activate the changes you make in linuxconf.

Although linuxconf tries to make user administration quite simple, it often falls apart when you change something in your system. For example, when I upgraded my SMTP mail transport agent (sendmail), the user administration aspect of the linuxconf stopped being nice. It could not locate a program (makemap) that comes with sendmail, and therefore it kept asking me (even after I specified the path to the program) about it every time I wanted to add, modify, or delete a user. After I upgraded to the latest version, it was fixed.

Using Disk Quotas for Users

Disk space on a multiuser system can be quite a scarce resource. Experience shows that as soon as you plug in a new drive with lots of space, users tend to use it up quite rapidly. So, the more you add, the more you need. The best way to ensure that you have enough disk space for your system is to enforce disk quotas. This section explains how.

Installing disk quota software

The official Red Hat CD-ROM comes with quota software. For example, to install the quota software for an *x*86 machine, the following command can be run from the CD-ROM's /RedHat/RPMS directory:

```
rpm -ivh quota-version.i386.rpm
```

After the quota software is installed, you are ready to configure it.

Configuring your system to support disk quotas

First, decide which partitions you want to bring under disk quotas. Typically, these are the partition(s) for user home directories and Web space. Also decide whether you want to enforce quotas per user, per group, or both. This discussion assumes that you want to enable disk quotas for the /home and /www partitions, and want to enforce only the per-user disk quota for the /home partition and the per-group disk quota for the /www partition. It also assumes that you have a /etc/fstab file that looks like the following:

```
/dev/sda1    /home    ext2    defaults    1 2
/dev/sda5    /www     ext2    defaults    1 2
```

To enforce user-level disk quotas on /home, you have to modify the first line as follows:

```
/dev/sda1    /home    ext2    defaults,usrquota    1 2
```

The new option in the mount option field in the preceding fstab line is needed to enable disk quotas for users. Similarly, to enable group-level disk quotas on /www, the second fstab line would have to be modified as follows:

```
/dev/sda5   /www   ext2   defaults.grpquota  1 2
```

Tip

You can also use both usrquota and grpquota for a single partition if you plan to enforce quotas for both users and groups.

After you complete these modifications, you need to modify the /etc/rc.d/rc.local script as follows:

```
# Check quota and then turn quota on.
if [ -x /sbin/quotacheck ]; then
        echo "Checking quotas. This may take some time..."
        sbin/quotacheck -avug
        echo " Done."
   fi
if [ -x /sbin/quotaon ]; then
        echo "Enabling disk quota .."
        /sbin/quotaon -avug
        echo " Done."
   fi
```

When this script is run after the file systems have been loaded, it enables quota checking and then turns on the disk quota feature.

Next, you need to create quota files for each file system you have placed under quota control. So, create the quota files as follows:

```
touch /home/quota.user
touch /www/quota.group
```

Make sure that these two files have read and write permissions for only the root user. Now you have completed the system-level quota configuration; before you continue with the quota assignments for users and groups, you should reboot the system. This will run the quotacheck program, which will create disk usage information in the quota files.

Assigning disk quotas to users

After you reboot the system with the new quota configuration, you are ready to assign disk quotas for each user. To assign disk quotas per user, use the edquota command. For example, to allocate a disk quota for a user named kabir, run the following:

```
edquota -u kabir
```

This brings up the default text editor (such as vi or whatever is set in the $EDITOR environment variable) with contents similar to the following:

```
Quotas for user kabir:
/dev/sda5: blocks in use: 0, limits (soft = 0, hard = 0)
          inodes in use: 0, limits (soft = 0, hard = 0)
```

Here, the user kabir has so far used 0 blocks (in K) on disk partition /dev/sda5 (under usrquota control), and the limits (soft or hard) are not set yet. Similarly, this user has not yet owned any files (inodes), and no limit (soft or hard) has been set yet.

As you can see, you can simultaneously set limits for the amount of space (in blocks) a user can consume, and control how many files can be owned by the user. The soft limit specifies the maximum amount of disk space (blocks) or files (inodes) a user can have on the file system. The hard limit is the absolute amount of disk space (in blocks) or files (inodes) a user can have.

For example, suppose that you want to allow user kabir to have a soft limit of 1MB (1,024K) and a hard limit of 4MB (4,096K) for disk space. Also, suppose that you want to allow this user a soft limit of 128 files/directories (inodes) and a hard limit of 512 files/directories. You can set the quota limit using edquota −u kabir as follows:

```
Quotas for user kabir:
```

```
/dev/sda5: blocks in use: 0, limits (soft = 1024, hard =
4096)
          inodes in use: 0, limits (soft = 128, hard = 512)
```

After you save the configuration, the user no longer can exceed the hard limits. If the user tries to go over any of these two (disk space and inode count) limits, an error message will be displayed. For example, in the following, user kabir tries to create a new directory in /home, but the quota limit for this quota has been exceeded, so the error message is displayed:

```
[kabir@picaso /home]$ mkdir eat_space
mkdir: cannot make directory `eat_space': Disc quota
exceeded
```

If you have many users to assign quotas to, the preceding method could be quite time-consuming. To aid you with such a situation, the edquota program includes a −p *prototype user* option that allows you to copy the prototype user's disk quota configuration for others. For example, suppose that you want to use the quota configuration you just created for user kabir for three other users (sheila, jennifer, and mrfrog). You can run the following:

```
edquote -p kabir  -u sheila jennifer mrfrog
```

Now, all three of these users have the same quota configuration as kabir.

Placing groups under disk quota control is very similar. The edquota syntax for configuring a group quota requirements is as follows:

```
edquota -g group name
```

To enforce the soft limit for either user or group quotas, you need to configure the grace period by using the edquota −t command. When you run this command, your editor will display something similar to the following:

```
Time units may be: days, hours, minutes, or seconds
Grace period before enforcing soft limits for users:
/dev/sda5: block grace period: 0 days, file grace period:
0 days
```

You can specify the grace period in days, hours, minutes, or even seconds. For example, in the following, the grace period for the disk space limit (in blocks) is 7 days, and the grace period for the number of files (inodes) is only 5 hours:

```
Time units may be: days, hours, minutes, or seconds
Grace period before enforcing soft limits for users:
/dev/sda5: block grace period: 7 days, file grace period:
5 hours
```

Monitoring disk usage

To find out how much of your disk space a particular user is using, run the quota command as follows:

```
quota -u username
```

For example:

```
quota -u kabir
Disk quotas for user kabir (uid 500):
Filesystem blocks quota limit grace files quota limit
grace
/dev/sda5  0     1024 4096       1    128   512
```

You can run the same command to monitor disk usage of a group, as follows:

```
quota -g group
```

When you find users or groups that are over the limit, you can send them e-mail messages, so that disk usage is brought down to acceptable limits.

Chapter 6

Process Administration

Controlling and Monitoring Processes

Daemon processes typically are started by the init process at boot time. You can control which daemons are run at boot time by reconfiguring /etc/inittab and run-level configuration files and scripts in the /etc/rc.d directory. Except for the daemon processes, the other kinds of processes that you run are called the user processes or interactive processes. You run an interactive process via a shell. Every standard shell provides a command line where a user enters the name of a program. When a user enters a valid program name in the command line, the shell creates a copy of itself as a new process and replaces the new process with the named program from the command line. In other words, the shell runs the named program as another process.

To get information about all the running processes on your system, you run a utility called ps.

Using ps to get the status of processes

This nifty utility produces a report of all the processes in a system. For example, when I run ps from a login shell, it shows the following output:

```
PID   TTY STAT TIME COMMAND
31795 p7  S    0:00 -tcsh
31811 p7  R    0:00 ps
```

As you can see, ps provides a tabular report. Here, ps shows that I'm running two processes: the –tcsh shell, which really is the /bin/tcsh shell run as a login shell, and the ps process itself. Table 6-1 explains the meaning of the common output fields for ps.

Table 6-1 *Output Fields for ps*

Field	Explanation
USER or UID	Process owner's username.
PID	Process ID.
%CPU	CPU utilization of the process. Because the time base over which this is computed varies, it is possible for this to exceed 100 percent.
%MEM	Percentage of memory (in kilobytes) utilization of the process.
SIZE	Size (in kilobytes) of virtual memory used by the process.
RSS	Resident set size or size of real memory (in kilobytes) used by the process.
TTY	Terminal (tty) associated with the process. Usually, the tty name is shortened. For example, p7 is displayed for /dev/ttyp7.
STAT	State of the process. Process states are represented by characters, such as R (running or ready to run), S (sleeping), I (idle), Z (zombie), D (disk wait), P (page wait), W (swapped out), N (lowered priority by nice), T (terminated), < (execution priority raised by superuser), and so on.
START	Process start time or date.
TIME	Total CPU time used by the process.
COMMAND	Command line being executed.
NI	The nice priority number.
PRI	Process priority number.
PPID	Process ID (PID) of the parent process.
WCHAN	Name of the kernel function where a process is sleeping. The name of the function is retrieved from the /boot/System.map file.
FLAGS	A numeric flag associated with the process.

The ps utility also accepts several command-line arguments. Table 6-2 shows the commonly used options.

Table 6-2 *Commonly Used ps Options*

Options	Description
a	Show processes belonging to all users.
e	Show process environment variables after the command line being executed.
l	Show output in long format.
u	Show username and process start time.
w	Show output in wide format. Normally, output is truncated if it cannot fit in a line. Using this option, you can prevent truncation.
t*xx*	Show processes that are associated with *xx* tty device.
x	Show processes without controlling tty.

A few examples of using ps options are provided next.

To see all the processes you are running at any time, run the following:

```
ps u
```

An example of the output of the preceding command is shown here:

```
USER   PID %CPU %MEM  SIZE   RSS TTY STAT START TIME COMMAND
kabir  18  0.0  0.8  1556  1040  p5  S   08:41 0:00 -tcsh
kabir 135  0.0  0.8  1560  1040  p7  S   09:03 0:00 -tcsh
kabir 852 53.8  0.6  1604   788  p5  R   09:33 0:04 perl ./eatcpu.pl
kabir 855  0.0  0.3   848   484  p7  R   09:34 0:00 ps u
```

This shows all the processes that are running for a user called kabir. Notice that ps itself is listed in the output. The first two lines show that kabir is running two tcsh shell sessions. The third line is very interesting, because it shows that a Perl script called eatcpu.pl is utilizing approximately 53.8 percent of the CPU. The STAT flags indicate that the Perl script and the ps utility are the only running (or runnable) processes here. By looking at the TTY field, you can tell which process is attached to which tty.

In the next example, ps is told to display all the processes (excluding the one not associated with any controlling tty):

```
ps au
```

To find out what processes are owned by a particular user, run

```
ps au | grep username
```

where *username* is the name of the actual user.

For example, ps au | grep sheila will show all the interactive processes (processes associated with a tty) being run by a user called sheila. Typically, normal users are not allowed to run daemon processes or processes that are not associated with a tty. However, if you just want to find out whether any such processes exist for any user, run

```
ps aux
```

The x option tells ps to list processes that are detached from terminals. You can identify these processes by looking at the TTY field, which displays a ? character instead of a shortened name of a tty device such as p7 (/dev/ttyp7).

To find the PID of a process's parent, you can run

```
ps l PID
```

where *PID* is the PID of the process.

For example, if you want to find the parent of a process with PID 123, run **ps l 123**, and the parent's PID will be listed in the PPID field of the report.

To determine what initial environment variables are available to processes, run

```
ps e
```

The environment information is appended to the COMMAND field.

Caution

A normal user cannot use the e option to see the environment information of another user's processes. This is a security feature. Only root or superuser-equivalent users can view the environment information of all the processes.

Signaling a running process

Linux, and all UNIX in general, provides a way to send various signals to processes. A signal is an exception, which typically is used to tell the process to do something other than the usual. For example, if you need to kill a process, you can send it a signal to terminate. The command to signal a process is called kill. It is a confusing name, because kill can be used to send any valid signal, not just a signal to kill the process.

Using kill

The kill command can be a built-in shell command for many popular shells, such as csh and tcsh. However, there is also an external kill program, which typically is found in the /bin directory. Both versions work the same way. To find out what signals you can send to processes via kill, you can run the following:

```
kill -l
```

You should see a list similar to the following:

1) SIGHUP	2) SIGINT	3) SIGQUIT	4) SIGILL
5) SIGTRAP	6) SIGIOT	7) SIGBUS	8) SIGFPE
9) SIGKILL	10) SIGUSR1	11) SIGSEGV	12) SIGUSR2
13) SIGPIPE	14) SIGALRM	15) SIGTERM	17) SIGCHLD
18) SIGCONT	19) SIGSTOP	20) SIGTSTP	21) SIGTTIN
22) SIGTTOU	23) SIGURG	24) SIGXCPU	25) SIGXFSZ
26) SIGVTALRM	27) SIGPROF	28) SIGWINCH	29) SIGIO
30) SIGPWR			

The preceding output is produced by the built-in kill command in the GNU Bourne-Again Shell (/bin/bash). Other shells or the /bin/kill command might print the output a bit differently. For example, /bin/kill -l produces the following output:

```
HUP INT QUIT ILL TRAP IOT UNUSED FPE KILL USR1 SEGV USR2
PIPE ALRM TERM STKFLT CHLD CONT STOP TSTP TTIN TTOU IO
XCPU XFSZ VTALRM PROF WINCH
```

Notice that these two kill commands differ in the −1 output they produce. In fact, if you use /bin/csh (C shell) or /bin/tcsh (enhanced C shell) and run the built-in kill command with −1 option, you get another listing that does not match either of these. To determine for sure which signals are really available under Red Hat Linux, and to provide you with an interactive demonstration of how kill can be used to send various signals to a process, I wrote a Perl script called gen_signal_demo.pl, shown in Listing 6-1, to identify the signals available on my Red Hat Linux system.

Listing 6-1 *gen_signal_demo.pl*

```perl
#!/usr/bin/perl
#
# Chapter 6
#
# Written by kabir@integrationlogic.com
#
# Purpose: to generate a Perl script that installs
#          signal handlers for all possible signals.
#          This script is used to demonstrate in an
#          interactive way how signals are caught.
#
# Notes: I don't attempt to stop the script from not
#          installing useless signal handlers for
#          uninterruptible signals (KILL, STOP).
#
#          This script is strictly for demonstration use.
#
# Syntax:  gen_signal_demo.pl > signal_demo.pl
#-----------------------------------------------------------


# First generate the #!/usr/bin/perl line for the
#
print <<SBANG;
#!/usr/bin/perl
```

```
SBANG

foreach $signal (keys %SIG){

print <<SIG;
   \$SIG{$signal} = sub { print "Caught a $signal
signal.\\n"; };
SIG


}

print <<MAIN;

print "Hello, my PID is \$\$.\\n";
print "Use kill -signal \$\$ command to experiment on
me.\\n";

# Set a 10 sec. alarm event.
alarm(10);

# Loop forever.
while(1){
  sleep(1);  # Sleep for a second.
}

MAIN
```

This relatively small Perl script generates another Perl script. Run the script as follows:

```
gen_signal_demo.pl > signal_demo.pl
```

The generated script will have signal handlers for all the signals available on your system. The generated script defines signal handlers using the following construct:

```
$SIG{shortened signal name}   = sub { # handler code };
```

For example, the SIGINT handler is defined here:

```
$SIG{INT} = sub { print "Caught an INT signal.\n"; };
```

It prints "Caught an INT signal.\n" when the script is signaled with SIGINT. Run the signal_demo.pl script as follows:

```
./signal_demo.pl
```

The output will look something like the following:

```
Hello, my PID is XXXX
Use kill —signal XXXX command to experiment on me.
```

The *XXXX* string will be replaced by the real PID of the process. Before you can use the kill command to send various signals to this program, browse Table 6-3 to find more information on each signal.

Table 6-3 *Available Signals*

#	Name (Short Name)	Description
1	SIGHUP (HUP)	Hang up. This signal is often used to instruct a process to reload configuration files.
2	SIGINT (INT)	Interrupt.
3	SIGQUIT (QUIT)	Quit.
4	SIGILL (ILL)	Illegal instruction.
5	SIGTRAP (TRAP)	Trace trap.
6	SIGIOT (IOT)	IOT instruction.
7	SIGBUS (BUS)	Bus error.
8	SIGFPE (FPE)	Floating-point exception.
9	SIGKILL (KILL)	Kill. This signal cannot be caught (i.e., handled in a process), blocked, or ignored.
10	SIGUSR1 (USR1)	User-defined signal 1.
11	SIGSEGV (SEGV)	Segmentation violation.
12	SIGUSR2 (USR2)	User-defined signal 2.
13	SIGPIPE (PIPE)	Write on a pipe with no one to read it.
14	SIGALRM (ALRM)	Alarm clock.
15	SIGTERM (TERM)	Software termination signal. This is often sent before a KILL signal is issued. This allows a process to catch this signal and prepare to exit.

#	Name (Short Name)	Description
16	SIGSTKFLT	Stack fault on coprocessor.
17	SIGCHLD (CHLD)	Child status has changed.
18	SIGCONT (CONT)	Continue after STOP signal. This signal cannot be blocked.
19	SIGSTOP (STOP)	Stop. This signal cannot be caught (i.e., handled in a process), blocked, or ignored.
20	SIGTSTP (TSTP)	Stop signal generated from keyboard, typically using Ctrl+Z.
21	SIGTTIN	Background read attempted from control terminal.
22	SIGTTOU	Background write attempted to control terminal.
23	SIGURG	Urgent condition present on socket.
24	SIGXCPU	CPU time limit exceeded. See man setrlimit (2).
25	SIGXFSZ	File size limit exceeded. See man setrlimit (2).
26	SIGVTALRM	Virtual time alarm. See man setitimer (2).
27	SIGPROF	Profiling timer alarm. See man setitimer (2).
28	SIGWINCH	Window size change.
29	SIGIO	I/O is possible on a descriptor. See man fcntl (2).
30	SIGPWR	Power failure.
31	UNUSED	Not used.

After you have the signal_demo.pl script running, use another virtual console, login shell, or xterm (if you are on X Windows) to send signals to the process. When you run the script, it displays the PID, so you don't need to use ps to locate the PID of this process. Send any of the signals just listed to the process and see the message it displays. For example, if the PID of this process is 12345 and you run

```
kill -HUP 12345
```

it will display the following:

```
Caught a HUP signal.
```

Note that the script schedules an alarm event (using the alarm function) to occur after 10 seconds of execution that prints the following:

```
Caught a ALRM signal.
```

When you send it a KILL signal by using kill –KILL 12345, the process exits, because this signal cannot be caught by a signal handler. Similarly, if you send a STOP signal to the process, it will be suspended. When it is suspended, you see a message such as this:

```
Suspended (signal)
```

You can run ps to see that the STAT field shows a T flag, which means that the process is terminated. This is a bit misleading, because the process really is stopped and not terminated. To bring the process back to running mode, you can send it a CONT signal. An interesting thing about the suspended mode is that the process is still able to receive any pending signals that were sent during its suspended stage. In other words, if you suspend this process using the STOP signal and then send an HUP signal while the process is still suspended, this signal is sent to the process when it is run again because of a CONT signal.

Most of the signals listed in Table 6-3 are seldom used outside system programs. As a system administrator, you are likely to use only HUP, INT, TERM, STOP, and KILL. If you are not fond of typing or prefer numbers to letters, you can use the signal numbers with kill instead. For example, to issue a KILL signal, you can either use **kill –KILL** *PID* or **kill –9** *PID*. Or, better yet, you can just kill a process by name by using the killall utility.

Using killall

This nifty utility lets you kill a process by name. For example, if you have a process called signal_demo.pl and want to kill it without typing its PID, you can run

```
killall —KILL signal_demo.pl
```

When you do not provide a signal name, killall automatically sends the SIGTERM signal. However, be very careful when using killall, because it kills all instances of the named command. Sometimes, the convenience of not having to know the PID can go sour. For example, look at the following ps output:

```
PID  TTY STAT TIME COMMAND
1246 p8  S    0:00 -tcsh
2160 p6  S    0:00 -tcsh
```

```
2365  p1 S    0:00 -bash
2459  p6 S    0:00 vi bar.txt
2460  p8 S    0:00 vi foo.txt
2463  p1 R    0:00 ps
```

Suppose that for some reason you want to kill the vi process used for editing the foo.txt file. If you run killall vi foo.txt expecting it to terminate only this instance of vi, you will be surprised to find that all of your vi sessions have terminated. This occurs because killall expects command names as arguments and sends signals to all instances of a named program.

Caution

Be extremely cautious when running the killall command as a superuser, because it will remove every instance of the specified command from the entire system, which includes all the users.

Controlling process priority

Linux has two priority numbers associated with each process. For example, if you run ps –l, you see two fields, PRI and NI. The PRI (short for PRIORITY) field shows the actual process priority, which is dynamically computed by the OS. Among other factors, the NI (short for NICE) number is taken into account when the OS computes and updates the PRI number. The NI number is called the *nice* number or the *requested process execution priority* number. This number can be set by the owner or the superuser to influence the actual execution priority number (PRI). You can use the /bin/nice utility to change the NI number. The functionality of this utility often is built into popular shells, including /bin/csh, /bin/tcsh, and others.

Using nice to change process priority

By default, the built-in shell version of nice or the /bin/nice utility allows a user to *decrease* process priority only. Only the superuser is allowed to *increase* the priority of a process. The valid range of process priority is from –20 to 20, where the lower the number, the higher the priority. In other words, –20 is the highest NI priority, and 20 is the lowest. Before you can set the priority of a process, run **which nice** to determine whether you are going to be running the built-in shell version of nice or the /bin/nice utility. You need to do this because the syntax varies between these two versions.

For example, suppose you want to run a Perl script called foo.pl at the lowest priority (20), and the shell version of the nice command is

```
nice +10 foo.pl
```

and the /bin/nice version of the same command is

```
nice -10 foo.pl
```

Now, if you were a superuser and wanted to increase the priority of the foo.pl script to −10, the built-in shell version of the command would look like this:

```
nice -10 foo.pl
```

and the /bin/nice version of the same command would look like this:

```
nice --10 foo.pl
```

If this is too confusing to you, you can use another utility called snice (short for simple nice) to handle process priority upgrades or downgrades. Here is how:

1. Use ps to find the PID of the process whose priority you want to change.

2. To upgrade priority, run **snice** *−n PID*, where *n* is the new priority number. For example, snice −5 1234 increases priority of the process 1234 (the PID) by 5. Note that, as with nice, only a superuser can increase priority.

3. To downgrade priority, run **snice** *+n PID*, where *n* is the new priority number. For example, snice +5 1234 decreases the priority of process 1234 (the PID) by 5. As with nice, any user can lower priority of the processes she owns.

As with snice, you can use the renice utility to change the priority of a process. The preceding steps for snice also apply to renice.

To make sure that the priority changes are taking effect, you can run **ps** **−l** to determine the value of the NI field.

Running a process in the foreground or the background

Normally, when you run a process from a console, shell, or xterm, you run the program in the foreground. When a process runs in the foreground, you have to wait for it to finish. However, instead of waiting for a process to finish, you can run it in the background by specifying an & character at the end of the command line. This becomes very handy when you are running a process that takes a long time to finish and you'd rather do something useful while it works. For example, suppose that you want use the du command to get an idea about what files are taking up the most disk space in your system. You can run it in the background as follows:

```
du > /tmp/du.out  &
```

Here, the output is directed to a file, /tmp/du.out, because you do not want to be interrupted by du output while working on something else.

Tip

If you want to leave a program running in the background after you log off from a shell session, use the nohup program. It immunizes a command from getting SIGHUP and SIGTERM signals, and allows the process to continue without a tty. See the man page for details.

Monitoring Processes and System Load

Being able to monitor the state of the processes in a system at any time is very important for system administration. As a Red Hat Linux system administrator, you have a few tools to help you in the monitoring processes.

Using top

The top utility is one of my favorite process monitoring tools. Using top, you can monitor process activity in real time. The top screen is automatically updated to provide a fresh look at the running state of the system. Here are the descriptions for the first five header lines displayed by top.

- **Line 1.** The uptime line, which shows the current time of the system, how long the system has been up since the last reboot, how many users are currently on the system, and three load average numbers. The load averages are the average numbers of processes ready to run during the last 1, 5, and 15 minutes.

- **Line 2.** The process statistics line that shows the total number of processes running at the time of the last top screen update. This line also shows the number of sleeping, running, zombie, and stopped processes.

- **Line 3.** Displays CPU statistics, which include percentage of CPU time used by the user, system, niced, and idle processes.

- **Line 4.** Provides memory statistics, which include total available memory, free memory, used memory, shared memory, and memory used for buffers.

- **Line 5.** Provides virtual memory or swap statistics, which include total available swap space, used swap space, free swap space, and cached swap space. The rest of the lines are similar to a ps-generated report.

Using top, you can identify which processes are using most of your resources, simply by looking at the few entries in the ps-like output. The process that consumes the second-most resources is the top utility itself! When you run top to monitor other processes, top takes some resources to run, but you still get a good idea about which process is consuming what amount of resources. To exit top, type 'q' at any time.

Using vmstat

The vmstat utility also provides interesting information about processes, memory, I/O, and CPU activity. When you run this utility without any arguments, the output looks similar to the following:

```
procs         memory          swap    io  system     cpu
r b w  swpd free  buff cache si so bi bo  in  cs us sy id
0 0 0     8 8412 45956 52820  0  0  0  0 104 11 66  0 33
```

The following list describes the elements of this output:

- **procs fields.** Show the number of processes that are waiting for run time (r), that are blocked (b), and that are swapped out (w).

- **memory fields.** Show the amounts of swap, free, buffered, and cached memory, in K.

- **swap fields.** Show the amount (in K/sec) of memory swapped in (si) from disk and the amount of memory swapped out (so) to disk.

- **io fields.** Show the number of blocks sent (bi) and received (bo) to and from block devices per second.

- **system field.** Shows the number of interrupts (in) and context switches (cs) per second.

- **cpu field.** Shows the percentage of total CPU time in terms of user (us), system (sy), and idle (id) time.

If you want vmstat to update information automatically, you can run it as **vmstat** *nsec*, where *nsec* is the number of seconds you want it to wait before another update.

Using uptime

To get quick statistics on the state of your system regarding process load, you can run the uptime utility. It shows the current time of the system, how long the system has been up since last reboot, how many users are currently on the system, and three load average numbers. The load averages are the average number of processes ready to run during the last 1, 5, and 15 minutes.

Logging Processes

A process log is a system administrator's best friend. Log files often provide many clues to the system administrator about what's going on with a certain process. Virtually all widely used server software packages — sendmail, Apache, named, and so on — write logs. Server programs follow either of two trends when writing logs: some write custom log files, and some use a facility called syslog, which is a logging facility provided by the syslogd daemon. Typically, syslogd is started by init at run level 3 (multiuser). The syslog facility provides a centralized logging environment for processes that want to write logs.

Configuring syslog

Typically, syslog is already configured on most systems. The default Red Hat installation installs syslogd and its /etc/syslog.conf configuration file, which is shown in Listing 6-2.

Listing 6-2 *The syslogd Configuration File, /etc/syslog.conf*

```
# Log all kernel messages to the console.
# Logging much else clutters up the screen.
kern.*   /dev/console

# Log anything (except mail) of level info or higher.
# Don't log private authentication messages!
*.info;mail.none;authpriv.none   /var/log/messages

# The authpriv file has restricted access.
authpriv.*   /var/log/secure

# Log all the mail messages in one place.
mail.* /var/log/maillog

# Everybody gets emergency messages.
*.emerg *

# Save mail and news errors of level err and
#higher in a  special file.
uucp,news.crit  /var/log/spooler
```

The configuration file is quite simple. The blank lines and the lines starting with # are ignored. The structure of a syslogd configuration line is as follows:

```
facility.priority    destination
```

where *facility* can be one of the following keywords: auth, Authpriv, cron, daemon, kern, lpr, mail, news, syslog, user, uucp, and local0 through local7. A *priority* can be one of the following keywords, in ascending order of severity: debug, info, notice, warning, err, crit, alert, emerg, none. You can also use * as a wildcard for the facility or the priority part of the line to indicate all facilities or all priorities, respectively. You can use a comma-separated list of multiple facilities with the same priority in a line. For example, the following indicates that log entries (often called messages) of critical (crit) priority from uucp and news facilities (uucp and the news server program) are written to /var/log/spooler file:

```
uucp,news.crit   /var/log/spooler
```

You can also use a semicolon-separated list of multiple *facility.priority* pairs to assign a single destination to them. For example, the following indicates that all informative (info) log entries from all facilities are written to the /var/log/messages file with the exception of the informative messages from the mail and authpriv facilities:

```
*.info;mail.none;authpriv.none   /var/log/messages
```

The default syslogd configuration makes it write the log files in the /var/log directory.

Monitoring logs using tail

If you are experiencing some problem with a server process, find out whether the process writes log files. If it writes log files of its own or uses the syslog facility, you can monitor the log files as the process runs, by using the tail utility, which allows you to monitor growing log files by viewing the last part of a file. For example, to monitor the /var/log/ messages file, you can run the following:

```
tail -f  /var/log/messages
```

This allows you to view the file as new entries are written to the file. If you want to limit the number of lines you see, use the --line number option. For example, to view only the last three lines of the same file as the last example, you can run **tail –f --line 3 /var/log/messages**.

Note that syslogd-produced log files can grow very large in a very active system. Therefore, you need to rotate your log files using the logrotate facility. In fact, by default, the RPM package for syslogd installs a logrotate configuration file called syslog in the /etc/logrotate.d directory. The logrotate setup rotates the log files on a weekly basis and keeps compressed backups of back-logs, as well.

Scheduling Processes

Like all other forms of UNIX and UNIX-like OSs, Red Hat Linux provides you with two widely used process scheduling facilities. This section describes how to use both of these services.

Using at

The at utility allows you to queue a command for execution at a later time. For example, to run the disk usage summary generator utility called du at 8:40 p.m., you can run at as follows:

```
at 20:40
```

The at command displays a prompt such as at>, where you can enter the du command as follows:

```
at> du -a > /tmp/du.out
```

Here, the output of du is directed to a file. After you enter the command (the du command, in this example), at displays the prompt again. You can press Ctrl+D to exit. You will see a message similar to the one here:

```
at> <EOT>
warning: commands will be executed using /bin/sh
job 1 at 1999-12-06 20:40
```

This means that at has scheduled the du −a > /tmp/du.out job to be run by the at daemon (atd) at 8:40 p.m., 12/06/1999. You can use a wide variety of time formats to specify the time of execution. For example, instead of saying at 20:40, you can say at 8:40pm, as well. You can also specify the date along with the time. For example, 8:40pm feb 23, 10am + 5 days, 12:30pm tomorrow, midnight, and noon are all valid time specifications.

To verify that your job is in the job queue, run the atq command, which shows the currently scheduled jobs in the queue. All the scheduled jobs are stored in the /var/spool/at directory.

Tip

If you are the root user on a system, you can examine the files in the /var/spool/at spool directory to see the commands that will be run.

If for some reason you want to stop the scheduled job, you can run the atrm command to remove your job. You need to know the job sequence number to remove a job with atrm. To find out what jobs you have scheduled, run the atq command. To delete any job, use atrm *job#*. For example, to remove job #1, run **atrm 1**.

The scheduled job is run via the atd daemon process, which is started by init for run level 3 (multiuser mode). If you want to restrict use of the at facility, you can create an /etc/at.allow file and list all the users who are allowed to run it. Remember to enter a single username per line. Any user not listed in the allow file is refused access to the at facility. On the other hand, if you want to deny only a few users but allow the rest, you can create a similar file called /etc/at.deny. All usernames listed in this file are denied at access.

Although at provides you with process scheduling capabilities, another facility called cron is more widely used than at, because cron offers a more structured way of creating unattended process execution schedules for repetitive tasks.

Using cron

Many tasks (processes) in a Linux system need to be scheduled for unattended execution on a regular basis. For example, to rotate the log files syslogd creates, or to remove old files from the /tmp directory, you need to run a process every day or every week. The cron facility allows you to create a recurring task schedule.

The cron facility includes the crond daemon, which is started by the init process. The crond daemon reads task schedules from /etc/crontab and files in the /var/spool/cron directory. The latter is used to store schedule files (often called *crontab* or *cron table*) for normal users who are allowed to run cron jobs. As a superuser, you can specify a list of users in the /etc/cron.allow file who will be allowed to run cron jobs. Similarly, you can explicitly deny cron access to any user by specifying her name in the /etc/cron.deny file. Both files use a simple one-username-per-line format.

If a normal user is allowed to run cron jobs, she can use the crontab utility to create job schedules. For example, if a normal user is allowed to run cron jobs, he can run crontab −e to create and edit his cron job entries. A cron job specification has the following format:

```
minute(s) hour(s) day(s) month weekday username command
argument(s)
```

The first five time specification fields are discussed in Table 6-4.

Table 6-4 *cron Time Specification Fields*

Fields	Description	Range
Minutes(s)	One or more minutes in an hour. You can specify a comma-separated list of minutes.	0–59
Hour(s)	One or more hours in a day. You can specify a comma-separated list of hours.	0–23, where 0 is midnight
Day(s)	One or more days in a month. You can specify a comma-separated list of days.	1–31
Month	One or more months in a year. You can specify a comma-separated list of months.	1–12
Weekday	One or more days in a week. You can specify a comma-separated list of days.	1–7, where 1 is Monday

For any of the fields shown in Table 6-4, you can use * as a wildcard. The following is an example cron job specification:

```
01 * * * * root /some/script
```

This states that /some/script is to be run every first minute of every hour, every day, every month, and every weekday. The script will be run as the root user. To run this script every ten minutes, a cron job such as the following can be defined:

```
0,10,20,30,40,50 * * * * root /some/script
```

To run the same script but only once a month, a cron job can be scheduled as follows:

```
01 1 1 * * root /some/script
```

Here, the script will be run at 1:01 a.m. on the first day of every month. The default cron job for the system is /etc/crontab, which includes a few interesting cron job entries, such as the following:

```
SHELL=/bin/bash
PATH=/sbin:/bin:/usr/sbin:/usr/bin
MAILTO=root


# run-parts
01 * * * * root run-parts /etc/cron.hourly
02 4 * * * root run-parts /etc/cron.daily
22 4 * * 0 root run-parts /etc/cron.weekly
42 4 1 * * root run-parts /etc/cron.monthly
```

These cron jobs are used to run the run-parts script located in the /usr/bin directory. This script is run every hour, every day, every week, and every month using the four cron job specifications in the preceding listing. It takes a directory name as an argument and runs all the scripts or programs located in that directory. For example, consider the first cron entry in the preceding listing. It states that the run-parts script should be run at the first minute of every hour. The script is fed the argument /etc/cron.hourly. Because the script runs all the files located in this directory, the entire process effectively works as if all the files in the /etc/cron.hourly directory had been set up as cron jobs. This trick allows you to put new files in the /etc/cron.hourly directory and automatically have it scheduled for an hourly run. Similarly, the other three cron entries allow you to run any program on a daily, weekly, or monthly basis simply by placing them in the /etc/cron.daily, /etc/cron.weekly, or /etc/cron.monthly directory, respectively. This makes it easy to create cron jobs for most everything without really having to configure a cron entry.

For example, suppose that you want to synchronize your system time with a remote time server on a daily basis. You decide to use the rdate utility to set the time via the Internet. The command to run is the following:

```
/usr/bin/rdate -s  time.server.host.tld
```

Because the default /etc/crontab contains a cron entry that allows you to schedule daily cron jobs simply by placing the script or program in the

/etc/cron.daily directory, you can create a simple shell script such as the following and place it in the /etc/cron.daily directory:

```
#!/bin/sh
/usr/bin/rdate -s time.server.host.tld
```

Your job is done. Every day at 4:02 a.m., your script will run along with all the other scripts and programs in the /etc/cron.daily directory.

As you can see, setting up cron jobs is much more systematic than using at commands to queue tasks, and therefore cron is preferred over at. In fact, I recommend that you disable the at facility by removing the atd entry from your /etc/rc.d/rc3.d directory.

Chapter 7

Network Administration

Classifying IP Networks

IP numbers are used to identify network interfaces on host computers. These numbers are not randomly assigned. Each IP number carries two types of information in it. You can think of an IP address as follows:

IP = { Network Address } + {Interface address of the host computer}

For example, 192.168.2.10 is an IP address in the 192.168.2.0 network, and the interface address, which is often called the host address, is .10. In other words, this IP address points to the network interface .10 in the 192.168.2.0 network. Which part of the IP address is used to identify the network depends on the class of the network. Notice that when you are writing a network address, the interface identifier bytes are written as zeros.

The 32-bit IP address covers a range from 0.0.0.0 to 255.255.255.255 (2^{32}) addresses. They are classified (with exceptions) as follows.

Class A networks

Any IP address that ranges from 0.0.0.0 to 127.255.255.255 is a class A IP network. Figure 7-1 shows the possible range of IP addresses in this class.

Class A IP network

Network	Total address space	Usable address space
0.0.0.0	0.0.0.0. – 0.255.255.255	0.0.0.1 to 0.255.255.254
1.0.0.0	1.0.0.0. – 1.255.255.255	1.0.0.1 to 1.255.255.254
2.0.0.0	2.0.0.0. – 2.255.255.255	2.0.0.1 to 2.255.255.254
3.0.0.0	3.0.0.0. – 3.255.255.255	3.0.0.1 to 3.255.255.254
• • •	• • •	• • •
126.0.0.0	126.0.0.0 – 126.255.255.255	126.0.0.1 to 126.255.255.254
127.0.0.0	127.0.0.0 – 127.255.255.255	127.0.0.1 to 127.255.255.254

Figure 7-1 *Class A network addresses*

In this class, the network address is determined by the leftmost byte of the IP address. The rest of the three bytes are used to identify the network interface on a host. So, you can think of the class as *n.x.x.x*, where *n* is 0 to 127 and *x.x.x* can be any three-byte number from 0.0.0 to 255.255.255. In other words, the number of IP addresses per class A network is 2^{24} (16,777,216).

Notice that the first network is 0.0.0.0, which is one of two special class A networks. The 0.0.0.0 network is reserved and used to indicate the default route for a network; the 127.0.0.0 network is used as a loopback network. Each computer should use 127.0.0.1 as the loopback interface IP address. This address is used to test network software without having a physical network. For example, you can run **telnet 127.0.0.1** to test the Telnet client in a single, nonnetworked computer. In such a case, the Telnet client program will connect to the local host computer. You will also notice that the /etc/hosts file contains an entry that assigns this IP address to a host name called localhost — the only host name in the loopback network. Because these special class A networks have special meanings and are not used to identify any physical class A networks, technically, only 126 class A networks are available. Also note that the 10.0.0.0 network is reserved.

Class B networks

Any IP address that ranges from 128.0.0.0 to 191.255.255.255 is a class B network. Figure 7-2 shows the possible range of IP addresses in this class.

Class B IP network

Network	Total address space	Usable address space
128.0.0.0	128.0.0.0 – 128.0.255.255	128.0.0.1 to 128.0.255.254
128.1.0.0	128.0.0.0 – 128.1.255.255	128.1.0.1 to 128.1.255.254
•••	•••	•••
128.255.0.0	128.255.0.0 – 128.255.255.255	128.255.0.1 to 128.255.255.254
•••	•••	•••
191.255.0.0	191.255.0.0 – 191.255.255.255	191.255.0.1 to 191.255.255.254

Figure 7-2 *Class B network addresses*

In this class, the network address is determined by the leftmost two bytes. So, you can think of this class as $n1.n2.x.x$, where $n1$ can be 128 to 191, $n2$ can be 0 to 255, and $x.x$ can be any two-byte number between 0.0 and 255.255. However, 0.0 and 255.255 pairs are used for the network address (e.g. 128.0.0.0) and the broadcast address (128.0.255.255) and therefore the usable range is for x.x is 0.1 to 254.254. The number of IP addresses per class B network is 2^{16} (65,536). The number of class B networks between 128.0.0.0 and 191.255.0.0 is 2^{14} (16,384). Note that the 172.16.0.0 to 172.31.0.0 class B networks are reserved.

Class C networks

Any IP address that ranges from 192.0.0.0 to 223.255.255.255 is a class C IP network. Figure 7-3 shows the possible range of IP addresses in this class.

Class C IP network

Network	Total address space	Usable address space
192.0.0.0	192.0.0.0 – 192.0.0.255	192.0.0.1 to 192.0.0.254
192.0.1.0	192.0.1.0 – 192.0.1.255	192.0.1.1 to 192.0.1.254
•••	•••	•••
192.0.255.0	192.0.255.0 – 192.0.255.255	192.0.255.1 to 192.0.255.254
192.1.0.0	192.1.0.0 – 192.1.0.255	192.1.0.1 to 192.1.0.254
•••	•••	•••
192.255.255.0	192.255.255.0 – 192.255.255.255	192.255.255.1 to 192.255.255.254
193.0.0.0	193.0.0.0 – 193.0.0.255	192.255.255.1 to 192.255.255.254
•••	•••	•••
223.255.255.0	223.255.255.0 – 223.255.255.255	223.255.255.1 to 223.255.255.254

Figure 7-3 *Class C network addresses*

In this class, the network address is determined by the leftmost three bytes. So, you can think of this class as *n1.n2.n3.x*, where *n1* can be 192 to 223, *n2* can be 0 to 255, *n3* can be 0 to 255, and *x* can be a single-byte number between 0 to 255. The number of IP addresses per class C network is 2^8 (256). The number of class C networks between 192.0.0.0 and 223.255.255.0 is 2^{21} (2,097,152). Note that addresses below 223.255.255.255 (that is, 224.0.0.0 to 255.255.255.255) are reserved.

One of the easiest ways to quickly determine which IP address is in what network is demonstrated in Figure 7-4.

Simply look at the leftmost byte of an IP address and determine the class of the network. For example, the IP addresses in the class A network always has the leftmost byte set to 0 to 126 (127 is the loopback network). Similarly, the IP addresses in the class B network have the leftmost byte set to 128 to 191, and the IP addresses in class C network have the leftmost byte set to 192 to 223.

Leftmost byte of an IP address

Binary	Hex	Decimal	
0000 0000	00	0	Class A
0111 1110	7F	126	

Binary	Hex	Decimal	
1000 0000	80	128	Class B
1011 1111	BF	191	

Binary	Hex	Decimal	
1100 0000	C0	192	Class C
1101 1111	DF	223	

Figure 7-4 *A cheat sheet for recognizing IP networks*

The first and the last IP addresses in any network (A, B, or C) are not usable as IP addresses for network interfaces. For example, 206.171.50.0 is a class C network where the range is 206.171.50.0 to 206.171.50.255. However, the 206.171.50.0 address is the network address, and 206.171.50.255 is considered the broadcast address for that network and therefore should be assigned to any network interface.

Configuring a Network Interface

This section assumes that you have already installed an Ethernet adapter card (that is, a network interface card, or NIC) that works with Red Hat Linux. To find out which NICs are compatible with your version of Red Hat Linux, see the hardware compatibility section of the Red Hat Web site (http://www.redhat.com/corp/support/hardware/). In general, most popular NIC cards work fine with Red Hat Linux.

You can configure your network in several ways. The command-line, traditional method is presented first, because it's the most powerful (in the sense that you don't need to rely on any special tool other than your favorite text editor).

Configuring a new network interface

Before you do anything, run the dmesg program (or view the /var/log/ dmesg file) to find out whether your NIC is recognized by your current Linux kernel. If the Linux kernel recognizes your card, you should see some lines in the dmesg output pertaining to the kernel's discovery of your network device. For example, when I run the following command on a Red Hat Linux system with a generic (NE2000-compatible) Ethernet card:

```
dmesg | grep -I eth
```

it displays the following output:

```
NE*000 ethercard probe at 0x340: 00 c0 f6 98 37 37
eth0: NE2000 found at 0x340, using IRQ 5.
```

This tells me that my NE2000-compatible NIC is found by the kernel and is using Interrupt Request Line (IRQ) 5 as well as the I/O address space starting at 0x340. Also note that this device is called eth0 (Ethernet device 0).

After you confirm that your network device is being recognized by the kernel, you are ready to configure it. This example assumes that you want to configure the first Ethernet device, eth0, and you want a *persistent* configuration, meaning that it will be used every time you start your computer. This is done with the help of the /etc/rc.d/init.d/network script. When this script is linked (where the name of the link is S*xx*network; *xx* is any number) from the default run level directory (which could be /etc/rc.d/rc3.d), the /etc/rc.d/init.d/network script is run at boot time. This script loads the network interfaces using files stored in the /etc/sysconfig directory.

Now, take a look at how to configure eth0 so that it automatically starts at boot time. The very first file you have to modify is /etc/sysconfig/ network. Listing 7-1 shows an example of this file.

Listing 7-1 *The /etc/sysconfig/network File*
```
NETWORKING=yes
FORWARD_IPV4=yes
HOSTNAME=picaso.nitec.com
DOMAINNAME=nitec.com
```

```
GATEWAY=206.171.50.49
GATEWAYDEV=eth0
```

The following list explains the lines in this file:

- The NETWORKING=yes line states that you want to enable networking support.

- FORWARD_IPV4=yes should be set to yes if you want to allow forwarding of IP packets to and from your Red Hat Linux server. This is required only if a Red Hat Linux computer is going to act as a gateway or router (discussed in a later section) for a network. For example, if you plan to install proxy server software on your computer to allow Web access for other computers on your LAN, you should set this to yes. Conversely, if you plan to use this computer only as a co-located Web server on an ISP network, you can turn off IP forwarding by setting this to no.

- The next two lines specify the host name of the computer and the domain name of your network. The host name you specify must include the domain name you specify in the DOMAINNAME line. In other words, don't specify a host name that uses a different domain name from what you state in the DOMAINNAME line.

- The next two lines specify the information needed to determine the default gateway for a computer. A default gateway is a computer (or a router) that transfers packets to and from your computer. For example, if your Red Hat Linux computer is going to be connected to your LAN, where you have an ISDN router that connects the LAN to the Internet, you specify the IP address of the ISDN router's network interface as the default gateway. The GATEWAY-DEV is important when you have multiple network interfaces. If you have only one Ethernet device, this always should be set to eth0. If you have multiple Ethernet devices (eth0, eth1, and so on), you have to use the interface name that is connected to the default gateway.

After you configure the /etc/sysconfig/network file, you are ready to create the network interface file in the /etc/sysconfig/network-scripts directory. The network interface file uses ifcfg-*interface* as the naming convention. For example, the network interface filename for eth0 is ifcfg-eth0. An example of this file is shown in Listing 7-2.

Listing 7-2 *The /etc/sysconfig/network-scripts/ifcfg-eth0 File*

```
DEVICE=eth0
NETMASK=255.255.255.240
IPADDR=206.171.50.50
NETWORK=206.171.50.48
BROADCAST=206.171.50.63
ONBOOT=yes
```

Before you can configure the information in this file, you have to obtain from your ISP the network address, the network mask, the IP address for the network interface on the host, and the broadcast address. The network mask and broadcast address are discussed in a later section.

The following are explanations of the entries in the preceding file:

- The first line specifies the device name.
- The second line specifies the network mask (netmask) number.
- The third line specifies the IP address of the computer.
- The fourth line specifies the network address.
- The fifth line specifies the broadcast address.
- The sixth line contains the ONBOOT option, which should be set to yes if you want the network interface to be "up" (started) after boot.

After you configure these two files, you are ready to bring up the network. The easiest way to bring up the interface you just configured is to run the following:

```
/etc/sysconfig/network-scripts/ifup  eth0
```

The ifup script takes the device name as the argument and starts it. It also creates a default route for the network. After you run this command, you can use the ifconfig program to see whether the interface is up and running. To see whether or not device eth0 is up, run this:

```
ifconfig eth0
```

You should see output similar to the following:

```
eth0 Link encap:Ethernet HWaddr 00:C0:F6:98:37:37
inet addr:206.171.50.50  Bcast:206.171.50.63
Mask:255.255.255.240
```

```
UP BROADCAST RUNNING MULTICAST  MTU:1500  Metric:1
RX packets:9470 errors:0 dropped:0 overruns:0 frame:0
TX packets:7578 errors:0 dropped:0 overruns:0 carrier:0
collisions:0
Interrupt:5 Base address:0x340
```

Here, ifconfig reports that network interface device eth0 has Internet address (inet addr) 206.171.50.50, broadcast address (Bcast) 206.171.50.63, and network mask 255.255.255.240. The rest of the information shows how many packets this interface has received so far (RX packets), how many packets this interface has transmitted so far (TX packets), how many errors of different types have occurred so far, what interrupt address line is being used for this device, what I/O address base is being used, and so on.

You can run ifconfig without any arguments to get the full list of all the up network devices. Note that the ifup script uses ifconfig to bring up an interface. For example,

```
ifconfig eth0 206.171.50.50 netmask 255.255.255.240 \
broadcast 206.171.50.63
```

starts eth0 with IP address 206.171.50.50. You can also quickly take down an interface by using the ifconfig command. For example, the following command takes down the eth0 interface:

```
ifconfig eth0 down
```

After the interface is up and running, try to contact a computer in your network. You can use the ping *IP address* command see whether your new interface can be used to contact a host on the same network.

If your /etc/resolv.conf file was not set up properly during installation, you will not be able to ping a host using its host name. The /etc/resolv.conf file looks like the following:

```
search nitec.com
nameserver 206.171.50.50
```

This is set up during Red Hat Linux installation. If you have specified an invalid IP address for the name server, your computer will not be able to contact the name server. So, if your network interface is up but you are unable to ping a host using the host name, try using the IP address of the host (really the network interface address). If you can ping the other host on your network, your interface is set up properly; just correct the name-server line by fixing the IP address of the name server.

However, if you cannot ping a host using either the IP address or the host name, you might have a routing problem. If you haven't used the ifup script as shown earlier, and instead used ifconfig to bring up the interface, you need to create a default route to your network and a default gateway manually. To create a default route for your network, use the route command as follows:

```
route add -net network address netmask device
```

For example, to create a default route for the 206.171.50.48 network with a 255.255.255.240 netmask and eth0 as the interface, I can run:

```
route add -net 206.171.50.48 255.255.255.240 eth0
```

To set the default gateway, you can run the route command as follows:

```
route add default gw gateway address device
```

For example, to set the default gateway address to 206.171.50.49, I can run the following command:

```
route add default gw 206.171.50.49 eth0
```

You can verify that your network route and default gateway are properly set up in the routing table by using the following command:

```
route -n
```

Here is an example of output of the preceding command:

```
Kernel IP routing table
Destination    Gateway Genmask         Flags Metric Ref Use Iface
206.171.50.48 0.0.0.0 255.255.255.240 U      0       0    6  eth0
127.0.0.0     0.0.0.0 255.0.0.0        U      0       0    5  lo
0.0.0.0       206.171.50.49  0.0.0.0 UG      0       0   17  eth0
```

At this point, use the ping program to ping hosts inside and outside your network. If you are successful, your network is up. If you still do not get any replies from your ping attempts, go back to the beginning of this section and ensure that you have followed all the steps as suggested.

Aliasing multiple IP addresses with a single network interface

The first step in creating an IP alias is to determine whether you have the IP alias module loaded with the kernel. The simplest way to check this is to run the lsmod command and see whether ip_alias.o is listed anywhere in the output. If you don't see this module and haven't custom-compiled your kernel to include this module as part of the kernel, you can try to load the module by using the following command:

```
/sbin/insmod    /path/to/ip_alias.o
```

where */path/to/ip.alias.o* is the real path to ip_alias.o module. You can use **locate ip_alias.o** to locate the path in your system. Typically, the path is /lib/modules/*kernel version number*/ipv4/ip_alias.o. After you load the ip_alias.o module, run lsmod to ensure that it is loaded. Now, to create an alias for the eth0 device, do the following:

1. Copy your existing /etc/sysconfig/network-scripts/ifcfg-eth0 file to /etc/sysconfig/network-scripts/ifcfg-eth0:0 to create an alias device named eth0:0.

2. Modify the file such that you have the lines similar to the ones shown in Listing 7-3. Of course your network, netmask, and IP address will vary. Make sure you change only the DEVICE and IPADDR lines. The DEVICE line should be set to **eth0:0**, and IPADDR should be set to the IP address you want to use as an alias to what you have assigned for eth0.

Listing 7-3 *The /etc/sysconfig/network-scripts/ifcfg-eth0:0 File*
```
DEVICE=eth0:0
USERCTL=no
ONBOOT=yes
BOOTPROTO=
BROADCAST=206.171.50.63
NETWORK=206.171.50.48
NETMASK=255.255.255.240
IPADDR=206.171.50.58
```

3. To start the alias device, run **ifconfig eth0:0 up**, and you should see output similar to the following:

```
lo Link encap:Local Loopback
    inet addr:127.0.0.1  Bcast:127.255.255.255
Mask:255.0.0.0
    UP BROADCAST LOOPBACK RUNNING  MTU:3584  Metric:1
    RX packets:501 errors:0 dropped:0 overruns:0
frame:0
    TX packets:501 errors:0 dropped:0 overruns:0
carrier:0
        collisions:0


eth0 Link encap:Ethernet  HWaddr 00:C0:F6:98:37:37
    inet addr:206.171.50.50 Bcast:206.171.50.63
Mask:255.255.255.240
    UP BROADCAST RUNNING MULTICAST  MTU:1500
Metric:1
    RX packets:2 errors:0 dropped:0 overruns:0
frame:0
    TX packets:2 errors:0 dropped:0 overruns:0
carrier:0 collisions:4
    Interrupt:5 Base address:0x340


eth0:0 Link encap:Ethernet  HWaddr 00:C0:F6:98:37:37
    inet addr:206.171.50.58  Bcast:206.171.50.63
Mask:255.255.255.240
    UP BROADCAST RUNNING  MTU:1500  Metric:1
    RX packets:9 errors:0 dropped:0 overruns:0
frame:0
    TX packets:9 errors:0 dropped:0 overruns:0
carrier:0 collisions:0
```

As you can see, the eth0:0 device is up and running. You can create an alias of any other Ethernet device in the same way.

Using netcfg to configure a network interface card

You need to have X Windows working on your system to use netcfg. This program allows you to configure all aspects of the basic network configuration. You must run this as a superuser from X Windows. The initial window, shown in Figure 7-5, displays the current host name, domain name, and name server configuration.

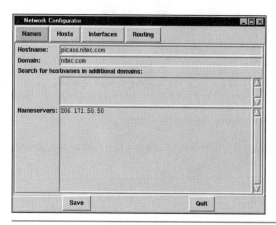

Figure 7-5 *The Names tab of the Network Configurator window*

To change the host name, the domain name, or the name servers, first click the Names tab. Simply modify the values and click Save. The program doesn't display any status message when you click Save, so it's a bit confusing at first. Also, the domain name displayed in the program comes from the search list (first entry in the list) in the /etc/resolv.conf file, so if you don't have any search list set up in this file, netcfg will not display any domain name.

To add, modify, or remove a network interface, click the Interfaces tab, shown in Figure 7-6, which displays the current network interfaces.

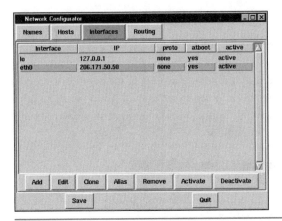

Figure 7-6 *The Interfaces tab of the Network Configurator window*

To add a new network interface, do the following:

1. Click Add to bring up the Choose Interface Type dialog box, shown in Figure 7-7.

Figure 7-7 *Adding a new network interface*

2. Click Ethernet to create a new Ethernet network interface configuration. After you click OK, you will see the Edit Ethernet/Bus Interface dialog box, shown in Figure 7-8.

3. Enter the IP address and the network mask for this new device. The netcfg program automatically calculates the network and broadcast addresses from the information you provide. If you want this interface to be active at boot time, click Activate interface at boot time. You should leave the Allow any user to (de)activate interface option

unchecked, because allowing just anyone to activate/deactivate your network interfaces is really a bad idea. If you are not using DHCP or BOOTP servers to dynamically assign IP addresses for this interface, select none as the interface configuration protocol. Click Done to complete the configuration; you will be asked to confirm that you want to save the configuration. Save the configuration by clicking OK. The new interface will appear in the interface list that shows up in the next screen.

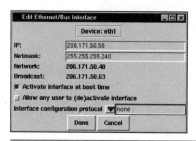

Figure 7-8 *Entering information about the new interface*

4. If you want to activate the interface right away, click Activate. The screen should update the status of the interface to be active. However, netcfg might show the interface as active when it really isn't. This happens when you try to configure a nonexistent NIC. One of the easiest ways to check the interface is to run the ifconfig *interface name* command from the command line to see which interfaces are up and running.

You just activated the new interface; now you need to set up a default gateway as follows:

1. Click Routing to bring up the Network Configurator window shown in Figure 7-9.

2. Enter the default gateway IP address. The gateway device name should be the device you just configured.

3. If you want to set up this device to forward IP packets to and from computers on your network, set the Network Packet Forwarding (IPV4) option.

4. Save the new settings and quit the program.

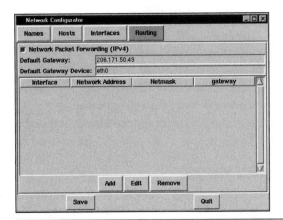

Figure 7-9 *Configuring a default gateway*

You have configured the new interface and set up a default gateway. Test your new interface by pinging a computer on your network, using the ping *IP address* command. If you can ping a remote host, you have successfully configured the new interface.

To modify an existing network interface, do the following:

1. Click Interfaces. Double-click the existing network interface line. Make changes as appropriate.

2. After you make and save the changes, deactivate the interface first and then activate it.

 Caution

If you are using X Windows on a remote terminal to run the netcfg program, do not ever deactivate the interface being used to provide network connectivity to your terminal. If you deactivate the interface that is needed for your remote X connection, your X session will not work any longer and you will not be able to activate the interface without local access.

To delete an existing network interface, do the following:

1. Click Interfaces. Select the existing network interface.

2. Click Delete to complete the process. The statements in the preceding Caution apply here.

Using a Default Gateway

Figure 7-10 shows two networks — network A (192.168.1.0) and network B (192.168.2.0).

Network A 192.168.1.0

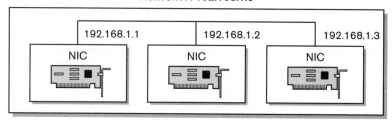

Network B 192.168.2.0

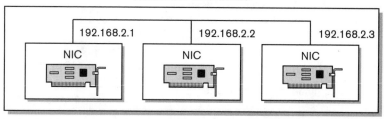

Figure 7-10 *Two distinct IP networks*

These two networks are completely separate. The computers in either network can see the hosts in the same network just fine. A user using the 192.168.1.1 computer in network A can ping the other two computers by using their network interface IP addresses. However, that user can't access any of the host computers on network B, because no way exists for the packets in network A to go to network B. Because two distinct networks can be physically wired together, these two networks can be joined by using a gateway computer or a router, as shown in Figure 7-11.

The new computer in the network is the gateway computer. It has two network interfaces. The network interface attached to network A has an IP address 192.168.1.100, and the network interface attached to network B has an IP address of 192.168.2.100. The computer is set up to forward IP packets between these two networks. For example, when the 192.168.1.1 computer wants to send a packet to 192.168.2.1, it forwards the IP packet to the 192.168.1.100 gateway computer. This gateway machine then places a modified version of the packet on its other interface (192.168.2.100), which becomes available to the destination computer. When the destination computer wants to respond, it follows a similar process such that the gateway computer will be able to send the packet to the source computer on network A.

So, the gateway computer is needed only if you want to communicate with two different networks. The gateway computer need not be a PC or a workstation; it could be specialized computer hardware, such as a router.

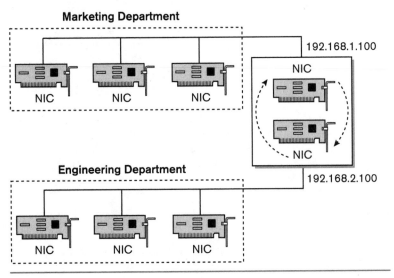

Figure 7-11 *Two distinct IP networks joined by a gateway*

Dividing a Network into Subnetworks

The network shown in Figure 7-12 has 100 host computers connected to a single network, 192.168.1.0.

Because all the computers share the same physical network cable, the traffic load is likely to be quite heavy at peak hours. For example, if all the marketing people start using the network at the same time as the engineers in the engineering department, things will become very slow, because every host has to share the network bandwidth. The solution is subnetworks, similar to the setup shown in Figure 7-13.

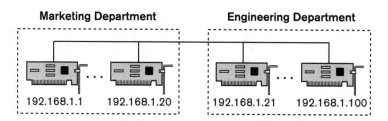

Network/netmask: 192.168.1.0/255.255.255.0

Figure 7-12 *A large network shared by 100 users*

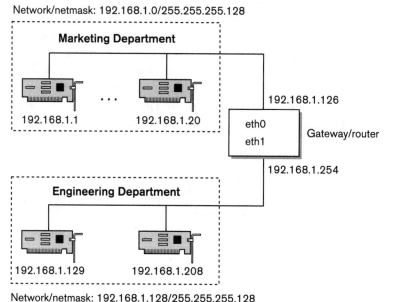

Figure 7-13 *Splitting a large network into subnetworks*

The 192.168.1.0 network has been divided into two subnetworks—192.168.1.0 and 192.168.1.128. These subnetworks are connected to each other using a gateway (or router) with two network interfaces. When each of the host computers on each of these two networks is configured properly, the network traffic will be separated between these networks. For example, when a user in the marketing department wants to communicate with another computer in the same department, the network traffic between these two computers will remain in their network. The same is true for the engineering side. Communication between different departments' computers is also allowed. Such internetwork traffic is forwarded to and from these networks by the gateway computer. The end result is a speedier network, because not all users are on the same, large network anymore. A description of how you can implement such a solution follows.

When a full network, such as 192.168.1.0, needs to be divided into subnets, the computer needs a way to determine which IP address belongs to which network. For example, the computer with the network interface 192.168.1.1 in the marketing department needs to know whether 192.168.1.129 is in the same network so that it can determine whether or not it should send packets destined for 192.168.1.129 to the gateway computer for further forwarding tasks. It can determine whether an IP address belongs to its own subnet by using a network mask, or netmask.

Before you can create a subnet from a network, you need to understand how to create a netmask. For example, suppose you want to determine the network mask for the network 192.168.1.0. This address in binary format looks as follows:

```
11000000.10101000.00000001.00000000
```

Because this is a class C address, the network bits are the first 24 bits (3 bytes). To create the mask, you must set all of these bits to 1's and set the remaining (host interface) bits to 0's. So, the netmask looks as follows:

```
11111111.11111111.11111111.00000000
```

In decimal format, this looks like 255.255.255.0. So, when creating a netmask, you simply need to remember that the network bits are all 1's and the host bits are all 0's. For example, the netmask for the class A network 10.0.0.0 is 255.0.0.0, and, similarly, the netmask for the class B network 129.1.0.0 is 255.255.0.0.

In a TCP/IP network, when a computer wants to send a packet to an IP address, it determines whether or not the IP address is local by performing a bitwise AND operation. For example, to determine whether 192.168.1.1

is local to a network with subnet mask 255.255.255.0, a host computer does the following:

```
Binary                                  Decimal
    11000000.10101000.00000001.00000001 => 192.168.1.1
AND 11111111.11111111.11111111.00000000 => 255.255.255.0
    --------------------------------------------------------
    11000000.10101000.00000001.00000000 => 192.168.1.0
```

As you can see, a bitwise AND operation returns the network address (192.168.1.0) of the IP address 192.168.1.1. Because a host computer knows to what network it belongs, it can very easily determine how to handle packets for such an IP address.

Because you are likely to deal with class C networks a lot, this class is used in all the examples in this section.

When a class C network is left in its entirety, the netmask is 255.255.255.0. To divide the network into subnets, you need to create a new netmask by setting one or more bits in the host interface part of the default class netmask (255.255.255.0) to 1's. Consider the ongoing example class C network—192.168.1.0. By setting the most significant bit in the host interface number part of the address to 1, you get:

```
11111111.11111111.11111111.10000000 => 255.255.255.128
```

This is a new netmask that splits the class in half. All IP addresses from 192.168.1.0 to 192.168.1.127 belong to the 192.168.1.0 network, and the rest of the IP addresses, 192.168.1.128 to 192.168.1.255, belong to the 192.168.1.128 network. Both networks use the 255.255.255.128 netmask. For example, to determine to which network an IP address called 192.168.1.10 belongs, you can perform the following bitwise AND operation:

```
Binary                                  Decimal
    11000000.10101000.00000001.00001010 => 192.168.1.10
AND 11111111.11111111.11111111.10000000 =>
255.255.255.128
    --------------------------------------------------------
    11000000.10101000.00000001.00000000 => 192.168.1.0
```

The netmask 255.255.255.128 tells you that the given IP address belongs to the 192.168.1.0 network. The following shows to which network an IP address called 192.168.1.200 belongs:

```
Binary                                  Decimal
    11000000.10101000.00000001.11001000 => 192.168.1.200
AND 11111111.11111111.11111111.10000000 =>
255.255.255.128

    ---------------------------------------------------
    11000000.10101000.00000001.10000000 => 192.168.1.128
```

The same netmask gives a different network address (192.168.1.128) for the given IP address. So, using this netmask, you have effectively separated the 192.168.1.0 networks into two subnets — 192.168.1.0 and 192.168.1128.

Because a full class C network has 256 possible IP addresses, each separate subnet has 128 IP addresses. However, not all of them are ever usable as host (interface) IP addresses. In a full class C network, such as 192.168.1.0 (with netmask 255.255.255.0), 192.168.1.0 is used as the network address, and 192.168.1.255 is used as the broadcast address. A broadcast address is used to communicate with all the host computers in the network. So, these two addresses are in a sense reserved. Therefore, in a full class C network, you have 254 (255 − network IP address − broadcast IP address) possible IP addresses. Similarly, when a network is subdivided, each subnet gets a network address and a broadcast address, so when a class C network is divided into two subnets, four IP addresses become unusable for host addressing. In the present example, this looks like the following:

```
Network: 192.168.1.0
Netmask: 255.255.255.128
First usable host IP address: 192.168.1.1
Last usable host IP address: 192.168.1.126
Broadcast address: 192.168.1.127

Network: 192.168.1.128
Netmask: 255.255.255.128
First usable host IP address: 192.168.1.129
Last usable host IP address: 192.168.1.254
Broadcast address: 192.168.1.255
```

The formula for determining how many subnets you can create out of a full class A, B, or C network is as follows: number of subnets = $2^{(\text{host bits} - 1)}$. For example, the number of host bits in a class C network is 8 (the last byte), so, technically, you can create 2^7 (128) equal-sized subnets from a single class C network. However, because of the loss of IP addresses (as network and broadcast addresses), most network administrators do not make more than 16 subnets out of a class C network.

If you are very new to the subnetting concept, you might find the ipcalc tool quite useful. For example, suppose that you want to make sure your subnet calculations are as expected. You can use this tool to reassure yourself that your numbers are right. For example, if you want to confirm that the subnets used in Figure 7-13 are correct, you can supply any IP in the 192.168.1.1 to 254 range to ipcalc, along with the subnet mask, to determine to which network the IP address will belong. Here are two examples:

```
ipcalc --broadcast --network 192.168.1.1 255.255.255.128
BROADCAST=192.168.1.127
NETWORK=192.168.1.0

ipcalc --broadcast --network 192.168.1.129
255.255.255.128
BROADCAST=192.168.1.255
NETWORK=192.168.1.12
```

In the first example, the ipcalc program is told to display the broadcast address (using the --broadcast argument) and the network address (using the --network argument) of an IP address 192.168.1.1 using the 255.255.255.128 netmask. It returns the broadcast address as 192.168.1.127 and the network address as 192.168.1.0. This is correct. In the second example, the program is asked to display the same information for an IP that belongs to the other half of the network, and it displays the correct addresses.

Gateway computer configuration

The gateway computer previously shown in Figure 7-13 must have two network interfaces. One of the interfaces has to be connected to each of the subnets. The /etc/sysconfig/network file for this computer is shown in Listing 7-4.

Listing 7-4 *The /etc/sysconfig/network File*

```
NETWORKING=yes
FORWARD_IPV4=yes
HOSTNAME=gateway.nitec.com
DOMAINNAME=nitec.com
```

The most important setting here is FORWARD_IPV4=yes, which enables IP forwarding in the kernel.

Tip

You must have IP forwarding support built into the kernel. You can use the cat /proc/sys/net/ipv4/ip_forward command to see whether IP forwarding is enabled in a running kernel. If the output is 1, then IP forwarding is set; a value of 0 signifies that IP forwarding is turned off. You can also turn it on or off by inserting a value of 1 or 0 using the echo *n* > /proc/sys/net/ipv4/ ip_forward command, where *n* is either 1 or 0.

Listings 7-5 and 7-6 show the two interface (eth0 and eth1) files.

Listing 7-5 *The /etc/sysconfig/network-scripts/ifcfg-eth0 File*

```
DEVICE=eth0
IPADDR=192.168.1.126
NETMASK=255.255.255.128
NETWORK=192.168.1.0
BROADCAST=192.168.1.127
ONBOOT=yes
```

Listing 7-6 *The /etc/sysconfig/network-scripts/ifcfg-eth1 File*

```
DEVICE=eth1
IPADDR=192.168.1.254
NETMASK=255.255.255.128
NETWORK=192.168.1.128
BROADCAST=192.168.1.255
ONBOOT=yes
```

After these files are set and the interfaces are up and running (either via a reboot or by using the ifup command), you need to create two default routes for the two networks, using the following route commands:

```
route add -net 192.168.1.0    255.255.255.128 eth0
route add -net 192.168.1.128 255.255.255.128 eth1
```

Each of the preceding route commands makes sure that packets destined for the named network are transmitted via the named interface device.

Host computer configuration

Each host computer on each of the subnets has to be configured so that each computer knows the network address, local subnet mask, and the gateway information. For example, assuming that all the host computers are also Linux workstations and each has a single Ethernet interface device (eth0), the /etc/sysconfig/network file on any of the host computers on the 192.168.1.0 network is shown in Listing 7-7.

Listing 7-7 The /etc/sysconfig/network File

```
NETWORKING=yes
FORWARD_IPV4=yes
HOSTNAME=marketing-1.nitec.com
DOMAINNAME=nitec.com
GATEWAY=192.168.1.126
GATEWAYDEV=eth0
```

The interface file on this same computer will look like the example shown in Listing 7-8.

Listing 7-8 The /etc/sysconfig/network-scripts/ifcfg-eth0 File

```
DEVICE=eth0
IPADDR=192.168.1.1
NETMASK=255.255.255.128
NETWORK=192.168.1.0
BROADCAST=192.168.1.127
ONBOOT=yes
```

In a similar fashion, the computers in the 192.168.1.128 network need to be set up. Each of the computers in this network will use the GATE-WAY=192.168.1.254 line in the /etc/sysconfig/network file and use

NETWORK=192.168.1.128 and BROADCAST=192.168.1.255 in their /etc/sysconfig/network-scripts/ifcfg-eth0 files.

Of course, if any of these computers are non-Linux systems, such as Windows 9*x*/2000, you have to use the appropriate network configuration tool to set these values.

After you set up the gateway computer and at least one host in each network, you are ready to test the subnets. The easiest way to test is to use the ping program. Here are some simple test and troubleshooting guidelines.

1. Use the ping program to ping a host computer in the same subnet. For example, run **ping 192.168.1.2** from the 192.168.1.1 computer. If you do not get ping replies, check the network configuration files (/etc/sysconfig/network and /etc/sysconfig/network-scripts/ ifcfg-eth0). Correct any problem you notice and restart the interface by first taking it down using **ifconfig eth0 down** and then bringing it up using **/etc/sysconfig/network-scripts/ifup eth0**. After you are able to ping a host in the same subnet, proceed to the next step.

2. Ping the gateway computer from each subnet. If you cannot perform this operation, check the gateway computer's network configuration files and correct any errors or typos. After you are able to ping the gateway computer from each subnet, proceed to the next step.

3. Try to ping a host in the other subnet. If you can't ping the host in the other subnet, try using **traceroute** *IP address* to determine whether the packets are even making it to the gateway machine. If traceroute shows that the packets are making it to the gateway but not being forwarded to the destination, the problem is at the gateway. You should ensure that IP forwarding is turned on for the computer. Run **cat /proc/sys/net/ipv4/ip_forward** on the gateway computer to see whether the returned value is 1 or 0. If it is not 1, IP forwarding is either turned off in the /etc/sysconfig/network file or not enabled in the kernel. In such a case, fix this problem and retry.

At this point, you should be able to send ping requests from any of the two subnets. If you can, then you have two working subnets.

Chapter 8

DNS Service

Configuring a DNS Client (Resolver)

Typically, the Red Hat installation program asks you about your DNS server and automatically configures the necessary resolver configuration file. However, it is often necessary to change the resolver configuration to reflect any changes to the DNS server you use. For example, if you configure your resolver during Red Hat installation and later change ISPs, you need to manually configure it again. Here is how.

If you plan to use your ISP's DNS server to resolve names and IP addresses, ask your ISP to give you the host name and the IP address of its DNS servers. After you have the required information, you can configure the resolver as follows:

1. First, you need to modify the resolver configuration file called /etc/resolv.conf. Listing 8-1 shows a typical /etc/resolv.conf file for a domain called `nitec.com`.

Listing 8-1 *The Resolver Configuration File /etc/resolv.conf*

```
# Default Domain
domain nitec.com

# Default search list
search nitec.com

# First name server
```

Continued

Listing 8-1 *Continued*

```
nameserver 206.171.50.50
# Second name server
nameserver 206.171.50.55
```

2. Set the Domain directive to the domain name for your system. If you do not have this line set to the domain name of your system, the default domain name is automatically extracted from the fully qualified host name of your system.

3. Set the Search directive to the domain name of your system. This directive is used to influence how the resolver searches for host names that are not fully qualified. For example, if you want to enter the ping www command in a shell on the system with the preceding resolver configuration file, the ping program will use the resolver to resolve www. Because www is a partial host name, the resolver creates a full host name by using the search list (for instance, www.nitec.com) and tries to resolve an IP for that host. For example, if you set the search directive to integrationlogic.com in the preceding listing and make the same ping request, the resolver returns the IP address for www.integrationlogic.com. If you do not provide a search directive, the default domain name is automatically applied when partial host names need to be resolved.

4. Set the Nameserver directive to the DNS server that the resolver should use to perform DNS queries. You can (and should) specify multiple nameserver directives in the configuration file. Each domain name server is queried in order of appearance in the configuration file. For example, if a program requests the resolver to resolve a host name called www.ad-engine.com, the resolver first tries to resolve the name to an IP using the 206.171.50.50 domain name server. If the 206.171.50.50 domain name server fails to return a response (that is, if the query times out), then the second domain name server, 206.171.50.55, is contacted. Currently, you are allowed to list only three nameserver directives in the configuration file. It is generally a good idea to have at least two nameserver directives set to two different name servers.

Caution

You can set the nameserver directive to any domain name server's IP address on the Internet. However, you should use only the closest name server IP addresses, to reduce delay in domain name resolution. Also, never use someone's domain name server IP address in your resolver configuration file without permission. It is considered rude and might have legal consequences if your resolver places a heavy load on someone's name server.

It is also possible to hard-code one or more IP addresses to their respective host names in the /etc/hosts file. This file has a very simple format, as follows:

```
IP address   host name   short-cut   host name
```

Here is an example of an /etc/hosts file:

```
206.171.50.50 picaso.nitec.com   picaso
127.0.0.1     localhost          localhost
```

The resolver can use this file to resolve an address when the remote DNS servers are not available. Also, if you have a small network and don't want to run a local DNS server, you may use this file to resolve local host names. However, when both the remote DNS server and the /etc/hosts file are available, the resolver needs to know which order to use to try to process DNS queries. You can set the order in the /etc/host.conf file by using the order directive. For example,

```
order hosts,bind
```

If your /etc/host.conf file has this order directive, then the resolver first attempts to use the /etc/hosts file to service the query. If the file does not contain an entry that can be used, the bind or DNS servers specified in the /etc/resolv.conf file will be used.

Tip

If you have a large user base, you can improve DNS-related performance by using a local DNS server over an /etc/hosts file, because reading the file for each new DNS request could be quite slow.

After you set up the files just described, your DNS resolver configuration is complete. The easiest way to test your DNS configuration is to try to ping a computer on the Internet. If the ping program fails because of an unknown host name, double-check your DNS resolver configuration for typos.

Setting Up a DNS Server

Red Hat Linux comes with the Berkeley Internet Name Domain (BIND) server software. If you did not install it during the OS installation phase, you can install the RPM version of the software. For example, to install the 8.2-6 version of BIND software for the Intel *x*86 platform, I located the bind-8.2-6.i386.rpm package in the Red Hat Linux CD-ROM's RPMS directory and ran the following command to install BIND:

```
rpm -ivh bind-8.2-6.i386.rpm
```

The RPM package of the BIND software just described installs the following four programs:

- **/usr/sbin/named.** The name server itself.
- **/usr/sbin/named-xfer.** An accessory program for the name server.
- **/usr/sbin/ndc.** A program to control the name server.
- **/usr/doc/bind-8.1.2/named-bootconf.pl.** An accessory Perl script to convert older configuration files to the new format.

Configuring a master/primary DNS server

Assume that I have the BIND domain name server (named) running on the ns.nitec.com host and I have just registered a domain called classifiedworks.com with InterNIC and want to set up named on ns.nitec.com to provide primary DNS for this new domain. Here is how.

First, I need to create the following zone statement in the /etc/named.conf file:

```
zone "classifiedworks.com" {
   type master;
   file "classifiedworks.db";
};
```

This states that my name server is the master name server for the
classifiedworks.com domain. Now, I need to create a zone file called
classifiedworks.db in the name server's working directory (specified by the
options { directory path_name}; statement. Listing 8-2 is an
example of such a zone file for the classifiedworks.com domain.

Listing 8-2 *A Zone File for the classifiedworks.com Domain*

```
@     IN   SOA  ns.nitec.com. kabir.nitec.com. (
                  1999020100    ; Serial
                  7200          ; Refresh - 2 hours
                  3600          ; Retry   - 1 hour
                  43200         ; Expire  - 12 hours
                  3600 )        ; Minimum - 1 hour


      IN   NS   ns.nitec.com.
      IN   MX   10 mail.nitec.com.


www   IN   CNAME www.nitec.com.
ftp   IN   A    206.171.50.55
```

I have set up SOA and NS records to state that ns.nitec.com is the
name server for the classifiedworks.com domain. Because I want to
receive mail for this domain on the mail.nitec.com host, I set up an
MX record that does just that. I set up an alias called www.classified
works.com for www.nitec.com. And, finally, I set up an A record for
ftp.classifiedworks.com to point to 206.171.55.

As you can see, by using the various RRs, you can configure the zone
file as you need to. After you configure the zone file and store it in the
working directory of the DNS server, the primary name server configuration for the domain is complete.

Configuring a slave/secondary DNS server

Configuring a slave or secondary DNS server is quite simple. The only file
you need to update by hand is the /etc/named.conf file. For example, suppose
that I want to use a DNS server called ns2.nitec.com as the secondary
name server for the classifiedworks.com domain. The first thing I need

to do is create a zone statement, such as the following, in the /etc/named.conf file of the ns2.nitec.com named server:

```
zone "classifiedworks.com" {
  type slave;
  file "classifiedworks.db";
};
```

Because this is a slave or secondary server, I do not need to create the classifiedworks.db file by hand. I can just grab the file from the primary name server for the classifiedworks.com domain by using a program called named-xfer, which comes with the named distribution. Because I know the name of the primary name server for the classifiedworks.com domain is ns.nitec.com, I can run the named-xfer command as follows:

```
named-xfer -z classifiedworks.com -f classifiedworks.db \
-s 0 ns.nitec.com
```

Here, the –z option is used to specify the zone name, the –f option is used to specify the zone filename, and the –s option is used to specify the name server on which the information currently resides.

After I run this program, a file called classifiedworks.db is created in the current directory. After I move the file to the working directory of the named server on the ns2.nitec.com machine, the secondary DNS configuration for the classifiedworks.com domain is complete.

Configuring a reverse DNS server

If you own your network IP addresses, you have to do reverse DNS for them. For example, if you own an IP network called 206.171.50.0 and use it in your forward DNS configuration for a domain called nitec.com, you have to set up a reverse DNS zone for this network. Here is how.

First, modify the /etc/named.conf file to include a new zone, as follows:

```
zone "50.171.206.in-addr.arpa" {
  type master;
  file "db.206.171.50";
};
```

The special zone name (50.171.206.in-addr.arpa) used in the preceding zone configuration is required to reverse your network number and append an in-addr.arpa at the end of the name to create a reverse DNS zone name.

Next, create db.206.171.50 in the working directory of the named server. The filename for the reverse DNS zone can be anything, but it is customary to use the db.*network-address* names. This file is similar to the other zone files shown so far; the only difference is that it will have PTR records instead of A, CNAME, and so on. Listing 8-3 shows an example of the db.206.171.50 file.

Listing 8-3 *An Example of a Reverse DNS Zone File (db.206.171.50)*

```
@    IN  SOA  ns.nitec.com. kabir.nitec.com. (
                1999020100  ; Serial
                7200        ; Refresh - 2 hours
                3600        ; Retry   - 1 hour
                43200       ; Expire  - 12 hours
                3600 )      ; Minimum - 1 hour


     IN  NS  ns.nitec.com.


51.50.171.206.in-addr.arpa.    IN  PTR  ns.nitec.com.
52.50.171.206.in-addr.arpa.    IN  PTR  mail.nitec.com.
53.50.171.206.in-addr.arpa.    IN  PTR  www.nitec.com.
```

Here, the PTR records are provided to map three different IP addresses to three different host names. You can also specify the preceding PTR records in shortened form, as follows:

```
51  IN  PTR  ns.nitec.com.
52  IN  PTR  mail.nitec.com.
53  IN  PTR  www.nitec.com.
```

In most cases, your ISP owns the IP addresses for your network and should be prepared to provide master reverse DNS service. However, for one special network, 127.0.0, you must provide reverse name service. This network is used for the local loopback interface IP (127.0.0.1). Because no one has authority over this loopback network, everyone must provide reverse

DNS service themselves, which is why you always need to have a special zone statement in your /etc/named.conf file that looks like the following:

```
zone "0.0.127.in-addr.arpa" {
   type master;
   file "named.local";
};
```

You also must have the named.local zone file in the working directory of your name server. This file is shown in Listing 8-4.

Listing 8-4 *The named.local File*

```
@    IN   SOA  localhost. root.localhost. (
               1999020100  ; Serial
               7200        ; Refresh -  2 hours
               3600        ; Retry   -  1 hour
               43200       ; Expire  - 12 hours
               3600 )      ; Minimum -  1 hour


     IN   NS   localhost.

1    IN   PTR  localhost.
```

Configuring a cache-only/slave DNS server

Technically, all DNS servers are cache-enabled; in other words, DNS servers use cache by default. However, if you don't want to provide DNS service for any Internet domains, and desire only to improve DNS query performance for your network, you can run a cache-only DNS server. Such a server will have an /etc/named.conf file, as shown in Listing 8-5.

Listing 8-5 *A Cache-Only DNS Server's /etc/named.conf File*

```
zone "." {
   type hint;
   file "named.ca";
};
```

```
zone "0.0.127.in-addr.arpa" {
  type master;
  file "named.local";
};
```

The first zone statement specifies that the name server use the named.ca file to determine root name server names at startup. The second zone statement is used to provide the reverse name service for the local loopback network. That's all you need to create a cache-only name server.

Controlling the DNS server

The named distribution comes with a nifty program called ndc that provides a simple command-line interface for controlling the name server.

Starting the name server

Your name server should be started automatically at boot. If it does not start automatically, you need to take the following steps:

1. Log in to your name server system as **root** and change the directory to /etc/rc.d/init.d. Make sure that you have a script called "named" in this directory. If you are missing this script, reinstall the BIND distribution RPM from your Red Hat CD-ROM.

2. After you confirm that you have the /etc/rc.d/init.d/named script, change the directory to your default system run-level (see /etc/inittab) rc directory. For most systems, the default run level is 3; if yours is the same, change the directory to /etc/rc.d/rc3.d/.

3. Make a symbolic link called S*XX*named that points to the /etc/rc.d/init.d/named script. Replace *XX* in S*XX*named with a high number, such as 55 or 85, to ensure that the system does not try to start the name server before network interfaces are set up properly. For example, to make a symbolic link called S55named to point to the named script, you can run the following:

   ```
   ln -s /etc/rc.d/init.d/named S55named
   ```

   After you create this link, your system will start the name server every time you boot your system. If, however, you prefer to run the name server manually, you can use the ndc program, as follows:

   ```
   ndc start
   ```

Reloading a new name server configuration

After you modify any of the zone files or the /etc/boot.conf file, you must restart the name server to make the changes effective. You can force the name server to reload the new configuration as follows:

```
ndc reload
```

Don't forget to modify the serial number in the SOA record for any zone file you modify, or else the name server will not load the new configuration.

To restart the name server by killing it first, you can use restart instead of reload in the preceding line.

Stopping the name server

If for any reason you need to stop the name server, run the ndc command as follows:

```
ndc stop
```

Viewing name server statistics

You can use the ndc program to generate various name server statistics in the working directory of the name server. Run the following to create a file called named.stats in the name server's working directory:

```
ndc stats
```

This statistics file shows various items of information, including the number of queries per RR.

Every time you modify your DNS information, don't forget to test the configuration using a name server query tool.

Testing Your DNS Server

Many tools are available for manually querying name servers. If you want to have a few commonly used query tools, install the bind-utils RPM distribution from your Red Hat CD-ROM. The bind-utils distribution comes with dig, dnsquery, host, nslookup, and more. My favorite, and the most widely used, is the nslookup utility, so it is used in this section for testing DNS configurations.

Suppose that you just registered a brand-new domain with InterNIC and have already set up the necessary DNS configuration on your name server. After restarting the name server, you want to test the configuration via nslookup.

When you run nslookup from the command line, it shows the host name and IP address of the name server it is going to use by default. If you are running nslookup on the name server system, you should see the name and IP of the name server. If you don't see the name server's information, make sure your /etc/resolv.conf file is configured properly.

On the other hand, if you are running nslookup on a computer other than the name server, you have to tell the program to use the name server you want to test. You need to do this only if InterNIC hasn't yet released the new domain's name server information to its root name servers. To tell nslookup to use a different name server from the default, enter **server _host name_** (where _host name_ is the host name of the server you want to test) from the nslookup command prompt. After you enter this command, nslookup uses the specified name server host for all queries.

The nslookup utility allows you to perform any type of DNS query using a simple syntax. For example, to locate the name server for a domain, run the following command from within the nslookup program:

```
set query=ns
domain.tld
```

The first line tells nslookup to perform an NS (Name Server RR) query for the next domain (domain.tld). Similarly, you can perform queries for A, MX, CNAME, and so on. If the responses you get don't look right, go back to the zone file and make sure you have no typos. One common mistake is to omit the period at the end of a full host name.

Managing DNS for Virtual Domains

A single name server can provide name service for many domains. This feature allows a single system to host numerous Internet domains. In fact, that's how most ISPs provide Web sites for their customers. Because such domains are hosted on another domain (for example, the ISP's own domain), they are called _virtual domains_, which are quite common these days. If you need to create a lot of virtual domains for your customers on a daily basis, you might want to automate the process as much as you can. Listing 8-6 shows a Perl script called makesite that you often can use to create a virtual domain.

Listing 8-6 *The makesite Script*

```perl
#!/usr/local/bin/perl -w

use strict;

#
# Purpose: makesite creates virtual sites.
# It uses a set of templates to create DNS and HTTPD
# configuration files.
#
# Note: this is a very *simple* script.
#
####################################################

use Time::localtime;

my $site              = $ARGV[0] or &syntax;
my $MAKESITE_DIR      = '/scratch/dns/makesite';
my $USER              = 'httpd';
my $GROUP             = 'httpd';
my $PERMISSION        = '2770';
my $BASE_DIR          = '/tmp';
my $HTDOCS            = 'htdocs';
my $CGIBIN            = 'cgi-bin';
my $NAMED_PATH        = '/var/named';
my $NAMED_FILE_EXT    = '.db';
my $NAMED_TEMPLATE    = "$MAKESITE_DIR/named.template";
my $NAMED_CONF        = '/etc/named.conf';
my $HTTPD_CONF        =
'/usr/local/apache/etc/httpd.conf';
my $VHOST_TEMPLATE    = "$MAKESITE_DIR/httpd.template";
```

```perl
my $LOG_FILE          = "$BASE_DIR/makesite.log";

my $dir = $site;
my @domain_types = qw(com net org edu);
my ($domain_ext, $thesite_dir, $public_dir,
    $htdocs_dir, $cgibin_dir, $named_file,
    $dir_len, $temp_len);

my $tm = localtime(time);
my $date = sprintf("%s-%02s-%02s-%02d-%02d", $tm-
>year+1900,

                                        $tm->mon+1,
                                        $tm->mday,
                                        $tm->hour,
                                        $tm->min);

my $serial = sprintf("%s%02d%02d000",          $tm-
>year+1900,

                                        $tm->mon+1,
                                        $tm->mday);

$site =~ y/[A-Z]/[a-z]/;

# Get the length with the EXT
$dir_len = length($dir);

foreach $domain_ext (@domain_types){ $dir =~
s/\.$domain_ext//g; }

# Get the new length without the EXT
$temp_len = length($dir);

# If the user has not entered an extension, then show
syntax.
```

Continued

Listing 8-6 *Continued*

```
&syntax if($temp_len == $dir_len);

$named_file = $NAMED_PATH . '/' . $dir . $NAMED_FILE_EXT
;
$thesite_dir = $BASE_DIR . '/' . $dir;
$htdocs_dir = $BASE_DIR . '/' . $dir . '/' . $HTDOCS;
$cgibin_dir = $BASE_DIR . '/' . $dir . '/' . $CGIBIN;

die "$thesite_dir already exist! Aborted!\n" if(-e
$thesite_dir);

system("mkdir $thesite_dir");
system("mkdir $htdocs_dir");
system("mkdir $cgibin_dir");

&createNamedFile($named_file,$site,"$dir$NAMED_FILE_EXT")
;
&createIndexFile($htdocs_dir,$site);
&createVirtualHostConf( domain=>$site,
                        website=>"www.$site",
                        cgibin=>$cgibin_dir,
                        htdocs=>$htdocs_dir);

system("chown -R $USER.$GROUP $thesite_dir");
system("chmod -R $PERMISSION $thesite_dir");

open(FP,">$LOG_FILE") || die "Can't write to log
file.\n";
print FP "$date created www.$site [$htdocs_dir] site.\n";
close(FP);

exit 0;

sub createNamedFile{
```

```perl
  my $file = shift;
  my $domain = shift;
  my $database = shift;
  my $line;

  open(OUT,">$file") || die "Can't write $file\n";
  open(FP,$NAMED_TEMPLATE) || die "Can't open
$NAMED_TEMPLATE\n";
    while($line=<FP>){
      $line =~ s/<DOMAIN>/$domain/g;
      $line =~ s/<SERIAL>/$serial/g;
      print OUT $line;
      }
    close(FP);
    close(OUT);

    open(FP,">$NAMED_CONF") || die "Can't open
$NAMED_CONF\n";
    print FP <<ZONE;

// $domain was created on $date
zone "$domain" {
        type master;
        file "$database";
};

ZONE
    close(FP);
    }

sub createIndexFile{
  my $htdocs = shift;
  my $domain = shift;
```

Continued

Listing 8-6 *Continued*

```
  open(FP,">$htdocs/index.html") || die "Can't write
index.html \n";
  print FP <<INDEX_PAGE;
  <HTML>
  <HEAD> <TITLE> $domain </TITLE> </HEAD>
  <BODY BGCOLOR="white">
  <CENTER>
   This is $domain Web site
   <p> It was created on $date </p>
  </CENTER>
  </BODY>
  </HTML>
INDEX_PAGE

  close(FP);
  }

sub createVirtualHostConf{

  my %params = @_;
  my $line;
  open(OUT,">$HTTPD_CONF") || die "Can't open $HTTPD_CONF
$!\n";

  open(FP,$VHOST_TEMPLATE) || die "Can't open
$VHOST_TEMPLATE $!\n";
  while($line=<FP>){
    $line =~ s/<DOMAIN>/$params{domain}/g;
    $line =~ s/<CGI-BIN-DIR>/$params{cgibin}/g;
    $line =~ s/<HTDOCS-DIR>/$params{htdocs}/g;
    $line =~ s/<WWW-SITE>/$params{website}/g;
    print OUT $line;

  }
```

```
    close(FP);
    close(OUT);
    }

sub syntax{
    print <<SYNTAX;

    makesite <virtual Internet domain>
    Example: makesite nitec.com

SYNTAX
    exit 0;
    }
```

The purpose of this Perl script is to allow you to create a virtual Web site with the proper DNS and Apache Web server configuration without doing many file-editing tasks. For example, suppose you want to create a new Web site called www.newdomain.com. To do this manually, you would have to do the following:

1. Add a new zone statement in the /etc/named.conf file for new domain.com.

2. Add a new zone file for newdomain.com in the working directory of the name server. I would have to create this from scratch or copy and modify an existing domain file.

3. Create a Web site document root and CGI script directory for the domain in the appropriate Web space on the server.

4. Modify the Apache Server configuration file so that Apache treats www.newdomain.com as a new Web site.

Because manually configuring these important files can be error-prone, you should write the makesite script to do all of these steps. For example, to create the www.newdomain.com site with the proper DNS and Apache configuration, you can run the following:

```
makesite newdomain.com
```

This command adds a zone statement such as the following in the /etc/named.conf file:

```
// newdomain.com was created on 1999-02-03-13-30

zone "newdomain.com" {
  type master;
  file "newdomain.db";
};
```

This statement creates a newdomain.db file in /var/named (the working directory for my name server), which is shown in Listing 8-7.

Listing 8-7 *The /var/named/newdomain.db File*

```
@  IN  SOA  newdomain.com. hostmaster.newdomain.com. (
                 19990206000  ; serial YYYYMMDDXXX
                 7200         ; refresh
                 3600         ; (1 hour) retry
                 1728000      ; (20 days) expire
                 3600)        ; (1 hour) minimal TTL

; Name Servers
   IN  NS  ns.nitec.com.
   IN  MX  10 mail.nitec.com.

; CNAME records
www  IN  CNAME  www.nitec.com.
```

The script then appends the following lines to the end of the Apache server configuration (httpd.conf) file:

```
#
# Domain Configuration for www.newdomain.com
#
```

```
<VirtualHost www.newdomain.com>
  ServerName www.newdomain.com
  ServerAdmin webmaster@newdomain.com

  DocumentRoot /tmp/newdomain/htdocs
  ScriptAlias /cgi-bin/ /tmp/newdomain/cgi-bin/

  ErrorLog logs/www.newdomain.com.error.log
  TransferLog logs/www.newdomain.com.access.log

</VirtualHost>

#
# End of Domain Configuration for www.newdomain.com
#
```

Finally, the script creates the following directory structure and the index.html page for the Web site:

```
/www/newdomain
/www/newdomain/htdocs -- the document root for the Web site
/www/newdomain/cgi-bin -- the cgi-bin directory
```

The index.html page is stored in the /www/newdomain/htdocs/ directory. The script also sets up the permissions for the Web site directories so that only a specified user and group have read/write permissions.

Because the script does all the dirty work, you can create many virtual sites without constantly worrying about configuration problems. And, when you are done making sites, you can restart the name server and the Web server to bring up all the sites online. This is really a simple yet useful tool.

The makesite script takes the domain name as the argument and uses two text template files to create the name server and the Web server configuration information. Listing 8-8 shows the named.template file used to create the name server configuration.

Listing 8-8 *The named.template File*

```
@   IN SOA <DOMAIN>.  hostmaster.<DOMAIN>. (
                    <SERIAL>    ; serial YYYYMMDDXXX
                    7200        ; refresh
                    3600        ; (1 hour) retry
                    1728000     ; (20 days) expire
                    3600)       ; (1 hour) minimal TTL


; Name Servers
    IN   NS   ns.nitec.com.
    IN   MX   10 mail.nitec.com.


; CNAME records
www  IN   CNAME  www.nitec.com.
```

The makesite script reads this template and replaces the `<DOMAIN>` and `<SERIAL>` tags with appropriate information. Because the idea is to create a virtual Web site with a proper DNS configuration, no A records need to be created. For example, the preceding configuration states that the `www.<DOMAIN>` (for instance, `www.newdomain.com`) is an alias of `www.nitec.com`. Using A records makes maintenance of many virtual Web sites time-consuming if IP changes are required. Thus, I use the CNAME record, so that if `www.nitec.com` host's IP needs to be changed, the virtual domain's configuration files do not need to be modified.

Listing 8-9 shows the httpd.template file used to create the Apache server configuration.

Listing 8-9 *The httpd.template File*

```
#
# Domain Configuration for <WWW-SITE>
#

<VirtualHost <WWW-SITE>
  ServerName <WWW-SITE>
  ServerAdmin webmaster@<DOMAIN>
```

```
DocumentRoot <HTDOCS-DIR>
ScriptAlias /cgi-bin/ <CGI-BIN-DIR>/

ErrorLog logs/<WWW-SITE>.error.log
TransferLog logs/<WWW-SITE>.access.log

</VirtualHost>

#
# End of Domain Configuration for <WWW-SITE>
#
```

As with the previous template, a few custom tags are used in this file and are replaced with appropriate information.

To use this Perl script in your own environment, modify the following code lines in the beginning of the script by making the change described after each line:

```
my $MAKESITE_DIR  = '/usr/local/src/makesite';
```

Change the directory path to where you are keeping all the makesite files.

```
my $USER   = 'httpd';
```

Change the username if you run your Apache Web server using another user, such as 'nobody' or something else.

```
my $GROUP  = 'httpd';
```

Change the group name if you run your Apache Web server using another group, such as 'nobody' or something else.

```
my $PERMISSION  = '2770';
```

Change the value (2770) as you see fit. This value allows only the $USER and $GROUP to have full access in the Web site directory.

```
my $BASE_DIR   = '/www';
```

Change this to the base directory of all of your Web sites.

```
my $HTDOCS  = 'htdocs';
```

Change this to the relative name of the document root directory name for httpd.conf file. The current setting creates $BASE_DIR/<*sitename*>$HTDOCS (default: /www/<*sitename*>/htdocs) as the document root for the Web site.

```
my $CGIBIN = 'cgi-bin';
```

Change this relative directory name to whatever is applicable if you do not want the Apache ScriptAlias directive to be set to $BASE_DIR/<*sitename*>/$CGIBIN (default: /www/<*sitename*>/cgi-bin).

```
my $NAMED_PATH = '/var/named';
```

Change this directory to the working directory of your name server.

```
my $LOG_FILE = "$BASE_DIR/makesite.log";
```

Change this to point to somewhere else if you do not want to write the makesite log file in the base directory. For example, you can set this to "/tmp/makesite.log" to write to the /tmp directory.

```
my $HTTPD_CONF = '/usr/local/apache/etc/httpd.conf';
```

Change this to point to the httpd.conf file of your Web server.

After you make the preceding changes, modify the named.template and httpd.template files as you see fit and store both of them in the directory where you keep the makesite script. Finally, make sure that the script is executable and that the Perl interpreter line (the #! bang line) is set up correctly. Hopefully, this will save you some work. If you know Perl programming, you can always fine-tune the script to your environment as much as you want.

Balancing Load Using the DNS Server

The idea is to share the load among multiple servers of a kind. This typically is used for balancing the Web load over multiple Web servers. This trick is called round-robin Domain Name Service.

Suppose that you have two Web servers, www1.yourdomain.com (192.168.1.10) and www2.yourdomain.com (192.168.1.20), and you want to balance the load for www.yourdomain.com on these two servers using the round-robin DNS trick. Add the following lines to your yourdomain.com zone file:

```
www1   IN   A   192.168.1.10
www2   IN   A   192.168.1.20

www    IN   CNAME   www1
www    IN   CNAME   www2
```

Restart your name server and ping the www.yourdomain.com host. You will see the 192.168.1.10 address in the ping output. Stop and restart pinging the same host, and you'll see the second IP address being pinged, because the preceding configuration tells the name server to cycle through the CNAME records for www. In other words, the www.yourdomain.com host is both www1.yourdomain.com and www2.yourdomain.com.

Now, when someone enters www.yourdomain.com, the name server gives out the first address once, and then gives out the second address for the next request, and keeps cycling between these addresses.

One of the disadvantages of the round-robin DNS trick is that the name server has no way to know which system is heavily loaded and which is not; it just blindly cycles. If one of the servers crashes or becomes unavailable for some reason, the round-robin DNS trick still returns the broken server's IP on a regular basis. This could be quite chaotic, because some people will be able to get to the sites and some won't.

If your load demands better management and checking your server's health is important, your best choice is to get a hardware solution using the new director products, such as the Web Director (www.radware.com/), Ace Director (www.alteon.com/), or Local Director (www.cisco.com/). I have used Web Director with great success.

Chapter 9

E-mail Service

Setting Up DNS for SMTP Server

Mail Exchange (MX) records in a DNS configuration are used to identify SMTP mail server resources for a domain. Suppose that you want to designate a host called `mail.yourdomain.com` as your SMTP mail server for the domain `yourdomain.com`. The Start of Authority (SOA) record for `yourdomain.com` must include a line such as

```
IN  MX  preference-value mail-server-hostname.
```

where *preference-value* is a positive (integer) number that is useful only when you have multiple SMTP mail servers. If you have a single SMTP mail server, this number can have any value. For example, the following sets the single SMTP mail server `mail.yourdomain.com` to preference level 5:

```
IN  MX  5  mail.yourdomain.com.
```

The following is an example of the multiserver scenario, in which the preference number plays a vital role:

```
IN  MX  10  fast-mail-server.ad-engine.com.
IN  MX  20  slow-mail-server.ad-engine.com.
```

When an SMTP mail server from anyone on the Internet wants to send mail to `someone@ad-engine.com`, it first performs a DNS query to locate the MX record for `ad-engine.com`. The MX record returned to the SMTP mail server will be the same as the one just shown. The SMTP mail server then selects `fast-mail-server.ad-engine.com` as the preferred mail server for the delivery, because it has the higher priority (that is, the lower preference number) of the two available servers.

The SMTP mail server then tries to initiate an SMTP connection (using port 25) with the `fast-mail-server.ad-engine.com` computer. If the `fast-mail-server.ad-engine.com` server is unavailable for any reason, the `slow-mail-server.ad-engine.com` server will be selected for delivery. So, having multiple MX records provides you with redundancy in your mail delivery system, which is very important if e-mail is a critical part of your organization.

Caution

Always use a host name in an MX record that has its own A record. In other words, do not use host aliases in MX records. See RFC 1123 for details.

After you set up DNS with appropriate MX records, test the configuration as follows:

1. Run the nslookup program from a shell.

2. When you are at the nslookup prompt, enter set q=mx totell nslookup that you want to perform an MX record query.

3. Enter your domain name.

   If you have configured DNS as discussed above, you will see the MX record(s) you have created earlier. On the other hand, if you do not get the MX records or nslookup returns an error, fix your DNS configuration, restart the DNS server and perform this test again.

Setting Up an SMTP Mail Server

The first step in setting up an SMTP server is to decide which SMTP mail server you want to use for your Red Hat Linux system. Many SMTP mail server products are available. However, sendmail stands out among the rest because of its long history of worldwide deployment. It is also the default SMTP mail server for Red Hat Linux. Hence, sendmail is used as the SMTP server for this chapter.

Installing sendmail

Like any other server software you have installed on your Red Hat system, sendmail comes in RPM packages. However, you need to install multiple RPM packages for sendmail:

- **sendmail-<*version*>.<*architecture*>.rpm.** The main distribution
- **sendmail-cf-<*version*>.<*architecture*>.rpm.** The mail sendmail configuration file distribution
- **sendmail-config-<*version*>.<*architecture*>.rpm.** The auxiliary configuration files distribution
- **sendmail-doc-<*version*>.<*architecture*>.rpm.** The documentation distribution

Installing these packages is quite simple; run **rpm –ivh** *package name* to install each package.

Tip

If you installed a previous version of sendmail during Red Hat Linux installation, remove the sendmail packages before you install a new version, because they might not be exactly compatible. To uninstall an RPM package, use the rpm –e *package name* command. You can also locate the exact package name of an RPM package by using the rpm –q *partial package name* command.

After you install the packages, you are ready to configure sendmail. The primary configuration file for sendmail is /etc/sendmail.cf.

Starting and stopping sendmail

Although you have not yet configured the sendmail server, you can still run it. To start sendmail manually, run the following command:

```
/usr/sbin/sendmail  -q<queue processing interval>
```

Replace *queue processing interval* with a time. Typically, time is specified in minutes or hours. For example, to have sendmail process the mail queue every 15 minutes, use **–q15m**; or, to process the queue every hour, use **–q1h**. You can also specify seconds (s), days (d), or weeks (w). For example, to have sendmail process the query every hour and a half, specify **–q1h30m**.

Tip

If you don't have a full-time Internet connection, you may use **/usr/sbin/sendmail –bd –o DeliveryMode=d** to start sendmail in deferred mode, which avoids use of DNS until it is run again via /usr/sbin/sendmail –q. If you connect periodically, you can put **/usr/sbin/sendmail –q** in a cron job so that when your connection is up, the queue is processed automatically.

If you want sendmail to start automatically after each boot, create a symbolic link (starting with S*xx*, where *xx* is a number) from your default run-level directory to the /etc/rc.d/init.d/sendmail script. For example, to run sendmail after each boot for a multiuser system (run level 3), I can create the following symbolic link:

```
ln -s /etc/rc.d/init.d/sendmail
/etc/rc.d/rc3.d/S85sendmail
```

This makes sure that sendmail starts automatically after each boot. The /etc/rc.d/init.d/sendmail script starts sendmail with the –bd option. You may want to modify the /etc/rc.d/init.d/sendmail script to reflect the queue interval requirements for your site. Also, you might want to add the following code just before the line:

```
daemon /usr/sbin/sendmail –bd
```

in the script to automatically run newaliases and makemap on the configuration files at boot:

```
newaliases
for i in virtusertable access domaintable mailertable
do
   if [ -f /etc/mail/$i ] ; then
       echo "Making $i database for sendmail..."
       makemap hash /etc/mail/$i < /etc/mail/$i
       sleep 1
   fi
done
sleep 1
```

This ensures that all the configuration databases are rebuilt each time you start the server process.

You can use the /etc/rc.d/init.d/sendmail script to start, stop, and restart sendmail quite easily, as well. To stop sendmail, run

```
/etc/rc.d/init.d/sendmail stop
```

To restart sendmail, run

```
/etc/rc.d/init.d/sendmail restart
```

You can also force sendmail to process its queue immediately by using the –q option:

```
/usr/sbin/sendmail -q
```

If you prefer to process the queue partially, you can use the –qS*string* option to process queues for only those messages that have the named string as part of the sender address. For example, the following forces sendmail to process all queued mail for sender kabir:

```
/usr/sbin/sendmail -qSkabir
```

This is handy when you have lots of mail waiting in a queue.

Tip

You can run the mqueue command to find what messages are currently in the queue.

You can also use –qR*string* to force sendmail to process messages that have the named string as part of the recipient address.

Understanding and configuring /etc/sendmail.cf

The /etc/sendmail.cf configuration file is considered the most complex configuration file UNIX administrators ever have to deal with.

A complete book can be (and has been) written about the configuration required for /etc/sendmail.cf. However, not every administrator needs to know the details of /etc/sendmail.cf configuration. In fact, in most cases, you don't even need to modify this configuration file, because it comes well-equipped with commonly required configurations.

This section provides a brief overview of how things are set up in the configuration file and enables you to follow instructions found at the sendmail Web site (`http://www.sendmail.org/`) to implement certain features, as needed. In other words, the information in this chapter is good enough to get you up and running and provides you with enough know-how to follow clearly written instructions in implementing configuration changes. This section does not explain how to create your own configuration rules, which requires extensive understanding of the inner workings of the sendmail configuration.

The sendmail.cf file contains the following types of configuration information:

- Blank lines are ignored.

- Comment lines, designated by a leading # sign, are also ignored.

- Lines starting with C, D, F, H, O, P, V, K, M, S, or R are configuration lines.

- Lines starting with a leading whitespace character are continuation lines.

The following sections show various configurations in brief so that you have an idea about which one does what.

S and R: address rewrite rules

An S line is used to mark the start of a new rewrite rule. The syntax for such a line is S*rule*, where *rule* is the rule name/number. For example, S3 marks the start of ruleset 3.

An R line defines an address rewrite rule. Think of a rewrite rule as a statement like the following:

```
If (current e-mail address matches rule's left-hand-side
pattern) then
     Replace current address
            with the rule's right-hand-side pattern
end
```

It has the following syntax:

```
R<LHS>    <RHS>   <optional comments>
```

LHS is the left-hand-side pattern, and *RHS* is the right-hand-side pattern of the rule. For example, in the following syntax,

```
R$* < $* > $* <@>        $: $1 < $2 > $3
```

the LHS pattern is $* < $* > $* <@>, and the RHS pattern is $: $1 < $2 > $3. Both the LHS and RHS patterns are composed of various metasymbols, such as $*, $+, $-, $=x, and $~x.

Rewrite rules are quite complex and usually don't require any changes on your part. However, if you plan to write your own rewrite rules, you should read the *Sendmail Installation and Operation Guide* bundled with the sendmail documentation.

D: define macro

D lines define a macro. The syntax is as follows:

```
D<macro name>   <string>
```

For example, the following syntax is the same as $P = someword, and whenever $P is referenced elsewhere, it is expanded to someword:

```
DP  someword
```

Typically, you do not need to add, delete, or remove any D macro definitions.

C and F: define classes

C lines are similar to D lines. The syntax for such a line is as follows:

```
C<class name> <string> <string> . . .
```

For example, the A class shown here is a list of str1, str2, and str3 strings:

```
CA  str1 str2 str3
```

F lines are the same as C lines, except that an F line is used to specify a class that is read from a file. In the following example, w class is a list of all the domain names in the /etc/mail/sendmail.cw file:

```
Fw/etc/mail/sendmail.cw
```

This file must contain a single entry per line. The only other F line you will notice in your sendmail.cf file is the following:

```
FR-o /etc/mail/relay-domains
```

The class R is a list of all domain names in /etc/mail/relay-domains. Notice the −o option, which makes the line optional. In other words, sendmail will not complain if this file is empty. Typically, you do not need to make any changes here. However, if you want sendmail to complain if no relay domains are defined, you can remove the −o option from the preceding FR line.

M: define mailer

An M line is used to create a mailer definition. The syntax for such a line is as follows:

```
Mmailer name field=value, field=value, . . .
```

In the following example, mailer SMTP is defined:

```
Msmtp,  P=[IPC], F=mDFMuX, S=11/31, R=21/31, E=\r\n, L=990,
        T=DNS/RFC822/SMTP
```

Typically, you don't need to make any changes in standard mailer definitions.

H: define header

An H line is used to create a header definition. The syntax for such a line is as follows:

```
H[?flags?]<header name>: <header template>
```

For example, each of the following H lines defines a mail header:

```
H?P?Return-Path: <$g>
HReceived: $?sfrom $s $.$?_($?s$|from $.$_)
        $.by $j ($v/$Z)$?r with $r$. id $i$?u
        for $u; $|;
        $.$b
H?D?Resent-Date: $a
H?D?Date: $a
```

```
H?F?Resent-From: $?x$x <$g>$|$g$.
H?F?From: $?x$x <$g>$|$g$.
H?x?Full-Name: $x
H?M?Resent-Message-Id: <$t.$i@$j>
H?M?Message-Id: <$t.$i@$j>
```

You should not make any changes in header definitions.

O: set option

The O lines are used to set global options for sendmail. The syntax for such a line is as follows:

```
O option name = value
```

Table 9-1 shows all the options available in the latest version (8.9.*x*) of sendmail.

Table 9-1 *Sendmail Options*

Option	Explanation
AliasFile=/etc/mail/aliases	Sets the name of the alias database file. Change only if you keep the aliases database some place other than /etc/mail/aliases.
AliasWait=30m	Default timeout (in minutes) for aliases to load at startup. Do not change.
AutoRebuildAliases=True	If set to True, sendmail tries to rebuild the aliases database if necessary and possible. Do not change.
BlankSub=.	Sets the blank substitution character. Do not change.
CheckAliases=False	If set to True, checks the right-hand side of an alias in the aliases database for validity. By default, set to False. No change recommended.
ClassFactor=1800	Used to compute priority of a message. Do not change.
ConnectionCacheSize=2	The maximum number of open connections that will be cached at any time.
ConnectionCacheTimeout=5m	The maximum time (in minutes) that a cached connection will be kept open during an idle period.
ConnectionRateThrottle=20	Allows no more than specified number of daemon processes for incoming connections per second. Setting this to 0 allows an unlimited (i.e., as much as is permitted by your system resources) number of daemon processes per second.

Continued

Table 9-1 *Continued*

DefaultUser=8:12	Default user and group for mailers. The UID 8 is default for user *mail* in /etc/passwd, and GID 12 is default for group "mail" in /etc/group. No change recommended.
DeliveryMode=background	Runs sendmail in the background. No change required.
EightBitMode=pass8	Sets how eight-bit data is handled. Keep the default.
ForkEachJob=False	When set to True, a separate process is forked to service each message in the queue. No change required.
ForwardPath=$z/.forward.$w+$h:$z/.forward+$h:$z/.forward.$w:$z/.forward	Sets the path for searching for the .forward file for each user. No change required.
HelpFile=/usr/lib/sendmail.hf	Sets the location of the help file.
HoldExpensive=False	When set to True, expensive mailers (marked using F=e flag in M line for the mailer) are not allowed to connect immediately. Keep the default.
HostStatusDirectory=.hoststat	Sets the directory name for the host status information. The default value sets the directory to /var/spool/mqueue/.hoststat. No change required.
HostsFile=/etc/hosts	Sets the name of the hosts file. No change required.
LogLevel=8	Sets the default log level. No change required.
MatchGECOS=False	When set to True, sendmail performs fuzzy search in the /etc/passwd file to locate a "similar" username in the GECOS field of each password entry. Default is recommended.
MaxDaemonChildren=40	Maximum number of forked child processes at any time.
MaxHopCount=30	Maximum length of time a message can be processed before it is rejected.
MaxMessageSize=5000000	Maximum size of a message, in bytes. Messages larger than this size won't be accepted.
MeToo=False	When an alias contains the sender herself, sendmail automatically removes the sender from the expansion. If this option is set to True, the sender receives the mail in such a case. You might want to set this to True, because it might reduce some tech-support calls from users who want to receive mail even if it originated from themselves.
MinFreeBlocks=100	Minimum number of free blocks that must be present before sendmail will accept a message. This enables you to ensure that someone can't wipe out your disk space by mail bombing (i.e., sending multiple copies of large mail messages) to your server. You might want to increase this to a number higher than the default.
MinQueueAge=10m	A message must be in the queue for at least the specified number of minutes before it is processed.

NoRecipientAction=add-to-undisclosed	When a message does not contain an appropriate recipient header, the specified action is taken. The default value creates a To: undisclosed-recipients header.
OldStyleHeaders=True	Toggle old/new header format. No change required.
OperatorChars=.:%@!^/[]+	List of token delimiter characters. No change required.
PrivacyOptions=needvrfyhelo, restrictmailq,restrictqrun,goaway	See the section on ensuring privacy under "Securing Sendmail" in this chapter for details.
QueueDirectory=/var/spool/mqueue	The fully qualified path name of the queue directory.
QueueLA=8	When the system's load average exceeds the specified number, do not send messages but instead queue them.
QueueSortOrder=Host	Sets the queue sort order. The default value allows sendmail to sort the queue using the host names of the recipients. You can change this to Priority to sort mail by priority header, or to Time to sort by submission time.
RecipientFactor=30000	Used to penalize the priority of a message that has a large number of recipients.
RefuseLA=12	When the system's load average exceeds the specified value, refuse incoming connections.
RetryFactor=90000	Used to lower priority. No change recommended.
RunAsUser=mail	Specifies the username sendmail uses for all of its child processes. In other words, sendmail child processes that are forked to service the actual requests do not run as the superuser; thus, this enhances security. No change recommended.
SendMimeErrors=True	When set to True, error messages are set using MIME formats. No change required.
SevenBitInput=False	When set to True, a message is converted into seven-bit data. Do not change the default value.
O SmtpGreetingMessage= $j Sendmail $v/$Z; $b	Sets the greeting message that sendmail issues when a connection is made. If you don't want to tell the world the version of sendmail you use, remove the $v/$Z variables from this line. This might provide fewer clues for someone who is trying to exploit any security holes.
StatusFile=/var/log/sendmail.st	The fully qualified path name of the status file.
SuperSafe=True	Toggle super safe mode. Default setting is recommended.
TempFileMode=0600	Sets the default mode for the temporary files in the queue.
Timeout.command=30m	Default timeout value for SMTP commands.
Timeout.connect=3m	Default timeout value for connection.
Timeout.datablock=1h	Default timeout value for data blocks.
Timeout.datafinal=1h	Default timeout value for final '.' in the data.

Continued

Table 9-1 *Continued*

Timeout.datainit=5m	Default timeout value for the DATA command.
Timeout.fileopen=60s	Default timeout value for opening .forward and :include: files.
Timeout.helo=5m	Default timeout value for the HELO command.
Timeout.hoststatus=10m	Host status becomes stale after the specified timeout period.
Timeout.iconnect=10s	Default timeout value for connection.
Timeout.initial=5m	Default timeout value for the initial greeting message.
Timeout.mail=10m	Default timeout value for the MAIL command.
Timeout.misc=2m	Default timeout value for the NOOP or VERB commands.
Timeout.queuereturn.non-urgent=7d	Length of time before nonurgent message is returned to sender.
Timeout.queuereturn.normal=5d	Length of time before normal message is returned to sender.
Timeout.queuereturn.urgent=2d	Length of time before urgent message is returned to sender.
Timeout.queuereturn=5d	Length of time before a message is returned to sender.
Timeout.queuewarn.non-urgent=12h	Length of time before a warning is sent to the sender because of yet-undelivered nonurgent message.
Timeout.queuewarn.normal=6h	Length of time before a warning is sent to the sender because of yet-undelivered normal message.
Timeout.queuewarn.urgent=2h	Length of time before a warning is sent to the sender because of yet-undelivered urgent message.
Timeout.queuewarn=6h	Length of time before a warning is sent to the sender because of yet-undelivered message.
Timeout.quit=2m	Default timeout value for the QUIT command.
Timeout.rcpt=30m	Default timeout value for the RCPT command.
Timeout.rset=5m	Default timeout value for the RSET command.
UnixFromLine=From $g $d	Defines the format used for UNIX-style From line. Do not change the default.
UnsafeGroupWrites=True	When set to True, files such as .forward and :include: are considered unsafe when they are writable by a group. Do not change the default.
UseErrorsTo=False	When set to True and an error occurs, sendmail uses the ErrorsTo header (if available) to report the error. Do not change the default.

P: precedence definitions

A P line is used to set values for the Precedence: header field. The syntax for such a line is as follows:

```
Pfield name = value
```

For example:

```
Pfirst-class=0
```

V: configuration version level

A V line is used for compatibility with older versions of a configuration. You do not need to make any changes to such a line.

K: key file declaration

A K line is used to define a map. The syntax for such a line is as follows:

```
Kmap name mapclass arguments
```

For example:

```
Kaccess hash -o /etc/mail/access.db
```

Configuring /etc/mail/* files

The sendmail configuration files found in the /etc/mail directory are discussed in this section.

Restricting access to your sendmail server using /etc/mail/access

This configuration file can be used to create an access restriction database for your sendmail server. You can control access to your sendmail server based on domain, subdomain, IP address, or network. The configuration lines in this file have the following format:

```
host or user  access control option
```

host or user can be a fully or partly qualified host name, domain name, IP address, network address, or e-mail address, such as wormhole.nitec.com, nitec.com, 192.168.1.10, 192.168.1.0, spammer@somewhere.com, and so on. The available configuration options are shown in Table 9-2.

Table 9-2 *Configuration Options for the /etc/mail/access Database*

Option	Description
OK	Accept mail even if other configuration rules want to reject mail from the specified host or the user.
RELAY	Act as an SMTP mail relay for the specified host. In other words, accept mail intended for users on the specified domain and also allow users on the specified domain to send mail via the server. Don't reject mail from the specified domain even if other rules want to do so.
REJECT	Reject all (incoming/outgoing) mail for the specified domain.
DISCARD	Discard the message completely by using the $#discard mailer. Discarded messages are accepted but silently kept undelivered so that the sender thinks they have been delivered.
501 <message>	Do not accept mail if the sender address partially or fully matches the specified *user@host*.
553 <message>	Do not accept mail if the sender address does not contain host name.
550 <message>	Do not accept mail for specified domain name.

Here is an example /etc/mail/access configuration:

```
any-spam-maker.com      REJECT
client-domain.com       RELAY
annoying-company.com    DISCARD
dumbguy@dumb-net.com    501 You can't use this mail server.
```

All mail from `any-spam-maker.com` will be rejected; all incoming and outgoing mail to and from `client-domain.com` will be relayed; all mail from `annoying-company.com` will be accepted but silently discarded; and all mail from `dumbguy@dumb-net.com` will be rejected with the "You can't use this mail server" message.

Note that sendmail does not directly use the /etc/mail/access configuration file. It uses a DBM database version of the file. To create the necessary DBM file for your /etc/mail/access file, run the following command:

```
makemap hash /etc/mail/access < /etc/mail/access
```

This creates the necessary DBM database file (such as /etc/mail/access.db) in the same directory. You don't need to restart the sendmail daemon after you modify this file.

Creating aliases for users using /etc/mail/aliases

This configuration file enables you to create an alias database for users. For example, suppose that you want to create an alias called carol.godsave for a user called carol. You can do so by using this configuration file, which has the following format:

```
alias name: comma-separated list of users
```

To create the carol.godsave alias, add a line in this configuration file as follows:

```
carol.godsave: carol
```

When sendmail receives mail for `carol.godsave@yourdomain.com`, it will be delivered to the carol account on your mail server.

One of the really useful uses of aliases is to create local groups. For example,

```
web-developers: keith, cynthea, jason
```

defines an alias web-developers, which can be used to send e-mail messages to the specified users.

The default /etc/mail/aliases file already contains a set of default aliases that you can change as you see fit. Also note that if you have a user with the same name as an alias, the e-mail will be sent to the user(s) specified in the alias. Here is an example of such an alias:

```
root: kabir
```

When mail is sent to `root@nitec.com`, even though a user account called root exists on the mail server, the mail will still be sent to user kabir.

You can also chain aliases. In the following example, alias root resolves to alias kabir, which resolves to mohammed:

```
root: kabir
kabir: mohammed
```

So, mail sent to `root@localhost` on my system can go to the mailbox of a user called mohammed.

Sendmail does not directly use the /etc/mail/aliases configuration file. It uses a DBM database version of the file. To create the necessary DBM file for your /etc/mail/aliases file, run the following command:

```
newaliases
```

This creates the necessary DBM database file (such as /etc/mail/ aliases.db) in the same directory. You don't need to restart the sendmail daemon when you modify this file.

TIP

Running newaliases is equivalent to running the sendmail –bi command.

Mapping domains using /etc/mail/domaintable

This configuration file can be used to create a domain name mapping database, such as the following, which maps yet-another-domain.com to yourdomain.com:

```
Yet-another-domain.com yourdomain.com
```

So, when mail is received for *user*@yet-another-domain.com, it is translated to *user*@yourdomain.com. The destination domain (your domain.com) must be a fully qualified domain name. Also, the domain mapping in the domain table is reflected into headers; that is, this is done in ruleset 3.

Sendmail does not directly use the /etc/mail/domaintable configuration file. It uses a DBM database version of the file. To create the necessary DBM file for your /etc/mail/domaintable file, run the following command:

```
makemap hash /etc/mail/domaintable < /etc/mail/domaintable
```

This creates the necessary DBM database file (such as /etc/mail/ domaintable.db) in the same directory. You do not need to restart the send-mail daemon when you modify this file.

Rerouting mail for domains using /etc/mail/mailertable

This configuration file can be used to create a database to override default mail routing for certain domains. The format of this file is as follows:

```
source-domain mailer:replacement-domain or user@host
```

For example:

```
visitor-01.mydomain.com  local:visitor1
```

When mail for `visitor-01.mydomain.com` arrives, it is rerouted to local user visitor1. You can use only the mailers that are specified in the /etc/sendmail.cf file using an M line. A quick look in the /etc/sendmail.cf file shows qsmtp, procmail, smtp, esmtp, smtp8, relay, usenet, uucp, uucp-ol, suucp, uucp-new, uucp-om, uucp-uuom, local, and prog to be defined as mailers.

You can also specify partial domain names as the source domain name. In the following example, mail for `*.mydomain.com` hosts will be relayed to `mail-hub.mydomain.com` server via the SMTP mailer:

```
.mydomain.com  smtp:mail-hub.mydomain.com
```

Caution

You must have the appropriate MX record for the source domain or else mail will never be delivered.

Consider another example, wherein all mail for `ad-engine.com` will be delivered to user kabir@integrationlogic.com via the SMTP mailer as long as `ad-engine.com` is listed in the /etc/mail/sendmail.cw file:

```
ad-engine.com  smtp:kabir@integrationlogic.com
```

Sendmail does not directly use the /etc/mail/mailertable configuration file. It uses a DBM database version of the file. To create the necessary DBM file for your /etc/mail/mailertable file, run the following command:

```
makemap hash /etc/mail/mailertable < /etc/mail/mailertable
```

This creates the necessary DBM database file (for instance, /etc/mail/ mailertable.db) in the same directory. You do not need to restart the send mail daemon when you modify this file.

Setting up mail relays using /etc/mail/relay-domains

The latest version of sendmail (v 8.9.*x*), by default, denies unauthorized relaying of mail. In other words, if sendmail is not explicitly told to accept mail destined for another domain, it refuses to do so. For example, suppose that you run the latest version of sendmail on a host called `mail.mydomain.com`. If an unauthorized user tries to use `mail.mydomain.com` to deliver mail to another SMTP server, your sendmail server will refuse such requests, by default. This is done to eliminate mail relay abuse by people who send unsolicited e-mail messages.

To allow legitimate domains to use your sendmail server as a relay, you must specify them in this file. Add your own domain and any other friendly domains for which you want to allow relay operation. For example:

```
nitec.com
integrationlogic.com
ad-engine.com
```

You can also use IP addresses in the form of a network address or a full IP. To test the relay configuration, run the following command:

```
echo '$=R' | sendmail -bt
```

This should display all the allowed domains.

Setting up local delivery destinations: /etc/mail/sendamil.cw

Use this file to specify the names of hosts and domains for which the sendmail server will receive e-mail. An example of this file is shown here:

```
nitec.com
ad-engine.com
classifiedworks.com
```

Each line specifies a domain name that the sendmail server will service.

Creating virtual mail servers using /etc/mail/virtusertable

To provide mail support for multiple domains, set up virtual mail service using sendmail. For example, to provide virtual mail service for a domain called yourclient.com, do the following:

1. Add the domain (yourclient.com) in the /etc/mail/sendmail.cw file so that sendmail will accept mail for this host.

2. Add the domain (yourclient.com) in the /etc/mail/relay-domains file so that sendmail will relay messages for this domain.

To map the virtual domain users to one or more local accounts, use the /etc/mail/virtusertable file as follows:

virtual e-mail address   real e-mail address

Here are some examples:

```
webmaster@yourclient.com  mike
mike@yourclient.com       mike
info@yourclient.com       jason
jason@yourclient.com      jason
```

In these examples, e-mail for virtual e-mail addresses such as web master@yourclient.com and mike@yourclient.com goes to local user mike; similarly, mail for info@yourclient.com and jason@your client.com goes to another local user, jason. This provides your client.com with a mail server it didn't have. To the rest of the world, yourclient.com appears to have a mail server. If you also provide the yourclient.com domain's DNS service for this domain, you can make the entire process look very professional by doing the following:

- Add an A record in the yourclient.com domain's DNS service that points to your sendmail server. For example, if your sendmail server host's IP address is 192.168.1.10, add the following line in the DNS configuration file for the yourclient.com domain:

  ```
  mail.yourclient.com.  IN   A   192.168.1.10
  ```

- Add an MX record in the yourclient.com domain's SOA record that points to mail.yourclient.com. For example:

  ```
  IN  MX 5 mail.yourclient.com.
  ```

This makes the rest of the (unsuspecting) world think that your client.com has a real mail server, as long as you have sendmail set up with the virtual configuration discussed previously.

Virtual mail service is often requested by Web site clients of ISPs. In other words, people or companies that pay an ISP to do Web site hosting (www.client-domain.com) also often request to have virtual mail service. In such a case, creating a single /etc/mail/virtusertable often is unmanageable. For example, if you are hosting hundreds of domains, /etc/mail/virtusertable will be a point of human error every time you (or your assistant administrators) modify the file. In such a case, you can create a more manageable solution. For example, to create two virtual mail services for two clients called client-a.com and client-b.com, do the following:

1. Create a separate virtual e-mail map file for each domain. Use a naming convention such as *domain*.ftr (.ftr is short for fake-to-real).

2. Create an /etc/mail/client-a.ftr file, which contains the content of what will normally go in /etc/mail/virtusertable for this domain. For example, this file could look like the following:

   ```
   user1@client-1.com   client1
   webmaster@client-1.com   unix@home-town-isp.com
   @client-1.com   client1
   ```

   In this example file, the user1@client-1.com address is mapped to the local account client1; the webmaster@client-1.com is mapped to a remote ISP account; and all other possible e-mail addresses for the domain are mapped to the local account. The last entry is quite useful and often requested by virtual domain owners. It allows the client-1.com domain owner to use whatever e-mail address s/hewants on theWeb site or other business publications and advertising, and still get the mail in the right place. For example, if www.client-1.com publishes an e-mail address called info@client-1.com, anyone sending mail to that account will be happily serviced by the client1 user.

3. Create the /etc/mail/client-b.ftr file for the second client. This file is likely to be similar to the previous example; but, suppose that the client-b.com owner wants all e-mail addresses to be automatically mapped to her existing accounts in your hometown ISP mail server. In such a case, this map file looks as follows:

```
@client-b.com   %1@home-town-isp.com
```

4. Now that you have two virtual user map files, create the final /etc/mail/virtusertable file by using the following commands:

```
touch /etc/mail/virtusertable
cat *.ftr > /etc/mail/virtusertable
```

The first command creates the /etc/mail/virtusertable file (if it doesn't already exist). The second command concatenates all the FTR files to /etc/mail/virtusertable. This effectively creates the final /etc/mail/virtusertable file.

5. Run the makemap program to create the database version of the file, as follows:

```
makemap hash /etc/mail/virtusertable <
/etc/mail/virtusertable
```

As this example demonstrates, creating multiple virtual user map files can help you keep track of individual domains quite easily. Any time you want to change a domain-specific map, just modify the domain's FTR file and create the final /etc/mail/virtusertable file using the technique just discussed.

Because most mail client programs allow users to set outgoing From: lines to whatever they wish, you may not need to do anything to map outgoing traffic for virtual sites. However, if you want to make sure outgoing mail from users of virtual mail sites translates to their virtual domains, you can use the /etc/mail/genericstable file.

For example, suppose you have a virtual mail site called `classified works.com`, for which you have an FTR file such as /etc/mail/classified works.ftr, which has the following line:

```
sales@classifiedworks.com   sheila
```

The `sales@classifiedworks.com` address is mapped to a local user called sheila. When sheila sends mail using the sendmail server, you want her mail to appear as `sheila@classifiedworks.com`, not `sheila@your domain.com`. In such a case, create a /etc/mail/genericstable file with the following line:

```
sheila   sales@classifiedworks.com
```

This reverses the content of the virtusertable file. In the spirit of keeping domain-specific information separate, you may want to create a separate reverse map file per domain. Suppose this file will have the extension .rtf (real-to-fake). After you create such a file for each domain for which you use virtual mail service, create a combined /etc/mail/genericstable file as follows:

```
touch /etc/mail/genericstable
cat *.rtf > /etc/mail/genericstable
```

Run the makemap program to create the database version of this file:

```
makemap hash /etc/mail/virtusertable
< /etc/mail/virtusertable
```

In summary, for each virtual mail domain, create an FTR file that maps fake e-mail addresses to real ones, and make another file to map real addresses to fake e-mail addresses. After you make these files, combine them to create an /etc/mail/virtusertable file (for *.ftr) and an etc/mail/genericstable file (for *.rtf). Then, run makemap to create the database versions of these files. This completes the process as long as you have each of the virtual domains listed in the /etc/mail/sendmail.cw and /etc/mail/relay-domains files.

Testing Sendmail Configuration

Sendmail configuration is complex and therefore it is often necessary to try out various configuration changes to achieve what you want. As a rule of thumb, always do the following:

- Back up your configuration before making any changes.
- Every time you make a change to your sendmail configuration, test it before proceeding too far.

This section presents a few examples of how to test typical configuration issues.

Testing sendmail address rewrite rules

To test how the sendmail rules behave, run sendmail as follows:

```
sendmail -bt
```

This runs sendmail in address mode and provides you a prompt to interact with it. At the prompt, enter a test command, such as the following:

```
<rewrite rule #s>  <test address>
```

For example, to see what sendmail's rewrite rule 0 does with kabir@nitec.com, run the following:

```
0 kabir@nitec.com
```

The output on my sendmail system is shown here:

```
ADDRESS TEST MODE (ruleset 3 NOT automatically invoked)
Enter <ruleset> <address>
> 0 kabir@nitec.com
rewrite: ruleset   0   input: kabir @ nitec . com
rewrite: ruleset 199   input: kabir @ nitec . com
rewrite: ruleset 199 returns: kabir @ nitec . com
rewrite: ruleset  98   input: kabir @ nitec . com
rewrite: ruleset  98 returns: kabir @ nitec . com
rewrite: ruleset 198   input: kabir @ nitec . com
rewrite: ruleset 198 returns: $# local $: kabir @
nitec . com
rewrite: ruleset   0 returns: $# local $: kabir @
nitec . com
```

The kabir@nitec.com address is delivered using the local mailer.

Consider another example, in which you have the following /etc/mail/ domaintable map:

```
ad-engine.com   nitec.com
```

The preceding map routes all mail destined for ad-engine.com to nitec.com. The following example tests this map:

```
ADDRESS TEST MODE (ruleset 3 NOT automatically invoked)
Enter <ruleset> <address>
> 3,0 kabir@nitec.com
rewrite: ruleset   3   input: kabir @ nitec . com
rewrite: ruleset  96   input: kabir < @ nitec . com >
```

```
rewrite: ruleset  96 returns: kabir < @ ad-engine . com . >
rewrite: ruleset   3 returns: kabir < @ ad-engine . com . >
rewrite: ruleset   0   input: kabir < @ ad-engine . com . >
rewrite: ruleset 199   input: kabir < @ ad-engine . com . >
rewrite: ruleset 199 returns: kabir < @ ad-engine . com . >
rewrite: ruleset  98   input: kabir < @ ad-engine . com . >
rewrite: ruleset  98 returns: kabir < @ ad-engine . com . >
rewrite: ruleset 198   input: kabir < @ ad-engine . com . >
rewrite: ruleset  90   input: < ad-engine . com > kabir < @
ad-engine . com . >
rewrite: ruleset  90   input: ad-engine . < com > kabir < @
ad-engine . com . >
rewrite: ruleset  90 returns: kabir < @ ad-engine . com . >
rewrite: ruleset  90 returns: kabir < @ ad-engine . com . >
rewrite: ruleset  95   input: < > kabir < @ ad-engine .
com . >
rewrite: ruleset  95 returns: kabir < @ ad-engine . com . >
rewrite: ruleset 198 returns: $# esmtp $@ ad-engine . com .
$: kabir < @ ad-engine . com . >
rewrite: ruleset   0 returns: $# esmtp $@ ad-engine . com .
$: kabir < @ ad-engine . com . >
```

The address kabir@nitec.com is rewritten as kabir@
ad-engine.com, and sendmail shows that it will deliver it via ESMTP
(expensive SMTP) mailer, because ad-engine.com is not listed in /etc/
mail/sendmail.cw. If it were, the preceding test would show the following
output:

```
ADDRESS TEST MODE (ruleset 3 NOT automatically invoked)
Enter <ruleset> <address>
> 3,0 kabir@ad-engine.com
rewrite: ruleset   3   input: kabir @ ad-engine . com
rewrite: ruleset  96   input: kabir < @ ad-engine . com >
rewrite: ruleset  96 returns: kabir < @ ad-engine . com . >
```

```
rewrite: ruleset   3 returns: kabir < @ ad-engine . com . >
rewrite: ruleset   0  input: kabir < @ ad-engine . com . >
rewrite: ruleset 199  input: kabir < @ ad-engine . com . >
rewrite: ruleset 199 returns: kabir < @ ad-engine . com . >
rewrite: ruleset  98  input: kabir < @ ad-engine . com . >
rewrite: ruleset  98 returns: kabir < @ ad-engine . com . >
rewrite: ruleset 198  input: kabir < @ ad-engine . com . >
rewrite: ruleset 198 returns: $# local $: kabir
rewrite: ruleset   0 returns: $# local $: kabir
```

Notice that 3,0 is used as the ruleset, because ruleset 3 is involved in the domaintable translation, and ruleset 0 is involved in parsing the address.

Testing /etc/mail/* database files

Any time you modify /etc/mail/access, /etc/mail/aliases, /etc/mail/domaintable, /etc/mail/mailertable, /etc/mail/virtusertable, and similar files, make sure sendmail can perform lookups properly. For example, suppose that you just created the following alias in the /etc/mail/alias file:

```
root: kabir
```

After you run the newaliases command, find out whether sendmail can do appropriate alias lookups, by running **sendmail −bt**. At the address test mode prompt, enter the following:

```
/map database name key
```

For example, to test the /etc/mail/aliases database for the alias root, I can run

```
/map aliases root
```

which shows the following output:

```
map_lookup: aliases (root) returns kabir
```

Using sendmail to see the SMTP transaction verbosely

You can also use sendmail to see how it delivers a message to the destination. For example, the –vt option in the following command tells sendmail to be verbose and scan for To:, From:, Cc:, and Bcc: headers in the input:

```
sendmail -vt
```

After you run the preceding command, it waits for user input. At this point, you can enter something like this:

```
To: kabir@integrationlogic.com
From: someone@somewhere.com
Subject: Testing sendmail

This is a test.

.
```

After you enter a short message, as shown here, press Ctrl+D to exit message entry mode. Sendmail then displays an SMTP transaction similar to the following:

```
kabir@integrationlogic.com... Connecting to
mail.integrationlogic.com. via esmtp...
220 wormhole.integrationlogic.com ESMTP Sendmail
8.9.3/8.9.3; Sun, 21 Feb 1999 19:57:00 -0500
>> EHLO picaso.nitec.com
250-wormhole.integrationlogic.com Hello picaso.nitec.com
[206.171.50.50], pleased to meet you
250-EXPN
250-VERB
250-8BITMIME
250-SIZE
250-DSN
250-ONEX
250-ETRN
```

```
250-XUSR
250 HELP
>> MAIL From:<kabir@picaso.nitec.com> SIZE=77
250 <kabir@picaso.nitec.com>... Sender ok
>> RCPT To:<kabir@integrationlogic.com>
250 <kabir@integrationlogic.com>... Recipient ok
>> DATA
354 Enter mail, end with "." on a line by itself
>> .
250 TAA16439 Message accepted for delivery
kabir@integrationlogic.com... Sent
(TAA16439 Message accepted for delivery)
Closing connection to mail.integrationlogic.com.
>> QUIT
221 wormhole.integrationlogic.com closing connection
```

The lines that start with >> are sent by the local sendmail server (picaso.nitec.com) to the remote sendmail server which is (mail. integrationlogic.com). This is very close to what I demonstrated earlier via a Telnet connection.

Using the sendmail debug flag

Use the −dX option (where X is a debug level) along with −bv to see what action sendmail will take for a particular address. For example,

```
sendmail -bv -d0 kabir@nitec.com
```

produces the following output on my sendmail server:

```
Version 8.9.3
 Compiled with: MAP_REGEX LOG MATCHGECOS MIME7TO8
MIME8TO7 NAMED_BIND NETINET NETUNIX NEWDB NIS QUEUE SCANF
SMTP USERDB XDEBUG


============ SYSTEM IDENTITY (after readcf) ============
      (short domain name) $w = picaso
  (canonical domain name) $j = picaso.nitec.com
```

```
(subdomain name) $m = nitec.com
    (node name) $k = picaso.nitec.com
==========================================================
```

kabir@nitec.com... deliverable: mailer local, user kabir

The −d0 option causes sendmail to display various items of information about sendmail itself. The last line shows how sendmail will handle the given address. Specifying −d without any debug level number shows all the debugging information you'll ever want.

Using a test configuration file

When you are modifying sendmail.cf, it is a good idea to create a test version of the /etc/sendmail.cf file and modify only the test copy, so that you don't lose any working configuration. Here is how you can test a new configuration:

1. Create a copy of /etc/sendmail.cf with a new name. For this example, call the test configuration /etc/sendmail-test.cf.

2. To run sendmail with your new test configuration file, use the −C option. For example, **/usr/sbin/sendmail −Csendmail-test.cf** uses /etc/sendmail-test.cf.

3. If you want to use a different queue (that is, other than /var/spool/mqueue) for the test configuration, use the −oQ option. For example, **/usr/sbin/sendmail −Csendmail-test.cf −oQ/var/ spool/test-mqueue** uses the /var/spool/test-mqueue directory for the test configuration.

At this point, you should have sendmail configured as expected.

Securing Sendmail

Being one of the oldest mail servers, sendmail has had its share of security holes and blame. The recent version of sendmail has been released with strict security in mind.

Securing your configuration files

Beginning with version 8.9.*x*, sendmail has tightened the restrictions on configuration file permissions. For example, if I run chmod −R 664 /etc/mail/* to change the file permissions for the configuration files, and then try to restart sendmail, I get the following error messages:

```
Starting sendmail: /etc/sendmail.cf: line 93: fileclass:
cannot open /etc/mail/sendmail.cw: Group writable directory

WARNING: Group writable directory /etc/mail
/etc/mail/virtusertable.db: could not create:
Permission denied

WARNING: Group writable directory /etc/mail
/etc/mail/access.db: could not create: Permission denied

WARNING: Group writable directory /etc/mail
/etc/mail/domaintable.db: could not create:
Permission denied

WARNING: Group writable directory /etc/mail
/etc/mail/mailertable.db: could not create:
Permission denied
```

In general, do the following to make sure sendmail is safe to run in your system:

- Ensure that the /etc/sendmail.cf and /etc/mail/* files and directories are readable by only the superuser or the username you specified in the RunAsUser line in the /etc/sendmail.cf file. All of these files and directories should be writable by the superuser only.

- Do not enable group write permission for any of the configuration files, directories, or any other files that sendmail needs to read.

Under no circumstances should you enable group write access for any of the configuration files. Although sendmail allows you to disable the security features related to file permissions and ownership by using the DontBlame Sendmail option, you instead should fix the permission/ownership problem and never disable the checks in sendmail. If you want to keep the security checks as is, ensure that user home directories in which .forward files are kept are not writable by any group. The .forward file itself should have a 644 (rw-r--r--) permissions setting. Also make sure that any directory that is in the path of a file sendmail reads has group write access disabled.

After you make sure that file/directory level permissions are set properly, and sendmail doesn't spit out any warning or error message because of permission/ownership of files and directories, make sure logging is properly enabled. By default, sendmail writes logs via syslogd, so include the following line in your /etc/syslog.conf:

```
mail.*            /var/log/maillog
```

You can change the log filename to your liking; typically, this file is named maillog or mail.log. Also make sure you that you have an entry such as the following in /etc/logrotate.d/syslog file:

```
/var/log/maillog {
    postrotate
        /usr/bin/killall -HUP syslogd
    endscript
}
```

This restarts syslogd after logrotate processes the /var/log/maillog file.

Ensuring a stricter mode of operating and privacy

You can force sendmail to enforce strict adherence to the SMTP protocol when clients connect to your server, and you can also control how users interact with sendmail. This is done by using an option line such as the following:

```
O PrivacyOptions=needvrfyhelo,restrictmailq,restrictqrun,
goaway
```

The values for PrivacyOptions are shown in Table 9-3.

Table 9-3 *Privacy Options for Sendmail*

Option	Explanation
public	Allow open access.
needmailhelo	Client must use HELO or EHELO before issuing a MAIL command.
needexpnhelo	Client must use HELO or EHELO before issuing an EXPN command.
noexpn	Client cannot use EXPN command.
needvrfyhelo	Client must use HELO or EHELO before issuing a VRFY command.
novrfy	Client cannot use VRFY command.
notrn	Client cannot use ETRN command.
noverb	Client cannot use VERB command.
restrictmailq	Restrict use of mailq command. When this option is set, only the superuser and the owner and group users of the queue directory can run the mailq command.
restrictqrun	Restrict the –q option. When this option is set, only the superuser and the owner of the queue directory can use this option.
noreceipts	Do not return success code upon success.
goaway	Do not allow SMTP status queries.
authwarnings	Insert X-Authentication-Warning: headers in messages.

Taking Antispam Measures

In this age of bulk unsolicited e-mail, your sendmail server may be vulnerable to abuse by outsiders. People who send unsolicited e-mail messages to thousands of people often use someone else's mail server to do their dirty work. This is called third-party mail relay vulnerability.

Confronting third-party mail relay vulnerability

Until recently, sendmail allowed mail relaying for anyone by default. In other words, someone totally unrelated to you or your organization could use your sendmail server as an SMTP mail relay to send mail to someone else you don't know about. In such a case, both the sender and the recipient are unknown or unrelated to you or your organization. This was formerly permissible because it provided mail administrators with debugging capabilities to locate mail connectivity problems. However, the bulk e-mailers, or *spammers*, are now rampant on the Internet, and they seek out unprotected relays to do their large mailing jobs. This abuses your system resources and also subjects you or your organization to legal complications.

Many U.S. states are now passing laws against unsolicited e-mail, and the parties involved may be financially responsible for damages under these laws. If your mail server becomes involved in a legal matter related to unsolicited e-mail, handling the matter and proving your innocence may take additional legal and financial resources on your part. Also, if your server becomes involved in such a mailing, many recipients will simply assume that you are actively involved in this matter, and they are more than likely to send you hundreds of angry e-mail messages and report you to a spammers blacklist. This could damage your reputation or your organization's reputation. It also could interfere with your mail connectivity operations, because many mail servers check the spammers blacklist before they agree to exchange mail with a domain. Here is how to find out whether your sendmail is vulnerable to such a relay attack.

One of the easiest ways to check your mail server for relay vulnerabilities is to go to the URL `http://maps.vix.com/tsi/ar-test.html`, which is provided by the Mail Abuse Prevention System (MAPS) Transport Security Initiative (TSI) Web site. Enter the host name of your mail server in the target host entry box and click the GO button to determine whether your mail server is vulnerable to relay attacks.

If you want to permit one or more domains to use your sendmail server for relay purposes, add them to the /etc/mail/relay-domains file. Also, if you want to block known spammers from sending junk e-mail messages, use the /etc/mail/access file to explicitly deny them access to your mail server.

Sending spammers to the black hole

The Mail Abuse Prevention System's Realtime Blackhole List (RBL) can be used to automatically block known spammers from using your sendmail server. The Web site for RBL is at `http://maps.vix.com/`.

You can think of RBL as a database of known spammers. By querying the database, you can find out who is a spammer and reject mail services from the domain involved. MAPS RBL is a DNS-based spam checking and blocking system that can be queried to determine whether a certain IP address is blocked as a spammer. You can use the RBL two ways.

- Simply sign an agreement with MAPS RBL, transfer the entire database onto a local host, and create a local RBL for your own use.
- Query the master RBL database on a case-by-case basis.

The latest version of sendmail (8.9.*x*) comes with RBL. The Red Hat Linux RPM available for the latest version enables RBL in /etc/sendmail.cf, so you do not have to do anything to configure it. Here is how you test the RBL configuration in your sendmail.

1. Run the following:

```
sendmail -bt
```

2. At the address test mode prompt, enter:

```
.D{client_addr}127.0.0.1
Basic_check_relay <>
```

The output looks like the following:

```
ADDRESS TEST MODE (ruleset 3 NOT automatically
invoked)
Enter <ruleset> <address>
> .D{client_addr}127.0.0.1
> Basic_check_relay <>
rewrite: ruleset 190   input: < >
rewrite: ruleset 190 returns: OKSOFAR
```

This tells you that the address 127.0.0.1 (loopback address) is not blocked in RBL, because the rewrite result was OKSOFAR.

3. Now, duplicate the preceding test using 127.0.0.2 (the RBL-supplied test IP, which is blocked in RBL). You should see output similar to the following:

```
ADDRESS TEST MODE (ruleset 3 NOT automatically
invoked)
Enter <ruleset> <address>
> .D{client_addr}127.0.0.2
> Basic_check_relay <>
rewrite: ruleset 190   input: < >
```

```
rewrite: ruleset 190 returns: $# error $@ 5 . 7 . 1
$: "Mail from " 127 . 0 . 0 . 2 " refused by
blackhole site rbl.maps.vix.com. Email from your
server is blocked.  Contact your local Systems
Administrator or ISP."
```

As you can see, this IP is blackholed or blacklisted in RBL, and therefore sendmail will not allow this IP to relay messages.

You can also perform a real test using an autoresponder that Russell Nelson has put together. According to the autoresponder owner, you must send mail to `nelson-rbl-test@crynwr.com` from the server whose RBL blocking you want to test. Expect one reply from `ns.crynwr.com` with the SMTP conversation. If you get another reply from `linux.crynwr.com`, your RBL setup is not working.

Tip

If you want to know which mail transactions are rejected because of RBL, simply run **grep "maps.vix.com" /var/log/maillog** to see the rejected requests.

Setting Up POP Mail Service

The latest version of the POP protocol is 3, so install a POP3 server. The IMAP package included on your Red Hat CD-ROM includes a POP3 server. So, to install POP3, simply install the IMAP package by using the **rpm –ivh** *package name* command.

After you install the server, configure it as follows:

1. Modify the /etc/inetd.conf file so that you have a line such as the following:

   ```
   pop-3    stream  tcp     nowait  root    /usr/
   sbin/tcpd ipop3d
   ```

   If you have a pop-2 line, comment it out, because POP2 is not widely used and most recent POP clients support POP3.

2. Check the /etc/services file to make sure you have the following lines:

   ```
   pop-3    110/tcp    # PostOffice V.3
   pop      110/tcp    # PostOffice V.3
   ```

3. Restart the inetd daemon using **killall –HUP inetd** to allow it to listen for POP3 requests on TCP port 110. When requests for POP3 connections come to the system, the inetd daemon will launch the ipop3d daemon to handle the request.

Your POP3 server is now ready to service requests. However, if you want to enhance system security, you might want to limit access to your POP3 server by using the /etc/hosts.allow and /etc/hosts.deny files used by the TCP wrapper (tcpd).

Configuring SMTP/POP Mail Clients

After you configure both your SMTP and POP3 servers, you need to set up mail client software for your users. If your users are going to access their mail by Telneting to the mail server, you need to install one or more mail client packages, such as mail, pine, and procmail. People who use Telnet to access their mail can use the mail-forwarding feature quite easily.

For example, a user who wants to send her mail to a different account or to another mail server can add a .forward file in her home directory to make sendmail deliver mail to the requested address. The format of the .forward file is quite simple. For example, to forward all mail for a user called mrfrog to `mrfrog@freemail-domain.net`, edit ~mrfrog/.forward such that the `mrfrog@freemail-domain.net` address is in a line by itself. Also, make sure that the file permissions for .forward allow only the owner to read and write the file; everyone else should have only read access to it.

In most cases, however, users access mail via a Windows machine running a POP3 client. To enable users to configure a typical Windows POP3/SMTP mail client, supply the following information to each user:

- Username
- Password
- Incoming POP3 mail server IP or host name
- Outgoing SMTP mail server IP or host name

You have to permit such clients to use your sendmail server as a relay, or else the client won't be able to send mail. For example, if your mail server is accessed via America Online, add `aol.com` to your /etc/mail/relay-domains.

Chapter 10

FTP Service

Using wu-ftpd: The Default FTP Server

The Red Hat Linux distribution ships with the Wuarchive-ftpd, more affectionately known as wu-ftpd. Developed at Washington University, wu-ftpd is the most popular FTP server on the Internet, being used on thousands of FTP sites all around the world.

If you choose to install FTP service during the Red Hat Linux installation, the wu-ftpd server is installed by default. However, if you aren't sure whether you already installed the wu-ftpd server, simply query the RPM database of installed packages:

```
rpm —qa | grep wu-ftpd
```

The rpm —qa command lists all the installed RPM packages, and the piped grep wu command matches the wu-ftpd pattern in the package names output by the rpm command, thus allowing you to see whether any package has the "wu-ftpd" string pattern in its name. For example, the preceding command shows "wu-ftpd-2.4.2vr17-3" on my Red Hat machine. The version number on your system will vary, because a new version of the wu-ftpd server is likely to be shipped with a later version of Red Hat Linux.

If you don't get any output for the preceding command, then you currently don't have the wu-ftpd server installed, and need to proceed with the installation as described in the text that follows. On the other hand, if you see that a version of wu-ftpd is already installed, skip the installation section and go right to the section on configuring FTP service.

Installing the wu-ftpd server

You have two options for installing the wu-ftpd server:

- Install the precompiled RPM package version of wu-ftpd.
- Get the source from `ftp://ftp.academ.com/pub/wu-ftpd/private/` and compile it yourself.

Because the Red Hat-provided wu-ftpd RPM package is quite suitable for most people, the second process is not described in this chapter. Use the wu-ftpd RPM package unless you have a very special reason for compiling and installing from the source. In the latter case, make sure you read the bundled documentation with great care.

Installing from your Red Hat CD-ROM

To install from your Red Hat CD-ROM:

1. Log in to your Red Hat server as root.

2. Mount your Red Hat CD-ROM and change the directory to RedHat/RPMS. Run

   `ls | grep wu-ftpd`

   to locate the RPM package for the wu-ftpd server.

3. After you locate the filename of the RPM package for wu-ftpd, run the following command to install the package:

   `rpm -ivh name of the wu-ftpd package`

   For example,

   `rpm -ivh wu-ftpd-2.4.2vr17-3.i386.rpm`

   installs the 2.4.2vr17-3 version of wu-ftpd for *x*86 computers. Your version number and system architecture may vary.

Installing from a Red Hat FTP server

If you do not have the Red Hat CD-ROM or want to install the latest version from the Internet, run the following command:

```
rpm —ivh URL
```

For example, to install the wu-ftpd-2.4.2vr17-3.i386.rpm package from an anonymous FTP server called `ftp://ftp.cdrom.com/` that mirrors the Red Hat distribution, I ran the following command:

```
rpm —ivh ftp://ftp.cdrom.com/pub/linux/redhat/redhat-\
5.2/i386/RedHat/RPMS/wu-ftpd-2.4.2vr17-3.i386.rpm
```

If you want to install from such a server, always make sure that you first determine the right URL by browsing the site via a Web browser. The URL will vary with your system architecture (i386, Alpha, Sparc, or what have you), as well as with the versions of Red Hat Linux and the wu-ftpd software.

If you are trying to install a newer version of wu-ftpd while keeping an older version, you have to supply the —force option in the preceding code line.

After you install wu-ftpd or confirm that you installed it as part of the Red Hat installation, you are ready to configure your new FTP server.

Configuring FTP server

Your FTP server configuration consists of the following files in the /etc directory:

- services
- inetd.conf
- ftpaccess
- ftpconversions
- ftpgroups
- ftphosts
- ftpusers

The wu-ftpd server, like many other TCP/IP-based servers, runs via the Internet superserver called inetd, which listens for an FTP connection on port 21; when such a connection request is detected, inetd launches the wu-ftpd server. At startup, inetd looks at two files, /etc/services and /etc/inetd.conf, to determine which service (port) is associated with a server.

/etc/services

The /etc/services file describes the TCP/IP services available on your Linux server. The following are the relevant lines for the FTP server configuration:

```
ftp-data        20/tcp
ftp             21/tcp
```

These two lines tell inetd which ports to use for the data and command functions, respectively, of the FTP service. The default port declarations are standard and should not be changed.

The preceding lines tell inetd what ports belong to the FTP service, but inetd still needs to know which server software is responsible for the service. This is defined in the /etc/inetd.conf file.

/etc/inetd.conf

The line that is relevant for the FTP configuration is shown here:

```
ftp stream tcp nowait root /usr/sbin/tcpd in.ftpd -l -a
```

The service named ftp is tied with the server software called in.ftpd, which is the name of the wu-ftpd executable. This line tells inetd how to implement the service. Here is how inetd interprets this line:

```
service name: ftp
socket type: stream
protocol: tcp
wait/nowait[.max]: nowait
user[.group] :   root
server program: /usr/sbin/tcpd
server program arguments: in.ftpd  -l -a
```

Notice how inetd is told that the name of the server program is /usr/sbin/tcpd, and how /usr/sbin/tcpd takes the arguments in.ftpd −l −a instead of running the bare server program in.ftpd. This is done to trick inetd into running the TCP wrapper program /usr/sbin/tcpd, which in turn runs the in.ftpd program with the −l and −a arguments.

The −l and −a options are specified by default. The −l option specifies that each FTP session be logged via the syslog facility, and the −a option specifies that the access control configuration specified in /etc/ftpaccess be enabled. These two arguments are very useful and should not be removed. For other options, see the ftpd man page.

Running the FTP server without the TCP wrapper (/usr/sbin/tcpd) is possible, but it is strongly discouraged. However, if you have a very compelling and sound reason for running it without the TCP wrapper, you have to change the default /etc/inetd.conf line for FTP service as follows:

```
ftp stream tcp nowait root /usr/sbin/in.ftpd -l —a
```

This assumes that your in.ftpd executable is in the /usr/sbin directory.

If you make any changes to /etc/inetd.conf or /etc/services, tell inetd to reload the configuration by sending a SIGHUP signal, as follows:

```
kill -HUP PID of inetd
```

or

```
killall -HUP inetd
```

/etc/ftpaccess

This is the main configuration file for the FTP server. This file contains configuration information in the following format:

```
keyword   one or more options
```

The default /etc/ftpaccess file is shown in Listing 10-1.

Listing 10-1 *The Default /etc/ftpaccess File*
```
class    all    real,guest,anonymous   *

email root@localhost

loginfails 5

readme   README*    login
readme   README*    cwd=*
```

Continued

Listing 10-1 *Continued*

```
message /welcome.msg          login
message .message              cwd=*


compress   yes   all
tar        yes   all
chmod      no    guest,anonymous
delete     no    guest,anonymous
overwrite  no    guest,anonymous
rename     no    guest,anonymous


log transfers anonymous,real inbound,outbound


shutdown /etc/shutmsg


passwd-check rfc822 warn
```

This is the most important configuration file for the server, and hence it is discussed in great detail in this chapter. You can specify five types of configuration information in this file.

Access configuration Access configuration can be specified using the class, deny, limit, noretrieve, loginfails, private, autogroup, and guestgroup keywords.

class

```
Syntax: class  classname>  typelist    addrglob
Default: class  all   real,guest,anonymous   *
```

The class keyword is used to define a class name and specify the type of users that belong to the class. It also specifies the IP addresses or the domain names from which the class members can access the FTP server. The arguments are as follows:

- *classname.* An arbitrary name for the class.
- *typelist.* A comma-separated list of user types. Three types of users are available: real, anonymous, and guest. A real user is someone who has a valid username and password in the /etc/passwd or /etc/shadow file.

■ *adrglob.* Can be an IP address of a host, a partial IP address with wildcards (such as 206.171.50.*), a host name (such as `blackhole.nitec.com`), or a partial domain name with wildcards (such as `*.nitec.com`).

The default /etc/ftpaccess file contains a class definition called all, which specifies that users of type real, guest, and anonymous can access the FTP server from anywhere. The wildcard character * is used to denote "anywhere."

In the following example, FTP access is granted only to real users who access the server from the 206.171.50.0 network:

```
class    all    real 206.171.50.*
```

You can also use domain names instead of IP addresses, as in the following example:

```
class    all    real *.nitec.com *.ad-engine.com
```

The preceding class definition allows real users to log in from any machine in the `nitec.com` and `ad-engine.com` domains.

If you don't plan to allow anonymous or guest accounts on your FTP server, you can remove the guest and anonymous keywords from the default *typelist* for the all class.

deny

Syntax: deny *addrglob   message_file*
Default: none

This keyword is used to deny FTP service to hosts that match the IP addresses or domain names specified. For example,

```
deny  *.edu
```

tells the FTP server to deny access to anyone trying to access the server from a U.S. university. Here is another example:

```
deny  *.com  /etc/goaway.msg
```

This configuration denies FTP access to anyone in a `.com` domain and also displays the /etc/goaway.msg file.

limit

Syntax: limit *class n times message_file*
Default: none

This keyword limits the number of simultaneous user logins for the named class. The arguments are as follows:

- *n.* The number of users to be allowed access.
- *times.* Specifies when the limit should apply. The time can be specified in a 24-hour-clock format. For example, 0700–1700 is a range that covers 7 a.m. to 5 p.m. The time format can also include days, as shown in Table 10-1.

Table 10-1 *The Time Format for limit*

Keyword	Meaning
Any	Any time
Wk	Any weekdays
Sa	Saturday
Su	Sunday
Mo	Monday
Tu	Tuesday
We	Wednesday
Th	Thursday
Fr	Friday

You can combine the days as well. For example: SaSu07–17 covers the weekend from 7 a.m. to 5 p.m. The following is an example configuration that sets limits on access:

```
class   local    real           *.nitec.com
class   remote   anonymous      *

limit local   200  Any /etc/msgs/msg.toomany
limit remote  100  Any /etc/msgs/msg.toomany
```

The preceding configuration allows up to 200 users from the `nitec.com` domain to log in at any time, and allows only 100 anonymous users to access the system at any time.

noretrieve

Syntax: noretrieve *filename filename* . . .
Default: none

This keyword denies FTP users the ability to retrieve named files. For example,

```
noretrieve /etc/passwd
```

denies anyone the ability to retrieve the /etc/passwd file. A message such as "/etc/passwd is marked unretrievable" is displayed. Note that if the filename does not include a fully qualified path name, all files with such names are marked unretrievable. For example,

```
noretrieve passwd core
```

prevents anyone from retrieving any file named passwd or core from any directory. Wildcards can't be used in the filename.

loginfails

Syntax: loginfails *number*
Default: loginfails 5

This keyword defines the number of times a user can attempt to log in before getting disconnected. When a user fails to enter a valid username/password pair for a login for the specified number of times, a error message is logged and the user is disconnected.

private

Syntax: private *yes or no*
Default: none

The wu-ftpd server provides an extended set of FTP commands that are nonstandard. One of these command is called SITE, which is considered a security risk. Therefore, use of the private keyword is not recommended. In fact, the SITE command is disabled in the default version of wu-ftpd shipped with Red Hat. You have to compile wu-ftpd yourself to enable the SITE command, which is not recommended.

guestgroup

Syntax: guestgroup *groupname groupname* . . .
Default: none

This keyword specifies the user groups that are to be considered as guest user accounts.

autogroup

Syntax: autogroup *groupname class* [*class* . . .]
Default: none

This keyword allows you to change the effective group ID for an anonymous user if she belongs to one or more classes specified.

Informational configuration An informational configuration can be specified using the banner, email, message, and readme keywords.

banner

Syntax: banner *filename*
Default: none

This keyword can be used to display the contents of the specified file. Typically, many systems use banners to identify the systems and to provide user policy and contact information.

If you use the banner keyword to display a file before login, some non-standard FTP clients may fail to log in, because they are unable to handle multiline responses from the server.

email

Syntax: email *user@host*
Default: email root@localhost

This keyword sets the e-mail address of the FTP site administrator.

message

Syntax: message *path* {*when* {*class* . . .}}
Default: message /welcome.msg login
   message .message cwd=*

This keyword is used to set the name of a file to be displayed when the user logs in to the system or uses the change directory command to change the directory. For example, the first default setting just shown displays the contents of the /welcome.msg file upon successful user login. The second default setting shows the contents of the .message file whenever the user changes a directory. Nothing is displayed when the file to be displayed is missing.

The file to be displayed can contain one or more of the magic cookie strings shown in Table 10-2.

Table 10-2 *Magic Cookie Strings for Message Files*

Cookies	Replacement Text
%C	The current working directory
%E	The maintainer's e-mail address as defined in ftpaccess
%F	Free space in partition of CWD (K)
%L	The local host name
%M	The maximum allowed number of users in this class
%N	The current number of users in this class
%R	The remote host name
%T	The local time (in the form "Thu Nov 15 17:12:42 1990")
%u	The username as determined via RFC 931 authentication
%U	The username given at login time

Listing 10-2 shows the /welcome.msg file that I use for my Red Hat system.

Listing 10-2 *An Example of a /welcome.msg File*

```
Hello %U


Welcome to %L.  You are user %N of possible %M users.
You are logging in from %R.


Local time is %T
```

Continued

Listing 10-2 *Continued*

```
Feel free to email (%E) if you have
any questions or comments.

Your current directory is %C (Free %F KB)
```

The message file is displayed only once per directory. If you plan to display message files for anonymous access, use relative paths to the base of the anonymous FTP directory tree.

readme

```
Syntax: readme  path  {when  {class . . .}  }
Default: readme README*  login
        readme README*  cwd=*
```

This keyword is similar to the message keyword discussed previously. However, instead of displaying the contents of the named file, it makes the FTP server notify the user about the existence of the file and also tells the user about the modification date and time of the file.

Logging configuration   A logging configuration can be specified using the log commands and log transfers keywords.

log commands

```
Syntax: log commands typelist
Default: none
```

This keyword allows you to log FTP commands for one or more types of users. For example,

```
log commands anonymous
```

logs all the FTP commands performed by all anonymous users.

log transfers

```
Syntax: log transfers typelist directions
Default: log transfers anonymous,real  inbound,outbound
```

This keyword allows you to log file transfers to and from the system. The default setting makes the server log both inbound and outbound file transfers for anonymous and real users.

Permission configuration The following keywords allow you to control file/directory permission settings for users.

chmod

Syntax: chmod *yes|no typelist*

Default: chmod no guest,anonymous

This keyword enables or disables the chmod command (site chmod) for user types specified in the list. For example, the default setting disables this command for both guest and anonymous users. By default, the chmod command is not available.

delete

Syntax: delete *yes|no typelist*

Default: delete no guest,anonymous

This keyword enables or disables the delete (del) command for users specified in the type list. For example, the default setting disables the delete command for both guest and anonymous users.

overwrite

Syntax: overwrite *yes|no typelist*

Default: overwrite no guest,anonymous

This keyword enables or disables the overwriting of files by the users specified in the typelist. For example, the default setting disables file overwriting for both guest and anonymous users.

rename

Syntax: rename *yes|no typelist*

Default: rename no guest,anonymous

This keyword enables or disables the rename command for specified users in the typelist. For example, the default setting disables the rename command for both guest and anonymous users.

umask

Syntax: umask *yes|no typelist*

Default: none

This keyword enables or disables the umask command (site umask) for specified users in the typelist. By default, the umask command is not available.

passwd-check

Syntax: passwd-check *none|trivial|rfc822 (enforce|warn)*
Default: passwd-check rfc822 warn

This keyword defines the type of passwords that are required for anonymous users. The default setting requires the password for an anonymous access to be an e-mail address; however, this rule is not enforced if the user fails to enter a valid e-mail address — the server simply warns the user about the invalid password. When no password checking is desired, set the passwd-check keyword as follows:

passwd-check none

If you set the checking to be trivial, the server checks only for the existence of an @ character in the password.

path-filter

Syntax: path-filter *typelist mesg allowed_charset*
{disallowed regexp . . .}
Default: none

This keyword allows you to restrict certain filenames to be used in file uploads that are done by the users specified in the typelist.

upload

Syntax: upload *root-dir dirglob yes|no owner group*
Default: none

This keyword allows you to enable or disable an upload directory. For example,

upload /home/ftp /dropbox yes root ftp 0600

enables the /dropbox directory as an upload directory where files are owned by root and the group ownership is set to ftp. The uploaded files have a permission setting of 0600. Note that /home/ftp must be the home directory of the user ftp. If you don't want to allow the uploader to create new subdirectories under the /dropbox directory, then change the preceding upload line to the following:

```
upload /home/ftp /dropbox  yes root ftp 0600 nodirs
```

On the other hand, if you want to allow the uploader to create subdirectories, then replace nodirs with **dirs**.

Miscellaneous configuration The following keywords allow you to control miscellaneous settings.

alias

```
Syntax: alias string dir
Default: none
```

This keyword allows you to create an alias for a directory. For example,

```
alias redhat  /pub/linux/distributions/redhat
```

allows a user to type the cd redhat command to change to the /pub/linux/distributions/redhat directory.

cdpath

```
Syntax: cdpath dir
Default: none
```

This keyword adds the specified directory to the search path of the change directory (cd) command. For example:

```
cdpath /pub/linux/redhat
```

If a user enters the command cd RPMS, then the server first looks for a directory called RPMS in the user's current directory. If it fails to find one, it looks for an alias called RPMS. If it still fails to find one, then it tries to change the directory to /pub/linux/redhat/RPMS.

compress

```
Syntax: compress yes|no class [classg . . .]
Default: compress yes all
```

This keyword enables or disables the compression feature for specified classes. The default setting enables the compression feature for the class called all, which, by default, covers all real, anonymous, and guest users.

When the default is left alone and the ftpconversions file is not modified, all the users who use the FTP service are able to compress files on the fly. For example, a user who wants to get the entire contents of a directory as a compressed file can enter the command get directoryname.tar.gz, and a compressed tar file will be downloaded.

tar

```
Syntax: tar yes|no classg [class . . .]
Default: tar yes all
```

This keyword enables or disables the tar (**tape ar**chive file) feature for specified classes. The default setting allows the compression feature for the class called all, which, by default, covers all the real, anonymous, and guest users. When the default is left alone and the ftpconversions file is not modified, all the users who use the FTP service are able to tar files on the fly. For example, a user who wants to get the entire contents of a directory as a compressed file can enter the command get directoryname.tar, and a tar file will be downloaded.

shutdown

```
Syntax: shutdown path
Default: shutdown  /etc/shutmsg
```

This keyword specifies the file that the FTP server monitors from time to time to detect a shutdown event. This file can be created using the ftp-shut command. For example, to shut down the server immediately, run the following command:

```
ftpshut now
```

You also can schedule a shutdown in such a way that the logged-in users have some time before the shutdown begins. For example, suppose the current date is Monday, July 03, 2000, and the time is 1600 (in 24-hour format). To shut down the system in an hour, issue the following command:

```
ftpshut -d 30 1700
```

This creates the /etc/shutmsg file, as follows:

```
2000 06 03 17 00 0010 0030
System shutdown at %s
```

The format of the first line is as follows:

```
YYYY MM DD HH MM   HHMM HHMM
```

YYYY is the year, *MM* is the month (0–11), *DD* is the day (1–31), *HH* is the hour (0–23), and *MM* is the minute (0–59). The first *HHMM* pair is the offset in time for denying new connections, and the second *HHMM* pair is the offset in time for disconnecting current connections. The –d 30 option sets the last *HHMM* pair to 0030 in the preceding example file. The deny offset for new connections is ten minutes, by default, but you can change that with the –l option. Also note that you can supply a more customized warning message than the default "System shutdown at %s" by using one or more of the magic cookies shown in Table 10-3.

Table 10-3 *Magic Cookies for ftpshut Warning Message*

Magic Cookie	Replacement Text
%s	The time the system is going to shut down
%r	The time new connections will be denied
%d	The time current connections will be disconnected

In addition to these cookies, you can use all the cookies previously shown in Table 10-2. To create such a message, run the ftpshut command as follows:

```
ftpshut -d MM -l MM HHMM "Shutdown at %s. Be done by %d."
```

Don't forget to replace *MM*, *HHMM*, and so on with appropriate values. When you are ready to restart the FTP service, you have to remove the /etc/shutmsg file.

virtual

Syntax: virtual *address root|banner|logfile path*
Default: none

Use this keyword if you have multiple IP addresses for your Linux system and want to offer virtual FTP services. See the section "Creating virtual FTP sites," later in the chapter, for details.

/etc/ftpconversions

The ftpconversions file stores the FTP server's conversion database. The default configuration for this file is sufficient for almost all installations. If you need more information, see the man page for ftpconversions.

/etc/ftpgroups

The file /etc/ftpgroups is important only if you allow the nonstandard SITE commands. The Red Hat-shipped wu-ftpd package comes with the SITE commands disabled, to enhance security, because SITE commands have been known to create security holes in earlier versions of the server. For the sake of completeness, the purpose of this file is described, but its use is strongly discouraged.

When a not-so-security-savvy FTP administrator enables the SITE commands, she needs to set up the /etc/ftpgroups file as follows:

```
groupname:encrypted password:realgroup
```

Typically, the SITE GROUP and SITE GPASS commands are used to allow an already-logged-in FTP user to upgrade her group privileges. The /etc/ftpgroups file provides the necessary mapping for a user of *groupname* to be upgraded to the *realgroup* when a valid password is entered using the SITE GPASS command. Also note that the *realgroup* must be a group in the /etc/group file.

/etc/ftphosts

The file /etc/ftphosts is used to control FTP access to specific accounts from various hosts. To allow a user to log in from one or more hosts, use a line such as the following:

```
allow   username   addrglob [addrglob. . .]
```

This allows the specified user to log in from the specified hosts. For example,

```
allow   joegunchy *.nitec.com
```

allows the user joegunchy to log in from any machine in the `nitec.com` domain. To deny a user the ability to log in to the server from one or more hosts, use the following line:

```
deny username   addrglob [addrglob. . .]
```

For example, to prevent joegunchy from logging in to the server from the 206.171.50.0 network, use the following line:

```
deny joegunchy  206.171.50.*
```

/etcftpusers

The file /etcftpusers specifies the list of users who are not allowed to access the FTP server. The default /etc/ftpusers file contains the following users:

root	halt
bin	mail
daemon	news
adm	uucp
lp	operator
sync	games
shutdown	nobody

These accounts are not allowed to log in, because they are not real user accounts. If you need to stop a real user from being able to FTP to the server, put the username in this file.

At this point you have learned about all the configuration files necessary to run the FTP server. Now I will discuss some common FTP server configuration issues in the following sections.

Tip

Because a lot of configuration is needed for proper FTP service, having a way to verify your configuration files periodically is useful. A utility called ftpck, which you can download from ftp://ftp.landfield.com/wu-ftpd/ftpck/, provides this type of periodic verification.

Creating an anonymous FTP site

Having an anonymous FTP site can be a mixed blessing. It can be a great medium for distributing files that need to be widely distributed. In fact, all the free software packages (including the Red Hat Linux distribution) that you can download from the Internet are stored in many anonymous FTP sites all around the world. Just think what a nightmare it would be if you needed accounts on each of the FTP servers on the Internet to get access to free software. It simply isn't practical. This problem has been solved with anonymous FTP service. However, anonymous FTP service is also a common gateway for hackers to get into a system. So, think twice before you decide to create an anonymous FTP server.

Fortunately, Red Hat makes creating an anonymous FTP server very easy. You simply need the anonftp RPM package. First, query your RPM database to find out whether you have already installed the anonftp package:

```
rpm -qa  | grep anonftp
```

This displays the package name, such as anonftp-2.8-1, if you have already installed the anonftp package as part of your Red Hat Linux installation. If you haven't, however, the preceding command won't produce any output. In such a case, get the latest anonftp package from your Red Hat CD-ROM and run the following:

```
rpm -ivh anonftp-2.8-1.i386.rpm
```

If you want to install the latest version from a Red Hat mirror site, run the following command:

```
rpm —ivh ftp://ftp.cdrom.com/pub/linux/redhat/redhat-\
6.0/i386/RedHat/RPMS/anonftp-2.8-1.i386.rpm
```

Your anonftp package name will vary with your system architecture and anonftp version. Also, the anonftp package won't install if you don't already have an FTP server, such as wu-ftpd.

After you install the anonftp package, you have an anonymous FTP server ready to run.

Tip

You must have the user account called ftp, without any password, in the /etc/passwd file before you can use anonymous FTP service. The FTP user account line in your /etc/password should look similar to this:

```
ftp:*:14:50:FTP User:/home/ftp:/bin/true
```

If you want to know what the package has installed, run the following:

```
rpm -qlp anonftp-2.8-1.i386.rpm
```

Notice that it has installed all the files under the ~ftp directory (the home directory of the ftp account — see the /etc/passwd file). These files are described next in detail.

Change the directory to ~ftp and enter **ls –l**. You will see the following directories:

```
[kabir@picaso ~ftp]# ls -l
total 4
d--x--x--x  2 root     root     1024 Nov  5 19:29 bin
d--x--x--x  2 root     root     1024 Nov  5 19:29 etc
drwxr-xr-x  2 root     root     1024 Nov  5 19:29 lib
dr-xr-sr-x  2 root     ftp      1024 Sep 10 17:21 pub
```

Change the directory to the bin subdirectory and run **ls –l**, as before; you will see something like the following:

```
[kabir@picaso ~ftp/bin]# ls -l
total 313
---x--x--x 1 root    root  15236 Nov  5 20:02 compress
---x--x--x 1 root    root  46356 Nov  5 20:02 cpio
---x--x--x 1 root    root  45436 Nov  5 20:02 gzip
---x--x--x 1 root    root  29980 Nov  5 20:02 ls
---x--x--x 1 root    root  62660 Nov  5 20:02 sh
---x--x--x 1 root    root 110668 Nov  5 20:02 tar
lrwxrwxrwx 1 root    root      4 Nov  5 20:02 zcat - gzip
```

These are the utilities needed to provide a reasonable anonymous FTP service. The ls utility is used to provide the directory listings, and the compression utilities are used to provide on the fly compression/decompression facilities. These files are provided because the server needs to perform a chroot to the ~ftp directory when someone accesses the anonymous FTP server. The chroot program allows the server to treat the ~ftp directory as the root directory of the system. In other words, when an anonymous FTP user logs in to the server, the server does a chroot to ~ftp and thus hides the real file system, showing only what is under the ~ftp directory. This is why you need a copy of the etc, bin, and lib directories with an absolutely minimal number of files. The lib directory contains the system library files that are needed for the programs in the bin directory. The ~ftp/pub directory is where you should keep the publicly distributable files.

If you need an incoming or dropbox directory to which anonymous users can upload files, do the following:

1. Create a subdirectory in the ~ftp directory that will be used for uploads. This directory typically is called "incoming," so that name is used here.

2. Add the following line in your /etc/ftpaccess file:

    ```
    upload  /home/ftp  /incoming yes root ftp 0600
    nodirs
    ```

3. Change /home/ftp to the appropriate directory. For example, if your ~ftp is really /data/ftp, then change /home/ftp to /data/ftp in the preceding line. Also, if you want to allow anonymous users to be able to create subdirectories under ~ftp/incoming, remove the nodirs option in the preceding line.

4. Run the following commands:

    ```
    chown -R root.ftp ~ftp/incoming
    chmod -R 1733 ~ftp/incoming
    ```

    The chown command sets root as the owner and ftp as the group for the incoming directory. The chmod command changes the incoming directory permissions so that root has read, write, and execute (rwx) permissions and the group and the world have write and execute (wx) permissions. It also sets the sticky bit for the directory and all of its files, which protects the files from being deleted by regular users. Normally, when a directory has write and execute permissions set for everyone, any user of that system can delete a file in that directory. The sticky bit stops that by allowing only the creator of the file to delete the file. Because the FTP server writes the file with root as the owner, no one but root is allowed to delete the uploaded files.

5. Make sure that you have the anonymous user type listed in at least one of the class definitions in your /etc/ftpaccess file. By default real, guest, and anonymous are all included in the default all class, so you don't need to do anything unless you have altered the default class definitions.

After you complete these steps, FTP to the server as an anonymous user and make sure you can upload files only in to the specified directory.

Because you don't have read access to the ~ftp/incoming directory, you shouldn't be able to see the files you upload using the ls command. However, you still can download the uploaded files if you supply the proper filenames.

Enhancing anonymous FTP security

Creating an anonymous FTP site is already a security risk, and having an uploadable directory increases that risk. However, many organizations have successfully run anonymous FTP servers for years, so don't be extremely discouraged — just be cautious. Here are some guidelines for enhancing anonymous FTP server security:

- Ensure that the ftp account in /etc/passwd is using an invalid password. For example, your ftp account entry in the passwd file should look like this:

  ```
  ftp:*:14:50:FTP User:/home/ftp:/bin/true
  ```

- The ~ftp/bin directory should be owned by root and not by the ftp account. The binaries, such as ls, compress, and tar, that you have in the ~ftp/bin directory also must be owned by the root user. The ~ftp/bin directory and its contents should be executable only. Run the following to ensure that all files in the ~ftp/bin directory are executable only:

  ```
  chown -R root.root ~ftp/bin; chmod -R 111 ~ftp/bin
  ```

- The ~ftp/etc directory should be owned by the root user, and it must be executable only. You can make it so by using the following commands:

  ```
  chown -R root.root ~ftp/etc; chmod 111 ~ftp/etc
  ```

- Contents of the ~ftp/etc directory must be read-only and must be owned by root. Run the following to make sure the permissions are set up correctly:

  ```
  chown -R root.root ~ftp/etc; cd ~ftp/etc; chmod 444 *
  ```

- Never copy your /etc/passwd or /etc/group files into the ~ftp/etc directory. The ~ftp/etc/passwd and ~ftp/etc/group files are dummy files needed to satisfy programs that look for them when running under ~ftp as the root directory because of the server's chroot to ~ftp.

- As a general security rule, make sure that no files or directories in ~ftp are owned by the ftp user.

Creating a guest FTP account

A guest FTP account is a real account with a real username and password. When a guest user logs in to an FTP server, the server does a chroot operation to the guest user's home directory, thus making the home directory of the guest user appear as the entire file system.

The easiest way to set up a guest account is to use the anonftp package, even if you do not want to provide anonymous FTP service. Just install the package temporarily for the purpose of creating a single guest account. Here are the steps needed to create a guest account:

1. **Create the guest user account.** Become root and create the guest user account in the same manner that you create a real user account. This example assumes this guest user account is called mrfrog and that it was created using the usual useradd command, as follows:

   ```
   useradd mrfrog
   ```

   Set a desired password for mrfrog, using the following command:

   ```
   passwd mrfrog
   ```

2. **Stop Telnet access.** Change mrfrog's default shell to /bin/true, using the following command:

   ```
   chsh mrfrog
   ```

   When prompted for the new shell path, enter **/bin/true**. This disallows mrfrog from telneting to the system, to ensure that mrfrog can't use telnet to access the server and browse other user or system files.

   Edit the /etc/passwd file and append **/./** to the existing home directory path. For example, if the /etc/passwd file has a line similar to the following:

   ```
   mrfrog:1dev33vylewv.:516:519::/home/mrfrog:/bin/true
   ```

   then change it to this:

   ```
   mrfrog:1dev33vylewv.:516:519::/home/mrfrog/./:/bin/
   true
   ```

   The **/./** sequence is used to tell the FTP server to perform chroot operationon the /home/mrfrog directory.

Edit the /etc/shells file and add /bin/true at the end of the file. This makes the /bin/true program a valid shell option. Note that the /bin/true program does nothing and exits immediately after it is run. This makes it a good candidate for a shell that needs to be validated but denies the user anything and then exits. Because an exit from the shell logs out the user, the user never gets a chance to do anything when a Telnet connection is attempted.

3. **Install the anonftp package.** If you already have the anonftp package installed on your system, skip this step and go to Step 4. Otherwise, get the latest anonftp package and install it by running the rpm command:

```
rpm -ivh anonftp-2.6-1.i386.rpm
```

Your anonftp package name will vary based on your system architecture and anonftp version. Also, the anonftp package won't install if you don't already have an FTP server, such as wu-ftpd.

4. **Copy the anonftp package files to the guest user's home directory.** Change the directory to ~ftp and use the following command to copy all the files and directories to ~mrfrog:

```
tar cvf - * | ( cd ~mrfrog ;  tar xvf  -)
```

All you really need are the ~ftp/bin, ~ftp/etc, and ~ftp/lib directories. You can delete the ~ftp/pub directory or any other directory that you might already have in your ~ftp directory.

5. **Update the ~mrfrog/etc/passwd and ~mrfrog/etc/group files.** Edit the ~mrfrog/etc/passwd file and remove the line for the FTP user. Append the exact password line for mrfrog from the /etc/passwd file. However, remove mrfrog's password and replace it with a * to make it invalid. For example:

```
mrfrog:1dev33vylewv.:516:519::/home/mrfrog/./:/bin/
true
```

This line needs to be copied to ~mrfrog/etc/passwd, and the password needs to be replaced such that the line looks like the following:

```
mrfrog:*:516:519::/home/mrfrog/./:/bin/true
```

Modify the ~mrfrog/etc/group file and add the mrfrog line found in /etc/group. This assumes that you have not somehow disabled Red Hat's default feature for automatic creation of a private group by the same name as the new user. In other words, when you create a user by using the useradd program, it automatically creates a private group for that user with the same name. So, when you created mrfrog, you should have also automatically created a group called mrfrog in the /etc/passwd. If you have changed the default behavior of the useradd program or manually created the user, create a group for this user and add it to the ~mrfrog/etc/group file. Also, remove the ftp group from the ~ftp/etc/group file.

6. **Set directory and file permissions.** Change the directory/file permissions as follows:

```
chown mrfrog.mrfrog ~mrfrog
chmod 750 ~mrfrog
```

The chown command sets the user and group ownership to mrfrog's user and group. The chmod command makes the ~mrfrog directory accessible only to the mrfrog user and group.

```
chown -R root.root ~mrfrog/etc  ~mrfrog/bin
~mrfrog/lib
```

This command changes the ownership of the etc, bin, and lib subdirectories under ~mrfrog to the root user and group.

```
cd ~mrfrog
chmod -R 111 *
```

The first command changes the directory to ~mrfrog, and the second command makes all the files and directories executable-only for everyone.

```
cd etc; chmod  444 *
```

These commands change the directory to the ~mrfrog/etc directory and change the file permissions to read-only for everyone.

7. **Set the guestgroup in /etc/ftpaccess.** Because you want the real user mrfrog to be a guest user, you need to add mrfrog's group (which is also called mrfrog) to the guestgroup group list. For example,

```
guestgroup mrfrog
```

allows any member of the mrfrog group (found in /etc/group) to be a guest user. In other words, the FTP server will perform the chroot operation. For the mrfrog user, the FTP server will chroot to /home/mrfrog.

8. **Test the account.** FTP to the server and log in as mrfrog. If everything is set up correctly, you will see only the home directory of this user. Try to upload a file or create a directory. You should be allowed to do these operations. However, whether or not mrfrog is allowed to delete, overwrite, or rename files depends on what you have set for these operations in /etc/ftpaccess. For example, the default /etc/ftpaccess includes the following lines:

```
chmod      no   guest,anonymous
delete     no   guest,anonymous
overwrite  no   guest,anonymous
rename     no   guest,anonymous
```

These lines prohibit the guest accounts from performing chmod, delete, overwrite, or rename operations. If you want to allow these operations for guest accounts, remove "guest" from the default type-list in these lines and turn them into the following lines:

```
chmod      no   anonymous
delete     no   anonymous
overwrite  no   anonymous
rename     no   anonymous
```

If you don't want to keep the anonftp package around or don't want to have anonftp capabilities on your FTP server, either remove the package files from the appropriate (~ftp) directory or simply run the following:

```
rpm -e anonftp-2.6-1.i386.rpm
```

Don't forget to use the appropriate filename, because your version or architecture might be different from what was just described.

Creating virtual FTP sites

If you have multiple domains and need to support separate FTP servers (ftp.domain-1.com, ftp.domain-2.com, and so on), you can use virtual FTP service, which allows you to share a single-server system for multiple domains. The wu-ftpd server can be configured at least two ways to support virtual FTP service, both of which are described here. Because both methods require that you have IP address aliases set up on your system, take a look at the IP aliasing issue first.

Creating IP aliases

To have virtual FTP servers, first you need to have appropriate DNS records for each FTP host. You need multiple IP addresses (one per FTP server host) to be routed to your FTP server machine. Using the IP aliasing technique, you have to create virtual Ethernet interfaces for all the IP addresses. For example, suppose that I have to create two virtual FTP servers (`ftp.client-01.com` and `ftp.client-02.com`) on an FTP server called `ftp.nitec.com`. Also assume that I have already set up DNS records for each domain, such that the following lines are true:

```
; In client-01.com DNS database
ftp.client-01.com.  IN  A   206.171.50.51
```

```
; In client-02.com DNS database
ftp.client-02.com.  IN  A   206.171.50.52
```

```
; In nitec.com DNS database
ftp.nitec.com.  IN  A   206.171.50.50
```

After I set up IP aliases and routes on the `ftp.nitec.com` machine, if I run

```
cat /proc/net/aliases
```

I see the following IP aliases:

```
Device  family  address
eth0:0  2       206.171.50.51
eth0:1  2       206.171.50.52
```

Creating a limited virtual FTP service

This method is simpler than the other method, but it is also quite limited. Although you will have virtual FTP service, you won't be able to customize

it as much as you would be able to by using the other method. If you want
a completely customizable service (like the primary FTP server), then skip
to the next section "Creating a complete virtual FTP service."

To create this limited version of virtual FTP service, you need to make
multiple copies of the anon-ftp package-created file/directory structure.
Simply install the anonftp package and make copies of it for each virtual
host. For the preceding example, I will create two virtual FTP site directories — /home/client1/ftp and /home/client2/ftp — and copy all the contents of the /home/ftp files and directories. One of the easiest ways to
make an exact copy of /home/ftp is to run the following commands:

```
cd /home/client1/ ; cp -a /home/ftp .
cd /home/client2/ ; cp -a /home/ftp .
```

These commands copy the /home/ftp file/directory structure in the virtual site directories. Now, edit the /etc/ftpaccess file to add virtual keywords, as follows:

```
virtual 206.171.50.51 root     /home/client1/ftp
virtual 206.171.50.51 banner
/home/client1/ftp/banner.msg
virtual 206.171.50.51 logfile /home/client1/ftp/xferlog

virtual 206.171.50.52 root     /home/client2/ftp
virtual 206.171.50.52 banner
/home/client2/ftp/banner.msg
virtual 206.171.50.52 logfile /home/client2/ftp/xferlog
```

Don't forget to replace IP addresses and directory paths with what you
chose earlier. Modify the banner.msg file for each host to reflect any site-
specific information you want to display. Also, you don't need the pub subdirectory for your virtual FTP sites, so remove it from each site.

After you create the preceding configuration, your virtual FTP servers
are ready for testing. FTP to each of the virtual IP addresses and notice
how the banner files are different for each host. Although this virtual setup
is quite easy to create, it lacks the capability to fully customize the look and
feel of the server. For example, you cannot use the email keyword in
/etc/ftpaccess to point to different e-mail addresses appropriate for the virtual sites.

The ftpshut command supplied with standard wu-ftpd does not support shutdown of virtual sites, because it writes the shutdown message file in only a single location specified by the shutdown keyword in the /etc/ftpaccess file. Also, when the time comes to restart the server, you need to manually remove the shutdown message file. To overcome these nuisances, you might want to get the replacement ftpshut/ftprestart utilities from the following Web site: `http://www.landfield.com/wu-ftpd/restart`. You have to compile and build these utilities yourself.

Creating a complete virtual FTP service

This method requires that you patch the wu-ftpd source and compile it on your own:

1. You can download the source code for wu-ftpd from `ftp://ftp.academ.com/pub/wu-ftpd/private/`. You also need the patch file from `ftp://ftp.meme.com/pub/software/wu-ftpd-2.4.2/`.

2. Read the README file that comes with the patch tar-ball and apply the patch to the wu-ftpd source you downloaded earlier. Compile and install the patched wu-ftpd per the instructions provided in the wu-ftpd source package. Install the new FTP server to the default location, /usr/sbin/in.ftpd.

3. The newly patched wu-ftpd program (in.ftpd) now accepts an argument for the −a option. Normally, −a tells the server that you want it to read the /etc/ftpacesss file. Now, the patched version allows it to specify a different path for the ftpaccess file. So, this allows the new server to look at different ftpaccess configuration files that will be needed to create virtual FTP sites.

4. Modify the /etc/inetd.conf file so that the FTP service has a line such as the following:

   ```
   ftp stream tcp nowait root /usr/sbin/tcpd in.ftpd
   ```

   This invokes the FTP server via the TCP wrapper (tcpd).

5. Modify the /etc/hosts.allow file such that you have lines similar to the ones that follow for each FTP server (that is, the primary server and all the virtual FTP servers):

   ```
   # For the primary server
   ftpd@206.171.50.50 : ALL : twist exec \
   ```

```
/usr/sbin/in.ftpd -l -a /etc/ftp/ftpaccess

# For the virtual FTP server
ftpd@206.171.50.51 : ALL : twist exec \
/usr/sbin/in.ftpd -l -a /etc/ftp/client1.ftpaccess

# For the second virtual FTP server
ftpd@206.171.50.52 : ALL : twist exec \
/usr/sbin/in.ftpd -l -a /etc/ftp/client2.ftpaccess
```

6. Create the /etc/ftp directory and move the /etc/ftpaccess file into that directory. Make two copies of the /etc/ftp/ftpaccess file so that you have /etc/ftp/client1.ftpaccess and /etc/ftp/client2.ftpaccess files. Remove any virtual keywords from the /etc/ftp/ftpaccess file used for the mail FTP server. Finally, modify the client1.ftpaccess file so that it has a line such as the following:

   ```
   virtual 206.171.50.51 root /home/client1/ftp
   ```

   Similarly, modify the client2.ftpaccess file to have a line such as this:

   ```
   virtual 206.171.50.52 root /home/client2/ftp
   ```

   Don't forget to replace the IP addresses and the directory path with your own.

7. Copy the anonftp files in the /home/client1/ftp and /home/client2/ftp directories.

8. After you create the preceding configuration, restart the inetd server using the following command:

   ```
   killall  -HUP  inetd
   ```

That's all there is to it. Now you have two virtual FTP sites that can be accessed via their respective host names or IP addresses.

Monitoring the transfer log

Logging is very important for FTP service, because you want to be able to tell who is doing what with your files. The wu-ftpd server logs transfers in the xfrlog file, which typically resides in the /var/log directory. You can customize logging by using the log commands and log transfers keywords discussed earlier.

If you are interested in monitoring xferlog on a regular basis, try Dumpxfer, which you can download from `ftp://ftp.microimages.com/tools/dumpxfer.1.2.tar.gz`.

Using a Commercial FTP Server

The wu-ftpd server is free and provides reasonably good configurability when it comes to providing standard FTP service. However, wu-ftpd's performance is deficient under heavy loads and does not have a very clean and customizable virtual FTP service solution. If you need a high-performance FTP server and don't mind paying for it, consider the NcFTPd package, a commercial FTP server that has the following interesting features:

- Does not run via inetd and therefore has much better startup performance than wu-ftpd. The inetd-based processes are never intended for high performance.

- Built-in directory listing capabilities, whereas wu-ftpd has to form an ls process per directory listing request. Thus, NcFTPd is better at handling directory listings. It can even cache directory listings in memory to provide faster transfer of such listings in a high-volume FTP site.

- Highly configurable virtual hosting capabilities. Each virtual host can have its own welcome message, anonymous FTP directory tree, password authentication scheme, user limit, and log files.

Try out this commercial FTP server by downloading it from `http://www.ncftp.com/download/`.

NcFTPd is free for educational organizations with certain top-level domains, such as `.edu` and `.us`.

Using a Trivial File Transfer Protocol Server

You may have installed a TFTP server already. It's called the tftpd server. It really isn't an FTP server, because it uses the Trivial File Transfer Protocol instead of the File Transfer Protocol. TFTP uses UDP over IP, an unreliable, packet-oriented transfer method. FTP uses TCP over IP, a reliable, stream-oriented transfer method. TFTP has no provisions for security. FTP has user-authentication provisions for security.

However, a TFTP server works pretty much the same way as an FTP server works. The only big difference is that it is *not* meant for anything but an anonymous FTP-like file transfer where no authentication is used.

Many people use TFTP primarily in conjunction with the bootp protocol to load diskless workstations, such as X Windows terminals. The TFTP service is disabled by default in the /etc/inetd.conf file. You can enable it by removing the # (comment sign) from the following line:

```
# tftp dgram udp wait root /usr/sbin/tcpd \
in.tftpd  /tftpboot
```

After you enable the preceding line, restart the inetd server so that the change will be effective. Note that /tftpbook is the directory that TFTP clients can access. Make sure this directory does not contain any files that you don't want to share with anyone. Remember that no authentication is required to access this file, so anyone who can access your server will have access to this directory. You might want to allow only read-only access to files in the directory, as well.

Chapter 11

Sharing Files and Printers with Samba

Installing Samba

If you chose the DOS/Windows-compatibility option during Red Hat Linux installation, the Samba RPM packages were automatically installed. However, if you did not install Samba packages during installation, you can always install them by using the rpm command. For example, to install the Samba client/server package for an *x*86 Red Hat Linux system, I ran the following command from the /RedHat/RPMS directory of the official Red Hat CD-ROM:

```
rpm -ivh samba-version.i386.rpm
```

When using this command to install the Samba package, do not forget to replace *samba-version.i386.rpm* with a real package filename.

If you plan to use Samba to mount your Windows disks on your Red Hat Linux system, you need to install another Samba file system package called smbfs. For example, to install the Samba file system package for an *x*86 Red Hat Linux system, I ran the following command from the /RedHat/RPMS directory of the official Red Hat CD-ROM:

```
rpm -ivh smbfs-version.i386.rpm
```

Again, when using this command to install the smbfs package, do not forget to replace *smbfs-version.i386.rpm* with a real package filename.

Configuring Samba

When you install the Samba RPM package, it installs a configuration file called smb.conf in your /etc directory. Listing 11-1 shows the default /etc/smb.conf.

Listing 11-1 *The Default /etc/smb.conf File*

```
# This is the main Samba configuration file.
# You should read the smb.conf(5) manual page
# in order to understand the options listed here.
# Samba has a huge number of configurable options
# (perhaps too many!) most of which are not shown
# in this example
#
# Any line which starts with a ; (semi-colon) or
# a # (hash) is a comment and is ignored. In this
# example we will use a '#' for commentary and a ';'
# for parts of the config file that you may wish to
# enable
#
# NOTE: Whenever you modify this file you should
# run the command "testparm" to check that you have
# not made any basic syntactic errors.
#
#======== Global Settings =================

[global]

# workgroup = NT-Domain-Name or Workgroup-Name
   workgroup = MYGROUP

# server string is the equivalent of the NT
# Description field
   server string = Samba Server
```

```
# This option is important for security. It allows
# you to restrict connections to machines which are on
# your local network. The following example restricts
# access to two C class networks and the "loopback"
# interface. For more examples of the syntax see
# the smb.conf man page
;   hosts allow = 192.168.1. 192.168.2. 127.

# If you want to automatically load your printer
# list rather than setting them up individually
# then you'll need this
    printcap name = /etc/printcap
    load printers = yes

# It should not be necessary to spell out the
# print system type unless yours is non-standard.
# Currently supported print systems include:
# bsd, sysv, plp, lprng, aix, hpux, qnx
;   printing = bsd

# Uncomment this if you want a guest account, you
# must add this to /etc/passwd
# otherwise the user "nobody" is used
;   guest account = pcguest

# This tells Samba to use a separate log file for
each machine
# that connects
    log file = /var/log/samba/log.%m

# Put a capping on the size of the log files (in Kb).
    max log size = 50

# Security mode. Most people will want user
```

Continued

Listing 11-1 *Continued*

```
# level security. See
# security_level.txt for details.
   security = user
# Use password server option only with
# security = server
;   password server = <NT-Server-Name>

# Password Level allows matching of _n_
# characters of the password for
# all combinations of upper and lower case.
;   password level = 8
;   username level = 8

# You may wish to use password encryption. Please read
# ENCRYPTION.txt, Win95.txt and WinNT.txt
# in the Samba documentation.
# Do not enable this option unless you have
# read those documents
;   encrypt passwords = yes
;   smb passwd file = /etc/smbpasswd

# Unix users can map to different SMB User names
;   username map = /etc/smbusers

# Using the following line enables you to
# customize your configuration
# on a per machine basis. The %m gets replaced
# with the netbios name of the machine that is
# connecting
;   include = /etc/smb.conf.%m

# Most people will find that this option gives
# better performance. See speed.txt and the manual
# pages for details
```

```
    socket options = TCP_NODELAY

# Configure Samba to use multiple interfaces
# If you have multiple network interfaces then you must
list them
# here. See the man page for details.
;    interfaces = 192.168.12.2/24 192.168.13.2/24

# Configure remote browse list synchronization here
# request announcement to, or browse list sync from:
# a specific host or from / to a whole subnet (see below)
;    remote browse sync = 192.168.3.25 192.168.5.255

# Cause this host to announce itself to local
# subnets here
;    remote announce = 192.168.1.255 192.168.2.44

# Browser Control Options:
# set local master to no if you don't want Samba to
# become a master browser on your network.
# Otherwise the normal election rules apply
;    local master = no

# OS Level determines the precedence of this
# server in master browser elections. The default
# value should be reasonable
;    os level = 33

# Domain Master specifies Samba to be the Domain
# Master Browser. This allows Samba to collate browse
# lists between subnets. Don't use this if you already
# have a Windows NT domain controller doing this job
;    domain master = yes
```

Continued

Listing 11-1 *Continued*

```
# Preferred Master causes Samba to force a local
# browser election on startup and gives it a slightly
# higher chance of winning the election
;    preferred master = yes


# Use only if you have an NT server on your
# network that has been configured at install time
# to be a primary domain controller.
;    domain controller = <NT-Domain-Controller-SMBName>


# Enable this if you want Samba to be a domain
# logon server for Windows95 workstations.
;    domain logons = yes


# If you enable domain logons then you may want
# a per-machine or per user logon script run a
# specific logon batch file per workstation (machine)
;    logon script = %m.bat
# run a specific logon batch file per username
;    logon script = %U.bat


# Where to store roving profiles (only for Win95
# and WinNT) %L substitutes for this servers
# netbios name, %U is username
# You must uncomment the [Profiles] share below
;    logon path = \\%L\Profiles\%U


# All NetBIOS names must be resolved to
# IP Addresses 'Name Resolve Order' allows
# the named resolution mechanism to be specified
# the default order is "host lmhosts wins bcast".
# "host" means use the unix system gethostbyname()
# function call that will use either /etc/hosts OR
# DNS or NIS depending on the settings of
```

```
# /etc/host.config, /etc/nsswitch.conf and the
# /etc/resolv.conf file. "host" therefore is system
# configuration dependant. This parameter is most
# often of use to prevent DNS lookups in order to
# resolve NetBIOS names to IP Addresses. Use with care!
# The example below excludes use of name resolution
# for machines that are NOT on the local network segment
# - OR - are not deliberately to be known via lmhosts
# or via WINS.
; name resolve order = wins lmhosts bcast


# Windows Internet Name Serving Support Section:
# WINS Support - Tells the NMBD component of Samba
# to enable its WINS Server
;   wins support = yes


# WINS Server - Tells the NMBD components of Samba
# to be a WINS Client
# Note: Samba can be either a WINS Server, or a
# WINS Client, but NOT both
;   wins server = w.x.y.z


# WINS Proxy - Tells Samba to answer name resolution
# queries on behalf of a non WINS capable client, for
# this to work there must be at least one WINS Server
# on the network. The default is NO.
;   wins proxy = yes


# DNS Proxy - tells Samba whether or not to try
# to resolve NetBIOS names via DNS nslookups. The
# built-in default for versions 1.9.17 is yes, this has
# been changed in version 1.9.18 to no.
    dns proxy = no
```

Continued

Listing 11-1 *Continued*

```
# Case Preservation can be handy - system default
# is _no_ NOTE: These can be set on a per share basis
;   preserve case = no
;   short preserve case = no


# Default case is normally upper case for all
# DOS files
;   default case = lower


# Be very careful with case sensitivity - it can
# break things!
;   case sensitive = no


#========= Share Definitions =============
[homes]
    comment = Home Directories
    browseable = no
    writable = yes


# Un-comment the following and create the netlogon
# directory for Domain Logons
;  [netlogon]
;     comment = Network Logon Service
;     path = /home/netlogon
;     guest ok = yes
;     writable = no
;     share modes = no


# Un-comment the following to provide a specific
# roving profile share the default is to use the
# user's home directory
;[Profiles]
;      path = /home/profiles
;      browseable = no
```

```
;     guest ok = yes


# NOTE: If you have a BSD-style print system there
# is no need to  specifically define each
# individual printer
[printers]
   comment = All Printers
   path = /var/spool/samba
   browseable = no
# Set public = yes to allow user 'guest account'
# to print
   guest ok = no
   writable = no
   printable = yes


# This one is useful for people to share files
;[tmp]
;    comment = Temporary file space
;    path = /tmp
;    read only = no
;    public = yes


# A publicly accessible directory, but read only,
# except for people in the "staff" group
;[public]
;    comment = Public Stuff
;    path = /home/samba
;    public = yes
;    writable = yes
;    printable = no
;    write list = @staff


# Other examples.
```

Continued

Listing 11-1 *Continued*

```
 #
 # A private printer, usable only by fred. Spool data
 # will be placed in fred's home directory. Note that
 # fred must have write access to the spool directory,
 # wherever it is.
 ;[fredsprn]
 ;    comment = Fred's Printer
 ;    valid users = fred
 ;    path = /homes/fred
 ;    printer = freds_printer
 ;    public = no
 ;    writable = no
 ;    printable = yes

 # A private directory, usable only by fred. Note
 # that fred requires write
 # access to the directory.
 ;[fredsdir]
 ;    comment = Fred's Service
 ;    path = /usr/somewhere/private
 ;    valid users = fred
 ;    public = no
 ;    writable = yes
 ;    printable = no

 # A service which has a different directory for
 # each machine that connects this allows you to
 # tailor configurations to incoming machines. You
 # could also use the %u option to tailor it by user
 # name. The %m gets replaced with the machine name
 # that is connecting.
 ;[pchome]
 ;    comment = PC Directories
 ;    path = /usr/pc/%m
```

```
;  public = no
;  writable = yes


# A publicly accessible directory, read/write to
# all users. Note that all files created in the directory
# by users will be owned by the default user, so any user
# with access can delete any other user's files. Obviously
# this directory must be writable by the default user.
# Another user could of course be specified, in which case
# all files would be owned by that user instead.
;[public]
;   path = /usr/somewhere/else/public
;   public = yes
;   only guest = yes
;   writable = yes
;   printable = no


# The following two entries demonstrate how to
# share a directory so that two users can place files
# there that will be owned by the specific users. In this
# setup, the directory should be writable by both users
# and should have the sticky bit set on it to prevent
# abuse. Obviously this could be extended to as many
# users as required.
;[myshare]
;   comment = Mary's and Fred's stuff
;   path = /usr/somewhere/shared
;   valid users = mary fred
;   public = no
;   writable = yes
;   printable = no
;   create mask = 0765
```

If you remove all the comment lines from the default /etc/smb.conf file, only three special configuration sections are defined in the file. They are discussed next.

Setting the [global] parameters

The [global] section defines Samba parameters that apply to all other configuration sections (that is, services that they define). The default [global] configuration is as follows:

```
[global]
    workgroup = MYGROUP
    server string = Samba Server
    printcap name = /etc/printcap
    load printers = yes
    log file = /var/log/samba/log.%m
    max log size = 50
    security = user
    socket options = TCP_NODELAY
    dns proxy = no
```

Here is how you configure each of these parameters.

workgroup

Set this parameter to the Windows workgroup or Windows NT domain name that you want Samba to participate in as a node. For example, I use NITEC as the Windows NT domain name so that I can set workgroup to NITEC. When a Windows 9*x* or NT system on my network browses the Network Neighborhood, it sees the Samba server under the NITEC Windows NT domain. Set this to whatever workgroup or domain name is appropriate for your LAN.

server string

Set this parameter to provide a description for your Samba server. This description will be visible to Samba clients (such as a Windows 9x machine.)

printcap name

Use this parameter to set the printcap file path. The default value, /etc/printcap, should work for you. The /etc/printcap file is used to describe your printer's capabilities. If you have one or more printers attached to your Linux server and you want to make all of your printers available to the Windows systems on your LAN, set this parameter along with the load printers parameter.

load printers

Use this parameter to tell Samba to automatically make local printers available to any SMB client computer on the network. Set this to yes if you want to enable this feature; set it to no if you prefer to specify printer configurations in individual configuration sections.

log file

Use this parameter to set the filename of the Samba log file. The default setting writes a log file per client. This is done using the %m macro, which expands to the client name. For example, if you keep the log file setting as is and access the Samba server from a Windows machine called r2d2, a log file called /var/log/samba/log.r2d2 is created.

max log size

Use this parameter to control the maximum log file size, in kilobytes.

security

The security parameter is the most important of all the global parameters. Use it to tell Samba about how to perform client authentication. The following are the three possible values for security, along with a description of what the Samba server does when security is set to each:

- **user.** The Samba server tells the client to supply a username/ password pair for authentication. If you use the same username/password pairs on your Windows systems and Linux systems, set the security parameter to user. For example, if you have a user called joe on a Windows NT Server and have the same user on the Samba server with the same password, set this parameter to user.

- **share.** The Samba server expects a password with each request for a service. No usernames are required. Use this setting if your Windows systems and the Linux Samba server do not have the same set of username/password pairs.

- **server.** The Samba server tells the client to supply a username/ password pair, just like when you set this parameter to user, but the Samba server does not verify the username/password pair itself. It uses another SMB server to authenticate the user. For this reason, when you set security to server, you must also set the password server parameter, which is used to name a SMB server that will be responsible for authentication. If you want to centralize your usernames/passwords for SMB activity on a Windows NT Server, set the password server parameter to point to the Windows NT Server.

Caution

If you use a Windows NT Server as your password server to do all the authentication for Samba, make sure that you do not have the guest account on the Windows NT system enabled. If the guest account is enabled, any time that a username/password pair fails because of an incorrect password, Windows NT will still provide a valid response to the Samba server, because Windows NT will simply assign guest privileges to the failed authentication attempt and return a success response to the Samba server.

The default setting for security is user, which means that a client has to supply a plain-text password along with a username. The Samba server verifies this username/password pair by using the /etc/password file. However, the later versions of Windows 9*x* and Windows NT OSs don't use plain-text (also known as clear-text) passwords, by default. Microsoft decided to use encrypted passwords as part of upgrades to its OS service packs. Because these Windows clients do not supply plain-text passwords, they can't be verified; therefore, the Samba server refuses to service them. To remedy this problem, you have two options:

- Enable plain-text passwords on Windows systems. This option is acceptable if any of the following conditions is true:

- You already allow plain-text-based services, such as FTP and Telnet, between your Windows machine and Red Hat Linux server.

- Your network is not connected to the Internet, so use of plain-text passwords does not pose a great threat to your organization.

- You just want to get Samba working first and then deal with either encrypted passwords or plan on delegating all authentication tasks to a Windows NT Server in the long run.

- Use encrypted passwords for authentication.

You probably will choose the first option, so it is described next. The details of using encrypted passwords for authentication are provided in the last section of this chapter, "Securing Your Samba Server."

If you are using Windows 98, Windows 95 with Service Pack 3 or higher, or Windows NT 4 with Service Pack 3 or higher, follow these steps to enable plain-text passwords:

1. Run the Windows Registry editor program called RegEdit.

2. For Windows 9*x*, locate the following Registry key:

```
/HKEY_LOCAL_MACHINE
    /System
        /CurrentControlSet
            /Services
                /VxD
                    /VNETSUP
```

For Windows NT 4 with Service Pack 3 or higher, locate the following Registry key:

```
/HKEY_LOCAL_MACHINE
    /SYSTEM
        /CurrentControlSet
            /Services
                /Rdr
                    /Parameters
```

3. After you locate the VNETSUP branch (for Windows 9*x*) or the Parameters branch (for Windows NT) in the Registry tree, select Edit ⇨ New and choose to create a new DWORD value.

4. RegEdit will insert a new DWORD value called New Value #1 in the Registry. Rename this new value **EnablePlainTextPassword** and double-click this new name.

5. A dialog box pops, enabling you to set a value for the EnablePlainTextPassword you just created. Enter 1 as the value and close RegEdit as usual.

6. Reboot your Windows 9*x*/NT system.

This ensures that your Windows 9*x*/NT system is able to use plain-text passwords for SMB authentication.

socket options

By default, the socket options parameter in the global configuration section is set to TCP_NODELAY, which enhances Samba performance on certain platforms. You should leave this parameter as is.

dns proxy

This parameter affects how the Samba suite's built-in Windows Internet Name Server (nmbd) behaves when a Windows system name (NetBIOS name) cannot be resolved to an IP address. If you set this parameter to yes, the nmbd server will treat the NetBIOS names as an Internet domain name and try to resolve it by using the DNS protocol. Keeping the default setting is recommended.

Setting the [homes] parameters

The [homes] section is a special configuration section that allows you to set up home directory access from Windows systems. In other words, a user with a valid username/password on the Red Hat system can access her home directory on the Linux system from a Windows system. The default [homes] configuration is as follows:

```
[homes]
   comment = Home Directories
```

```
browseable = no
writable = yes
```

Here is how you can change these parameters.

- **comment.** Exactly what its name suggests. Set this to whatever you wish.

- **browseable.** Controls whether or not home directories are visible in a browser list (such as the Network Neighborhood) or when the NET VIEW command is used from the Windows command prompt. Set this to yes or no depending on your needs.

- **writable.** Controls whether or not a user can write to her own home directory. For most practical purposes, this needs to be set to yes. If you set this to no, a user will have read-only access to her own home directory.

Setting the [printers] paramters

The [printers] section is useful only if you have one or more printers attached to your Red Hat Linux system. The default [printers] configuration is as follows:

```
[printers]
    comment = All Printers
    path = /var/spool/samba
    browseable = no
    guest ok = no
    writable = no
    printable = yes
```

Here is how you can change these parameters.

- **comment.** Exactly what its name suggests. Set this to whatever you wish.

- **path.** Set this to the directory where printer data files will be spooled. If you have a lot of users, make sure you have plenty of disk space for this directory.

- **browseable.** By default, printers are not visible in a browser (such as Network Neighborhood) or NET VIEW command output. To change this behavior, set this to yes.

- **guest ok.** By default, printer services are not available to guest users who do not have passwords. To change this behavior, set this to yes.

- **printable.** By default, this parameter permits printing. If this is set to no, printing is completely disabled.

The default configuration includes many commented configuration parameters and additional sections. Carefully investigate these options and enable anything that you want to use. However, if you are using Samba for the first time, first get it working using the default configuration.

Managing Samba via Web

Using the new Web based configuration tool, SWAT, shipped with Samba, you can manage the Samba using a standard Web browser. Here is how you can use SWAT.

1. Verify that your /etc/services file has the following line:

   ```
   swat                901/tcp
   ```

   If the above line is not present, add this line and save /etc/services file.

2. Verifiy that your /etc/inetd.conf file has the following line:

   ```
   swat  stream  tcp  nowait.400 root /usr/sbin/swat swat
   ```

   If the above line is missing or commented out, add or uncomment it and save /etc/inetd.conf file. In such a case restart inetd daemon using killall –HUP inetd command.

3. Next, run your favorite Web browser which can access your Samba server. Enter the following URL:

   ```
   http://your-samba-server:901/
   ```

4. You will be asked to enter a username and password. Enter root as the username and the corresponding password. If you have entered an appropriate username/password pair, you will see the SWAT welcome screen.

5. Click on the available links to manage various aspects of Samba.

If you plan to access SWAT from machines other than the Samba server itself, you should secure it as follows:

1. Edit /etc/inetd.conf such that you have the following line:

```
swat   stream   tcp   nowait.400 root   /usr/sbin/tcpd
/usr/sbin/swat swat
```

2. Edit /etc/hosts.deny to have the following line:

```
swat: ALL
```

3. Next, edit /etc/hosts.allow to have a line such as the following:

```
swat: IP-address-of-machine
```

Here *IP-address-of-machine* is the IP address of the machine where you plan to run the Web browser that will access SWAT.

You can have multiple IP addresses listed as long as they are separated by at least a space character.

Testing the /etc/smb.conf configuration

Any time you change a Samba configuration file, run the testparm utility that is bundled with the Samba package. When you run this nifty utility from the command line, it checks the syntax of the /etc/smb.conf file and gives you useful warning and error messages. Because a misconfigured /etc/smb.conf file can be a security hole, use this utility whenever you modify this file.

Starting, stopping, and restarting the Samba service

After you make sure that your /etc/smb.conf file is error-free, you are ready to start Samba. Two daemons come with the Samba package. The smbd daemon is the Samba server, and the nmbd daemon is the NetBIOS name server. To start the daemons, run the following command as root:

```
/etc/rc.d/init.d/smb start
```

You can then start accessing the Samba server from your Windows computers. To stop the Samba server, run the same command with a stop argument. You can also restart the daemons by using the same command with a restart argument.

If you want to start the Samba service at boot time, create a symbolic link as follows:

```
ln -s /etc/rc.d/init.d/smb   /etc/rc.d/rc3.d/S91smb
```

This starts the Samba service when your Red Hat Linux server enters run level 3, which is the default run level for all multiuser systems.

If you use an X Window System-based login (using XDM) and want to start Samba automatically, create the following link:

```
ln -s /etc/rc.d/init.d/smb   /etc/rc.d/rc5.d/S91smb
```

Using a Linux File Server on Windows

Using a Linux file server on Windows probably is the most common reason why a Linux administrator in a Linux/Windows shop may consider using Samba. For example, suppose you want to make a Linux partition (or directory) called /intranet available to a group of Windows users (john, mary, and phil) on your LAN. Here is what you do:

1. If you set the security parameter in the [global] configuration section to user or share, create three user accounts (john, mary, and phil) on your Linux system. These user accounts need to be set up such that the password for each account matches its Windows counterpart. For example, if jennifer's password on her Windows system is set to tsk#tsk, then you must set her Linux account with the same password. Also, create a group called intranet in /etc/group that includes users jennifer, chad, and phil as the only members.

2. Modify the /etc/smb.conf file to add the following:

```
[Intranet]
    comment = Intranet Directory
    path = /intranet
```

```
public = no
writable = yes
write list = @intranet
printable = no
```

The preceding [Intranet] configuration specifies that /intranet is not publicly accessible, and write permission is given for the intranet group. After you run testparm to make sure that the /etc/smb.conf file contains no syntax errors, you can restart the Samba service.

Now, you can have john, mary, and phil access the /intranet partition or directory from their Windows machines. If you want to create a read-only file server, set the writable parameter to no and remove the write list parameter from the preceding configuration. To force the file permissions in this shared partition (or directory) to remain the same, use the force create mode parameter. For example,

```
force create mode   0750
```

makes sure that all files created in the shared space have full access (read, write, and execute) for the owner, and read and execute access for everyone in the group. Anyone outside the group will not have any access to these files.

Using a Windows File Server on Your Linux System

If you have a Windows file server that you want to make available to your Linux users, you can use smbfs (SMB file system) to mount Windows disks and directories onto your Linux system. For example, to mount the default drive (C drive) of a Windows NT Server called PLUTO on a Linux Samba server, do the following:

1. On the Windows NT system, double-click the My Computer icon to open the My Computer window. Select the C drive icon and then right-click it. In the pop-up window that displays, select the Sharing option. This opens the Properties dialog box with the Sharing tab selected.

2. Click the Shared As radio button and select a name for the share from the drop-down Share Name list. In this example, the share name is C. Write a comment line to help identify the share when browsed from other computers.

3. Click Apply and exit the window.

You just enabled SMB sharing for the C drive. Now, simply mount this share on your Linux system. The smbfs file system comes with a command called smbmount that enables you to mount an SMB share. The common syntax is shown here:

```
smbmount //WINDOWS-SERVER/path  /mount-point  \
-U WindowsUser -P WindowsUserPassword
```

//WINDOWS-SERVER is the Windows system with the share (path); /mount-point is the mount directory on the Linux system; WindowsUser is a user on the Windows system that has at least read access to the share; and WindowsUserPassword is the password for that user. If your Windows NT system is set up correctly, only the Administrator user (or an equivalent user) should have full access to the entire drive. So, this example uses the Administrator user to mount the C drive. Here is an example smbmount that mounts the C drive from PLUTO:

```
smbmount //PLUTO/c /mnt/pluto-c  -U Administrator -P gowent
```

If you get an error message when you run your version of the preceding command, make sure you have entered the proper password. Also, try the −I option to specify the IP address of the Windows NT Server, just in case it does not advertise its IP address. When the command is successful, you will see /mnt/pluto-c in your df listing and will be able to access all the files from the C drive of your Windows system. If you prefer to mount the C drive such that only certain users and groups on the Linux system can access the drive, use the −u *UID* and −g *GID* options, as in the following example:

```
smbmount //PLUTO/c /mnt/pluto-c  -U Administrator -P gowent \
-u root -g admin
```

Here, only user root and anyone in group admin have access to PLUTO's C drive, which is mounted on the Linux system under /mnt/pluto-c.

To unmount or remove an SMB file system from the Linux system, run the smbumount command. For example, the following command unmounts the //PLUTO/c share from the Linux system:

```
smbumount /mnt/pluto-c
```

Sharing printers between Linux and Windows

Sharing printers is a common benefit of a LAN environment. Using Samba, you can share printers between both Linux and Windows.

Sharing a Windows printer with Linux

On your Windows system attached to the printer, create an account that can use the printer and that doesn't require a password. For example, on a Windows NT Workstation or Server, follow these steps to create such an account:

1. Use the User Administrator program to create an account called **printeruser**. Do not assign any password for this user and assign the user to the regular user group only.

2. Select your printer from the My Computer folder and right-click it to open the Printer Properties window. Select the Security tab and click Permissions. If Everyone has print access, you don't need to do anything. If Everyone does not have print access, add the printeruser to the list, with the privilege to print to the selected printer. After you configure the Windows NT account to print, you are ready to test it.

From the Linux system, use the smbclient program to connect to the printer, as follows:

```
smbclient //WINDOWS-SYSTEM/SharedPrinter -U
printeruser -N -P
```

Replace *WINDOWS-SYSTEM* with your Windows system name, and replace *SharedPrinter* with the printer name. The –N and –P options are used to instruct the smbclient program to use the null password for connection.

At the smbclient program prompt, type **printmode text** to set print mode to text and enter a command such as **print /path/to/a/linux/textfile** to print the file. If your printer prints the file, you are halfway done.

3. Configure the Linux side. The easiest way to configure an SMB-based printer is to use the X Windows-based printtool utility that comes with Red Hat. Run printtool from an xterm and click Add. In the dialog box that appears, select the Lan Manager Printer (SMB) option and click OK to continue. This enables you to edit the Lan Manager printer (SMB) entry.

4. If this is your first printer, the name will be set to lp, which you can change to whatever you want. This name is used by print commands, such as lpr, to identify this printer. The spool directory should also be set to /var/spool/lpd/lp. If you change the printer name, make sure you also change the spool directory path to reflect the name change. The File Limit option should be left as is, unless you are setting up the printer in an environment in which users can send large files. In such a case, use a reasonable limit, such as 2048K (2MB). The host name of the printer should be set to the Windows NT system to which the printer is attached. The IP address of this host is optional. The printer name is the share name you created for the printer. The username should be the printer user (printuser) you created earlier. The password field should be left blank, because you have not assigned a password to this user.

5. Click Input Filter Select to modify the input filter. The Configure Filter dialog box appears. Select the printer type and printer options as appropriate. Click OK to complete the filter configuration, and click OK to add the new printer.

6. Test the printer. From the Red Hat Linux Print System Manager screen, select the newly created printer and then click the Tests menu and select a test option to test your printer. If you get output on the printer, your configuration is working. However, if your output is pretty much garbage, go back to the input filter configuration dialog box and make changes to get better or appropriate output.

If you successfully test-printed in the last step, you are done with the printer configuration and can use the printer from your Linux applications. For example, to use the printer to print a text file from the command line, use the lpr command as follows:

```
lpr -Pprintername  /path/to/file
```

If the printer name is lp and you want to print the /etc/smb.conf file, use the following command:

```
lpr -Plp  /etc/smb.conf
```

Use the lpq command to see the print queue, and use the lprm command to remove print jobs from the queue. Note that when the file being printed is transferred to the Windows print spooler, its status is no longer available to you.

Sharing a Linux printer with Windows

To share a Linux printer with Windows, modify your /etc/smb.conf file as follows:

1. In the [global] configuration section, set the following:

```
printcap name = /etc/printcap
load printers = yes
```

2. In your [printers] configuration section, set the following:

```
comments = All Printers
path = /var/spool/lpd
writable = no
printable = yes
```

If you want the printer list to appear in the browser list, set the browseable parameter to **yes** in the preceding configuration. Similarly, if you want to allow the guest account to use the printer, set guest ok to **yes** in the [printers] configuration.

That's all that is required to set up all of your printers. However, if you prefer to make one or more printers privately available to one or more users, you can specify a separate section for each of these users. For example, if I want to create private printer (fancyjet) access for a user called bigboss, I can create a configuration such as the following:

```
[fancyjet]
comment = Big Boss Only Printer
valid users = bigboss
path = /home/bigboss/fancyjet
guest ok = no
browseable = no
writable = no
printable = yes
```

The valid users parameter enables you to specify a space-separated list of users who have access to the printer.

After you modify and test the /etc/smb.conf file, restart the Samba service, and you should be able to access the Linux printers from your Windows computers.

Using an interactive Samba client

The Samba package comes with a program called smbclient that enables you to access a Samba resource interactively. For example, if you want to access a disk share on a Windows system from your Linux system, use the smbclient program to access it as follows:

```
smbclient //WINDOWS-SERVER/resource  -U username -P
password
```

In the following example, smbclient is used to access the C drive on PLUTO as user kabir:

```
smbclient //PLUTO/c -U kabir -P foobar
```

If the authentication is successful (in other words, PLUTO allows connection), smbclient displays an FTP client-like prompt and allows you to perform many FTP client commands. Typing **help** or **?** at any time provides more information about the commands.

You can use smbclient to list the available Samba resources on a remote computer. In the following example, the –L option specifies the Samba server to be interrogated using username kabir:

```
smbclient -L reboot -U kabir
```

The example output is shown in Listing 11-2.

Listing 11-2 *Example Output of smbclient*
```
Server time is Sat Feb 13 19:48:03 1999
Timezone is UTC-8.0
Password:
Domain=[NITEC] OS=[Windows NT 4.0] Server=[NT LAN
Manager 4.0]
security=user


Server=[REBOOT] User=[] Workgroup=[NITEC] Domain=[]

        Sharename      Type        Comment
        ---------      ----        -------
        ADMIN$         Disk        Remote Admin
        C              Disk        C Drive on PLUTO
        C$             Disk        Default share
        F              Disk
        home           Disk
        IPC$           IPC         Remote IPC
        OkidataO       Printer     Okidata OL-600e
        print$         Disk        Printer Drivers
        sheila         Disk
        TEMP           Disk
```

Conitinued

Listing 11-2 *Continued*

```
This machine has a browse list:

        Server                  Comment
        ---------               -------
        PICASO                  Picaso Samba Server
        PLUTO
        R2D2                    Nitec Laptop (r2d2)
        REBOOT


This machine has a workgroup list:

        Workgroup               Master
        ---------               -------
        NITEC                   PLUTO
```

As you can see, the smbclient program can be used to determine what resources are being shared from other Samba-compliant systems.

The smbclient program also allows you to send Windows pop-up messages to Windows computers that have enabled this service. For example, when you run

```
smbclient -M reboot
```

smbclient enables you to type text messages that it will display as pop-up messages on the target Windows computer.

Securing Your Samba Server

If used correctly, Samba can turn a mixed environment (Linux/Windows) into a smoother computing environment. However, like any other useful service, when Samba is misconfigured, it can be a potential source of security holes. This issue is especially important if your Samba server is connected to the Internet. I recommend that you do not connect a Samba server to the Internet or enable Samba services over the Internet. This section discusses a few security measures that you can take to reduce risks involving Samba.

An earlier section of this chapter reviews how to enable plain-text passwords on later versions of Windows 9x and NT systems. This works well for those systems, but it might not be suitable for a LAN or WAN environment, where a potential for illegal TCP/IP packet sniffers exists. In other words, if you believe that your network might be vulnerable to packet sniffers, implement encrypted passwords. The encrypted password-based authentication that the SMB protocol permits never transmits any passwords between a Samba client and server. This ensures a higher degree of security and hence is very desirable in high-risk scenarios in which security and confidentiality are of utmost importance. Two ways exist to use encrypted passwords, both of which are described next.

Using a Windows NT Server as a password server

A Windows NT Server, by default, can provide encrypted password services. So, if you have a Windows NT Server on your network, consider making it your password server. You can centralize all of your user accounts on the Windows NT Server so that Samba services can be enabled using encrypted passwords. To use a Windows NT Server as your encrypted password server, do the following:

1. Create a Windows NT Server account for each user who needs Samba access.

2. Modify the /etc/smb.conf file so that you have the password server parameter set to the name of the Windows NT Server. Also, set the security parameter to **server**.

3. Run the testparm command to ensure that all configuration lines are syntactically correct in the /etc/smb.conf file.

4. Restart the Samba service.

To test your new configuration, use one of the Windows NT Server user accounts to access the Samba server.

Using encrypted passwords on your Samba server

The Samba package shipped with Red Hat is precompiled with encrypted password support, so you don't need to download the Samba source code and compile it with encrypted password support. To enable encrypted passwords, take these steps:

1. Use the mksmbpasswd.sh script supplied with the Samba package to create a replacement password file for /etc/passwd. Run the following command:

   ```
   cat /etc/passwd | mksmbpasswd.sh > /etc/smbpasswd
   ```

   This creates a special password file that has lines such as the following:

   ```
   root:0:XXXXXXXXXXXXXXXXXXXXXXXXXXXXXXXX:XXXXXXXXXXXX
   XXXXXXXXXXXXXXXXXXXX:root:/root:/bin/tcsh
   ```

2. Use the smbpasswd program to create an encrypted Samba password for each user. For example, to create an encrypted Samba password for a user called sheila, run the following:

   ```
   smbpasswd sheila
   ```

3. Modify the /etc/smb.conf file so that the following line appears in the [global] configuration file:

   ```
   encrypt passwords = yes
   ```

4. Test your new configuration by running the testparm program; if the test is successful, restart the Samba service. On the other hand, if testparm shows errors, review and modify your configuration as needed.

Test the Samba service from your Windows systems. If you have modified your Windows Registry to use plain-text passwords, remove the Registry entry you created so that encrypted passwords can be used.

Chapter 12

Web Service Using Apache

Getting Apache from the Internet

Although the official copy of Red Hat Linux comes with an RPM-packaged version of a prebuilt Apache Web server, you may still want to download the latest version from the official Apache Web site at http://www.apache.org/.

If you are not in the United States, it might be faster to get Apache source and binaries from a nearby Apache mirror site. Use the URL http://www.apache.org/dyn/closer.cgi to locate a good mirror site near you. This discussion assumes that you are getting the software from the official Apache Web site. The software (both source and binaries) can be found at http://www.apache.org/dist/.

You will see many recent versions of Apache distributions archived using various compression programs, such as the following:

```
Apache_1.3.91.3.9.tar.gz
Apache_1.3.91.3.9.tar.Z
```

These are examples of Apache version 1.3.91.3.9 source distribution. The only difference is in their size, resulting from a difference in the compression technique used. Download one of these files. No matter which format you download, you need the tar utility and either the gnuzip or gzip utility to decompress the files. For example, to decompress the Apache 1.3.91.3.9.tar.gz file on my Red Hat 5.2 system, I use the following command:

```
tar xvzf apache_1.3.91.3.9.tar.gz
```

Or I could use

```
gzip -d apache_1.3.91.3.9.tar.gz
tar xvf apache_1.3.91.3.9.tar
```

which decompresses and extracts all the files in a subdirectory while keeping the relative path for each file intact.

The binaries are usually kept in a different directory, where each OS has a subdirectory of its own. It's a good idea to compile the Apache source yourself instead of using someone else's binary. When you use a downloaded binary file, you are letting someone else (possibly someone you don't know) decide which modules and features are enabled in your Web server. Occasionally, downloaded binary files may not work at all on your system, because of incompatibilities between the library files required by the binary and what is available on your system. If this is acceptable or if compiling is not an option for you, make sure the site from which you download the binaries is reputable. This chapter assumes that you will compile your own copy.

Creating a Custom Apache Server

After you extract the source code into a directory of your choice, you are ready to configure and compile your custom copy of Apache. You can either configure Apache manually or use the new Autoconf-style interface called APACI. The APACI method is recommended because it is quicker and requires less knowledge of Apache configuration details; in other words, you have to read fewer README and INSTALL files to get the job done. Hence, it is also the recommended method.

Configuring Apache source using APACI

In the top-level directory of the source distribution is a script called configure, which is what you need to configure Apache using APACI. Run this script as follows:

```
./configure --help
```

This enables you to see all the available options.

The first step in configuring Apache is to determine where you want to install it. For example, to install Apache in a directory called /usr/local/apache, run the configuration script as follows:

```
./configure --prefix=/usr/local/apache
```

This installs all Apache files under the specified directory. However, if you need to install certain files outside the directory, you can use the following --prefix options:

Prefix Option	Description
--exec-prefix=DIR	Installs architecture-dependent files in DIR
--bindir=DIR	Installs executables in DIR
--sbindir=DIR	Installs sys-admin executables in DIR
--libexecdir=DIR	Installs program executables in DIR
--mandir=DIR	Installs manual (man) pages in DIR
--sysconfdir=DIR	Installs configuration files in DIR
--datadir=DIR	Installs read-only data files in DIR
--includedir=DIR	Installs include files in DIR
--localstatedir=DIR	Installs modifiable data files in DIR
--runtimedir=DIR	Installs run-time data in DIR
--logfiledir=DIR	Installs log file data in DIR
--proxycachedir=DIR	Installs proxy cache data in DIR
--compat	Installs according to the Apache 1.2 installation paths

For example, if you keep your logs in a separate partition called /logs and you want Apache to write logs there, run the configure script as follows:

```
./configure --prefix=/usr/local/apache --logfiledir=/logs
```

If you want to be 100 percent sure about which file is going to be installed in what directory, use the --layout option. For example,

```
./configure --prefix=/usr/local/apache  --layout
```

shows the following output:

```
Configuring for Apache, Version 1.3.91.3.9

Installation paths:
prefix: /usr/local/apache
exec_prefix: /usr/local/apache
bindir: /usr/local/apache/bin
sbindir: /usr/local/apache/bin
libexecdir: /usr/local/apache/libexec
mandir: /usr/local/apache/man
sysconfdir: /usr/local/apache/etc
datadir: /usr/local/apache/share
includedir: /usr/local/apache/include
localstatedir: /usr/local/apache/var
runtimedir: /usr/local/apache/var/run
logfiledir: /usr/local/apache/var/log
proxycachedir: /usr/local/apache/var/proxy

Compilation paths:
HTTPD_ROOT: /usr/local/apache
SUEXEC_BIN: /usr/local/apache/sbin/suexec
SHARED_CORE_DIR: /usr/local/apache/libexec
DEFAULT_PIDLOG: var/run/httpd.pid
DEFAULT_SCOREBOARD: var/run/httpd.scoreboard
DEFAULT_LOCKFILE: var/run/httpd.lock
DEFAULT_XFERLOG: var/log/access_log
DEFAULT_ERRORLOG: var/log/error_log
TYPES_CONFIG_FILE: etc/mime.types
SERVER_CONFIG_FILE: etc/httpd.conf
ACCESS_CONFIG_FILE: etc/access.conf
RESOURCE_CONFIG_FILE: etc/srm.conf
```

The --layout option allows you to verify the directory structure before it is
actually used. If you are upgrading Apache from 1.2 and want to keep the

old directory structure, you can use --compat, which uses the old-style directory structure.

Tip

If you find yourself constantly overriding the default layout, you can simply create a custom layout in the configure.layout file. The simplest way to create a custom layout is to edit the configure.layout file in the top-level Apache source distribution. Copy the existing Apache layout starting with the <Layout apache> line and ending with </Layout>. Then, change the directory paths as you please and replace the layout name from Apache to whatever you like. You can then use this layout by using the --with-layout=<*name of your custom layout*> option.

The next step in configuring Apache is to decide whether you want to use the standard module configuration provided by the developers of Apache. If this is your first time compiling Apache, stick to the standard configuration, simply to get used to the entire process.

The standard, or default, configuration file for APACI-based configuration is Configuration.apaci, which is stored in the src subdirectory. This file contains three types of information:

- **EXTRA_* lines.** Used by the configure script to add extra flags in the Makefile, which in turn is needed to compile Apache.
- **Rule lines.** Used by the script to turn on/off certain functions.
- **AddModule lines.** Enable Apache modules that should be part of your Apache executable.

Makefile configuration options

For most systems, you do not need to modify any of these extra flags. Also note that the configure script will try to figure out which C compiler you use on your system. If you think it might fail to find your compiler for some reason, uncomment the #CC= line and send it to your compiler. For example: CC = gcc.

In such a case, you also might have to supply extra compiler flags in the following lines:

```
EXTRA_CFLAGS=
EXTRA_LDFLAGS=
```

If your system requires special libraries or include files, specify them using the following lines:

```
EXTRA_LIBS=
EXTRA_INCLUDES=
```

The configure script automatically sets code optimization to −O2. If you want a different setting, first uncomment the following line:

```
#OPTIM=-O2
```

Then, change the value to whatever you desire, if your C compiler supports it. For most installations, the default settings work fine, just as they did for me on a Red Hat 5.2 Linux system.

Rules configuration options

As with the Makefile flags, you should not need to modify the Rules lines. However, if you must modify these rules, you can use the configure script. To enable a rule, use the --enable-rule=*NAME* option, where *NAME* is the name of the rule. For example:

```
./configure --prefix=/usr/local/apache --enable-
rule=SOCKS4
```

Similarly, disable a rule by using the --disable-rule option.

The first two Rule lines (SHARED_CORE and SHARED_CHAIN) relate to Dynamic Shared Object (DSO) support and should be left as is.

The SOCKS4 functionality is turned off by default. SOCKS is a control system in which all TCP/IP network application data flows through the SOCKS daemon. This enables SOCKS to collect, audit, screen, filter, and control the network data. Most people use it as a software-based firewall. If you want to make Apache SOCKS4-compliant, you need to turn on this feature by setting it to Yes using the --enable-rule=SOCKS4 option in the command line of the configure script. Also, modify the EXTRA_LIBS setting in the Makefile configuration area, to point to your SOCKS4 library file. Otherwise, the configure script will set it to −. Similarly, if you want SOCKS5 support, turn it on by setting it to Yes using the --enable-rule=SOCKS5 option in the command line of the configure script.

The IRIXNIS rule is for people who want to use Apache on a Silicon Graphics system running IRIX and NIS. The IRIXN32 option is also meaningful for systems running an IRIX operating system. It tells Apache to use n32 libraries instead of o32 libraries.

The PARANOID rule allows you to see whether any Apache module is executing any shell scripts during configuration. Apache 1.3 allows modules to execute custom shell scripts when the configure script is run. This rule is turned off by default. If you want to enable it, set this to Yes using the --enable-rule=PARANOID option in the command line of the configure script.

The WANTHSREGEX option is automatically set to Default. This specifies that you want to use the regular expression package included with Apache. If you'd rather use your own system's regular expression package, however, you can set this option to No using the --disable-rule=WANTH-SREGEX option in the command line of the configure script.

Modules configuration options

The default set of modules is added to the standard Apache by using the AddModule lines. The modules are listed in reverse priority order. If you plan to add other modules, do not manually modify this file. Use the configure script to add, remove, enable, or disable modules.

To enable a module that is not already enabled by default, use the --enable-module=NAME option. To disable a module, use the --disable-module=NAME option. For example, to disable the CGI module, use the following:

```
./configure --prefix=/usr/local/apache --disable-
module=cgi
```

Or, to enable the user-tracking module, run configure as follows:

```
./configure --prefix=/usr/local/apache --enable-
module=usertrack
```

After you run the configure script successfully using one or more of the options discussed previously, you are ready to compile and install Apache.

Compiling and installing Apache

Compiling and installing Apache is very simple after you have run the configure script. Simply run the make command from the top-level directory of your Apache source distribution. If everything goes well, you will not see any error messages. In such a case, you can install Apache by running the make install command. If you get error(s) when running make, write down the error message(s) and go through the configuration steps again. If you are still having problems, go to the Apache Web site and read the FAQ to find out whether you need to do something else to get Apache running. In my experience, the standard Apache source distribution compiles on Red Hat without a single hitch. So, if things are not working, double-check your steps before you seek help from Usenet newsgroups such as comp.infosystems.www.servers.unix and linux.redhat.

After you compile and install Apache, run make clean to remove all the object files that get created during compilation.

Compiling and installing Apache support tools

When you configure Apache using the configure (or config.status) script, it automatically installs a set of support tools. The only exception is the logresolve.pl Perl script, which you need to install manually. If you don't want to install any of the support tools, you can supply the --without-support option when running the configure (or config.status) script. I highly recommend leaving the default settings alone, because the support tools are very helpful in administering various aspects of Apache.

apachectl

Using this script, you can now control Apache. To determine which command -line options it accepts, run it without any command-line options or use the help option as follows:

```
/path/to/apache/bin/apachectl help
```

To start the server, run the script as follows:

```
/path/to/apache/bin/apachectl start
```

To stop the server, run the script as follows:

`/path/to/apache/bin/apachectl stop`

To restart the server, run the script as follows:

`/path/to/apache/bin/apachectl restart`

To perform a graceful restart, run the script as follows:

`/path/to/apache/bin/apachectl graceful`

For the curious, the restart argument makes apachectl send a SIGHUP signal to Apache, and the graceful argument makes it send a SIGUSR1 signal instead. Because the latter is user-defined (by the Apache developers), it is much more agreeable to the running server.

To get the full status of the running server, run the script as follows:

`/path/to/bin/apachectl fullstatus`

You get a page of information showing various server status data. Redirecting the status information to a file is recommended, because it most likely will be more than a full screen of details. Here is how to redirect the data to a file called /TMP/STATUS:

`/path/to/apache/sbin/dir/apachectl fullstatus >`
`/tmp/status`

To test the server configuration files for syntax errors, run the apachectl script as follows:

`/path/to/apache/sbin/dir/apachectl configtest`

ab

This utility allows you to run benchmarks on your Web server. Run the program without any options to find out about the command-line options it takes.

apxs

This utility helps in compiling modules for dynamic loading. It is not useful unless you have Dynamic Shared Object (DSO) support enabled on your Apache server, and your OS supports DSO.

logresolve.pl

This Perl script does not get installed automatically, but you can manually copy it in an appropriate place from the src/support directory of your Apache source distribution. This script resolves IP addresses found in an Apache log file to their host names. This script spawns child processes and uses the parent process to provide caching support to speed up DNS lookups, which are often very slow.

logresolve

This utility works practically the same way as the logresolve.pl script, except that this executable program gets installed by default. To learn about the command-line syntax, run it with the −h option.

htpasswd

This utility allows you to create username/password pairs for per-directory authentication schemes. To see the usage syntax, run the program without any arguments. Unlike the previously mentioned support tools, this utility gets installed in the bin directory of your Apache server installation directory.

dbmmanage

This utility allows you to manage DBM-based username/password pairs for DBM-based authentication schemes. To see the usage syntax, run the program without any arguments. This utility is also installed in the bin directory of your Apache server installation directory.

htdigest

This utility allows you to create username/password pairs for MD5 digest-based authentication schemes. To see the usage syntax, run the program without any arguments. This utility is also installed in the bin directory of your Apache server installation directory.

Customizing Apache with optional or third-party modules

Try out the standard Apache first before you add any third-party modules, to make sure that everything is working before you add any third-party code to the picture. After the standard Apache is running on your system, you can customize it as you please. In such a case, you no longer need to run the configure script in the same manner you did the first time. A script called config.status is automatically created when you run the configure script. The config.status script maintains a history of the options you supplied to configure script. For example, if you run the configure script once as follows:

```
./configure --prefix=/usr/local/apache --disable-module=cgi
```

the config.status script will look like this:

```
#!/bin/sh
##
##    config.status -- APACI auto-generated
##                       configuration restore script
##
##    Use this shell script to rerun the APACI
##    configure script for restoring your configuration.
##    Additional parameters can be supplied.
##


./configure \
"--prefix=/usr/local/apache" \
"--disable-module=cgi" \
"$@"
```

Suppose that you want to enable the usertrack module. Run configure again as follows:

```
./configure --prefix=/usr/local/apache \
--disable-module=cgi —enable-module=usertrack
```

Or, run the following:

```
./config.status --enable-module=usertrack
```

The config.status script makes it easier to work with configure, so use it for all future compilations. If you decide to start fresh, you can simply delete config.status and run configure to create a new config.status script.

Adding FastCGI support

Before you can add FastCGI support in your Apache, you have to download the latest FastCGI module (mod_fastcgi.c) from the FastCGI Web site, `http://www.fastcgi.com/` and follow the steps below:

1. The first step is to extract the FastCGI module distribution. Next, copy or move the distribution to the src/modules/fastcgi directory of your Apache source distribution. Then, change directories to your top-level Apache source distribution directory and run the configuration script as follows:

   ```
   ./configure \
   —activate-module=src/modules/fastcgi/libfastcgi.a
   ```

2. If you previously compiled Apache using APACI and want to keep the existing configuration along with the new mod_fastcgi.c module update, run the following command instead:

   ```
   ./config.status \
   —activate-module=src/modules/fastcgi/libfastcgi.a
   ```

3. Now, rebuild the Apache server executable (httpd) by running the make command. If you get no error messages, run the make command again with the install option to reinstall the Apache executable.

4. After you build the new Apache executable, check to verify that the mod_fastcgi.c module is included in the executable. The easiest way to verify this is to run the following command:

   ```
   /path/to/your/apache/httpd -l
   ```

5. Use the appropriate path instead of */path/to/your/apache*, as shown earlier. You should see mod_fastcgi.c listed in the output produced by the −l option. If you don't see it, you have missed one or more steps in compiling Apache, so go back and verify your steps.

Adding an embedded Perl interpreter in Apache

Make sure you have the latest Perl version installed on your system. Check the version number of your installed Perl by using the **perl –v** command and verify what the latest version available is at http://www.perl.com/. If you don't have the latest version, download and install it.

After you install the latest Perl version on your target system, download the latest version of mod_perl from http://perl.apache.org/.

Also, many of the tests used for verifying a mod_perl installation use the LWP Perl modules, so install LWP modules along with LWP's prerequisite modules. If you have installed Perl properly, you can install the LWP modules quite easily using the CPAN module. Run CPAN as follows:

```
perl  -MCPAN –install LWP
```

After you complete these prerequisite tasks, you can install the mod_perl module as follows:

1. Installing mod_perl support into your Apache server involves two parts: update your Perl distribution with mod_perl, and then update your Apache distribution with mod_perl. To make things simpler, this discussion assumes that you have downloaded and decompressed the mod_perl source distribution from http://perl.apache.org/ into a directory such that both Apache source and mod_perl source share the same top-level directory as their parent directory; in other words, both Apache source and mod_perl source distributions are subdirectories of a single parent directory. For this example installation, assume that the Apache server is in /usr/local/build/apache-1.3.91.3.9, and the mod_perl source distribution is in /usr/local/build//usr/local/build/mod_perl-1.16. (Your version numbers for both Apache and mod_perl may vary.)

2. Change directories to the source distribution (/usr/local/build//usr/local/build/mod_perl-1.16) and run the following command:

```
perl  Makefile.PL APACHE_SRC=../apache-
1.3.91.3.9/src \
DO_HTTPD=1  \
USE_APACI=1  \
PREP_HTTPD=1  \
EVERYTHING=1
```

3. This builds the Perl side of mod_perl and prepares the Apache side of mod_perl. Next, run the following commands, as long as any error messages do not stop you:

```
make
make test
make install
```

4. If you are compiling Apache for the first time, run the following command from the Apache source distribution directory to complete the Apache side of the mod_perl installation:

```
./configure
-prefix=/path/to/where/you/want/to/install/apache \
--activate-module=src/modules/perl/libperl.a
```

If you have already compiled Apache, use the following command instead:

```
./config.status --activate-
module=src/modules/perl/libperl.a
```

This preserves all the previous options that you supplied to the configure command.

5. Next, run the following commands to install Apache with mod_perl support:

```
make
make test
make install
```

6. To verify that mod_perl is part of your Apache executable (httpd), use the httpd -l command.

Adding PHP scripting support

Before you can install PHP support, make sure you have already compiled Apache at least once. After you have downloaded the latest PHP distribution from http://www.php.net/, extract it into an appropriate directory, and follow the steps below:

1. Enter the top-level PHP distribution directory, running its own configure script as follows:

```
./configure \
—-with-
apache=/path/to/your/apache/distribution/directory
```

After you configure it with Apache, run the make command followed by a make install if you do not get any compilation errors. This will build PHP on your system, and then you can proceed with the Apache part of this installation.

2. Change directories to your Apache source distribution and run the configure (or config.status) script as follows:

```
./configure —activate-
module=src/modules/php3/libphp3.a
```

3. After you run the preceding command, run make followed by a make install to install the PHP support in Apache. After you compile and install Apache, you are ready to get it up and running.

Getting Apache Up and Running

Every Apache source distribution comes with the following set of default configuration files:

- httpd.conf
- srm.conf
- access.conf
- magic
- mime.types

The last two files should be left as alone in most cases. The magic file is used for a special module called mod_mime_magic, and the mime.types file controls what MIME types are sent to the client for a given file extension. If for some reason you need to create additional MIME types for your server, use the AddType directive instead of modifying this file.

The httpd.conf, access.conf, and srm.conf files are the ones that you have to customize. Although these are three separate files, they share the same structure. In fact, it is recommended that you put all the directives in httpd.conf and keep the other two files empty. The default versions of srm.conf and access.conf provided with the Apache distribution contain only comments, which also recommend that you don't use these two files. Thus, heed the advice and only use httpd.conf for all server-specific configurations.

The httpd.conf file is a text file that has two types of information: optional comments (begin with #) and server directives. The comments have no purpose for the server software; they serve as a form of documentation for the server administrator. You can add as many comment lines as you want; the server simply ignores all comments when it parses these files.

The server treats all lines other than comments and blank lines as either complete or partial directives.

The default httpd.conf file, stored in the conf subdirectory of your Apache installation directory, is the only file you need to configure to get Apache operational.

Running Apache as a standalone or inetd server

The first directive in the default httpd.conf configuration file is ServerType, which specifies how the Web server is run. The server can be run using either of two methods: standalone or inetd. Although these methods may appear to be virtually identical in their functionality, a big difference exists between them in the performance of the server. An inetd-run server process exits as soon as it finishes servicing a request. In standalone mode, the child Web server processes hang out for a certain amount of time before they cease to exist, giving them a chance to be reused by future requests. Because the overhead of launching a new process per request is absent in the standalone mode, this mode is more efficient. So, the default value (standalone) should work for most sites. If you prefer to run Apache as an inetd server, then set ServerType to inetd.

Edit your /etc/inetd.conf file to add a new record for Apache. This text file has a specific record format, which you should be able to determine by looking at the existing entries in the file. For Red Hat Linux systems, the inetd.conf record syntax is as follows:

```
service_name sock_type proto flags user server_path args
```

As the preceding line indicates, the service is run as a particular user. Thus, decide which user you want to run the Apache server as. The simplest method is either to use the nobody user or to create a special user named httpd to run the server process. If you use the nobody user for other services, then don't use it again for Apache. Reusing nobody for Web service might affect what is accessible to the Web server when you modify a directory/file setting for the other service using the nobody account. I recommend creating a special httpd account and using it as follows:

```
httpd stream tcp nowait httpd /path/to/httpd -f
/path/to/httpd.conf
```

After you modify the inetd.conf file, modify the /etc/services file, which has a record structure as follows:

```
service name port number/protocol name service entry in
inetd.conf
```

Add the following line in /etc/services:

```
httpd 80/tcp httpd
```

The preceding entry describes the httpd service available and used by the inetd server. It specifies that the HTTP service is available on port 80. If you want to use a different port for your Web (HTTP) service, replace 80 with a port number that is not already being used by another service. Because all port numbers below 1024 are reserved for standard services, use a port address higher than 1024 (for example, 8080) and lower than 65535.

Restart your inetd process. First, you need its process ID (PID), which you can obtain by using the following commands:

```
ps auxw | grep inetd
```

Piping the output of ps to the grep utility enables grep to search the lines for any line that matches the word inetd, and print the line onscreen (standard output). Although the ps output format varies on different systems, usually the first numeric column in the output is the PID for the process on that line.

Use the kill utility as follows, replacing *PID of inetd* with the actual PID:

```
kill -HUP PID of inetd
```

The kill utility sends a SIGHUP (HUP is the shortened name) signal to the named PID. This restarts your inetd server and enables it to reread the configuration files you modified. Now, your inetd configuration is complete.

After you assign the Apache directive ServerType to inetd and configure the /etc/inetd.conf and /etc/services files, the User and Group directives in the httpd.conf file have no effect. However, make sure the username you used in the /etc/inetd.conf file has access privileges both to your Web directories and to where you store the log files for the server.

I recommend that you run Apache as an inetd server only if your system has very little RAM to spare, or if you do not expect to have a high-traffic Web site.

A port for the standalone server

The Port directive has no effect if you choose to run your Apache server as an inetd process. On the other hand, if you kept the default ServerType setting (standalone), you can use this directive to tell Apache which port address to listen to.

The default HTTP port is 80, and this should be used in typical Web sites. If you are not the root user of the system, however, and want to run the Web server, you need to use a port number greater than 1023 and lower than 65535. All ports below 1024 are considered standard reserved ports and require inetd-level (root-level) access to start a service on these ports. If you are just experimenting with Web servers on a nonroot account on a system, you can use a port higher than the mentioned range as long as it has not already been taken. If you try to use a port address that is already in use by another server, you will get an error message when you try to start the server. Also, if you use any port other than the standard HTTP port 80, you have to supply a port number along with all URL requests to the server. For example, if you set this directive as Port 8080, you need to request resources (such as a page called mypage.html) on this server as follows:

```
http://www.domain.tld:8080/mypage.html
```

A user and a group for the standalone server

Like the Port directive, the User and Group directives in the httpd.conf file
are meaningful only for a standalone server. The syntax for these directives
is as follows:

```
User  [username   |   #UID]
Group [group name  |   #GID]
```

These two directives are very important for security reasons. When the
primary Web server process launches a child server process to fulfill a
request, it changes the child's UID and GID according to the values set for
these directives.

If the child processes are run as root user processes, a potential security
hole is opened for attack by hackers. Allowing the capability to interact
with a root user process maximizes the risk of a potential breach of security
in the system; hence, this user capability is discouraged. Rather, choose to
run the child server processes as very low-privileged users belonging to a
very low-privileged group. The user named nobody (usually UID = −1) and
the group named nogroup (usually GID = −1) are low-privileged. Consult
your /etc/group and /etc/passwd files to determine these settings.

If you plan to run the primary Web server as a nonroot (regular) user, it
will not be able to change the UIDs and GIDs of child processes, because
only root user processes can change the UIDs or GIDs of other processes.
Therefore, if you run your primary server as the user named foobar, all
child processes will have the same privileges of foobar. Similarly, whatever
GID you have also will be the GID for the child processes.

If you plan to use the numeric format for UIDs and/or GIDs, you need
to insert a # symbol before the numeric value, which can be found in the
/etc/passwd and /etc/group files.

Configuring common directives

The standalone and inetd-based servers share the following common
directives:

```
CustomLog path/to/logfile
```

This directive sets the log file path for storing logs for successful access requests. It also sets the log format that needs to be used in logging the access requests. For example, the default setting uses the common log format specified using the LogFormat directive. If you choose to use a different log format, such as combined, then make sure you change the default value from common to combined.

```
ErrorLog path/to/logfile
```

This directive specifies the log file used for logging error messages. If you set this directive to a relative path (a path that does not start with a slash character), then the path is assumed to be relative to the ServerRoot directory. For example, if your ServerRoot directory is set as /usr/local/apache, and ErrorLog is set to var/logs/error_log, then it is the equivalent of the following:

```
ErrorLog /usr/local/apache/logs/error_log
```

Whatever directory you keep the logs in, make sure that only the primary server process has write access in that directory. This is a major security issue; allowing other users or processes to write to the log directory poses the potential of someone unauthorized being able to take over your primary Web server process UID, which is normally the root account.

```
HostnameLookups on | off
```

When this directive is set to off, it tells Apache not to do DNS lookups to determine host names of requesting clients. Because DNS lookups are time-consuming, using the default value off is a very good idea. Turning this on may cause clients to time out if their ISP has not properly set up the client's reverse-DNS settings.

```
LogFormat format
```

The LogFormat specifies the format for server log files and assigns a nickname to that format. The default httpd.conf file contains multiple LogFormat directives but uses only one with the CustomLog directive. For example:

```
LogFormat "%h %l %u %t \"%r\" %>s %b \"%{Referer}i\"
\"%{User-Agent}i\"" combined
```

This log format nicknamed "combined" specifies all the Common Log Format (CLF) fields and adds the referrer and user-agent fields. The next format in the default configuration is as follows:

```
LogFormat "%h %l %u %t \"%r\" %>s %b" common
```

This format is simply the CLF, and hence is nicknamed "common." The last two LogFormat directives in the default httpd.conf file are the following:

```
LogFormat "%{Referer}i -> %U" referer
LogFormat "%{User-agent}i" agent
```

These two directives create nicknames for log formats that store only the referrer and user-agent information. By default, the common format is used with the CustomLog directive. However, because most log-analysis programs accept the combined format, you may want to set that as the default. After all, more log information is always better for determining who is accessing your site and how.

```
LogLevel [emerg | alert | crit | errors | warn | debug ]
```

This directive specifies the level of logging for the ErrorLog directive. The default value, warn, is normally sufficient. It tells Apache to log all emergency (emerg) error conditions, alert (alert) conditions, critical (crit) errors, and all warnings (warn). If you plan to do much debugging, set this to debug, which will catch just about all types of errors, warnings, and informative messages from the server. Also remember that the more disk I/O that you have the server perform, the slower it gets, so keeping the LogLevel at debug is not ideal for production servers.

```
ServerAdmin e-mail address
```

This directive sets the e-mail address of the server admin. The e-mail address is displayed when the server generates an error message page. Typically, it is set as follows:

```
ServerAdmin webmaster@domain.tld
ServerName hostname
```

This directive sets the server's Internet host name. Normally, you want to enter a host name such as www.*yourcompany*.com. Be sure, however, that the host name you enter here has proper DNS records that point it to your server machine.

`ServerRoot` *path*

This directive specifies the top-level directory where the server's configuration, error, and log files are kept. This is the parent directory for all server-related files. If you compiled and installed Apache using the APACI interface, the default ServerRoot is set to the value of the PREFIX value you supplied as the parameter to the configure script. For example, if you run the configure script from your Apache distribution directory as follows:

```
./configure  --PREFIX=/usr/local/apache
```

ServerRoot will be set to /usr/local/apache by default. However, if you compiled Apache manually, you might have to change the default value to point to an appropriate directory.

`Timeout` *number*

Using this directive you can set the number of seconds that Apache will wait for the client. The default value should be just fine.

`UseCanonicalName on | off`

When set to on, this directive tells Apache to use ServerName- and Port-specified values when creating self-referencing URLs. Conversely, when it is set to off, the server constructs self-referencing URLs using the server name and port information the client supplied. If the client does not supply any such information, the server then uses ServerName- and Port-specified values. Most sites do not use self-referencing URL addresses, so this is not going to be an important directive for most administrators.

The next set of directives that you need to configure are used to tell the server what resources you want to offer from your Web site, and where and how to offer them.

`AccessFileName` *filename filename filename* . . .

This directive sets the directory access control filename. Some Web administrators change the default (.htaccess) to enhance security, because the .htaccess name is widely known. If you plan to change the name, choose a name that starts with a period so that it won't show up in directory listings. Also note that the default access.conf file prohibits Apache from looking into any directory level access control file. If you plan to use such access control files, make sure you modify the httpd.conf file accordingly. For example, the default httpd.conf file has the following configuration segment:

```
<Directory />
  Options FollowSymLinks
  AllowOverride None
</Directory>
```

This configuration uses the AllowOverride directive to prohibit Apache from looking into the AccessFileName-specified file. If you are interested in allowing Apache to look for an access control file in a certain subsection of your site, use the following configuration:

```
<Directory "/path/to/your/dir">
  Options FollowSymLinks
  AllowOverride All
</Directory>
```

This configuration allows you to have an access control file such as .htaccess in the */path/to/your/dir* directory or in any of the subdirectories below it. It also allows you to override all the allowed directives. If you are interested in a more restricted setting, set AllowOverride to one of the following settings:

- **AuthConfig:** Allows the authorization directives, such as AuthDBMGroupFile, AuthDBMUserFile, AuthGroupFile, AuthName, AuthType, AuthUserFile, and require.

- **FileInfo:** Allows the document types directives, such as AddEncoding, AddLanguage, AddType, DefaultType, ErrorDocument, and LanguagePriority.

- **Indexes:** Allows the directory indexing directives, such as AddDescription, AddIcon, AddIconByEncoding, AddIconByType, DefaultIcon, DirectoryIndex, FancyIndexing, HeaderName, IndexIgnore, IndexOptions, and ReadmeName.

- **Limit:** Allows the host access directives, such as allow, deny, and order.

- **Options:** Allows the directory options directives, such as Options and XbitHack.

```
AddEncoding MIME-encoding file-extension file-extension .
. .
```

This directive assigns MIME encoding information with filename extensions. Keep the defaults as they are.

```
AddIcon icon name name . . .
```

This directive sets the icon filename for a specific file extension. When FancyIndexing is turned on, Apache displays this icon next to each file matching the extension specified in this directive. Keep the default as is.

```
AddIconByEncoding icon MIME-encoding mime-encoding . . .
```

This directive sets the icon to display next to files with MIME-encoding for FancyIndexing. Keep the default as is.

```
AddIconByType icon MIME-type MIME-type . . .
```

This directive also sets the icon to display next to files with MIME-encoding for FancyIndexing. Keep the default as is.

```
AddLanguage MIME-language file-extension file-extension .
. .
```

This directive assigns language-specific MIME encoding information with filename extensions. Keep the defaults as they are.

```
Alias URL-path path
```

You can create an alias for a physical directory using this directive. The default alias /icons/ points to the directory where the server's icon images are stored. If the path is incorrect, modify it as appropriate. The icon images are used to create fancy directory listings.

BrowserMatch *variable*[=*value*] [. . .]

This directive defines environment variables based on the User-Agent HTTP request header field. Keep the default as is.

DefaultIcon *url*

This directive sets the icon to display for files when no specific icon is known. Keep the default as is.

DefaultType *MIME-type*

The default content type is set using this directive. When the server can't determine a document's MIME type using the mapping information stored in mime.types or other means (such as AddType directives), it uses the value set by this directive. Keep the default as is.

DirectoryIndex *filename filename filename* . . .

This directive specifies which file the Apache server should consider as the index for the directory being requested. For example, when a URL such as www.yourcompany.com is requested, the Apache server determines that this is a request to access the / (document root) directory of the Web site. If the DocumentRoot directive is set as follows:

DocumentRoot "/www/www.yourcompany.com/public/htdocs"

the Apache server looks for a file named /www/www.yourcompany .com/public/htdocs/index.html; if the server finds the file, Apache services the request by returning the content of the file to the requesting Web browser. If the DirectoryIndex is assigned welcome.html rather than the default index.html, however, the Web server instead looks for /www/www.yourcompany.com/public/htdocs/welcome.html. If the file is absent, Apache returns the directory listing by creating a DHTML page. You also can specify multiple index filenames in the DirectoryIndex directive. For example,

```
DirectoryIndex index.html index.htm welcome.htm
```

tells the Web server that it should check for the existence of any of the three files, and if any one is found, it should be returned to the requesting Web client.

Listing many files as the index may create two problems:

- The server has to check for the existence of many files per directory request, which could potentially make it a bit slower than usual.

- Your site could become a bit difficult to manage from the organizational point of view.

If your Web site content developers use various systems to create files, however, it may be a practical solution to keep both index.html and index.htm as index files. For example, a Windows 3.*x* machine is unable to create filenames with extensions longer than three characters, so a user working on such a machine may need to manually update all of his or her index.html files on the Web server. Using the recommended index filenames eliminates this hassle.

```
DocumentRoot "path"
```

This directive tells the server to treat the supplied directory name as the root directory for all documents. The default typically is set to Apache's own htdocs directory, where server documentation is kept. You will have to change the default. This is a very important decision for you to make. For example, if the directive is set as follows:

```
DocumentRoot /
```

every file on the system becomes accessible by the Web server. Of course, you can protect files by providing proper file permission settings, but setting the document root to the physical root directory of your system is definitely a major security risk. Instead, you want to point the DocumentRoot to a specific subdirectory of your file system.

A potentially better option, however, is to create a Web directory structure for your organization. For example, if you are planning to host more than one Web site (such as virtual hosts) using your Apache server, you may want to create a partition specifically for Web documents and scripts. I typically use a separate disk partition, such as /www, to store all the Web sites that I manage. I keep each site as a subdirectory of the /www directory. Here is a reasonably good directory structure:

- Directory structure for `www.nitec.com` on port 80

  `/www/www.nitec.com/public`
  `/www/www.nitec.com/public/htdocs`   `Document Root Dir`
  `/www/www.nitec.com/public/cgi-bin`   `CGI Script Dir`
- Directory structure for `www.nitec.com` on port 8080

  `/www/www.nitec.com/staging`
  `/www/www.nitec.com/staging/htdocs`   `Document Root Dir`
  `/www/www.nitec.com/staging/cgi-bin`   `CGI Script Dir`
- Directory structure for `www.nitec.com` on port 9000

  `/www/www.nitec.com/dev`
  `/www/www.nitec.com/dev/htdocs`   `Document Root Dir`
  `/www/www.nitec.com/dev/cgi-bin`   `CGI Script Dir`

This is the directory structure I use for the entire production of my company Web site (`www.nitec.com`). Having such a directory structure allows me to develop, stage, and produce the Web site in a systematic fashion. For example, when some new development work is done for the site, it is accessible from the `www.nitec.com:9000` site. Then, after it is approved, the newly developed content moves to `www.nitec.com:8080`. Finally, the content moves to the public site.

Just because your document root points to a particular directory does not mean the Web server cannot access directories outside of your document tree. You can easily enable it to do so by using symbolic links (with proper file permission) or aliases. From an organizational and security perspective, I don't recommend using a lot of symbolic links or aliases to access files and directories outside of your document tree. Nonetheless, it is sometimes necessary to keep a certain type of information outside the document tree, even if you need to keep the contents of such a directory accessible to the server on a regular basis.

If you have to add symbolic links to other directory locations outside the document tree, make sure that when you back up your files, your backup program is instructed to back up symbolic links properly.

`FancyIndexing on | off`

This directive sets the FancyIndexing option for a directory. When a request for a directory is made and none of the files in the directory matches any name specified in the DirectoryIndex directive, the server generates a dynamic directory listing. This feature is turned on and off by this directive. Also, note that FancyIndexing and IndexOptions directives override each other. Instead of using the FancyIndexing directive, you can use the IndexOptions directive as follows:

`IndexOptions FancyIndexing`

which also turns on fancy indexing for server-generated directory listings.

`HeaderName` *filename*

This directive sets the filename that will be embedded in the directory listings created by the server. This file is inserted before the actual listing, thus creating the effect of a header.

`IndexIgnore` *filename filename filename . . .*

This directive sets the filenames that will be ignored by the server when creating a dynamic directory listing. The filenames can be simple regular expressions separated by space characters. Keep the default.

`LanguagePriority` *MIME-language MIME-language . . .*

This directive sets the precedence of languages in order of decreasing preference. Keep the default as is if English (en) is your preferred language.

`ReadmeName` *filename filename filename . . .*

This directive sets the filename that will be appended at the end of a directory listing created by the server. This file is inserted after the actual listing, thus creating the effect of a footer. This file must be in the same directory.

`TypesConfig` *filename*

This directive sets the location of the MIME types configuration file. Keep the default unless you move the mime.types file.

`UserDir` *directory*

This directive is used to tell Apache which directory to consider as the DocumentRoot for users on your system. This applies only if you have multiple users on the system and want to allow each one to have his or her own Web directory. The default value is public_html, which means that if you set up your Web server's name to be www.yourcompany.com, and you have two users, joe and jenny, their personal Web site URLs and Web directories would be as follows:

```
http://www.yourcompany.com/~joe    ~joe/public_html
http://www.yourcompany.com/~jenny   ~jenny/public_html
```

The tilde (~) character extends to a user's home directory. The directory specified by the UserDir directive resides in each user's home directory, and Apache must have read and execute permissions to read files and directories within the public_html directory. This can be accomplished by using the following commands:

```
chown -R <user>.<Apache server's group name> \
   ~<user>/<directory assigned in UserDir>
chmod -R 770 ~<user>/<directory assigned in UserDir>
```

For example, if the username is joe, Apache's group is called httpd, and public_html is assigned in the UserDir directive, the preceding commands will look like this:

```
chown -R joe.httpd  ~joe/public_html
chmod -R 2770 ~joe/public_html
```

The first command, chown, changes ownership of the ~joe/public_html directory (as well as all files and subdirectories within it) to joe.httpd. In other words, it gives the user joe and the group httpd full ownership of all the files and directories in the public_html directory. The next command, chmod, sets the access rights to 2770; in other words, only the user (joe) and the group (httpd) have full read, write, and execute privileges in public_html and all files and subdirectories under it. It also ensures that when a new file or subdirectory is created in the public_html directory, the newly created file has the GID set. This enables the Web server to access the new file without the user's intervention.

If you create user accounts on your system by using a script (such as the /usr/sbin/useradd script on Linux systems), you may want to incorporate the Web site creation process in this script. Just add a mkdir command to create a default public_html directory (if that's what you assign to the UserDir directive) to create the Web directory. Add the chmod and chown commands to give the Web server user permission to read and execute files and directories under this public directory.

The final set of directives that you need to configure are used to set access permissions for items such as files, directories, and scripts on your Web site. The first directive you need to modify has the following syntax:

```
<Directory "path"> . . . </Directory>
```

<Directory> and </Directory> are used to enclose a group of directives. The scope of the enclosed directives is limited to the named directory path (with subdirectories); however, you may use only directives that are allowed in a directory context. The named directory is either the full path to a directory or a wildcard string.

The first <Directory /> . . . </Directory> container configuration segment is very restrictive; it enables the server to follow only symbolic links, and disables per-directory-based access control files (.htaccess) for all directories starting with the root directory of the system. Keep this configuration segment as is. The idea is both to open things that need to be opened and to lock everything else. For example, the <Directory "/usr/local/apache/htdocs"> . . . </Directory> configuration segment allows directory indexing and the FollowSymLinks feature for the DocumentRoot directory.

You may need to change the directory /usr/local/apache/htdocs to whatever you set earlier as the argument for the DocumentRoot directive in the httpd.conf file. The default setting, which includes multiple directives such as Options and AllowOverride, tells the server the following:

- The named directory and all subdirectories under it can be indexed. In other words, if an index file exists, it will be displayed; in the absence of an index file, the server creates a dynamic index for the directory. The Options directive specifies this.

- The named directory and all subdirectories under it can have symbolic links that the server can follow (that is, use as a path) to access information. The Options directive also specifies this.

- No options specified in the directory container can be overridden by a local access control file (specified by the AccessFileName directive in srm.conf; the default is .htaccess). This is specified using the AllowOverride directive.
- Access is permitted for all.

The default setting should be sufficient at this early stage. If your server is going to be on the Internet, however, you may want to remove the FollowSymLinks option from the Options directive line. Leaving this option creates a potential security risk. For example, if a directory in your Web site does not have an index page, the server displays an automated index that shows any symbolic links you may have in that directory. This could cause sensitive information to be displayed or may even allow anyone to run an executable that resides in a carelessly linked directory.

The <Directory "/usr/local/apache/cgi-bin"> ... </Directory> container specifies the options for the /usr/local/apache/cgi-bin directory. This is the directory in which the distributed CGI scripts are kept. Because the contents of the CGI scripts are not to be browsed or made available via directory indexing, there is no need to allow any per-directory control on that directory; hence, the default is to remove all options.

Configuring directives for a standalone server

The following directives in the default httpd.conf file are meaningful only for Apache running in standalone mode.

```
KeepAlive on | off
```

This directive enables or disables the KeepAlive feature built into Apache. Simply speaking, KeepAlive is a feature that allows a persistent connection between the server and the client. Having a persistent connection helps speed up the delivery of the content, because no time is lost in establishing new connections for each request. Keep the default as is, because it is a part of the HTTP 1.1 specification.

```
KeepAliveTimeout
```

This directive specifies the maximum time (in seconds) the server will wait for a subsequent connection before it disconnects from the client. Keep the default as is.

`MaxClients` *number*

This directive sets the limit on the number of simultaneous requests that can be supported. The maximum possible value is 256. If you feel that you need to handle more than 256 simultaneous connections, edit the src/include/httpd.h header file and set the HARD_SERVER_LIMIT constant to the desired limit. After you compile the new server, you will be able to set this directive to the desired limit.

`MaxKeepAliveRequests` *number*

This directive specifies the maximum number of requests to be serviced per KeepAlive connection. Keep the default as is. Note that setting the value to 0 disables the KeepAlive feature.

`MaxRequestsPerChild` *number*

This directive sets the limit on the number of requests a child server process will service before it dies. If you set the value to 0, the child server processes will never die. Keep the default as is.

`MaxSpareServers` *number*

This directive specifies the maximum number of spare (idle) servers that Apache will run. You should experiment with this directive only if you are running Apache to host very busy Web sites.

This directive is useless with the Windows version of Apache.

`MinSpareServers` *number*

This directive sets the minimum number of spare (idle) servers that the primary server will keep around. You should experiment with this directive only if you are running Apache to host very busy Web sites. Apache can automatically adjust to load, so I recommend that you do not use a large number here.

This directive is useless with the Windows version of Apache, because it does not use a pool of servers to service requests.

`PidFile` *path/filename*

This directive is used to specify a filename for storing the primary server's PID information. This file can be used by scripts to easily determine what the PID of the primary server is. For example, if the PidFile is set as follows:

```
PidFile /usr/local/apache/var/run/httpd.pid
```

I can restart the Apache server by using the kill command as follows:

```
kill -HUP `cat /usr/local/apache/var/run/httpd.pid`
```

Whatever directory you keep this file in, make sure that only the primary server process has write access in that directory. This is a major security issue; allowing other users or processes to write to this directory potentially enables someone unauthorized to take over your primary Web server process UID, which is normally the root account.

ScoreBoardFile *path*/*filename*

This directive is set to a filename that the primary server uses to communicate with its child server processes. This is needed for only a few OS platforms. If you have to use a ScoreBoardFile, then you may see improved speed by placing it on a RAM disk. Consult your OS manuals.

StartServers *number*

This directive sets the initial number of child server processes that Apache will launch at startup. Apache can automatically adjust to load, so you don't need to change the default.

Controlling the Apache server

Apache 1.3.*x* comes with a nifty shell script called apachectl, which can be used to control the server in many ways. This section discusses this script in detail. However, before you can control Apache, you must become the superuser on your system, unless you have configured Apache to run on a port above 1023.

If you properly set up the inetd configuration for httpd, you don't need to do anything to start or stop the Apache server, because inetd runs it when it receives a request for access on the HTTP port.

Starting the server

To start the server, run the apachectl script as follows:

```
/path/to/apache/bin/apachectl start
```

If you want your server to start automatically after a system reboot, add the preceding line to your /etc/rc.local file or a similar file in your rc.d directory. I use the script shown in Listing 12-1 for automatic Apache startup and shutdown at boot and reboot, respectively.

Listing 12-1 *The httpd.sh Script*

```
#!/bin/sh
#
# httpd    This shell script starts and stops the Apache
server
# It takes an argument 'start' or 'stop' to start and
# stop the server process, respectively.
#
# Notes: You might have to change the path information
used
# in the script to reflect your system's configuration.
#
[ -f /usr/local/apache/bin/apachectl ] || exit 0

# See how the script was called.
case "$1" in
  start)
        # Start daemons.
        echo -n "Starting httpd:"
        /usr/local/apache/bin/apachectl start
        touch /var/lock/subsys/httpd
        echo
        ;;
  stop)
        # Stop daemons.
        echo -n "Shutting down httpd:"
```

```
        /usr/local/apache/bin/apachectl stop

        echo "done"
        rm -f /var/lock/subsys/httpd
        ;;
    *)
        echo "Usage: httpd {start|stop}"
        exit 1
esac
exit 0
```

I put this script in the /etc/rc.d/init.d directory and made the following symbolic links:

```
/etc/rc.d/rc3.d/S80httpd -> /etc/rc.d/init.d/httpd.sh
/etc/rc.d/rc3.d/K80httpd -> /etc/rc.d/init.d/httpd.sh
```

When the system starts up, it loads the Apache server automatically. The script also stops the Apache server at system shutdown or reboot.

Stopping the server

To stop the server, run the apachectl script as follows:

```
/path/to/apache/bin/apachectl stop
```

Restarting the server

To restart the server, run the apachectl script as follows:

```
/path/to/apache/bin/apachectl restart
```

To perform a graceful restart, run the apachectl script as follows:

```
/path/to/apache/bin/apachectl graceful
```

For the curious, the restart command sends a SIGHUP signal to Apache and the graceful command sends a SIGUSR1 signal instead. Because the latter is user-defined (by the Apache developers), it is much more agreeable to the running server.

Getting full status of the server

Before you can get the full status of the server, make sure you have the Lynx text-based Web browser installed on your system. You can get this nifty Web browser from the following URL: `http://lynx.browser. org/`.

After you install Lynx, you can get the full status of the running server when you run the apachectl script as follows:

`/path/to/apache/bin/apachectl fullstatus`

You will get a page full of information showing various server status data. Redirect the status information to a file, because it most likely will be more than a full screen. Here is how you can redirect the data to a file called /tmp/status:

`/path/to/apache/bin/apachectl fullstatus > /tmp/status`

Checking server configuration files

To test the server configuration files for syntax errors, run the apachectl script as follows:

`/path/to/apache/bin/apachectl configtest`

Testing the Apache server

Run your favorite Web browser and point it to the Web site running your newly configured Apache server. If you are running the Web browser on the same system that is running Apache, you can use the following URL: `http://localhost/`.

In all other cases, however, you need to specify the exact host name (such as `www.yourcompany.com`). If you haven't made any changes to the default htdocs directory, you will see a page that tells you "It Works!" This page is shipped with the Apache distribution and needs to be changed with your own content.

Finally, make sure the log files are updated properly. To check your log files, enter the log directory and run the following command:

`tail -f [/path/to/access_log]`

The tail part of the command is a utility that enables viewing of a growing file (when the –f option is specified). Now, use a Web browser to access the site or, if you are already there, simply reload the page you currently have on the browser. You should see an entry added to the listing on the screen. Click the Reload button a few more times to ensure that the access file is updated accordingly. If you see the updated records, your access log file is working. Press Ctrl+C to exit the tail command session. If you do not see any new records in the file, check the permission settings for the log files and the directory in which they are kept.

Another log to check is the error log file. Use the following to view the error log entries as they come in:

```
tail -f [/path/to/error_log]
```

Simply request nonexistent resources (such as a file you don't have) on your Web browser, and you will see entries being added. If you observe this, the error log file is properly configured.

If all of these tests were successful, then you have successfully configured your Apache server. Congratulations!

Managing Your Apache Server

This section reviews typical Web server management issues.

Configuring Apache for CGI scripts

Configuring Apache to process CGI requests includes telling Apache where you store your CGI programs, setting up CGI handlers for specific file extensions, and indicating which file extensions should be considered CGI programs. Keep your CGI programs in one central directory to maintain better control of them. Scattering CGI programs all over the Web space might make the site unmanageable, and could create security holes that would be hard to track.

Creating a CGI program directory

Creating a central CGI program directory is just the beginning to setting up a secured CGI environment. Keeping this central CGI program directory outside of your DocumentRoot directory is recommended, so that CGI programs can't be accessed directly. When it comes to CGI programs, you want to provide as little information as possible to the outside world. This ensures better security for your site(s). The less someone knows about where your CGI programs are physically located, the less harm that person can do.

The first step is to create a directory outside of your DocumentRoot directory. For example, if /www/mycompany/public/htdocs is the DocumentRoot directory of a Web site, then /www/mycompany/public/cgi-bin is a good candidate for the CGI program directory. To create the alias for your CGI program directory, use the ScriptAlias directive.

If you are setting up CGI support for the primary Web server, edit the httpd.conf file and insert a ScriptAlias line with the following syntax:

```
ScriptAlias  /alias/ /path/to/CGI-program-dir/
```

For example,

```
ScriptAlias /cgi-bin/ /www/mycompany/public/cgi-bin/
```

If you are setting up CGI support for a virtual site, add a ScriptAlias line in the <VirtualHost ... > container that defines the virtual host. For example, the following uses the /apps/ alias to create a CGI program directory alias:

```
NameVirtualHost 206.171.50.60
<VirtualHost 206.171.50.60>
ServerName blackhole.nitec.com
ScriptAlias /apps/ /www/nitec/blackhole/public/cgi-bin/
</VirtualHost>
```

If a CGI program called feedback.cgi exists in the /www/nitec/blackhole/public/cgi-bin directory, it can be accessed *only* via the following:

```
http://blackhole.nitec.com/apps/feedback.cgi
```

After you set up the ScriptAlias directive, make sure that the directory permission permits Apache to read and execute files found in the directory.

The directory pointed to by ScriptAlias should have very strict permission settings. No one but the CGI program developer or the server administrator should have full (read, write, and execute) permissions for the directory. Note that you can define multiple CGI program directory aliases, and the ScriptAlias-specified directory is not browseable, by default, for security reasons.

When requested, Apache attempts to run any executable (file permission-wise) file found in the ScriptAliased directory. For example:

```
http://blackhole.nitec.com/apps/foo.cgi
http://blackhole.nitec.com/apps/foo.pl
http://blackhole.nitec.com/apps/foo.bak
http://blackhole.nitec.com/apps/foo.dat
```

All of the preceding URL requests prompt Apache to attempt to run the various foo files.

I am not particularly fond of the idea that any file in the ScriptAlias-specified directory can be run as a CGI program. I prefer a solution that enables me to restrict the CGI program names such that only files with certain extensions are treated like CGI programs. This is accomplished with the AddHandler handler. For example:

```
Alias /cgi-bin/ "/path/to/cgi/dir/outside/doc/root/"

<Directory "/path/to/cgi/dir/outside/doc/root/">
  Options ExecCGI -Indexes
  AddHandler cgi-script .pl .cgi
</Directory>
```

The Alias directive line tells Apache to create an alias called cgi-bin for the */path/to/*cgi/dir/outside/doc/root/ directory. The Options ExecCGI -Indexes line tells Apache to permit CGI program execution from within this directory and to now allow anyone to browse the contents of the directory. The AddHandler cgi-script .pl .cgi line tells Apache to treat the list of named extensions as CGI program extensions (in other words, whenever Apache encounters a URL requesting a file that has one of the named extensions, it must execute it as a CGI program).

Enabling cgi-bin access for your users

At least two ways exist to provide cgi-bin access for users on an Apache Web server. You need to implement only one of the following methods.

Using Directory or DirectoryMatch containers   When the UserDir directive is set to a directory name, Apache considers it as the top-level directory for a user Web site. For example:

```
ServerName www.yourcompany.com
UserDir public_html
```

Now, when a request for www.yourcompany.com/~username arrives, Apache locates the named user's home directory (usually by checking the /etc/passwd file) and then appends the UserDir-specified directory to create the path name for the top-level user Web directory. For example,

```
http://www.yourcompany.com/~joe
```

makes Apache look for /home/joe/public_html (assuming /home/joe is joe's home directory). If the directory exists, the index page for that directory will be sent to the requesting client.

One way to add CGI support for each user is to add the following configuration in one of your Apache configuration files:

```
<Directory ~ "/home/[a-z]+/public_html/cgi-bin">
  Options ExecCGI
  AddHandler cgi-script .cgi .pl
</Directory>
```

Or, if you are using the latest Apache server, you can use the following configuration:

```
<DirectoryMatch "/home/[a-z]+/public_html/cgi-bin">
  Options ExecCGI
  AddHandler cgi-script .cgi .pl
</DirectoryMatch>
```

In both methods, Apache translates www.yourcompany.com/~username/cgi-bin/ requests to /home/username/public_html/cgi-bin/ and permits any CGI program with the proper extension (.cgi or .pl) to execute.

Note that all usernames must be lowercase characters for this to work. If you have usernames that are alphanumeric, you have to use a different regular expression.

Using ScriptAliasMatch Using the ScriptAliasMatch directive also enables you to support CGI program directories for each user. For example,

```
ScriptAliasMatch ~([a-z]+)/ \
cgi-bin/(.*)/home/$1/public_html/cgi-bin/$2
```

matches username to $1, where $1 is equal to ~([a–z]+), and matches everything followed by /cgi-bin/ to $2, where $2 is equal to (.*). Then, it uses $1 and $2 to create the actual location of the CGI program directory. For example:

```
http://www.yourcompany.com/~joe/ \
cgi-bin/feedback.cgi?book=dummies&author=kabir
```

In this example, ~([a–z]+) will map one or more lowercase characters following the tilde mark (~) to $1. In other words, the pair of parentheses enables you to capture everything between the tilde (~) and the trailing forward slash (/) after the username. So, $1 is set to kabir and (.*) maps everything following the cgi-bin/ and the parentheses pair in this regular expression, and enables you to put everything in $2. Thus, $2 is set to search.cgi?book=dummies&author=kabir.

Now, Apache can create the physical path of the CGI program directory using the following:

```
/home/$1/public_html/cgi-bin/$2
```

This regular expression results in the following path for the previous example:

```
/home/kabir/public_html/ \
cgi-bin/search.cgi?book=dummies&author=kabir
```

Because this is where the CGI program search.cgi is kept, it executes.

If, like me, you aren't fond of having the CGI program directory under public_html (that is, the UserDir-specified directory), you can keep it outside by removing the public_html part of the expression, as follows:

```
ScriptAliasMatch ~([a-z]+)/cgi-bin/(.*) /home/$1/cgi-
bin/$2
```

This maps the example call

```
http://www.yourcompany.com/~joe/ \
cgi-bin/feedback.cgi?book=dummies&author=kabir
```

to the following physical file:

```
/home/kabir/cgi-bin/search.cgi?book=dummies&author=kabir
```

Of course, if you are not too fond of keeping a user subdirectory world readable (that is, public_html), you can remedy this by creating a Web partition (or a directory) for your users and giving them individual directories from which to host their home pages.

Creating new CGI extensions using AddType

If you want to create new CGI program extensions in a particular directory, you can also use the .htaccess file (or a file specified by the AccessFileName directive).

Before you can add new extensions using the per-directory access control file (.htaccess), you have to create a <Directory> container as follows:

```
<Directory "/path/to/your/directory">
  Options ExecCGI
  AllowOverride FileInfo
</Directory>
```

The first directive tells Apache that you want to enable CGI program execution in this directory. The second directive tells Apache to enable the FileInfo feature in the per-directory access control file (.htaccess). This feature enables you to use an AddType directive in the per-directory access control file.

To add a new CGI program extension (.wizard), simply create an .htaccess (or whatever you specified in the AccessFileName directive) file in the directory with the following:

```
AddType application/x-httpd-cgi .wizard
```

Now, rename an existing CGI program in that directory to have the .wizard extension, and request it via your browser. Make sure all the file permission settings for the directory and the CGI programs are set to read and execute by Apache.

Configuring Apache for server-side includes

CGI scripts are not the only way to create dynamic content; using server-side includes (SSIs) is another option. Again, Apache makes it quite easy to add SSI support for your Web sites.

Although the mod_include.c module, required for server-side include (SSI) support, is compiled by default in the standard Apache executable, the SSI parsing of HTML pages is not enabled by default. To enable SSI support for Apache, you need to perform the following steps:

1. Add a new handler for SSI pages.
2. Add a new file extension for SSI pages.
3. Enable SSI parsing for a directory.

When these steps are completed for a directory called chapter12, under a virtual host called **apache.nitec.com**, the configuration appears as follows:

```
<VirtualHost 206.171.50.50>


ServerName apache.nitec.com
DocumentRoot "/data/web/apache/public/htdocs"
ScriptAlias /cgi-bin/ /data/web/apache/public/cgi-bin


<Directory "/data/web/apache/public/htdocs/chapter12">
```

```
AddHandler server-parsed .shtml
AddType text/html .shtml
Options +Include
</Directory>

</VirtualHost>
```

Caution

The use of Include in the Options directive enables all SSI commands. If you plan to disable execution of external programs via SSI commands, use IncludesNOEXEC instead. This disables execution of external programs. However, it also disables loading of external files via the SSI command Include.

The preceding steps involved in enabling SSI support are described in the following sections.

Add a new handler for SSI pages

Suppose that you want to use .shtml as the SSI file extension for all HTML pages that will contain one or more SSI commands. You need to tell Apache that the file extension .shtml should be treated as an SSI-enabled page. You can do that by using the AddHandler directive as follows:

```
AddHandler server-parsed .shtml
```

The AddHandler directive tells Apache that an .shtml file needs to be handled by the server-parsed handler, which is found in the mod_include module.

If, for some reason, you have to use the .html and .htm extensions as the SSI extensions, do not use the following:

```
AddHandler server-parsed .html
AddType text/html .html


AddHandler server-parsed .htm
AddType text/html .htm
```

This would degrade your server performance. Apache would process all the
.html and .htm files, which would mean that files without any SSI commands would be parsed, therefore increasing the delay in file delivery. Try
hard to avoid using the .html or .htm extensions for SSI; if you must use
them, however, use the XbitHack directive. For example,

```
<Directory "/some/path/">
  Options +Includes
  XbitHack on
</Directory>
```

enables SSI parsing for each .html (and .htm) file in the /some/path/
directory as long as its owner has read and execute permissions for the file.

Add a new file extension for SSI pages

Although Apache now knows how to handle the .shtml file, it needs to be
told what to tell the Web browser about this file. Web servers send header
information for each request to tell the Web browser what type of content
is being sent as the response. Therefore, you need to tell Apache that when
responding to an .shtml file request, it should tell the browser, by setting
the content type, that the information being sent is still an HTML document. This way, the Web browser will render the content onscreen as usual.
The MIME type for HTML content is text/html. The following line
shows how to instruct Apache to generate a text/html content type header
when transmitting the output of an .shtml page:

```
AddType text/html   .shtml
```

For backward-compatibility, documents with the MIME type text/x-
server-parsed-html or text/x-server-parsed-html3 will also be parsed (and
the resulting output is given the MIME type text/html).

Enable SSI parsing for a directory

Both Apache and Web browsers know how to handle the new .shtml files; however, Apache is still not ready to parse the .shtml pages.

Using the Options directive, you need to tell Apache that you want to enable Includes support. First, however, you need to determine where to put this Options directive.

If you want to enable SSI support in the entire (primary) Web site, add the following directive in one of the global configuration files (such as access.conf):

```
Options +Includes
```

If you want to enable SSI support for a virtual Web site, put the preceding directive inside the appropriate <VirtualHost . . .> container. Or, if you want to be able to control this option from directory to directory, put this directive inside a <Directory . . .> container or in the per-directory access control file (.htaccess).

If you use a per-directory access control file (.htaccess) to enable SSI support, make sure the AllowOverride directive for the site owning that directory allows the Includes option to be overridden. For example, if the AllowOverride is set to None for a site, no SSI parsing will occur.

If you do not use the + sign in the Options line in the preceding example, all the options except Includes will be disabled.

Using SSI commands

SSI commands are embedded in HTML pages in the form of comments. The base command structure looks like this:

```
<!--#command argument1=value argument2=value
argument3=value -->
```

The value is often enclosed in double quotes; many commands allow only a single attribute-value pair. The comment terminator (-->) should be preceded by whitespace to ensure that it isn't considered part of the SSI command.

Next, the config, echo, exec, fsize, flastmod, include, printenv, and set SSI commands are examined.

config The config command enables you to configure error messages and output formats. Here is the syntax:

```
config [errmsg="error message"] [sizefmt=["bytes" |
"abbrev"] [timefmt=format string]
```

For example,

```
<!--#config errmsg="This is a custom SSI error message."
-->
<!--#config errmsg_typo="This is a custom error message."
-->
```

The first command is a valid config errmsg command that sets the error message to the string "This is a custom SSI error message." The second command is an invalid SSI command that causes a parse error; the error message "This is a custom SSI error message." is displayed as a result. The message appears where the invalid command is found. It is possible to enter HTML tags or even insert client-side script in the string of the error message.

To configure the output format for the file size, use the config sizefmt=["bytes" | "abbrev"] command. Acceptable format specifiers are "bytes" or "abbrev." For example,

```
<!-- config sizefmt="bytes" -->
```

shows file sizes in bytes. To show files in kilobytes or megabytes, use the following:

```
<!-- config sizefmt="abbrev" -->
```

To configure the display format for time, use the config timefmt=*format string* command. The commonly used value of the format string may consist of the following identifiers:

For example, the following shows the time in the format 05/20/1998:

```
<!--#config timefmt="%m/%d/%Y" -->
```

echo The echo command prints one of the Include variables or any of the CGI environment variables. Here is the syntax:

```
echo var="variable name"
```

Identifier	Description
%a	The abbreviated weekday name according to the current locale
%A	The full weekday name according to the current locale
%b	The abbreviated month name according to the current locale
%B	The full month name according to the current locale
%c	The preferred date and time representation for the current locale
%d	The day of the month as a decimal number (range 01 to 31)
%H	The hour as a decimal number using a 24-hour clock (range 00 to 23)
%I	The hour as a decimal number using a 12-hour clock (range 01 to 12)
%j	The day of the year as a decimal number (range 001 to 366)
%m	The month as a decimal number (range 01 to 12)
%M	The minute as a decimal number
%p	Either a.m. or p.m., according to the given time value or locale
%S	The second as a decimal number
%w	The day of the week as a decimal, Sunday being 0
%x	The preferred date representation for the current locale without the time
%X	The preferred time representation for the current locale without the date
%y	The year as a decimal number without a century (range 00 to 99)
%Y	The year as a decimal number including the century
%Z	The time zone name or abbreviation
%%	A literal % character

If the value of the variable is not available, it prints "(none)" as the value. Any dates printed are subject to the currently configured timefmt. For example,

```
<!--#config timefmt="%m/%d/%Y" -->
<!--#echo var="DATE_LOCAL" -->
```

prints a date, such as 05/20/1998, due to the specified timefmt string.

exec The exec command enables you to execute an external program, which can be a CGI program or any other type of executable, such as shell scripts or native-binary files. Here is the syntax:

```
exec [cgi="path/to/cgi/program"]
[cmd="path/to/other/program "]
```

If you use the IncludesNOEXEC value for the Options directive, the exec command is disabled. The exec cgi command runs the named program as a CGI script, and the exec cmd command runs the named program using the sh (/bin/sh) shell as an external program.

fsize The fsize command prints the size of the specified file. Here is the syntax:

```
fsize [ file="path" ] [ virtual="URL"]
```

When the first syntax (file="path") is used, the path is assumed to be relative to the directory containing the current SSI document being parsed. You can't use ../ in the path, nor can absolute paths be used. You can't access a CGI script in this fashion. You can, however, access another parsed document. For example:

```
<!--#fsize file="download.zip">
```

If the second syntax is used (virtual="URL"), the virtual path is assumed to be a (%-encoded) URL path. If the path does not begin with a slash (/), then it is taken to be relative to the current document. You must access a normal file this way, but you cannot access a CGI script in this fashion.

flastmod The flastmod command prints the last modification date of the specified file. Here is the syntax:

```
flastmod [ file = "path" ] [ virtual="URL"]
```

The output is subject to the timefmt format specification. For example:

```
<!--#flastmod file="free_software.zip">
<!--#flastmod virtual="/download/free_software.zip">
```

If you are unclear about the syntax difference, see the previous section regarding the fsize command as an example. To control how the modification date is printed, see the earlier description of the config command.

include The include directive inserts the text of a document into the SSI document being processed. Here is the syntax:

```
include [ file = "path" ]  [ virtual="URL"]
```

See the previous description of the fsize command for an explanation of the difference between file and virtual mode.

Any included file is subject to the usual access control. If the directory containing the parsed file has the option IncludesNOEXEC set, and including the document would cause a program to be executed, then it is not included. This prevents the execution of CGI scripts. Otherwise, CGI scripts are invoked as they normally are, using the complete URL given in the command, including any query string. For example,

```
<!--#include file="copyrights.html" -->
```

includes the copyrights.html file in the current document. Recursive inclusions are detected, and an error message is generated after the first pass.

printenv The printenv command prints a listing of all existing variables and their values. Here is the syntax:

```
printenv
```

For example, the following prints all the Include and CGI environment variables available:

```
<!--#printenv -->
```

Use the <PRE> tag pair to make the output more readable. Also note that displaying the output of this command in a publicly accessible page might give away somewhat sensitive information about your system. Therefore, use this command only for debugging purposes.

set The set command sets the value of a user-defined variable. Here is the syntax:

```
set var="name" value="something"
```

For example,

```
<!--#set var="home" value="index.shtml" -->
```

Note that any variable set using the preceding command is not persistent. In other words, every time a page that uses the set command is loaded, all the variables are reset.

Using SSI variables

The SSI module makes available to all SSI files a set of variables, in addition to the CGI environment variables, called the include variables. These variable can be used by SSI commands (echo, if, elif, and so on) and by any program invoked by an SSI command. The include variables are the following:

- **DATE_GMT.** The current date in Greenwich Mean Time.
- **DATE_LOCAL.** The current date in the local time zone.
- **DOCUMENT_NAME.** The current SSI filename.
- **DOCUMENT_URI.** The (%-decoded) URL path of the document.
- **LAST_MODIFIED.** The last modification date of the current file. The date is subject to the config command's timefmt format.

The include variables and the CGI variables are preset and available for use. Any of the variables that are preset can be used as arguments for other commands. The syntax for using defined variables is as follows:

```
<!--#command argument1="$variable1"
argument2="$variable2" . . . -->
```

The variable name is prefixed by a $ sign. Here's another example:

```
<!--#config errmsg="An error occurred in $DOCUMENT_NAME
page." -->
```

When using variables in a var="variable" field, the $ sign is not necessary. For example:

```
<!--#echo var="DOCUMENT_NAME" -->
```

If you need to insert a literal dollar sign into the value of a variable, you can insert the dollar sign by using backslash quoting. For example,

```
<!--#set var="password" value="\$cheese" -->
<!--#echo var="password" -->
```

prints $cheese as the value of the variable "password."

Also, if you need to reference a variable name in the middle of a character sequence that might otherwise be considered a valid identifier on its own, use a pair of braces around the variable name. For example,

```
<!--#set var="uniqueid"
value="${DATE_LOCAL}_${REMOTE_HOST}" -->
```

sets uniqueid to something such as Tue May 20 06:47:48 1998_206.171.50.51, depending on the timefmt setting.

Using SSI flow control commands

As in programming languages, flow control is available in the SSI module. By using flow control commands, you can conditionally create different output. The simplest flow control (that is, conditional) statement is the following:

```
<!--#if expr="test_expression" -->
<!--#endif -->
```

The *test_expression* is evaluated, and if the result of the test is true, then all the text up to the endif command is included in the output. The *test_expression* can be a string, which is true if the string is not empty, or a comparison expression that involves two strings and a comparison operator, such as = (equal), != (not equal), < (less than), > (greater than), <= (less than or equal to), or >= (greater than or equal to). The following is an example of a string by itself:

```
<!--#if expr="foobar" -->
   This test is successful.
<!--#endif -->
```

This always displays "This test is successful" because the expression is true when the test_expression is a nonnull string. If expr="foobar" is changed to expr="" or expr="''", however, then the text within the if-endif block will never be part of the output.

The following is an example of a string equality test:

```
<!--#set var="quicksearch" value="yes" -->
<!--#if expr="$quicksearch = yes" -->
   Quick search is requested.
```

```
<!--#endif -->
```

The variable called quicksearch is being set with the value yes and is later being compared with yes. Because the set value and the comparison value are equal, the "Quick search is requested" line is the output. If you require more-complex flow control constructs, you can use the following forms:

```
<!--#if expr="test_condition1" -->

<!--#elif expr="test_condition2" -->

<!--#else -->

<!--#endif -->
```

The elif directive enables you to create an else-if condition. For example:

```
<!--#if expr="${HTTP_USER_AGENT} = /MSIE/" -->

    <!--#set var="browser" value="IE" -->
    <!--#include flie="vbscript.html" -->

<!--#elif expr="${HTTP_USER_AGENT} = /Lynx/" -->

    <!--#set var="browser" value="Lynx" -->
    <!--#include flie="simple-html.html" -->

<!--#else -->

    <!--#set var="browser" value="Navigator" -->
    <!--#include flie="javascript.html" -->

<!--#endif -->
```

The HTTP_USER_AGENT variable in the first line is checked to see whether it contains the string MSIE (a string used by Microsoft Internet Explorer browser). If it does contain this string, then the browser variable is set to "IE" and a file named vbscript.html is inserted in the current document. On the other hand, if the HTTP_USER_AGENT does not contain the MSIE string, it is assumed to be the other leading browser, Netscape Navigator, and thus the browser variable is set to "Navigator" and the javascript.html file is inserted in the current document. By using the if-then-else construct, this example sets a different value to the same variable and loads different files.

Hosting virtual Web sites

Apache supports two types of virtual hosts—IP-based virtual hosts and name-based virtual hosts. No matter what type of virtual host you choose to implement, proper Domain Name Service (DNS) configuration is a prerequisite. IP-based virtual host configuration requires unique IP addresses for each virtual host, and name-based virtual hosts are created using CNAME records.

Apache configuration for virtual hosts

You can configure Apache in two ways to enable it to support multiple hosts (the main server and the virtual servers):

- Run multiple daemons, so that each host has a separate httpd daemon.

- Run a single daemon that supports all the virtual hosts and the primary server host.

The second approach is widely used and preferable in most cases. Hence, only this method is discussed in this section.

A single httpd daemon launches child processes to service requests for the primary Web site and all the virtual sites; by default, Apache listens to port 80 on all IP addresses of the local machine, and this is often sufficient. If you have a more complex requirement, such as listening on various port numbers or listening only to specific IP addresses, the BindAddress or Listen directive can be used.

Apache uses the special container <VirtualHost> in the httpd.conf file to handle all the virtual host-specific configurations. An example of a minimal virtual host configuration might look like this:

```
<VirtualHost 192.168.0.50>
```

```
DocumentRoot "/www/apachehandbook/public/htdocs"
ServerName www.apachehandbook.com
</VirtualHost>
```

The first line marks the start of a virtual host (`www.apachehandbook.com`) configuration. The enclosed IP address needs to be a valid IP for `www.apachehandbook.com`. If a nonstandard (that is, not 80) port address needs to be used, it can be supplied as follows:

```
<VirtualHost IP-address:port>
```

For example,

```
<VirtualHost 192.168.0.50:8080>
```

Any directive inside a <VirtualHost> container applies only to that virtual host. Any directive that has been used outside the <VirtualHost> containers constitutes the primary server's configuration. Each virtual host inherits the primary server's configuration, unless a conflict exists. In a case in which the same directive is used both in the main server configuration and in a virtual host configuration (that is, inside a <VirtualHost> container), the directive inside the virtual host configuration overrides the primary server's setting for only that particular virtual host.

For example, if you have ServerName set to `www.yourcompany.com` in your primary server configuration (that is, outside any <VirtualHost> container), and you have a ServerName directive in a <VirtualHost> container set to `www.yourclient.com`, then obviously you want the virtual host to respond to `www.yourclient.com`. That's exactly what happens; the directive within the virtual host section overrides the main server's corresponding directive. It may be easier to think of the main server configuration as the global default configuration for all virtual hosts that you create using the <VirtualHost>. So, when configuring virtual hosts, you need to decide what changes need to be made in each of the virtual host configurations.

The directives either override the configuration given in the primary server or supplement it, depending on the directive. For example, the DocumentRoot directive in a <VirtualHost> container overrides the primary server's DocumentRoot, whereas the AddType directive supplements the main server's MIME types.

Now, when a request arrives, Apache uses the IP address and port on which it arrived to find a matching virtual host configuration. If no virtual host matches the address and port, it is handled by the primary server configuration. If it does match a virtual host address, Apache uses the configuration of that virtual server to handle the request.

In the previous example, the virtual host configuration used is the same as the primary server, except that the DocumentRoot is set to /www/apachehandbook/public/htdocs, and the ServerName is set to www.apachehandbook.com. Directives commonly set in <VirtualHost> containers are DocumentRoot, ServerName, ErrorLog, and TransferLog.

You can put almost any configuration directive in the VirtualHost container, with the exception of ServerType, StartServers, MaxSpareServers, MinSpareServers, MaxRequestsPerChild, BindAddress, Listen, PidFile, TypesConfig, ServerRoot, and NameVirtualHost. User and Group may be used inside VirtualHost containers if the suEXEC wrapper is used.

You can have as many <VirtualHost> containers as you want. You can have one or more of your virtual hosts handled by the primary server, or have a <VirtualHost> for every available address and port and leave the primary server with no requests to handle.

Apache configuration for IP-based virtual hosts Setting up IP-based virtual hosts in a single primary Apache server configuration is very simple. Simply create a <VirtualHost> container per virtual IP-address. For example, to create a virtual host called vhost1.domain.com (192.168.0.50) with /www/vhost1/ as the DocumentRoot directory, add the following lines in the httpd.conf file:

```
<VirtualHost 192.168.0.50>
   DocumentRoot "/www/vhost1"
   ServerName vhost1.domain.com
</VirtualHost>
```

Apache configuration for name-based virtual hosts Setting up name-based virtual hosts is also very easy. The first step is to set the NameVirtualHost directive to the IP address of the name-based virtual hosts. This directive specifies an IP address that should be used as a target for name-based virtual hosts. For example, suppose that you want to set up two virtual hosts, such as www.client1.com and www.client2.com, on an Apache server that listens to IP address 192.168.0.50. Here is an example configuration for such a setup:

```
NameVirtualHost 192.168.0.50

<VirtualHost 192.168.0.50>
  ServerName www.client1.com
  DocumentRoot "/www/client1"
</VirtualHost>

<VirtualHost 192.168.0.50>
  ServerName www.client2.com
  DocumentRoot "/www/client2"
</VirtualHost>
```

You need only a single NameVirtualHost directive per IP address for all the name-based virtual hosts using that IP address. When a request comes for one of these virtual hosts from an HTTP/1.1-compliant browser, Apache matches the ServerName directive with the host name provided in the Host header of the request. Thus, Apache is able to determine which virtual host was requested.

After you create the virtual host configuration for Apache, start (or restart) the Apache server so that the configuration takes effect. Also, don't forget to create any directories that you might be using in a virtual host configuration, before you restart your Apache server.

Tip

Starting with Apache 1.3.*x*, you can verify your virtual host configuration by running Apache using the –s option.

Using Apache as a proxy server

Proxy support in Apache comes from the mod_proxy module. This module is not compiled by default.

Compiling the proxy module

If you are using the APACI interface to compile and install Apache, then building a new Apache executable with the proxy module is as easy as performing the following steps in your Apache source distribution directory:

1. If you are running the configure script for the first time, enter the following command:

   ```
   ./configure
   -prefix=/dir/where/you/want/to/install/apache \
   --enable-mode=proxy
   ```

   Conversely, if you have already run the configure script to compile Apache, enter the following:

   ```
   ./config.status  --enable-module=proxy
   ```

   Your previous configuration options will be applied when creating a new configuration file.

2. Run the make command. If it returns no error messages, run the make install command to install the newly compiled Apache executable in the appropriate directory.

Proxy module directives

The proxy module for Apache comes with the set of directives that you need to use the module. All of these directives are usable in both the main server configuration and any virtual server configuration context.

ProxyRequests on | off

This directive allows you to enable or disable the caching proxy service. However, it does not affect the functionality of the ProxyPass directive. The default value is off.

ProxyRemote *match remote-proxy-server-URL*

This directive enables you to interface your proxy server with another proxy server. The value of match can be either the name of a URL scheme (http, ftp, and so on) or a partial URL.

remove-proxy-server-URL can be http://remote-proxy-*hostname*: *port*. Currently, only the HTTP protocol is supported. In other words, you can specify only a proxy server that deals with the HTTP protocol; however, you can forward FTP requests from your proxy server to one that supports both HTTP and FTP protocols, as follows:

```
ProxyRemote ftp http://ftp.proxy.nitec.com:8000
```

This sends all FTP requests that come to the local proxy server to `ftp://ftp.proxy.nitec.com`. The requests will be sent via HTTP, so the actual FTP transaction will occur at the remote proxy server.

If you just want to forward all proxy requests for a certain Web site to its proxy server directly, you can do that with the ProxyRemote directive. For example,

```
ProxyRemote http://www.isp.com/ http://web-
proxy.isp.com:8000
```

sends all requests that match **www.isp.com** to **web-proxy.bigisp.com**. If you want to forward all of your proxy requests to another proxy, however, you can use the asterisk as the match phrase. For example,

```
ProxyRemote * http://proxy.domain.com
```

sends all local proxy requests to the proxy server at **proxy.domain.com**.

```
ProxyPass relative-URL destination-URL
```

This directive enables you to map a Web server's document tree onto your proxy server's document space. For example,

```
ProxyPass /internet/microsoft      www.formserv.com/
```

The above ProxyPass directive, found in the httpd.conf file of a proxy server called **proxy.nitec.com**, permits users of the proxy server to access the FormServ Web site using the URL:

```
http://proxy.nitec.com/internet/formserv
```

This directive (ProxyPass) makes proxy.nitec.com act like a mirror of the www.formserv.com Web site. Any request that uses the *relative-URL* will be converted internally into a proxy request for the *destination-URL*.

```
ProxyPassReverse relative-URL destination-URL
```

This directive is useful when you want to create a reverse proxy server using Apache. In such a reverse proxy setup, this directive fixes the Location headers that might be returned by the actual Web server. For example, in the following, `www.nitec.com` is the proxy server that gets all the pages from another server called `realserver.nitec.com`:

```
<Virtualhost 206.171.50.50>
  ServerName www.nitec.com
  ProxyRequests on
  ProxyPass / realserver.nitec.com/
  ProxyPassReverse / realserver.nitec.com/
</VirtualHost>
```

The ProxyPass directive enables this feature. However, if a page on `realserver.nitec.com` sends a Location header in response, the ProxyPassReverse directive fixes it so that the proxy server `www.nitec.com` is not bypassed by the client.

ProxyBlock *partial or full host name . . .*

This directive enables you to block access to a named host or domain. For example,

ProxyBlock gates

blocks access to any host that has the word "gates" in its name. This way, access to `http://gates.ms.com` or `http://gates.friendsof-bill.com` will be blocked. You also can specify multiple hosts, as follows:

ProxyBlock apple orange.com banana.com

This directive blocks all access to any host that matches any of the preceding words or domain names. The mod_proxy module attempts to determine the IP addresses for these hosts during server startup and caches them for matching later.

To block access to all hosts, use the following:

ProxyBlock *

This effectively disables your proxy server.

NoProxy *Domain name| Subnet | IP Address | Hostname*

This directive gives you some control over the ProxyRemote directive in an intranet environment. You can specify a domain name, subnet, IP address, or host name not to be served by the proxy server specified in the ProxyRemote directive. For example:

```
ProxyRemote   *  http://firewall.yourcompany.com:8080
NoProxy          .yourcompany.com
```

All requests for *anything*.yourcompany.com (such as www.yourcompany.com) will be served by the local proxy server, and everything else will go to the firewall.yourcompany.com proxy server.

ProxyDomain *Domain*

This directive specifies the default domain name for the proxy server. When this directive is set to the local domain name on an intranet, as in the following example, any request that does not include a domain name will get this domain name appended in the request:

```
ProxyDomain    .nitec.com
```

When a user of the nitec.com domain sends a request for a URL such as http://marketing/us.html, the request will be regenerated as the following URL:

```
http://marketing.nitec.com/us.html
```

Note that the domain name you specify must have a leading period.

ProxyReceiveBufferSize *bytes*

This directive sets the network buffer size for outgoing requests from the proxy server. It has to be greater than 512. However, to use the system's default buffer size, set this directive to 0.

CacheRoot *directory*

This directive allows you to enable disk caching. You can specify a directory name to which the proxy server can write cached files. The Apache server running the proxy module must have write permission for the directory. For example,

```
CacheRoot /www/proxy/cache
```

tells Apache to write proxy cache data to the /www/proxy/cache directory. You need to specify the size of the cache using the CacheSize directory before the proxy server can start using this directory for caching. You also may need to use other cache directives, such as CacheSize, CacheMax Expire, CacheDefaultExpire, CacheGcInterval, and CacheDirLength, to create a usable disk caching proxy solution.

CacheSize *n kilobytes*

This directive specifies the amount of disk space (in K) that should be used for disk caching. The cached files are written in the directory specified by the CacheRoot directive. Note that it is possible for the proxy server to write more data than the specified limit, but the proxy server's garbage collection scheme will delete files until the usage is at or below this setting. The default setting (5K) is unrealistic; I recommend anywhere from 10MB to 1GB, depending on your user load.

CacheGcInterval *n hours*

This directive specifies the time interval (in hours) at which Apache should check the cache directories to delete expired files. This is also when Apache enforces the disk space usage limit specified by the CacheSize directive.

CacheMaxExpire *n hours*

This directive specifies the time (in hours) when all cached documents expire. In other words, if you specify this directive as

CacheMaxExpire 48

all the cached documents will expire in 48 hours, or 2 days. This directive overrides any expiration date specified in the document itself; so, if a document has an expiration date later than the maximum specified by this directive, the document is still removed. The default value is 24.

CacheLastModifiedFactor *floating point number*

This directive specifies a factor (the default is 0.1) used to calculate the expiration time when the original Web server does not supply an expiration date for a document. The calculation is done using the following formula:

```
expiry-period = (last modification time for the
document) * (floating point number)
```

So, if a document was last modified 24 hours ago, the default factor of 0.1 makes Apache calculate the expiration time for this document to be 2.4 hours. If the calculated expiration period is longer than that set by CacheMaxExpire, the latter takes precedence.

CacheDirLength *length*

When disk caching is on, Apache creates subdirectories in the directory specified by the CacheRoot directive. This directive specifies the number of characters (the default is 1) used in creating the subdirectory names. You really do not need to change the default for this directive.

CacheDirLevels *levels*

This directive specifies the number of subdirectories that Apache will create to store cache data files (the default value is 3). See CacheDirLength for related information.

CacheDefaultExpire *n hours*

This directive provides a default time (in hours) that is used to expire a cached file when the last modification time of the file is unknown (the default value is 1). CacheMaxExpire does not override this setting.

CacheForceCompletion *percentage*

This directive tells the proxy server to continue transferring a document from the remote HTTP/FTP server even if the request is canceled. The percentage specified in the directive makes the proxy server determine whether it should continue with the transfer. The default value is 90 percent, which tells the proxy server to continue transferring when 90 percent of the document is already cached. You can change the value from 1 to 100.

NoCache *Domain name| Subnet | IP Address | Hostname . . .*

The NoCache directive specifies a list of hosts, domain names, and IP addresses, separated by spaces, for which no caching is performed. This directive should be used to disable caching of local Web servers on an intranet. Note that the proxy server also matches partial names of a host. If you want to disable caching altogether, use the following:

```
NoCache *
```

To enable the proxy server, you need to set the ProxyRequests directive to On. After that, the additional configuration depends on what you want to do with your proxy server. Whatever you decide to do with it, any proxy configuration that you choose should go inside a special <Directory . . .> container that looks like the following:

```
<Directory proxy:*>
. . .
</Directory>
```

Any directives that you want to use to control the proxy server's behavior should go inside this container. The asterisk is a wildcard for the requested URL. In other words, when a request for www.nitec.com is processed by the Apache server, it looks like this:

```
<Directory proxy:http://www.nitec.com/>
. . .
</Directory>
```

You also can use the <Directory ~ /RE/> container, which uses regular expressions; for example,

```
<Directory ~ proxy:http://[^:/]+/.*>
. . .
</Directory>
```

Caching remote Web sites

Because a great deal of Web content on both the Internet and intranets is likely to be static, caching it on a local proxy server could save valuable network bandwidth. A cache-enabled proxy server will fetch requested documents only when the cache contains an expired document or when the requested document is not present in the cache. To enable caching on your proxy server, you need to specify caching directives inside a special directory container. For example, the following configuration defines a caching proxy server that writes cache files to the /www/cache directory:

```
<Directory proxy:*>
CacheRoot /www/cache
CacheSize 1024
CacheMaxExpire 24
</Directory>
```

It is permitted to write 1,024K of data (1MB), and the cache must expire after each day (24 hours).

To prevent outside people from abusing your proxy, you can restrict proxy access either by host or by username/password authentication.

To control which hosts have access to the proxy server, create a configuration such as the following, which denies access to all but myhost.nitec.com:

```
<Directory proxy:*>
AuthType Basic
AuthName Proxy
order deny,allow
deny from all
allow from myhost.nitec.com
</Directory>
```

If you want to use username/password authentication, you can use something similar to the following:

```
<Directory proxy:*>
AuthType Basic
AuthName Proxy
AuthUserFile /path/to/proxy/.htpasswd
AuthName Proxy
require valid-user
</Directory>
```

Create the .htpasswd file by using the htpasswd utility that comes with Apache.

You also can restrict access for a protocol, as shown in the following example:

```
<Directory proxy:http:*>
. . .
</Directory>
```

This enables you to control how HTTP requests are processed by your proxy server.

Similarly, you can use the following to control how each of these protocols is handled by the proxy server:

```
<Directory proxy:ftp:*>
. . .
</Directory>
```

You can also create a virtual host exclusively for your proxy server. In that case, the directives should go inside the proxy host's <VirtualHost> container:

```
<VirtualHost proxy.host.com:*>
. . .
</VirtualHost>
```

Mirroring a Web site

A mirror Web site is a local copy of a remote Web site. For example, if you want to mirror the www.apache.org Web site so that your users can connect to your mirror site for quick access to Apache information, you can use the proxy server to create such a mirror, as follows:

```
ProxyPass / www.apache.org/
ProxyPassReverse / www.apache.org/
CacheRoot /www/cache
CacheDefaultExpire 24
```

This makes a proxy server a mirror of the www.apache.org Web site. For example, this configuration turns my proxy server blackhole.nitec.com into a www.apache.org mirror. Users who enter http://

blackhole.nitec.com as the URL receive the Apache mirror's index page just as if they had gone to www.apache.org.

Caution

Before you mirror someone else's Web site, you must get their permission, because copyright issues may be involved.

Creating a reverse proxy server

Reverse proxy servers are needed when the real HTTP/FTP server is behind a firewall or some load-balancing scheme needs to be in place to speed up or distribute delivery of the content. Creating a reverse proxy server is quite easy with the latest proxy module found in Apache 1.3.*x*. Suppose that you have a Web server with host name realserver.your-company.com and you want to have everyone visit it via a reverse proxy server called www.yourcompany.com (11.22.33.44). You can create the following virtual host on .yourcompany.com server:

```
<VirtualHost 11.22.33.44>
  ServerName www.yourcompany.com
  ProxyPass / realserver.yourcompany.com/
  ProxyPassReverse / realserver.yourcompany.com/
  CacheRoot /www/cache
  CacheDefaultExpire 24
</VirtualHost>
```

This makes the proxy server a reverse proxy for realserver.yourcom-pany.com. To your visitors, it appears as if they are accessing www.your-company.com.

Authenticating Web users

Knowing how to create password-protected, restricted areas in a Web site is a must for any Web administrator. By default, Apache supports authentication schemes such as host-based authentication and basic HTTP authentication.

Using host-based authentication

In this authentication scheme, access is controlled by the host name or the host's IP address. When a request is made for a certain resource, the Web server first checks whether the requesting host is allowed access to the resource, and then takes action based on its findings. The standard Apache distribution includes a module called mod_access, which provides this access control support by using directives such as Allow, Deny, Order, Allow from env=variablename, and Deny from env=variablename.

```
Allow from host1 host2 host3 . . .
```

This directive enables you to define a list of hosts (containing one or more hosts or IP addresses) that are allowed access to a certain directory. When more than one host or IP address is specified, they should be separated with space characters. Table 12-1 shows the possible values for the directive.

Table 12-1 *Possible Values for the allow Directive*

Value	Example	Description
All	allow from all	This reserved word allows access for all hosts. The example shows how to use this option.
A fully qualified domain name (FQDN) of a host	allow from wormhole. nitec.com	Only the host that has the specified FQDN is allowed access. The allow directive in the example allows access only to `wormhole.nitec. com`. Note that this compares whole components; thus, `toys.com` would not match `etoys.com`
A partial domain name of a host	allow from .mainoffice. nitec.com	Only hosts that match the partial host name are allowed access. The example permits all hosts in the `.mainoffice.nitec. com` network to access the site. For example, `developer1. mainoffice.nitec. com` and `developer2. mainoffice.nitec. com` have access to the site, but `developer3. baoffice.nitec.com` is not allowed access.

Continued

Listing 12-1 *Continued*

Value	Example	Description
A full IP address of a host	allow from 206.171.50.50	Only the specified IP address is allowed access. The example shows a full IP address (all four octets of IP are present), 206.171.50.50, that is allowed access.
A partial IP address	Example 1: allow from 206.171.50 Example 2: allow from 130.86	When not all four octets of an IP address are present in the allow direc tive, the partial IP address is matched from left to right, and hosts that have the matching IP address pattern (that is, it is part of the same subnet) are allowed access. In the first example, all hosts with IP addresses in the range of 206.171.50.1 to 206.171.50.255 have access. In the second example, all hosts from the 130.86 network are allowed access.
A network/netmask pair	Allow from 206.171.50.0/ 255.255.255.0	This enables you to specify a range of IP addresses by using the network and the netmask address. The exam- ple allows only the hosts with IP addresses in the range of 206.171.50.1 to 206.171.50.255 to have access. This feature is available in Apache 1.3 or later.
A network/nnn CIDR specification	Allow 206.171.50.0/24	Similar to the previous entry, except the netmask consists of *nnn* high- order 1 bits. The example is equiva- lent to allow from 206.171.50.0/ 255.255.255.0. This feature is available in Apache 1.3 or later.

```
deny from host1 . . .
```

This directive is the exact opposite of the allow directive. It enables you to define a list of hosts that are denied access to a specified directory. Like the allow directive, it can accept all the values shown in Table 12-1.

```
order deny, allow | allow, deny | mutual-failure
```

This directive controls how Apache evaluates both allow and deny directives. For example, the following denies the host `myboss.mycompany.com` access and allows all other hosts to access the directory:

```
<Directory "/mysite/myboss/rants">
  order deny, allow
  deny from myboss.mycompany.com
  allow from all
</Directory>
```

The value for the order directive is a comma-separated list, which indicates which directive takes precedence. Typically, the one that affects all hosts is given lowest priority. In the preceding example, because the allow directive affects all hosts, it is given the lowest priority When this directive is set to mutual-failure, only those hosts appearing on the allow list but not on the deny list are to be granted access. In all cases, every allow and deny directive is evaluated.

`allow from env=variable`

This directive, a variation of the allow directive, allows access when the named environment variable is set. This is useful only if you are using other directives, such as BrowserMatch, to set an environment variable. For example,

```
BrowserMatch "MSIE" ms_browser
<Directory "/path/to/Vbscript_directory">
  order deny,allow
  deny from all
  allow from env=ms_browser
</Directory>
```

Here, the Apache server will set the ms_browser environment variable for all browsers that provide the MSIE string as part of the User-Agent header. The allow directive will allow only browsers for which the ms_browser variable is set.

`deny from env=variable`

This directive, a variation of the deny directive, denies access capability for all hosts for which the specified environment is set. For example,

```
BrowserMatch "MSIE" ms_browser
<Directory "/path/to/Vbscript_directory">
  order deny,allow
  allow from all
  deny from env=ms_browser
</Directory>
```

blocks access for all Web browsers that send MSIE string as part of the User-Agent header in a request.

Using HTTP-specified basic authentication

Support for HTTP-specified basic authentication in Apache has been around for quite a while. By default, Apache provides authentication support using the mod_auth.c module.

Using standard mod_auth

This module is compiled by default in the standard distribution. Standard mod_auth-based basic HTTP authentication uses usernames, groups, and passwords stored in text files to confirm authentication. This works well when you are dealing with few users. However, if you have a lot of users (thousands or more), use of mod_auth might have a performance penalty. In such a case, you can use something more advanced, such as DBM files, Berkeley DB files, or even a SQL database. The default authentication module offers the following directives:

```
AuthUserFile filename
```

This directive sets the name of the text file that contains the usernames and passwords used in the basic HTTP authentication. You must provide a fully qualified path to the file to be used. For example:

```
AuthUserFile /www/nitec/secrets/.htpasswd
```

This file is usually created using a support utility called htpasswd. The format of this file is very simple. Each line contains a single username and an encrypted password. To enhance security, keep the AuthUserFile-specified file resides outside the document tree of your Web site.

`AuthGroupFile` *filename*

This directive specifies a text file to be used as the list of user groups for basic HTTP authentication. The filename is the absolute path to the group file. You can create this file using any text editor. The format of this file is as follows:

`groupname:` *username1 username2 username3* . . .

To enhance security, make sure the AuthGroupFile-specified file resides outside the document tree of your Web site.

`AuthAuthoritative` on | off

If you are using more than one authentication scheme for the same directory, you can set this directive to **on** so that when a username/password pair fails with the first scheme, it is passed on to the next (lower) level.

The following is an example of basic authentication that shows how to create a restricted directory that requires a username and a password for access. To simplify the example, assume the following are settings for a Web site called **apache.nitec.com**:

```
DocumentRoot "/data/web/apache/public/htdocs"
AccessFileName .htaccess
AllowOverride All
```

Also assume that you want to restrict access to the following directory, such that only a user named "reader" with the password "bought-it" is able to access the /www/IDGbooks/readers/ directory. Follow these steps to create the restricted access.

Step 1: Create a user file using htpasswd The standard Apache distribution comes with a utility program called htpasswd, which creates the user file needed for the AuthUserFile directive. Use the program as follows:

```
htpasswd -c /data/web/apache/secrets/.htpasswd reader
```

The htpasswd utility asks for the password "reader." Enter **bought-it** and then reenter the password again to confirm that you didn't make a typo. After you reenter the password, the utility creates a file called .htpasswd in the /data/web/apache/secrets directory. Note the following:

- Use the −c option to tell htpasswd that you want to create a new user file. If you already had the password file and wanted to add a new user, you would not want this option.

- Place the user file outside the document root directory of the apache.nitec.com site, because you do not want anyone to download it via the Web.

- Use a leading period (.) in the filename so that it will not appear in the ls output unless the −a option is specified. This is a simple attempt to hide files from prying eyes.

To save future headaches, execute the following command:

```
cat /data/web/apache/secrets/.htpasswd
```

This should show a line similar to the following (the password won't be exactly the same as this example):

```
reader:hulR6FFh1sxK6
```

This confirms that you have a user called reader in the .htpasswd file. The password bought-it is encrypted by the htpasswd program using the standard crypt() function.

Step 2: Create an .htaccess file   Using a text editor, add the following lines to a file named /data/web/apache/public/htdocs/chapter12/.htaccess:

```
AuthName "IDG Readers Only"
AuthType  Basic
AuthUserFile /data/web/apache/secrets/.htpasswd
require user reader
```

The following list describes the directives in the preceding syntax:

- **AuthName.** Sets the realm of the authentication. This is really just a label that is sent to the Web browser so that the user will be provided with some clue about what he or she is about to access. In this case, the "IDG Readers Only" string indicates that only IDG readers can access this directory.

- **AuthType.** Specifies the type of authentication to be used. Because only basic authentication is supported, AuthType is always set to Basic.

- **AuthUserFile.** Specifies the filename for the user file. The path to the user file is provided here.

- **require.** Specifies that a user named "reader" is allowed access to this directory.

Step 3: Set file permissions After you create the .htaccess and.htpasswd files, it is important to make sure that only Apache can read the files. No users except the file owner and Apache should have access to these files.

Step 4: Test Use a Web browser to access the following URL: http://apache.nitec.com/chapter 12. Apache will send the 401 status header and WWW-Authenticate response header to the browser with the realm (set in AuthName) and authentication type (set in AuthType) information. The browser will display a pop-up dialog box that requests a username and password.

Check whether you can get in without a username or password, by entering nothing in the entry boxes in the dialog box and pressing the OK button. This should result in an authentication failure. The browser receives the same authentication challenge again, so it displays another dialog box.

Choosing the Cancel button results in the browser showing the standard "Authentication Required" error message from Apache.

Pressing the Reload button on the browser requests the same URL again, and the browser receives the same authentication challenge from the server. This time, enter **reader** as the username, enter **bought-it** as the password, and press the OK button. Apache will now allow you to access the directory.

You can change the "Authentication Required" message if you want by using the ErrorDocument directive:

```
ErrorDocument 401 /nice_401message.html
```

Insert this line in your httpd.conf file and create a nice message in the nice_401message.html file.

Instead of allowing a single user called reader to access the restricted area, as demonstrated in the previous example, in the next example, you will allow anyone belonging to a group named asb_readers to access the same directory. Assume this group has two users: pikejb and bcaridad. Follow these steps to give the users in group asb_readers directory access.

Step 1: Create a user file using htpasswd Using the htpasswd utility, create the users **pikejb** and **bcaridad**.

Step 2: Create a group file Using a text editor such as vi, create a file named **/data/web/apache/secrets/.htgroup**. This file has a single line, as follows:

```
asb_readers: pikejb bcaridad
```

Step 3: Create an .htaccess file Using a text editor, create a file named **/www/IDGbooks/readers/.htaccess** and add the following lines:

```
AuthName "IDG Readers Only"
AuthType  Basic
AuthUserFile /data/web/apache/secrets/.htpasswd
AuthGroupFile /data/web/apache/secrets/.htgroup
require group  asb_readers
```

This is almost the same configuration discussed in the previous example, but with two changes: the addition of a new directive, AuthGroupFile, which points to the .htgroup group file created earlier, and the require directive line, which now requires a group called "asb_readers." In other words, Apache will allow access to anyone that belongs to that group. Note that you could have just as easily used the following line:

```
require user pikejb bcaridad
```

instead of

```
require group asb_readers
```

However, listing all users in the require line could become cumbersome and cause unnecessary headaches. Using group, you can easily add or remove multiple users. As in the previous example, make sure the .htaccess, .htpasswd, and .htgroup files are readable only by Apache, and that no one but the owner has write access to the files.

You can also mix Apache's host-based access control with the basic HTTP authentication scheme. For example,

```
AuthName "IDG Readers Only"
AuthType  Basic
AuthUserFile /data/web/apache/secrets/.htpasswd
AuthGroupFile /data/web/apache/secrets/.htgroup
require group  asb_readers
order deny, allow
deny from all
allow from .nitec.com
```

This is same as the last example, but it adds three host-based access control directives:

- **order.** Tells Apache to evaluate the deny directive before the allow directive.
- **deny.** Tells Apache to refuse access from all hosts.
- **allow.** Tells Apache to allow access from the `apache-train-ing.nitec.com` domain. This effectively tells Apache that any hosts in the `.nitec.com` domain are welcome to this directory.

Here, Apache will assume that both host-based and basic HTTP authentication are required for this directory. If you want to allow access when a user enters a valid username/password pair or makes the request from the `nitec.com` domain, you need to add satisfy any at the end of the preceding configuration.

Monitoring server status

The module mod_status.c enables Apache administrators to monitor the server via the Web. An HTML page is created with server statistics. This module also produces a page that is machine-readable. The information displayed on both pages includes: server version and compilation date/time stamp; current time on the server system; time when the server was last restarted; server uptime; total number of accesses served so far; total bytes transferred so far; the number of idle servers and their status; averages of the number of requests per second, number of bytes served per second, and number of bytes per request; CPU usage by each child server and total load placed on the server by Apache processes; and the list of virtual hosts and requests currently being processed.

This module is not compiled by default in the standard Apache distribution, so you need to compile it into your Apache executable (httpd) yourself. After you do so, you need to define a URL location that Apache should use to display the information. In other words, you need to tell Apache which URL will bring up the server statistics on your Web browser.

Suppose that your domain name is yourdomain.com and you want to use the following URL: www.mydomain.com/apache-status. Using the <Location . . .> container, you can tell the server that you want it to handle this URL by using the server-status handler found in the mod_status module. The following lines will do the job:

```
<Location /apache-status>
   SetHandler server-status
</Location>
```

The SetHandler directive sets the handler (server-status) for the previously mentioned URL. This configuration segment typically should go in the access.conf file, but it really can go inside any of the three configuration files.

After you add the configuration in one of the three files, you can restart the server and access the preceding URL from a browser. Note that the <Location . . .> container in this example enables anyone to see the server status using this URL, which may not be desirable as far as security is concerned. To make sure that only machines on your domain can access the status page, replace the preceding configuration with the following:

```
<Location /apache-status>
  SetHandler server-status
  order deny, allow
  deny from all
  allow from .yourdomain.com
</Location>
```

where *yourdomain.com* should be replaced with your own domain name. If you want only one or more selected hosts to have access to this page, simply list the host names in the allow directive line.

Tip

You can have the status page update itself automatically if you have a browser that supports the refresh command. Access the page   `http://www.yourdomain.com/server-status?refresh=N` to refresh the page every *N* seconds.

To simplify the status display, add **?auto** at the end of the URL. This query string tells Apache to display simplified output.

Logging hits and errors

By default, the standard Apache distribution includes a module called mod_log_config, which is responsible for the basic logging, and writes Common Log Format (CLF) log files by default. You can alter this behavior by using the LogFormat directive. However, CLF covers logging requirements in most environments.

The CLF file contains a separate line for each request. A line is composed of several tokens separated by spaces:

```
host ident authuser date request status bytes
```

If a token does not have a value, then it is represented by a hyphen (–). Tokens have the following meanings:

- **Host.** The fully qualified domain name of the client, or its IP address.

- **Ident.** If the IdentityCheck directive is enabled and the client machine runs identd, this is the identity information reported by the client.

- **Authuser.** If the requested URL required a successful Basic HTTP authentication, this is the username.

- **Date.** The date and time of the request.

- **Request.** The request line from the client, enclosed in double quotes.

- **Status.** The three-digit HTTP status code returned to the client.

- **Bytes.** The number of bytes in the object returned to the client, excluding all HTTP headers.

The date field can have the following format:

```
date = [day/month/year:hour:minute:second zone]
```

For example,

```
[02/Jan/1998:00:22:01 -0800]
```

Four directives are available in the mod_log_config module, the first of which follows:

```
TransferLog filename | "| /path/to/external/program"
```

This directive sets the name of the log file or program where the log information is to be sent. By default, the log information is in the CLF format, which can be customized using the LogFormat directive.

When the TransferLog directive is found within a virtual host container, the log information is formatted using the LogFormat directive found within the context. If a LogFormat directive is not found in the same context, however, the server's log format is used.

The TransferLog directive takes either a log file path or a pipe to an external program as the argument. The log filename is assumed to be relative to the ServerRoot setting if no leading / character is found. For example, if the ServerRoot is set to /etc/httpd, then the following tells Apache to send log information to the /etc/httpd/logs/access.log file:

```
TransferLog logs/access.log
```

When the argument is a pipe to an external program, the log information is sent to the external program's standard input (STDIN).

Note that a new program is not started for a virtual host if it inherits the TransferLog directive from the main server. If a program is used, then it is run under the user who started httpd. This will be the root if the server was started by the root. Be sure that the program is secure.

`LogFormat` *format* [*nickname*]

This directive sets the format of the default log file named by the TransferLog directive. The default value is "%h %l %u %t \"%r\" %s %b." If you include a nickname for the format on the directive line, you can use it in other LogFormat and CustomLog directives rather than repeat the entire format string. A LogFormat directive that defines a nickname does nothing else — that is, it only defines the nickname; it doesn't actually apply the format.

`CustomLog` *file-pipe* *format-or-nickname*

Like the TransferLog directive, the CustomLog directive enables you to send logging information to a log file or an external program. Unlike the TransferLog directive, however, it enables you to use a custom log format that can be specified as an argument.

The argument format specifies a format for each line of the log file. The options available for the format are exactly the same as for the argument of the LogFormat directive. If the format includes any spaces (which it will in almost all cases), it should be enclosed in double quotes.

Instead of an actual format string, you can use a format nickname defined with the LogFormat directive. (Nicknames are available only in Apache 1.3 or later.) Also, the TransferLog and CustomLog directives can be used multiple times in each server to cause each request to be logged to multiple files.

`CookieLog` *filename*

The CookieLog directive sets the filename for the logging of cookies. The filename is relative to the ServerRoot. This directive is included only for compatibility with mod_cookies and is deprecated; therefore, use of this directive is not recommended. Use the user-tracking module's directive instead. The user-tracking module mod_usertrack is discussed later in this chapter.

Customizing server log files

Although CLF meets most log requirements, sometimes you'll want to be able to customize your logging data. For example, you may want to log the type of browsers that are accessing your site, so that your Web design team can determine what type of browser-specific HTML to avoid or use. Or, perhaps you want to know which Web sites are sending (referring) visitors to your sites. All of this is accomplished quite easily in Apache. The default logging module, mod_log_config, supports custom logging.

Custom formats are set with the LogFormat and CustomLog directives of the module. The format argument to LogFormat and CustomLog is a string that can have both literal characters and special % format specifiers. When literal values are used in this string, they are copied into the log file for each request. The % specifiers, however, are replaced with corresponding values. The special % specifiers are described here:

Specifier	Description
%b	Bytes sent, excluding HTTP headers.
%f	The filename of the request.
%{variable}e	The contents of the environment variable VARIABLE.
%h	The remote host that made the request.
%{ IncomingHeader }i	The contents of IncomingHeader – that is, the header line(s) in the request sent to the server. The i character at the end denotes that this is a client (incoming) header.
%l	If the IdentityCheck directive is enabled and the client machine runs identd, then this is the identity information reported by the client.
%{MODULE_NOTE }n	The contents of the note MODULE_NOTE from another module.
%{ OutgoingHeader }o	The contents of OutgoingHeader – that is, the header line(s) in the reply. The o character at the end denotes that this is a server (outgoing) header.
%p	The port to which the request was served.
%P	The process ID of the child that serviced the request.
%r	The first line of the request.
%s	The status returned by the server in response to the request. When the request gets redirected, the value of this format specifier is still the original request status. If you want to store the redirected request status, use %.>s instead.

Continued

Continued

Specifier	Description
%t	The time of the request. The format of time is the same as in CLF format.
%{format}t	The time, in the form given by format. (Look at the strftime man page.)
%t	The time taken to serve the request, in seconds.
%u	If the requested URL required a successful Basic HTTP authentication, then the username is the value of this format specifier. The value may be bogus if the server returned a 401 status (Authentication Required) after the authentication attempt.
%u	The URL path requested.
%v	The name of the server or the virtual host to which the request came.

You can include conditional information in each of the preceding specifiers. The conditions can be presence (or absence) of certain HTTP status code(s). For example, suppose you want to log all referring URLs that pointed a user to a nonexistent page. In such a case, the server produces a 404 status (Not Found) header. So, to log the referring URLs you can use the format specifier:

```
'%404{Referer}i'
```

Similarly, to log referring URLs that resulted in an unusual status, you can use the following:

```
'%!200,304,302{Referer}i'
```

Notice the use of the ! character to denote the absence of the server status list.

Similarly, to include additional information at the end of the CLF format specifier, you can extend the CLF format, which is defined by the format string:

```
"%h %l %u %t \"%r\" %s %b"
```

For example, the following logs CLF format data and adds the Referer and User-agent information found in client-provided headers in each log entry:

```
"%h %l %u %t \"%r\" %s %b \"%{Referer}i\" \"%{User-
agent}i\""
```

Using error logs

If you don't log errors, you won't be able to determine what's wrong and where the error occurs. Interestingly, error logging is supported in the core Apache. The ErrorLog directive enables you to log all types of errors that Apache encounters. You can either specify a filename or use the syslog daemon (syslogd) to log all errors. For example,

```
ErrorLog /logs/error_log
```

causes Apache to write error messages to the /logs/error_log file. To log use of the syslog facility, use the following:

```
ErrorLog syslog
```

Using the LogLevel directive, you can specify what type of messages Apache should send to syslog. For example, the following instructs Apache to send debug messages to syslog:

```
ErrorLog syslog
LogLevel debug
```

If you want to store debug messages in a different file via syslog, then you need to modify /etc/syslog.conf. For example,

```
*.debug    /var/log/debug
```

Add this line in /etc/syslog.conf, restart syslogd (killall –HUP syslogd), and Apache will enable you to store all Apache debug messages to the /var/log/debug file. Also note that you can set LogLevel to any of the following settings:

- **emerg.** Emergency messages
- **alert.** Alert messages
- **crit.** Critical messages
- **error.** Error messages
- **warn.** Warnings
- **notice.** Notification messages
- **info.** Information messages

■ **debug.** Messages logged at debug level will also include the source file and line number where the message is generated, to help debugging and code development

Tip

If you want to see updates to your syslog or any other log files as they happen, use the **tail** utility with the **-f** */path/to/log* option.

Analyzing server log files

Many third-party Web server log analysis tools are available. Most of these tools expect the log files to be in CLF format, so make sure you have CLF formatting in your logs. Here are some of those tools and where you can find them:

■ **WebTrends:** http://www.webtrends.com/

■ **Wusage:** http://www.boutell.com/wusage/

■ **wwwstat:** http://www.ics.uci.edu/pub/websoft/wwwstat/

■ **http-analyze:** http://www.netstore.de/Supply/http-analyze/

■ **pwebstats:** http://www.unimelb.edu.au/pwebstats.html

■ **WebStat Explorer:** http://www.webstat.com/

■ **AccessWatch:** http://netpressence.com/accesswatch/

The best way to find out which one works for you is to try them out, or at least visit their Web sites for feature comparisons. Two utilities that I find very useful are Wusage and wwwstat. Wusage is my favorite commercial log-analysis application. It is highly configurable and produces great graphical reports using the company's well-known GD graphics library. I also like the free wwwstat program. It is written in Perl, so you need to have Perl installed on the system on which you want to run it.

Maintaining server log files

On Apache sites with high hit rates or many virtual domains, the log files can become huge in a very short time, which could easily cause a disk crisis. When log files become very large, you should rotate them. You have two options for rotating your logs: use a utility that comes with Apache called rotatelog, or use logrotate.

Using rotatelog   Apache comes with a support tool called rotatelog. You can use this program as follows:

```
TransferLog "| /path/to/rotatelogs logfile rotation time
in seconds"
```

For example, if you want to rotate the access log every 86,400 seconds (24 hours), use the following line:

```
TransferLog "| /path/to/rotatelogs /var/logs/httpd 86400"
```

You will have each day's access log information stored in a file called /var/logs/httpd.*nnnn*, where *nnnn* represents a long number.

Using logrotate   The logrotate utility rotates, compresses, and mails log files. It is designed to ease the system administration of log files. It enables the automatic rotation, compression, removal, and mailing of log files on a daily, weekly, or monthly basis, or on a size basis. Normally, logrotate is run as a daily cron job. You can create a file called /etc/logrotate.d/apache as follows:

```
/path/to/apache/access_log {
compress
rotate 5
main webmaster@yourdomain.com
errors root@yourdomain.com
size=1024K
postrotate
kill -HUP 'cat /path/to/httpd.pid'
endscript
}
```

This configuration specifies that the */path/to/apache/*access_log file be rotated whenever it grows over 1MB (1,024K) in size, and that the old log files be compressed and mailed to webmaster@*yourdomain*.com after going through five rotations, rather than being removed. Any errors that occur during processing of the log file are mailed to root@*yourdomain*.com.

Enhancing Web server security

To reduce security risks, you have to be on alert at all times. The number of things that you can do to your Web server to make it 100-percent secure is unlimited. Retaining a high degree of security is an ongoing process; you must keep yourself up to date on what is happening in the computer security area and take preventive measures as needed. This section discusses a few security issues specific to a Web server.

Installing Apache and not a Trojan horse

Apache is freely available software, so make sure to obtain it from a reliable source. Do not ever download Apache binaries or source code from just any Web or FTP site. Always check with the official site, www.apache.org, first. In the future, Apache source will be PGP (Pretty Good Privacy) signed.

Using a dedicated user and group for Apache

If you run Apache as a standalone server, create a dedicated user and group for Apache. Do not use the nobody user or the nogroup group, especially if your system has already defined these. Chances are good that your system is using them for other services or in other places. This might lead to administrative and security problems. Instead, create a fresh new user and group for Apache, and use them with the User, and Group directives.

Protecting ServerRoot and log directories

Make sure that the ServerRoot directories (especially the log directories and files) are not writable by anyone but the root user. You do not need to give Apache user/group read or write permission in log directories. Enabling anyone other than the root user to write files in the log directory could lead to a major security hole.

Disabling default access

A strict security model dictates that no default access exists, so get into the habit of permitting no access at first. Permit specific access only to specific locations. To implement no default access, use the following configuration segment in one of your Apache configuration files:

```
<Directory />
    Order deny,allow
    Deny from all
</Directory>
```

This disables all access first. Now, if you need to enable access to a particular directory, use the <Directory . . .> container again to open that directory. For example, if you want to permit access to /www/mysite/public/htdocs, add the following configuration:

```
<Directory "/www/mysite/public/htdocs">
    Order deny,allow
    Allow from all
</Directory>
```

This method—opening only what you need—is a preventive security measure and is highly recommended.

Disabling user overrides

If you don't want users to override server-configuration settings using the per-directory configuration file (.htaccess) in a directory, disable this feature as follows:

```
<Directory />
    AllowOverride None
    Options None
    allow from all
</Directory>
```

This disallows user overrides and, in fact, speeds up your server, because the server no longer looks for the per-directory access control files (.htaccess) for each request.

Reducing CGI risks

The biggest security risk on the Web comes in the form of CGI applications. CGI is not inherently insecure, but poorly written CGI applications are a major source of Web security holes. Actually, the simplicity of the CGI specification makes it easy for many inexperienced programmers to write CGI applications. These inexperienced programmers, being unaware of the security aspects of internetworking, create applications that work but also create hidden back doors and holes on the system on which the applications run.

Here are the three most common security risks that CGI applications may create:

- **Information leaks.** Such leaks help hackers break into a system. The more information a hacker knows about a system, the better he or she gets at breaking into the system.

- **Execution of system commands via CGI applications.** In many cases, remote users have succeeded in tricking an HTML form-based mailer script to run a system command or give out confidential system information.

- ___Consumption of system resources. **A poorly written CGI application can be made to consume system resources such that the server becomes virtually unresponsive.**

Of course, you should take careful steps in developing or installing CGI applications when your Apache server will run these applications as an unprivileged user, but even carefully written applications can be a security risk.

Most of the security holes created by CGI applications are caused by user input.

Limiting CGI risks with wrappers

The best way to reduce CGI-related risks is not to run any CGI applications at all; however, in the days of dynamic Web content, this is unrealistic. Perhaps you can centralize all CGI applications in one location and closely monitor their development, to ensure that they are well-written.

In many cases, especially on ISP systems, all users with Web sites want CGI access. In this situation, it might be a good idea to run CGI applications under the UID of the user who owns the CGI application. By default, CGI applications that Apache runs use the Apache UID. If you run these applications using the owner's UID, all possible damage is limited to what the UID is permitted to access. In other words, a bad CGI application run with a UID other than the Apache server UID can damage only the user's files. The user responsible for the CGI application will now be more careful, because the possible damage will affect his or her content solely. In one shot, you get increased user responsibility and awareness and, simultaneously, a limited area for potential damage. To run a CGI application using a UID other than the Apache server, you need a special type of program called a *wrapper*, which enables you to run a CGI application as the user who owns the file rather than as the Apache server user. Some CGI wrappers do other security checks before they run the requested CGI applications. The following sections cover two popular CGI wrappers.

suEXEC

Apache comes with a support application called suEXEC that provides Apache users with the ability to run CGI and SSI programs under UIDs that are different from the UID of Apache. suEXEC is a setuid wrapper program that is called when an HTTP request is made for a CGI or SSI program that the administrator designates to run as a UID other than that of the Apache server. When such a request is made, Apache provides the suEXEC wrapper with the program's name and the UID and GID. suEXEC runs the program using the given UID and GID.

Before running the CGI or SSI command, the suEXEC wrapper performs a set of tests to ensure that the request is valid. Among other things, this testing procedure ensures that the CGI script is owned by a user who is allowed to run the wrapper and that the CGI directory or the CGI script is not writable by anyone but the owner. After the security checks are successful, the suEXEC wrapper changes the UID and the GID to the target UID and GID via setuid and setgid calls, respectively. The group-access list is also initialized with all groups in which the user is a member. suEXEC cleans the process's environment by establishing a safe execution PATH (defined during configuration), as well as by passing through only those variables whose names are listed in the safe environment list (also created during configuration). The suEXEC process then becomes the target CGI application or SSI command and executes. This may seem like a lot of work—and it is—but this provides a greater security coefficient, as well.

Configuring and installing suEXEC If you are interested in installing suEXEC support in Apache, run the configure (or config.status) script as follows:

```
./configure --prefix=/path/to/apache \
             --enable-suexec \
             --suexec-caller=httpd \
             --suexec-userdir=public_html \
             --suexec-uidmin=100 \
             --suexec-gidmin=100
             --suexec-
safepath="/usr/local/bin:/usr/bin:/bin"
```

Here is the detailed explanation of this configuration:

- **--enable-suexec.** Enables suEXEC support.

- **--suexec-caller=*httpd*.** Change *httpd* to the UID you use for the User directive in the Apache configuration file. This is the only user who will be permitted to run the suEXEC program.

- **--suexec-userdir=*public_html*.** Defines the subdirectory under users' home directories where suEXEC executables are to be kept. Change *public_html* to whatever you use as the value for the UserDir directive, which specifies the document root directory for a user's Web site.

- **--suexec-uidmin=100.** Defines the lowest UID permitted to run suEXEC-based CGI scripts. In other words, UIDs below this number won't be able to run CGI or SSI commands via suEXEC. Look at your /etc/passwd file to make sure the range you chose does not include the system accounts that are usually lower than UIDs below 100.

- **--suexec-gidmin=100.** Defines the lowest GID permitted to be a target group. In other words, GIDs below this number won't be able to run CGI or SSI commands via suEXEC. Look at your /etc/group file to make sure that the range you chose does not include the system account groups that are usually lower than UIDs below 100.

- **--suexec-safepath="/usr/local/bin:/usr/bin:/bin".** Defines the PATH environment variable that gets executed by suEXEC for CGI applications and SSI commands.

Enabling and testing suEXEC After you install both the suEXEC wrapper and the new Apache executable in the proper location, restart Apache, which will write a message similar to this:

```
[notice] suEXEC mechanism enabled (wrapper:
/usr/local/sbin/suexec)
```

This tells you that the suEXEC is active. Now, test suEXEC's functionality. In the srm.conf file, add the following lines:

```
UserDir public_html
AddHandler cgi-script  .pl
```

The first directive (UserDir) sets the document root of a user's Web site to be ~*username*/public_html, where *username* can be any user on the system. The second directive associates the cgi-script handler with the .pl files. This is done to run Perl scripts with .pl extensions as CGI scripts. For this test, you will need a user account. In this example, I will use the host wormhole.nitec.com and a user called kabir. Copy the script shown in Listing 12-2 in a file called test.pl and put it in a user's public_html directory. In my case I put the file in the ~kabir/public_html directory.

Listing 12-2 *A CGI Script to Test suEXEC Support*

```
#!/usr/bin/perl
#
# Make sure the preceding line is pointing to the
# right location. Some people keep perl in
# /usr/local/bin.

my ($key,$value);
print "Content-type: text/html\n\n";
print "<h1>Test of  suEXEC<h1>";

foreach $key (sort keys %ENV){
    $value = $ENV{$key};
    print "$key = $value <br>";
    }
exit 0;
```

To access the script via a Web browser, I request the following URL: `http://wormhole.nitec.com/~kabir/test.pl`.

A CGI script is executed only after it passes all the security checks performed by suEXEC. suEXEC also logs the script request in its log file. The log entry for my request looks as follows:

```
[1998-12-23 16:00:22]: uid: (kabir/kabir) gid:
(kabir/kabir) cmd: test.pl
```

If you are really interested in knowing that the script is running under the user's UID, insert a sleep command (such as sleep(10);) inside the foreach loop, which will slow down the execution and allow you to run commands such as top or ps on your Web server console to find out the UID of the process running test.pl. You also can change the ownership of the script using the chown command, try to access the script via your Web browser, and see the error message that suEXEC logs. For example, when I change the ownership of the test.pl script in the ~kabir/public_html directory as follows:

```
chown root test.pl
```

I get a server error, and the log file shows the following line:

```
[1998-12-23 16:00:22]: uid/gid (500/500) mismatch with
directory (500/500) or program (0/500)
```

Here, the program is owned by UID 0, and the group is still kabir (500), so suEXEC refuses to run it, which means suEXEC is doing what it is supposed to do.

To ensure that suEXEC is going to run the test.pl program in other directories, I created a cgi-bin directory in ~kabir/public_html and put test.cgi in that directory. After determining that the user and group ownership of the new directory and file are set to user ID kabir and group ID kabir, I accessed the script by using the following command:

```
http://wormhole.nitec.com/~kabir/cgi-bin/test.pl
```

If you have virtual hosts and want to run the CGI programs and/or SSI commands using suEXEC, you must use User and Group directives inside the <VirtualHost ...> container. Set these directives to user and group IDs other than those the Apache server is currently using. If only one, or neither, of these directives is specified for a <VirtualHost> container, the server user ID or group ID is assumed.

For security and efficiency reasons, all suEXEC requests must remain within either a top-level document root for virtual host requests or one top-level personal document root for userdir requests. For example, if you have four virtual hosts configured, you need to structure all of your virtual host document roots off of one main Apache document hierarchy to take advantage of suEXEC for virtual hosts.

CGIWrap

CGIWrap is like the suEXEC program insofar as it permits users to use CGI applications without compromising the security of the Web server. CGI programs are run with the file owner's permission. In addition, CGIWrap performs several security checks on the CGI application and will not be executed if any checks fail.

CGIWrap is written by Nathan Neulinger; the latest version of CGIWrap is available from the primary FTP site on `ftp://ftp.cc.umr.edu/pub/cgi/cgiwrap/`. CGIWrap is used via a URL in an HTML document. As distributed, CGIWrap is configured to run user scripts that are located in the ~/public_html/cgi-bin/ directory.

Configuring and installing CGIWrap   CGIWrap is distributed as a gzip-compressed tar file. You can uncompress it by using gzip and extract it by using the tar utility.

Run the Configure script, which prompts you to answer many questions. Most of these questions are self-explanatory. Also note that there is a feature in this wrapper that differs from suEXEC. It enables you to create allow and deny files that can be used to restrict access to your CGI applications. Both of these files have the same format, as shown in the following:

```
User ID
mailto:Username@subnet1/mask1,subnet2/mask2. . .
```

You can either have a single username (nonnumeric UID) or a user mailto:ID@subnet/mask line where one or more subnet/mask pairs can be defined. For example, if the following line is found in the allow file (you specify the filename),

```
mailto:Myuser@1.2.3.4/255.255.255.255
```

user kabir's CGI applications are permitted to be run by hosts that belong in the 206.171.50.0 network with netmask 255.255.255.0.

After you run the Configure script, you must run the make utility to create the CGIWrap executable.

Enabling CGIWrap To use the wrapper application, copy the CGIWrap executable to the user's cgi-bin directory. Note that this directory must match what you have specified in the configuration process. The simplest way to get things going is to keep the ~username/public_html/cgi-bin type of directory structure for the CGI application directory.

After you copy the CGIWrap executable, change the ownership and permission bits as follows:

```
chown root CGIWrap
chmod 4755 CGIWrap
```

Create three hard links or symbolic links called nph-cgiwrap, nph-cgi-wrapd, and cgiwrapd to CGIWrap in the cgi-bin directory as follows:

```
ln [-s] CGIWrap cgiwrapd
ln [-s] CGIWrap nph-cgiwrap
ln [-s] CGIWrap nph-cgiwrapd
```

On my Apache server, I specified only the cgi extension as a CGI application; therefore, I renamed my CGIWrap executable to cgiwrap.cgi to get it working. If you have similar restrictions, you might try this approach or make a link instead.

Now, execute a CGI application as follows:

```
http://www.yourdomain.com/cgi-
bin/cgiwrap/username/scriptname
```

To access user kabir's CGI application test.cgi on the wormhole.nitec.com site, for example, I would have to use the following:

```
http://wormhole.nitec.com/cgi-bin/cgiwrap/kabir/test.cgi
```

If you want to see debugging output for your CGI, specify cgiwrapd instead of CGIWrap, as in the following URL:

```
http://www.yourdomain.com/cgi-
bin/cgiwrapd/username/scriptname
```

If the script is an nph-style script, you must run it using the following URL:

```
http://www.yourdomain.com/cgi-bin/nph-
cgiwrap/username/scriptname
```

Reducing server-side include risks

If you run external applications using SSI commands such as exec, the security risk is virtually the same as with the CGI applications. However, you can disable this command very easily under Apache, using the Options directive as follows:

```
<Directory />
  Options IncludesNOEXEC
</Directory>
```

This disables exec and includes SSI commands everywhere on your Web space; however, you can enable these commands whenever necessary by defining a directory container with narrower scope. The following is an example:

```
<Directory />
  Options IncludesNOEXEC
</Directory>

<Directory "/ssi">
  Options +Include
</Directory>
```

This configuration segment disables the exec command everywhere but the /ssi directory.

Using SSL for secured transactions

Electronic commerce on the Web is booming at an extraordinary rate. Many companies are putting up e-commerce Web sites to establish business on the Internet. One prerequisite for an e-commerce site is to have secure transaction capabilities, which are provided by Secure Sockets Layer (SSL). Unfortunately, due to U.S.-enforced legal restrictions on the export of cryptography, Apache does not readily come with SSL support. However, multiple choices for third-party SSL software are currently available for Apache. Table 12-2 should help you pick the right one for your needs.

Table 12-2 *SSL Solutions for Apache*

Software	Distribution	Restriction	Comments
Apache-SSL	Free	Commercial use in the U.S. may be restricted by copyright and patent laws	Not recommended, because it isn't the cleanest solution. Apache-SSL is basically a set of patches for Apache and isn't very well#documented.
mod_ssl	Free	Commercial use in the U.S. may be restricted by copyright and patent laws	A clean solution. Although partly based on Apache-SSL, it is much cleaner and better documented. Recommended by the author.
Red Hat Secure Server	Commercial	U.S. cryptography-related export restrictions apply for countries outside the U.S. and Canada	The cheapest commercial solution. Based on the mod_ssl module.
Raven SSL module	Commercial	None	A midrange solution, price-wise.
Stronghold Web Server	Commercial	None	The author's personal favorite SSL solution for serious e-commerce sites. It is the most expensive among the commercial options.

The mod_ssl module not only is a much cleaner approach than Apache-SSL, it's free. Although it is partly based on Apache-SSL, it is yet another well-documented module by Ralf S. Engelschall. I recommend using this if you are using the latest version of Apache.

Getting mod_ssl

The mod_ssl module is not distributed with the standard Apache source distribution. You have to download it from http://www.engelschall. com/sw/mod_ssl/. Because this module depends on the SSLeay package (like Apache-SSL), you also have to get the SSLeay package, from ftp://ftp.psy.uq.oz.au/pub/Crypto/SSL/. If you are a U.S. citizen and plan to use the SSL support in the U.S., you need to obtain the RSA Reference Implementation package from ftp://ftp.rsa.com/ rsaref/.

View the README file at the FTP site to locate the U.S.-citizens-only directory where the rsaref20.tar.Z package is kept.

You also need a working Perl 5 interpreter, and you must make sure that you have the latest Apache source from the Apache Web site or one of its mirror sites.

Compiling and installing mod_ssl

Extract all the packages into an appropriate directory. I typically use /usr/local/src for such purposes. Then, compile and install them using the following steps. This description assumes that you have extracted the necessary packages into the following directories:

- /usr/local/src/apache_1.3.9 for the Apache source distribution
- /usr/local/src/mod_ssl-2.0.13-1.3.9 for the mod_ssl source distribution
- /usr/local/src/SSLeay-0.9.0b for the mod_ssl source distribution
- /usr/local/src/rsaref-2.0/ for the RSAref package for U.S. citizens only

Your version numbers might vary, because this software is always being updated, so make sure you supply appropriate version numbers as you follow the instructions in this book.

Building the RSAref library

You do not need the RSAref package for mod_ssl if you are not in the U.S. If you are in the U.S. and don't already have the librsaref.a library module, follow these steps:

1. Change directories to /usr/local/src/rsaref-2.0.

2. Run the following commands:

```
cp -rp install/unix local
cd local
make
mv rsaref.a librsaref.a
```

After you create the librsaref.a library file, you can compile SSLeay.

Building SSLeay

Follow the steps below:

1. Change directories to /usr/local/src/SSLeay-0.9.0b and run the following command:

```
make -f Makefile.ssl links
```

2. If you are in the U.S., you need to tell SSLeay about the rsaref library package, so run the following commands:

```
perl ./Configure gcc -DNO_IDEA -DRSAref -lRSAglue \
-L`pwd`/../rsaref-2.0/local/ -lrsaref
cp rsaref/rsaref.h include/
```

Everyone else should run the following command, which does not specify the RSAref library package:

```
perl ./Configure gcc  -DNO_IDEA
```

3. Compile and test the package by running the following commands:

```
make
make test
```

Building mod_ssl and Apache

Change directories to /usr/local/src/mod_ssl-2.0.13-1.3.9 and run the configure script as follows:

```
./configure \
--with-apache=../apache_1.3.9   \
--with-ssleay=../ SSLeay-0.9.0b \
--with-rsaref=../rsaref-2.0/local   \
--prefix=/usr/local/apache
```

You do not need the --with-rsaref option if you are not in the U.S. Also, make sure you use the appropriate --prefix value for your desired Apache destination.

If you already have a working server certificate and a private key, you can supply the following options to the configure script:

```
--with-key=/path/to/your/server.key
--with-crt=/path/to/your/server.crt
```

Now, you can compile Apache as follows:

1. Change your document directory to /usr/local/src/apache_1.3.9 and run the following command:

   ```
   make
   ```

2. If you do not have a real server certificate and private key, you can make a test certificate by using the following command:

   ```
   make certificate
   ```

3. Run the following command to install the Apache server:

   ```
   make install
   ```

   You now have an SSL-enabled Apache server. All that remains is the Apache configuration.

Configuring Apache for mod_ssl

The mod_ssl package installs a copy of the httpd.conf.default file in the etc subdirectory of your Apache installation directory. You can use this file to test and configure your Apache server. An example of this file appears in Listing 12-3.

Listing 12-3 *The Default httpd.conf Installed with mod_ssl*

```
##
## httpd.conf -- Apache HTTP server configuration file
##


ServerType standalone
```

Continued

Listing 12-3 *Continued*

```
Port 80
<IfDefine SSL>
Listen 80
Listen 443
</IfDefine>

HostnameLookups off

User nobody
Group nobody
ServerAdmin kabir@picaso.nitec.com
ServerRoot "/usr/local/apache"
ErrorLog /usr/local/apache/var/log/error_log
LogLevel warn
LogFormat "%h %l %u %t \"%r\" %>s %b \"%{Referer}i\"
\"%{User-Agent}i\"" combined
LogFormat "%h %l %u %t \"%r\" %>s %b" common
LogFormat "%{Referer}i -> %U" referer
LogFormat "%{User-agent}i" agent
CustomLog /usr/local/apache/var/log/access_log common
PidFile /usr/local/apache/var/run/httpd.pid
ScoreBoardFile /usr/local/apache/var/run/httpd.scoreboard
ServerSignature on
UseCanonicalName on

Timeout 300
KeepAlive on
MaxKeepAliveRequests 100
KeepAliveTimeout 15

MinSpareServers 5
MaxSpareServers 10
StartServers 5
```

```
MaxClients 150
MaxRequestsPerChild 30

<IfModule mod_ssl.c>
#   We disable SSL globally.
SSLDisable

SSLCacheServerPath      /usr/local/apache/sbin/ssl_gcache
SSLCacheServerPort
/usr/local/apache/var/run/ssl_gcache_port
SSLSessionCacheTimeout 300

<IfDefine SSL>
<VirtualHost _default_:443>

#   Set up the general virtual server configuration.
DocumentRoot "/usr/local/apache/share/htdocs"
ServerName picaso.nitec.com
ServerAdmin kabir@picaso.nitec.com
ErrorLog /usr/local/apache/var/log/error_log
TransferLog /usr/local/apache/var/log/access_log

# Enable SSL for this virtual host.
SSLEnable
SSLRequireSSL
SSLCertificateFile
/usr/local/apache/etc/ssl.crt/server.crt
SSLCertificateKeyFile
/usr/local/apache/etc/ssl.key/server.key
SSLVerifyClient none
MD5:DES-CBC3-SHA
SSLLogFile /usr/local/apache/var/log/ssl_misc_log
CustomLog /usr/local/apache/var/log/ssl_log "%t %h
%{version}c \
```

Continued

Listing 12-3 *Continued*

```
%{cipher}c %{subjectdn}c %{issuerdn}c \"%r\" %b"
</VirtualHost>
</IfDefine>
</IfModule>
The first configuration segment in the file is as follows
<IfDefine SSL>
Listen 80
Listen 443
</IfDefine>
```

Here, Apache is made to listen to ports 80 and 443 only if a label called "SSL" is defined in the command line of the Apache executable (httpd). You can define the label when running the Apache executable directly as follows:

```
httpd -DSSL
```

or by using the apachectrl script from the sbin subdirectory of your Apache installation, as follows:

```
apachectl -sslstart
```

If this label is not defined, Apache listens only to port 80, which is set by the Port directive earlier in the configuration.

The mod_ssl-related directives found in the default httpd.conf file are enclosed in a <IfModule mod_ss.c> . . . </IfModule> container, which is used to make sure the enclosed directives are taken into consideration only if the mod_ssl.c module is compiled into the running Apache executable.

```
SSLDisable
```

This directive is used to disable SSL support everywhere, to later enable SSL support where needed. In this example, SSL support is enabled for the main server listening on port 443.

```
SSLCacheServerPath      /usr/local/apache/sbin/ssl_gcache
SSLCacheServerPort
/usr/local/apache/var/run/ssl_gcache_port
SSLSessionCacheTimeout 300
```

These three directives are used to set up path, port, and timeout values for the SSL session cache server. Then, again, the <IfDefine Label> container is used to make sure that the server was intended to run in SSL mode using the –DSSL or sslstart option provided at the command line.

Next comes the virtual host configuration for the default server running on port 443. This is the SSL-enabled server. After the usual DocumentRoot, ServerName, ServerAdmin, ErrorLog, and TransferLog directives, the SSLEnable directive is used to turn on SSL support for this virtual host.

Next, the SSLRequireSSL directive is used to ensure that only SSL-based access is permitted for this virtual host.

Author: Is the preceding syntax supposed to include the <IfDefine Label> container,

```
SSLCertificateFile \
/usr/local/apache/etc/ssl.crt/server.crt
```

```
SSLCertificateKeyFile \
/usr/local/apache/etc/ssl.key/server.key
```

These two directives set the server's certificate and private key file path, respectively. If you already have a real certificate and private key for your server, use them here.

The next directive, SSLVerifyClient, is set to none to allow any SSL-capable clients to access the site. If you want to allow only clients with client certificates, you can set this to require.

The SSLLogFile and the CustomLog directives are used to write SSL-related logging data in a custom file. This really isn't needed, because most of the SSL data is automatically written to the error log file of the virtual host.

If you are interested in running your main server as an SSL-enabled server, put the following directives outside any virtual host configuration:

```
Listen 443
SSLEnable
SSLRequireSSL
SSLCertificateFile
/usr/local/apache/etc/ssl.crt/server.crt
SSLCertificateKeyFile
/usr/local/apache/etc/ssl.key/server.key
```

```
SSLVerifyClient none
```

The directives used in mod_ssl are the same as the Apache-SSL directives.

Testing Apache built with mod_ssl

Testing your mod_ssl-enabled server is quite simple. Restart the server using the apchectl script with the sslstart or startssl option, and access it as `https://yourserver.domain.tld`. Be sure to type **https**, and not http, to access your SSL-enabled site. If you are using a certificate created using the make certificate command, the Web browser will display warning dialog boxes stating that the server is using SSL but the certificate is not issued by any known Certificate Authority. In such a case, apply for a real certificate from a known CA, such as VeriSign or Thawte.

Getting a CA-signed certificate

You simply need to get a browser-recognizable certificate from one of the well-known CAs. The following are a few CAs that are likely to provide you with a certificate for Apache-SSL:

- **VeriSign:** `http://www.verisign.com/`
- **Thawte Consulting:** `http://www.thawte.com/certs/ server/request.html`
- **IKS GmbH:** `http://www.iks-jena.de/produkte/ca/`

The certification process requires that you produce paper documents proving the authenticity of your business. Such documents have to be accompanied by letters from high authorities in your organization. It is possible to get a certificate for your personal Web server; you do not have to have a legally founded company. For personal server certificates, only proof of an existing bank account is required by most CAs.

Commercial SSL solutions

If you are in doubt about your legal ability to use a mod_ssl-based SSL solution, and can afford the cost, I recommend getting either Stronghold or the Red Hat Secure server. I have personally evaluated and used the Stronghold server and found it to be a solid product. The Red Hat Secure Server is not available for evaluation.

Chapter 13

Using NFS File Servers

Installing an NFS Server

You can install the NFS server software from the RPM package shipped with the Red Hat CD-ROM. For example, to install the NFS server package for an *x*86 Red Hat Linux system, I run the following command from the /RedHat/RPMS directory of the CD-ROM:

```
rpm -ivh nfs-server-version.i386.rpm
```

The NFS server package includes the NFS daemons and configuration files necessary to turn a Red Hat Linux system into an NFS server. However, because NFS is based on Remote Procedure Call (RPC), you need another package called the portmap. If you do not have this package already installed (check using **rpm –q portmap**), then you should install it from the CD-ROM.

Configuring an NFS Server

An NFS server needs to run a program called portmap (also called rpc.portmap), which is usually started at boot time via init. To check whether portmap is already running, use the following command:

```
ps auxw | grep portmap
```

When you install the portmap package, it also installs an init script in /etc/rc.d/init.d called portmap. This script should also be automatically linked in your default run level (typically run level 3 for a multiuser system) rc directory. Absence of such a symbolic link requires that you run portmap manually. In such a case, run

```
ln -s /etc/rc.d/init.d/portmap
/etc/rc.d/rc3.d/S11portmap
```

This creates a symbolic link that allows Red Hat Linux to automatically run portmap at boot. Similarly, you should have another script called nfs in your /etc/rc.d/init.d directory. This is used to start the NFS daemons (rpc.mountd, rpc.nfsd) at boot time. This should also be linked from your default run level directory, or else you have to run these daemons manually.

The next step is to create an /etc/exports file to tell the system what file systems or directories need to be exported to NFS clients. The syntax of this file is as follows:

```
/directory nfs-client-host-ip-or-name (access options)
```

Here is an example of the /etc/exports file:

```
/www        www1.nitec.com(ro) www2.nitec.com(ro)
/www-data   cgi.nitec.com(rw)  fastcgi.nitec.com(rw)
```

The /www directory on the NFS server is exported to the www1.nitec.com and www2.nitec.com NFS clients. Both of these machines are given read-only (ro) access to the exported directory. The second line is used to export the /www-data directory to cgi.nitec.com and fastcgi.nitec.com client systems. Both of these systems have read/write (rw) access to the exported directory. You can specify NFS clients in any of the following commonly used ways, as well:

- Specify an NFS client as an IP address in the /etc/export file. For example:

  ```
  /www        206.171.50.51(ro)
  ```

  The machine with the IP address 206.171.50.51 is given read-only NFS access to the /www directory.

- Specify an entire IP network, as shown in the following example:

  ```
  /           206.171.50.48/255.255.255.240 (rw)
  ```

  The entire 206.171.50.48 network (14 IP addresses in the range 206.171.50.48 to 206.171.50.63) has been given read/write permission to the root file system of the NFS server.

- Specify a set of hosts by using wildcards. For example:

```
/pc          *.nitec.com (rw)
```

All the hosts in the `nitec.com` domain can access the /pc directory on the NFS server.

- Use the ? character as a single character wildcard.

- Export a file system or a directory to all the NFS clients in the world, by omitting the NFS client list in the line used to export it. For example:

```
/pub          (ro)
```

The /pub directory is exported to any NFS client.

Granting read-only access to the exported directory

If you want to allow only read-only access to any directory or file system you export from your NFS server to the clients, use ro as the access option. For example,

```
/master-data    production.nitec.com (ro)
```

provides the `production.nitec.com` client system read-only access to the /master-data directory.

Granting read and write access to the exported directory

If you want to allow read and write access to any directory or file system you export from your NFS server to the clients, use rw as the access option. For example,

```
/intranet    *.nitec.com (rw)
```

gives all the NFS clients on the `nitec.com` domain read and write access to the /intranet directory.

Disabling access to a certain directory

When you export an entire file system or a directory, the subdirectories below the exported directory are automatically accessible using the same access options. However, this might not always be desirable. You might want to allow access to a directory called /pub but not to a directory called /pub/staff-only. In such a case, you need to use the noaccess access option, as follows:

```
/pub   weblab-??.nitec.com (ro)
/pub/staff-only   weblab-??.nitec.com (noaccess)
```

Here, all the `weblab-??.nitec.com` (where *??* is any two characters) computers have read-only access to the /pub directory, but they are not allowed to access the /pub/staff-only directory, because of the noaccess option in the next line.

Mapping users between the NFS server and the clients

One of the issues that will quickly come up after you set up an NFS server is the user mapping between the NFS server and the clients. For example, suppose that you are exporting a directory called /www that is owned by a user and group called webguru and webdev, respectively. The NFS client capable of mounting this directory has to have a user called webguru or a webdev group to access it. This is often not desirable. In particular, you do not want an NFS client root account to have root privileges on the NFS-mounted directory. This is why the NFS server, by default, enforces an option called root_squash.

This typically maps the root user (UID = 0) and root group (GID = 0) to user nobody on the client system. You can disable the default mapping of root user and root group to nobody by adding no_root_squash when defining your export lines. However, I recommend that you do not do this unless you have an extraordinary circumstance in which both NFS client and server are in an isolated, trusted environment.

If you want to map the root UID/GID pair to a particular UID/GID, use the anonuid and anongid access options. For example, the anonuid and anongid in the following line are specified to allow root squashing to UID 500 and GID 666:

```
/proj     *.nitec.com (anonuid=500 anongid=666)
```

If you prefer to squash all the UID/GID pairs to an anonymous UID/GID pair, use the all_squash option. For example:

```
/proj     *.nitec.com (anonuid=500 anongid=666
all_squash)
```

Here, the /proj directory is exported to all hosts in the nitec.com domain, but all accesses are made as UID 500 and GID 666.

If you want to specify a list of UIDs and GIDs that needs to be squashed using the anonymous UID/GID pair, use the squash_uids and squash_gids options. For example, the following squashes all the UIDs and GIDs in the range 0–100 using the anonymous UID 500 and GID 666:

```
/proj     *.nitec.com (anonuid=500 anongid=666 \
squash_uids=0-100 squash_gids=0-100)
```

You can also specify an external map file to map NFS client-supplied UIDs and GIDs to whatever you want. The map is specified using the map_static option. For example:

```
/proj     *.nitec.com (map_static=/etc/nfs.map)
```

Here, the /proj directory is exported to all the nitec.com hosts, but all NFS client-supplied UIDs and GIDs are mapped using the /etc/nfs.map file. An example of this map file is as follows:

```
uid  0-100  -  # squash all remote uids in the 0-100
range
gid  0-100  -  # squash all remote gids in the 0-100
range
uid  500    666 # map remove uid 500 to local uid 666
gid  500    777 # map remove gid 500 to local gid 777
```

That covers all the commonly used options for creating the /etc/export file. Whenever a change is made to the /etc/exports file, however, the NFS daemons need to be told about this change. A script called exportfs can be used to restart these daemons, as follows:

```
/usr/sbin/exportfs
```

To make sure both rpc.mountd and rpc.nfsd are running properly, run a program called rpcinfo, as follows:

```
rpcinfo -p
```

The output looks like this:

```
program  vers    proto    port
100000    2      tcp      111     rpcbind
100000    2      udp      111     rpcbind
100005    1      udp      635     mountd
100005    2      udp      635     mountd
100005    1      tcp      635     mountd
100005    2      tcp      635     mountd
100003    2      udp      2049    nfs
100003    2      tcp      2049    nfs
```

This shows that mountd and nfsd have announced their services and are working fine. At this point, the NFS server is set up, so the NFS client hosts now can be set up.

Installing an NFS Client

If you are also using Red Hat Linux systems as NFS clients, you need to install the NFS client software on them. The NFS client software also comes in an RPM package. You should install it from your Red Hat CD-ROM. For example, to install the NFS client package for an *x*86 Red Hat Linux system, I can run the following command from the /RedHat/RPMS directory of the CD-ROM:

```
rpm -ivh nfs-client-version.i386.rpm
```

After you install the NFS client package, you are ready to configure the clients.

Configuring an NFS Client

This section assumes that you are configuring Red Hat Linux-based NFS clients. If you are configuring an NFS client on a different platform, read the proper documentation if you need any help. The NFS client package comes with a program called showmount that gives you information on exported file systems or directories on an NFS server. You can run this command with the NFS server's host name or IP address as the argument to see what hosts are allowed to access the exported file systems or directories. For example,

```
showmount   nfs-server.nitec.com
```

shows the list of NFS clients that are allowed to import files from nfs-server.nitec.com. To see the NFS server's export list, run this command with the –e option. To see which client is allowed to import what file systems or directories, run the command with the –a option.

If the showmount command shows that the NFS client you currently are configuring is allowed to import a file system or directory, you are ready to continue with client configuration. If it does not show the host name or IP address of your current NFS client, you must reconfigure the /etc/exports file on the NFS server to allow this client access to whatever directory or file system you want to import.

To import a directory or file system from an NFS server, you need to mount it using the standard mount command. For example, to mount a directory called /www from an NFS server called nfs-server. nitec.com, use the following mount command:

```
mount nfs-server.nitec.com:/www   /www  -t nfs
```

This command mounts the /www directory from the nfs-server. nitec.com system to /www as an nfs file system that is specified using the –t option. However, if you plan to mount an NFS file system or directory on a regular basis and on boot, you have to add a new line in the /etc/fstab file of your client system. For example, to mount the /www directory from nfs-server.nitec.com at boot, add the following line in the /etc/ fstab file:

```
nfs-server.nitec.com:/www   /www   nfs
```

To make sure that your NFS client will automatically mount NFS file systems and directories at boot, check whether you have a symbolic link (starting with S*xx*, where *xx* is a two-digit number) to the /etc/rc.d/init.d/ nfsfs script in your default run level rc directory. Unmounting an NFS file system is exactly the same as unmounting the local file system.

After you mount the NFS server-exported files on your NFS client system, your users can start using the mounted file systems or directories immediately. Before you allow users access to your NFS exports, consider the following security issues.

Securing Your NFS Server

The portmap program, in combination with rpc.nfsd, can be fooled, making it possible for unauthorized persons to get to files on NFS servers without having any privileges. Fortunately, the portmap program that Linux uses is relatively secure against attack and can be made more secure by adding the following line in the /etc/hosts.deny file:

```
portmap: ALL
```

The system will deny portmap access for everyone. Next, the /etc/hosts.allow file needs to be modified as follows:

```
portmap: 192.168.1.0/255.255.255.0
```

This allows all hosts from the 192.168.1.0 network to have access to portmap-administered programs, such as nfsd and mountd.

Caution

Never use host names in the portmap line in /etc/hosts.allow, because use of host name lookups can indirectly cause portmap activity, which will trigger host name lookups in a loop.

One other security issue on the server side is whether to allow the root account on a client to be treated as root on the server. By default, Linux prohibits root on the client side of the NFS to be treated as root on the server side. In other words, an exported file owned by root on the server cannot be modified by the client root user. To explicitly enforce this rule, the /etc/exports file can be modified as follows:

```
/www www1.nitec.com(rw, root_squash)
```

Now, if a user with UID 0 (the root user) on the client attempts to access (read, write, or delete) the file system, the server substitutes the UID of the server's nobody account. This means the root user on the client can't access or change files that only the root on the server can access or change. To grant root access to an NFS file system, use the no_root_squash option instead.

Note that it is also possible to enhance NFS client security by not trusting the NFS server too much. For example, you can use the nosuid option to disable suid programs from working off the NFS file system. This means that the server's root user cannot make a suid-root program on the file system, log in to the client as a normal user, and then use the suid-root program to become the root on the client, too.

You also can forbid execution of files on the mounted file system altogether with the noexec option. Enter these options in the options column of the line that describes your NFS mount point in the /etc/fstab file.

Distributing Files Using rdist

The rdist program enables you to maintain identical copies of files over multiple hosts. It uses either the rcmd function calls or the remote shell (rsh) to access each of the target host computers.

The easiest way to get rdist working is to create a common account on all the machines involved and create .rhosts files for each target (that is, client) system so that the common user on the master host is allowed to run rsh sessions. Because an example will make this easy to understand, suppose that you want to create a file distribution environment in which a master computer called `master.an-university.edu` contains the master copy of the file, and two hosts called `student1.an-university.edu` and `student2.an-university.edu` need to get fresh copies of the files on the master computer on a daily basis. Also assume that each of these three computers shares a common user account called updater. Here is how to set up such an environment.

On each of the student computers, add an .rhosts file in the home directory of the updater user. This file contains a single line, such as the following:

```
master.an-university.edu
```

This file must be owned by the root user and must be read-only for everyone else. This allows a user called updater on `master.an-university.edu` to run remote shell sessions on each student system.

The next step is to create a file distribution configuration file for rdist. This file is often called the distfile. A distfile is a text file that contains instructions for rdist on how to perform the file distribution task. Listing 13-1 shows one such distfile, rdist_distfile.

Listing 13-1 *The rdist_distfile File*

```
#
# Distfile for rdist
#
# This is used to distribute files from
# master.an-university.edu to student[12].an-
university.edu
# systems
#
# $Author$ (kabir@nitec.com)

# $Version$
# $Date$
# $Id$


# List all the hosts that need to be updated.
# The list is created using user@hostname entries where
each
# entry is separated by a whitespace character.
#
HOSTS = (updater@student1.an-university.edu \
        updater@student2.an-university.edu)

# List the directories that need to be updated.
#
FILES = ( /csc101)

# List the directories that need to be excluded from
# the update process.
EXCLUDE_DIR = (/csc101/instructor /csc101/secret)
```

```
# Here are the commands:
# Install all directories listed in FILES for
# all hosts listed in HOSTS except for the directories
# that are listed in EXCLUDE_DIR
#
${FILES} -> ${HOSTS}
  install ;
  except ${EXCLUDE_DIR};
```

This very simple distfile defines a variable called HOSTS that has two entries as values: `updater@student1.an-university.edu` and `updater@student2.an-university.edu`. This tells rdist to use the updater user account on both `student1.an-university.edu` and `student2.an-university.edu` for connection.

The next variable, FILES, defines the directories for rdist to distribute. Here, only the /csc101 directory is being distributed.

The third variable is EXCLUDE_DIR, which is set to list all the files and directories that you want to exclude from being distributed. The values that you see in the example are /csc101/instructors (this could contain files that only the instructor should have access to) and /cs101/secret (a directory that students should not have access to).

The rest of the file describes a simple command:

```
${FILES} -> ${HOSTS}
  install ;
  except ${EXCLUDE_DIR};
```

This command takes all the files and directories that the FILES variable points to and installs them on the hosts indicated by the HOSTS variable. It also tells rdist to exclude the files and directories specified by the EXCLUDE_DIR variable. To run rdist (as updater), from the command line, do the following:

1. Log in as **updater**. (If you are root on the master system, you can use su to change the UID to updater, as well.)

2. Run the following command as updater:

   ```
   /usr/bin/rdist -p /usr/sbin/rdistd -oremove,quiet \
   -f /usr/local/rdist/ rdist_distfile
   ```

The following is a description of the options:

- **−p.** Specifies the location of the rdistd program needed by rdist.
- **−o.** Specifies that one or more options are to follow—in this case, remove and quiet.
- **remove.** Tells rdist to remove any extraneous files found in the target system in target directories. This provides an easy method for maintaining an identical copy of the files on each student system.
- **quiet.** Tells rdist to be as quiet as possible during the operation.
- **−f.** Specifies the location of the distfile.

To reduce human error in running this command, create an sh script called **rdistribute.sh**, as shown in Listing 13-2.

Listing 13-2 *The rdistribute.sh Script*

```
#!/bin/sh
#
# This script runs rdist to update Web servers via the
# non-routable lan an-university.edu. The script is run
# by cron at a fixed interval.
#
# /etc/rc.d/rc.local starts the script to clean up
# left-over tempfiles that might have been left
# at shutdown. This process also removes the
# log file.
#
# $Author$ (kabir@nitec.com)
# $Version$
# $Id$
# $Date$
# $Status
##########################################################
#####

# If the script is called with an
# argument then
```

```
case "$1" in

boot)

   # since the argument is 'boot' the script is being
   # called at system start-up so remove all old lock
   # files and logs.
   echo -n "Cleaning up rdistribute.sh tmp files: "
      rm -f /tmp/rdist.lck
         rm -f /tmp/rdist.log
   echo "complete."
   exit 0;
   ;;

   # since the argument is 'restart' the script
   # needs to clean up as if the system just booted.

restart)
   $0 boot
   ;;

esac

# If the lock file exists then don't do anything.
if [ -f /tmp/rdist.lck ]; then
   exit 0
fi

# Otherwise create the lock file using /bin/touch
/bin/touch   /tmp/rdist.lck

# Run rdist
```

Continued

Listing 13-2 *Continued*

```
/usr/bin/rdist -p /usr/sbin/rdistd -
oremove,nochkgroup,nochkmode,nochkowner,quiet -f
/usr/local/rdist/rdist_distfile

# Remove the lock file
rm -f /tmp/rdist.lck

# Write the time and date in the log file
echo `date` > /tmp/rdist.log

# Exit the script
exit 0
```

This script is smart enough to detect in progress the rdistribute.sh process by using a lock file, which can tell when a previous rdistribute.sh is already in progress and continuing. This can happen when numerous files are being updated over multiple servers. The script also accepts an argument called boot that can be used to clean up the lock file and the log file it creates during the boot process. The script should be called from /etc/rc.d/rc.local as follows:

```
/usr/local/rdistribute.sh boot
```

This script can be scheduled to run by a cron entry in /etc/crontab. For example, to run this script every hour, the following cron entry can be added in /etc/crontab:

```
01 * * * * updater /usr/local/rdistribute.sh > /dev/null
```

The cron daemon will run the script as updater. Alternatively, you can create a link to rdistribute.sh from /etc/cron.hourly (or /etc/cron.daily, /etc/cron.monthly, or what have you) as you see fit.

Chapter 14

Configuring X Window

Installing XFree86

When you install Red Hat Linux from the official CD-ROM, you get a chance to install and configure XFree86. If you haven't done that already, you can install XFree86 quite easily using the RPM packages on your CD-ROM. To install XFree86 from the RPMS directory of your CD-ROM, run the following command:

```
rpm -ivh XFree86*.rpm
```

This installs all the XFree86 packages from the CD-ROM.

Configuring XFree86

Before you can configure XFree86 for your system, you need to know the following:

- How much video memory you have
- What kind of chipset your video card uses
- The maximum resolution of your monitor
- The horizontal and vertical refresh rates, make, and model of your monitor

If you do not know the information for your video card, run the SuperProbe utility, included with XFree86, to determine it:

```
/usr/X11R6/bin/SuperProbe
```

Here is an example of SuperProbe output:

```
WARNING - THIS SOFTWARE COULD HANG YOUR MACHINE.
          READ THE SuperProbe.1 MANUAL PAGE BEFORE
          RUNNING THIS PROGRAM.


          INTERRUPT WITHIN FIVE SECONDS TO ABORT!


First video: Super-VGA
          Chipset: S3 Trio64V+ (Port Probed)
          Memory:  2048 Kbytes
          RAMDAC:  Generic 8-bit pseudo-color DAC
                   (with 6-bit wide lookup tables (or in 6-
bit mode
```

Caution

As the warning message in the output clearly indicates, this program can make your system unresponsive. Be sure to read the man pages before you run this program.

After you ascertain the information about your system, you need to decide how you want to configure XFree86. You have three choices:

- Use a full-screen, menu-driven utility called Xconfigurator.
- Use a command-line, prompt-oriented utility called xf86config.
- Create the XF86Config file manually. This is the primary configuration file needed to create a usable X Windows environment in XFree86. It usually resides in the /etc/X11 directory, and typically a symbolic link (/usr/X11R6/lib/X11/XF86Config) is pointed back to /etc/X11/XF86Config.

Using Xconfigurator to create the XF86Config file

The Xconfigurator utility allows you to create the XF86Config file quite easily:

1. Run the program as follows:

```
/usr/X11R6/bin/Xconfigurator
```

This displays a screen stating what the program is all about. As suggested in the opening screen, you should read the /usr/X11R6/lib/X11/doc/README.Config file to learn about the latest details on the structure of the file.

2. Click OK to continue. If for some reason the /usr/X11R6/lib/X11/XF86Config symbolic link is broken, Xconfigurator displays a screen asking you to fix the problem.

3. Click OK to create the symbolic link. If you didn't have the symbolic link problem or just fixed it, you will the see result in the next screen, which lists the video card information and the selected X server name.

4. Click OK to continue. Select the monitor type by using the up- and down-arrow keys to scroll to locate your monitor brand and model. If you find your monitor in the list, select it and press OK to continue. If your monitor isn't listed here, select the Custom monitor and press OK to continue. The next screen tells you to specify your monitor's vertical refresh rate and horizontal sync rate. Consult your monitor's manual to find these numbers. If you still can't locate information on your monitor, check the /usr/X11R6/lib/X11/doc/Monitor file.

Tip

If you lost or threw away the monitor manual, you might be able to find information on your monitor vendor's Web site.

5. Click OK to proceed with the monitor specification. The next screen presents a list of monitor resolutions. Select the most appropriate resolution and horizontal refresh rate for your monitor. If you do not know what these settings should be, call your monitor or computer vendor to find this information. Don't experiment with these settings unless you care very little about the health of your monitor. Be warned that if you give XFree86 the wrong monitor settings, it might harm your monitor.

6. After you specify the resolution and the horizontal refresh rate, click OK to continue to specify the vertical refresh rate. When you finish, click OK.

7. A dialog box appears stating that Xconfigurator will now probe your video card using the selected X server. Click OK to continue. Wait for the probing to complete. As warned by the previous dialog box, the screen might become blank a few times as part of the probing procedure. After the probing is complete (hopefully without any problem), a screen displays the default video mode (color depth and resolution size).

8. If the default video mode is not satisfactory, click the Let Me Choose option to select the video modes you want. Selecting this option is recommended, so that you can customize your video modes.

9. Using the up- and down-arrow keys, select an appropriate resolution for each color mode by pressing the spacebar. You can also toggle a selection by using the spacebar. After you select all the desired resolutions for each color mode, click OK.

10. A dialog box confirms the creation of the XF86Config file. Before you start the X server, review the XF86Config file.

Understanding the XF86Config file

Like any typical UNIX configuration file, the XF86Config file ignores blank lines and any lines that start with a leading # character, which are treated as comments. The XF86Config file is divided into multiple sections. Each section provides a particular type of information to the X server. Also, each section starts with the Section "*<name of the section>*" line and ends with a EndSection line. The following list describes the sections:

■ **Files section.** Used to specify font and color database paths. Here is an example of such a section:

```
Section "Files"

    RgbPath      "/usr/X11R6/lib/X11/rgb"


    FontPath     "/usr/X11R6/lib/X11/fonts/misc/"
    FontPath     "/usr/X11R6/lib/X11/fonts/Type1/"
    FontPath     "/usr/X11R6/lib/X11/fonts/Speedo/"
    FontPath     "/usr/X11R6/lib/X11/fonts/75dpi/"
```

```
FontPath      "/usr/X11R6/lib/X11/fonts/100dpi/"
```

```
EndSection
```

If you add new fonts to your system, you can use the FontPath option to specify the directory for the fonts you installed.

Other commonly used options that you can add in this section are listed in Table 14-1.

Table 14-1 *Options for the Files Section of XF86Config*

Option	Description
AllowNonLocalXvidtune	Allows the xvidtune program to connect from a remote host
DisableVidMode	Disables certain video mode extensions used by the xvidtune program
AllowNonLocalModInDev	Allows a remote X client to change keyboard and mouse settings
DisableModInDev	Disables certain input device extensions that can normally be set dynamically
AllowMouseOpenFail	Allows the X server to start without a mouse

- **Server flags section.** Used to specify general options to the X server. Here is an example of such a section:

```
Section "ServerFlags"

# Uncomment this to cause a core dump at the
# spot where a signal is received.  This may leave
# the console in an unusable state, but may provide
# a better stack trace in the core dump to aid in
debugging
#NoTrapSignals

# Uncomment this to disable the <Ctrl><Alt><BS>
# server abort sequence This allows clients to
receive
# this key event.
#DontZap
```

```
# Uncomment this to disable the
# <Crtl><Alt><KP_+>/<KP_-> mode switching sequences.
# This allows clients to receive these key events.
#DontZoom
```

```
EndSection
```

The following are the options in this section:

- **NoTrapSignals.** Should be turned on by removing the leading # sign only if you are an X Windows developer and know what you are doing.

- **DontZap.** Disallows you to terminate the X Windows server using Ctrl+Alt+Backspace. If you have an X application that requires this key sequence, you can uncomment the DontZap line so that this key sequence can be passed to the application.

- **DontZoom.** Disallows you to switch back and forth between different screen resolutions using Ctrl+Alt+Keypad-Plus and Ctrl+Alt+Keypad-Minus. If you have an X application that requires these key sequences, you can uncomment the DontZoom line so that these key sequences can be passed to the application.

- **Keyboard section.** Used to set up keyboard devices. An example of this section is shown here:

```
Section "Keyboard"

    Protocol    "Standard"

    # when using XQUEUE, comment out the above line,
    # and uncomment the following line
    #Protocol    "Xqueue"

    AutoRepeat  500 5

    LeftAlt     Meta
    RightAlt    Meta
    ScrollLock  Compose
    RightCtl    Control
```

```
XkbRules        "xfree86"
XkbModel        "pc101"
XkbLayout       "us"
```

EndSection

The following are the options in this section:

- **Protocol.** Specifies the keyboard option. It should be set to standard for all Linux systems.

- **AutoRepeat.** Sets the auto repeat delay (first argument) and rate (second argument).

- **LeftAlt, RightAlt, ScrollLock, and RightCtl.** Allow you to map the Left Alt key, Right Alt key, Scroll Lock key, and Right Ctrl key, respectively, to either Meta, Compose, or Control values.

- **XkbModel.** Used to set a non-U.S. 102-key keyboard to pc102. Similarly, can be used to set a Microsoft Natural Keyboard to Microsoft.

- **XkbLayout.** Used to set the language, using the two-digit language code, to any language other than U.S. English, which is the default (us). For example, to set your keyboard language to French, use fr as the XkbLayout option.

- **XkbOptions.** Used to swap the Ctrl key for a regular keyboard's Caps Lock key (that is, Caps Lock becomes Ctrl) for those who prefer the setup of Sun Microsystems' keyboards. For example,

```
XkbOptions "ctrl:swapcaps"
```

swaps Caps Lock with Ctrl. The default is to leave the keys as is.

- **XkbRules.** Used to specify the rules file. The default rules file is xfree86.

Other commonly used options that you can add in this section are listed in Table 14-2.

Table 14-2 *Options for the Keyboard Section of XF86Config*

Option	Description
XkbTypes	Use to set the keyboard type. The default is default; other possible values are basic, cancel, complete, iso9995, mousekeys, nocancel, and pc.
XkbCompat	Use to set keyboard compatibility. The default value is default; other possible values are accessx, basic, complete, group_led, iso9995, japan, keypad, misc, mousekeys, norepeat, pc, pc98, and xtest.
XkbSymbols	Use to set the keyboard symbol. The default value is us; other possible values are amiga, ataritt, be, bg, ca, cs, ctrl, czsk, de, de_CH, digital, dk, dvorak, en_US, es, fi, fr, fr_CH, fujitsu, gb, group, hu, iso9995-3, it, jp, keypad, lock, nec, no, pc104, pl, pt, ru, se, sgi, sony, sun, and th.
XkbGeometry	Use to set the keyboard geometry parameters. The default value is pc; other possible values are amiga, ataritt, dell, digital, everex, fujitsu, keytronic, kinesis, Microsoft, nec, northgate, sgi, sony, sun, and winbook.
XkbKeycodes	Use to set the key codes for the keyboard. The default value is xfree86; other possible values are amiga, ataritt, digital, fujitsu, hp, ibm, sgi, sony, and sun.

■ **Pointer section:** Used to set up the pointer device, which is typically a mouse. An example of this section is as follows:

```
Section "Pointer"


    Protocol      "Microsoft"
    Device        "/dev/mouse"


EndSection
```

The following are the options in this section:

● **Protocol.** Sets the protocol for the pointer device. The protocol can be Auto, BusMouse, GlidePoint, GlidePointPS/2, IntelliMouse, IMPS/2, Logitech, Microsoft, MMHitTab, MMSeries, Mouseman, MouseManPlusPS/2, MouseSystems, NetMousePS/2, NetScrollPS/2, OSMouse, PS/2, SysMouse, ThinkingMouse, ThinkingMousePS/2, or Xqueue. If you do not know what protocol is appropriate for your late-model pointer device, try setting the protocol to Auto.

- **Device.** Specifies the device path. If you use a mouse as your pointing device and have it connected to serial port 1 (cua0) or serial port 2 (cua1), you can specify /dev/cua0 or /dev/cua1, respectively. However, the best method is to create a symbolic link called /dev/mouse that points to your serial port device (cua0 or cua1), and have the device set to /dev/mouse. This way, if you change the port, you simply need to readjust the link, and not the configuration file as well.

Other commonly used options that you can add in this section are listed in Table 14-3.

Table 14-3 *Options for the Pointer Section of XF86Config*

Option	Description
BaudRate	Use to set the baud rate for your pointer device.
Port	Same use as the Device option, described in the preceding list.
Button	Use to set the number of buttons.
Emulate3Buttons	Use to emulate a three-button mouse with a two-button mouse. When you press both buttons together, the third button is emulated.
Emulate3Timeout	Use to set the timeout (in milliseconds) for three-button emulation. The X server will wait for the specified number of milliseconds to decide whether or not a third button was pressed when you hold down both of the buttons.

- **Monitor section:** Used to describe your monitor. This is the most commonly modified section in the XF86Config file. Here is an example of this section:

```
Section "Monitor"

Identifier   "My Monitor"
VendorName   "Unknown"
ModelName    "Unknown"
HorizSync    31.5 - 82.0
VertRefresh  50-100


# This is a set of standard mode timings.
```

Continued

Continued

```
# Modes that are out of monitor spec
# are automatically deleted by the server
# (provided the HorizSync and VertRefresh lines
# are correct), so there's no immediate need to
# delete mode timings (unless particular mode
timings
# don't work on your monitor). With these modes,
# the best standard mode that your monitor
# and video card can support for a given resolution
# is automatically used.

# 640x400 @ 70 Hz, 31.5 kHz hsync
Modeline "640x400" 25.175 640  664  760  800    400
409  411  450

# 640x480 @ 60 Hz, 31.5 kHz hsync
Modeline "640x480" 25.175 640  664  760  800    480
491  493  525

# 800x600 @ 56 Hz, 35.15 kHz hsync
ModeLine "800x600" 36    800  824  896 1024    600
601  603  625

# 640x480 @ 72 Hz, 36.5 kHz hsync
Modeline "640x480" 31.5 640 680 720  864 480 488 491
521

# 800x600 @ 60 Hz, 37.8 kHz hsync
Modeline "800x600" 40 800 840 968 1056 600 601 605
628 +hsync +vsync

# 1024x768 @ 60 Hz, 48.4 kHz hsync
Modeline "1024x768" 65 1024 1032 1176 1344 768 771
777 806 -hsync -vsync
```

```
# 1024x768 @ 70 Hz, 56.5 kHz hsync
Modeline "1024x768" 75 1024 1048 1184 1328 768 771
777  806 -hsync -vsync

# 1024x768 @ 76 Hz, 62.5 kHz hsync
Modeline "1024x768"  85  1024 1032 1152 1360    768
784  787  823

# 1280x1024 @ 61 Hz, 64.2 kHz hsync
Modeline "1280x1024" 110 1280 1328 1512 1712  1024
1025 1028 1054

# 1280x1024 @ 74 Hz, 78.85 kHz hsync
Modeline "1280x1024" 135 1280 1312 1456 1712  1024
1027 1030 1064

# 1280x1024 @ 76 Hz, 81.13 kHz hsync
Modeline "1280x1024" 135 1280 1312 1416 1664  1024
1027 1030 1064
```

EndSection

The following are the options in this section:

- **Identifier.** Used to set a unique identifier for the monitor. Each monitor needs to have a unique identifier that can be referenced in the Screen section.

- **VendorName and ModelName.** Used to specify the vendor name and model of the monitor.

- **HorizSync.** Used to set the horizontal refresh (sync) rate in KHz. If you want to specify this rate in megahertz or in hertz, use MHz or Hz, respectively, at the end of the line.

- **VertRefresh.** Used to set the vertical refresh (sync) rate in Hz. If you want to specify this rate in megahertz or in kilohertz, use MHz or KHz, respectively, at the end of the line.

- **ModeLine.** Used to specify video modes. Each ModeLine option has the following format:

```
ModeLine mode  clk-rate Horizontal-timing Vertical-
timing Flags
```

   clk-rate is the rate of the pixel clock for this mode. This is a single positive (integer) number. *Horizontal-timing* and *Vertical-timing* are a set of four timing (integer) numbers. The *Flags* are optionally used to specify additional characteristics of the mode. A ModeLine can be written in multiple lines using the *mode* option. For example:

```
ModeLine "1024x768i" 45 1024 1048 1208 1264 768 776
784 817 Interlace
Mode "1024x768i"
DotClock        45
HTimings        1024 1048 1208 1264
VTimings        768 776 784 817
Flags           "Interlace"
EndMode
```

   Both of the preceding video mode descriptions are identical.

- **Graphics Device section.** Used to set options for the video card. Here is an example section:

```
# Device configured by Xconfigurator:

Section "Device"
    Identifier  "Trio32/Trio64"
    VendorName  "Unknown"
    BoardName   "Unknown"

EndSection
```

   The following are the options in this section:

   - **Identifier.** Used to set a unique identifier for the monitor. Each monitor needs to have a unique identifier that can be referenced in the Screen section.

- **VendorName.** Used to specify the vendor name.
- **BoardName.** Used to specify the name of the video card. Typically, the X server detects the features installed on your video card, including the amount of RAM, the chipset, and so on.

■ **Screen section.** Used to specify how the video hardware (monitor and video card) should be used by the X server. Here is an example of this section:

```
Section "Screen"
    Driver      "accel"
    Device      "Trio32/Trio64"
    Monitor     "My Monitor"


    Subsection "Display"
        Depth       8
        Modes       "640x480" "800x600" "1024x768"
"1280x1024"
        ViewPort    0 0
        Virtual     1280 1024
    EndSubsection


    Subsection "Display"
        Depth       16
        Modes       "640x480" "800x600" "1024x768"
        ViewPort    0 0
        Virtual     1024 768
    EndSubsection


    Subsection "Display"
        Depth       32
        Modes       "640x480" "800x600"
        ViewPort    0 0
        Virtual     800 600
    EndSubsection
```

```
EndSection
```
The following are the options in this section:

- **Driver.** Sets the driver name. Supported driver names are accel, mono, svga, vga2, and vga16.
- **Device.** Sets the name of the video card that is to be used.
- **Monitor.** Sets the name of the monitor that is to be used.

A Display subsection is used to specify a set of parameters for a particular display type. The Depth option is used to set color depth; the Modes option is used to set video modes or resolutions; the ViewPort option is used to set the top-left corner of the initial display; the Virtual option is used to specify the virtual video resolution. A Screen section may have multiple display subsections.

The video resolutions specified as the arguments for a Modes option in a Display section can be selected or deselected by using the Ctrl+Alt+Keypad-Plus and Ctrl+Alt+Keypad-Minus keys.

Using X Windows

You can start X Windows in any of several ways. You can run xinit, which starts the X Windows server and also runs the first X client application. The client application it runs depends on the .xinitrc script in a user's home directory. For example, if you run xinit as root, the ~root/.xinitrc script will be used to determine what X client application needs to be started after the X Windows server is up and running. If no client application is specified in the command line, or if the *~<user home directory>/* .xinitrc file does not exist, it will use the following command as a default:

```
xterm -geometry +1+1 -n login -display :0
```

In other words, it will start an xterm session as the sole client application. When this client application exits, the X Windows server will also terminate.

To provide better user control over what gets started, an sh script called startx is distributed. You can run startx without any argument to start the X Windows server. This script is really a front end for the xinit program.

By default, the startx script looks for .xserverrc in the user's home directory, and if it can't find it, startx looks for a system-wide xserverrc file in the

/usr/X11R6/lib/X11/xinit directory. The ~<*user home directory*>/.xserverrc file or the /usr/X11R6/lib/X11/xinit/xserverrc file is used to determine which X Windows server needs to be started.

The startx script also looks for .xinitrc in the user's home directory, and if it can't find it there, it looks for a system-wide xinitrc file in the /usr/X11R6/lib/X11/xinit directory. The ~<*user home directory*>/.xinitrc or the /usr/X11R6/lib/X11/xinit/xinitrc file is used to determine which client applications are going to be run after the X Windows server has been started.

You can provide command-line arguments to alter the default settings found in any of these files. However, if you keep overriding the defaults, you might as well put your chosen settings in these files, so that you don't have to type them every time you want to run this script.

If you prefer, start X Windows in a different color mode, by specifying the color mode in the command line. For example, the following starts X Windows in 256 color mode:

```
startx -- -bbp 8
```

To start X Windows in true color mode, use the following command:

```
startx -- -bbp 32
```

The double dashes are required, to pass arguments directly to the xinit program.

When you run startx for the first time, your home directory likely won't have a preinstalled .xinitrc file; therefore, the system-wide xinitrc file will be used. To create your own .xinitrc file, run the locate xinitrc command to locate a copy of the file in /usr/X11R6/lib/X11/xinit or in /etc/X11/xinit. Copy this file to your home directory by renaming it with a period as the first character, so that the final name is .xinitrc.

Configuring .xinitrc

As mentioned before, the .xinitrc script is used to launch client applications per a user's preference. When such a script is found in a user's home directory, startx will run it; when the .xinitrc script exits, it will terminate the X Windows server. Therefore, you must call a client application in the script so that control does not fall through to the bottom of the script (causing it to exit) until you terminate that client application. Typically, this is accomplished by running all but the last client program in the background. The last client program is usually an X Windows manager. Listing 14-1 shows an example .xinitrc file.

Listing 14-1 *An Example .xinitrc File*

```
#
# Example .xinitrc
#

# start xclock (in the background)
xclock -geometry 50x50-1+1 &

# start two xterms (in the background)
xterm -geometry 80x50+494+51 &
xterm -geometry 80x20+494-0 &

#
# now start a window manager in
# the foreground
#

# If my favorite fvwm95 is there, start it
if [ -f /usr/X11R6/bin/fvwm95 ]; then
    exec fvwm95

# Ok, no fvwm95, try fvwm2
elif [ -f /usr/X11R6/bin/fvwm2]; then
    exec fvwm2

# Ok, no fvwm95 or fvwm2, try just fvwm
elif [ -f /usr/X11R6/bin/fvwm]; then
    exec fvwm

# Ok, no fvwm of any kind, so try afterstep
```

```
elif [ -f /usr/X11R6/bin/afterstep ]; then
    exec afterstep

# Ok, not even afterstep, try twm
else
    exec twm
fi
```

As you can see, instances of X applications such as xclock and xterm are executed in the background by using the & operator. Only the X Windows manager application is run in the foreground. Start with a simple .xinitrc file, such as the preceding one, and modify it to include X applications that you need to start by default.

You can run X Windows without a window manager by running xinit directly; however, most people find that window managers are must-have tools to work under X Windows. The popular X Windows managers are fvwm2, fvwm, afterstep, twm, wmaker, and wmx, among others. Each window manager has its own look and feel and thus provides a different appeal to different users. I recommend that you install the popular X Windows managers and try them out.

Customizing the look and feel of window managers

An X Windows manager controls the look and feel of the entire X Windows environment, so you need to control how your chosen window manager behaves.

Red Hat Linux comes with a program called wmconfig that allows you to do just that. For example, to create a custom configuration file for the fvwm2 window manager, run

```
wmconfig --output=fvwm2 > .fvwm2rc
```

After you create such a configuration file and enable fvwm2 as your window manager in your .xinitrc, it will run using the configuration in the .fvwm2rc file in your home directory. If you already have a .fvwm2rc file, you may want to rename it before you run the preceding command, so that you don't delete your existing configuration. Also, you can edit the

.fvwm2rc file manually, to add or remove further customization. If you want to enable users who are using fvwm2 on your system to have a consistent environment, you may want to copy the customized .fvwm2rc file to the /usr/lib/X11/fvwm2 directory.

Similarly, wmconfig allows you to create and customize configurations for other window managers, such as fvwm95, afterstep, mwm, anotherlevel, icewm, wmaker, and kde. If you enter the wmconfig command without any argument, it will show you the supported window managers in the --output option line.

Customizing the look and feel of client applications

When you run an X client application, such as an xterm or a calculator (xcalc), the default look and feel of the application typically comes from a file in /usr/X1R6/lib/X11/app-defaults. For example, the default look and feel of xcalc (the calculator) comes from the /usr/X1R6/lib/X11/app-defaults/XCalc file. You can modify these defaults to provide a customized look and feel for you and/or your users. Be sure to back up each file you want to modify.

If you are interested only in changing the look and feel of a few applications for yourself, you can create an .Xresources file in your home directory and add lines using the following syntax:

```
<application><resource key>: <resource value>
```

For example, I placed the following line in my .Xresources file to change the default background color (black) of the digital display of the xcalc program:

```
XCalc*bevel.Background:  red
```

To identify which resource is responsible for changing this particular color, I first looked at the /usr/X1R6/lib/X11/app-defaults/XCalc file. After I located the resource, I copied it into my .Xresources file and prefixed the line with the name of the application (XCalc). If you use an .xinitrc file in your home directory, put **xrdb -merge $HOME/.Xresources** in it before loading any client applications. Any time you add or modify resources in your .Xresources file, you can run this command from the command line to integrate resource changes to your current X environment.

Using xdm, the X Display Manager

If you want to provide a graphical user authentication interface, xdm, or X Display Manager, is your answer. Using xdm, you can authenticate users via a graphical login screen and take them straight to their X Windows environment. The purpose of this program is to provide services similar to getty and login. Start the display manager as follows:

```
xdm &
```

The xdm configuration files are located in the /usr/X11R6/lib/ X11/xdm directory. The file xdm-config is used to configure how the login screen appears to users, and Xsetup_0 is used to tell xdm what programs should be launched when X is started. The default Xsetup_0 is shown here:

```
#!/bin/sh
```

```
/usr/X11R6/bin/xconsole -geometry 480x130-0-0 -daemon \
-notify -verbose -fn fixed -exitOnFail
```

```
/usr/X11R6/bin/xbanner
```

This file starts the xconsole and xbanner programs when a user is authenticated. These are practically useless for most users; hence, modify this to whatever is appropriate for you. For example, you might use the xv program to set the background of the X environment to something appropriate for your organization. Or, perhaps you can start up a few applications that are typically run by most users, such as the xmailbox.

The xdm can be run automatically after boot by changing the default run level to 5. To change the run level of your system to 5, modify the following line in the /etc/inittab file:

```
id:3:initdefault:
```

Replace the 3 with 5 and make sure that you have the following line in the same file:

```
x:5:respawn:/usr/bin/X11/xdm -nodaemon
```

Using XFree86 with MS Windows 9x/2000

To run X Windows applications on MS Windows 9x/2000, you need to run an X Windows server on such a platform. Many commercial X Windows server software packages are available for MS Windows 9x/2000. This section uses Micro X-Win32, which I have used for over a year and find very easy to install and support.

Getting Micro X-Win32

You can download an evaluation copy of X-Win32 from StarNet Communications Corporation at http://www.starnet.com/. The evaluation version of the product runs exactly like the product version; the only limitation is that you can use the evaluation version for only two hours per session; after every two-hour period, you have to restart the X Windows server on the MS Windows side. Because none of the features are crippled in the evaluation version, this constraint is not much of a problem. After all, if you use it, you should pay for it.

After you download an evaluation copy, which typically comes in a self-extracting executable file, extract the files by double-clicking the executable; the installation will begin automatically. You are asked to select a destination directory for the installation. After it is installed, you are ready to use the X Windows server on MS Windows, and your Red Hat Linux server's X client applications can be run on the MS Windows system running the local X Windows server.

Before you can run an X client from your Red Hat Linux X installation, you need to configure Micro X-Win32 using the X-Util32 program provided with the distribution. Do the following:

1. Run the X-Util32 program.

2. From its menu, select Sessions ⇨ Edit sessions. From this menu, select an existing session entry, such as sun. This will display a dialog box with information on the current session.

3. Rename the session entry by typing a new name in the Session name field. This can be any name. Next, select the connection method: rsh (remote shell), rexec (remote exec), or XDMCP (for use with xdm). Choose the one most appropriate for your Red Hat Linux X Windows environment. For example, if you are running xdm on the Linux side, choose XDMCP.

   If you choose to use the remote shell option, you must have an .rhosts file in the Linux user's home directory. This file must contain the host name or the IP address of the MS Windows system.

   Also make sure you haven't disabled the rsh or rexec lines in /etc/inetd.conf. For security, you may want to disallow anyone from using rsh or rexec via the /etc/hosts.deny file and only allow hosts that are specifically allowed such services in the /etc/hosts.allow file.

4. If you want to automatically start this session every time you start X-Win32, click the Auto startup option. Also, make sure the Windows setting is set to the Switch to multiple windows option.

5. Enter the host name of the Red Hat Linux server on which the X application will reside.

6. Enter the username in the Login field. If you choose the remote exec (rexec) option, you are asked to enter a password every time you want to connect your session. If you prefer to enter the password only once, enter it in the Password field, which appears only when you select the rexec option.

7. In the Command field, enter the command you want to run. Typically, you will want to run an xterm here. So, set this field to this value:

   `/usr/bin/X11/xterm -ls -display $DISPLAY.`

8. Save the modified session and exit the X-Util32 application.

Now, you are ready to run the new session. Click the X-Win32 icon in your taskbar, select the Sessions menu, and then select the modified session name. If you are connecting via rexec, you are asked to enter the password.

After you are successfully authenticated, an xterm (or whatever application you put in the Command field while editing this entry in X-Util32) appears on your MS Windows system. If you do not see the application in a few seconds, however, go back to the X-Win32 icon on your taskbar, click the Show Messages option, and try to run your application again. Watch for any permission errors in the message window. If you do get permission errors, either you have forgotten to enable the rexec or rsh service in /etc/inetd.conf, you have forgotten to restart the inetd server after modifying the /etc/inetd.conf file, or you have not yet set up the .rhosts file for rsh-only sessions. Make sure your .rhosts file is writable only by the owner; everyone else should have only read-only access to this file.

At this point, you should have an X Windows application running under the Micro X-Win32 server. If you prefer to start an X Windows manager, such as fvwm2 or openstep, and run all X Windows applications as usual (that is, as if you were on the Red Hat Linux system), do the following:

1. Using XUtil32, create or edit a session. Enter the host name, the login username, and the connection method (rsh, rexec), as you did before. Select the Switch to single window option and enter the following line as the command:

   ```
   fvwm2  -display $DISPLAY
   ```

2. Don't forget to replace fvwm2 with your favorite X Windows manager. Save the new (or edited) session.

Close any X Windows client sessions that you have already started; then, start the new session. You should see a large single window where your favorite X Windows manager is loaded. Now you can use X Windows as if you are running it from the console of the Red Hat Linux system. In case of a problem, read the online troubleshooting information for details.

Part III

Troubleshooting

Chapter 15

Security

Securing User Access

If you could keep a computer outside the reach of everyone, it likely would be completely secure. Of course, it also would be practically useless to anyone. Unfortunately, all security risks are associated with the users who access your computer. You will never hear about one computer attacking another by itself. The attack could come from a user who has rightful access to your computer or from someone who has acquired access to your computer by illegal means. In most cases, people who have rightful access do not attack the computer they use; however, they often unknowingly aid in attacks that come from people who gain illegal access. So, restricting a user's ability to do damage to your system makes perfect sense; such restrictions, in turn, enhance your system security. The following sections describe how to restrict unnecessary user interaction with your system.

Restricting physical access

All security measures will fail when someone capable of physically accessing your computer decides to do physical damage to your computer or the services and data it has to offer. Virtually no easy way exists to protect your computer from such a bad guy, who can pull out the power plug to bring your computer to a screeching halt, boot the computer with a floppy and steal or vandalize your data, or do anything else he wants.

The only way to ensure physical security for your system is to restrict who has such access to your computer. Know the people who can potentially access your computer. Keep your server away from public places where it is hard to know who is coming and going at all times. If it is impossible for you to restrict strangers from physically being near your computer, do the following:

- Password-protect access to the computer's BIOS. You should do this whenever you get a computer for the first time. If your computer is going to be in a public place, be assured that someone will try to get into the BIOS before you do and lock you out by adding a password. Recovering from such a problem could require calling your computer vendor or opening the computer to reset the BIOS by unplugging the battery for a short time. So, secure your BIOS by password-protecting it. No one but you should have access to your computer's BIOS.

- If your BIOS allows you to disable floppy seek at boot, turn that option on. Some newer BIOSs allow booting from the CD-ROM drive; if you have such a computer, disable that option, too. Do not allow your computer to boot from anything but your hard disk.

- Create or modify the /etc/shutdown.allow file and list only the users who are allowed to shut down your computer. If you allow only the root user to perform this task, create an empty /etc/shutdown.allow file. When anyone at the computer console presses the Ctrl+Alt+ Del keys to reboot the computer, the computer will check the file to make sure a specified user is logged in at the console before it shuts down. When someone who is not allowed to shut down presses these keys, the computer ignores the request and displays a warning message on the console. Of course, this does not stop anyone from pressing the reset button (if your computer has one) or turning off power to shut down the hard way. So, make sure you have some way of protecting these switches.

- Lock your computer to a large piece of furniture in the same way that you would lock a bike to a bike stand. This method is typically used to deter or delay theft of computer equipment.

Restricting normal user access

A Red Hat Linux system has two kinds of users: normal users and super-users. When a normal user account is used to illegally acquire superuser privileges, bad things start to happen to a computer. So, you (the superuser) need to make sure that user accounts have the least number of privileges required to get their job done. For example, if you create a Red Hat Linux server to provide e-mail and Web services for your users, you don't need to allow them Telnet (and so shell) access to your server. To restrict Telnet (shell) access for users that do not need such service, do the following:

1. Edit the /etc/shells file to insert **/bin/false** as a valid shell. You can either manually modify the file using an editor such as vi or use linuxconf.

2. Modify each user account, using either usermod or linuxconf, to set the login shell to **/etc/false**.

After you complete these steps, the modified account cannot be used for Telnet access. You can also create more restricted user accounts for FTP-only users by using the guest account feature found in the wu-ftpd server. A guest FTP account is a real account with a real username and password. However, when a guest user accesses an FTP server, she does not see anything other than her own home directory. In other words, when a guest user logs in to an FTP server, the server does a chroot operation to the guest user's home directory which makes the home directory of the guest user appear as the entire file system. The great advantage to this setup is that the user is unable to see anything else, such as system files and other user directories.

Restricting superuser access

Many people mistakenly associate superuser access with only the root account. They think that if you are not the root user, you aren't the superuser. In fact, what makes the root account a superuser is not the name but its user ID (UID) and the group ID (GID). The root account's UID and GID are set to 0, which makes it a superuser. So, it is possible to create multiple superuser accounts by assigning them the previously mentioned UID and GID values. Superuser accounts are very powerful and prone to abuse. Thus, superuser accounts should be used infrequently, only when necessary, and with extreme care. Just because someone has superuser privileges does not mean that he or she should use it at all times. As a superuser, you may want to follow these guidelines:

- Use superuser accounts only when necessary. In other words, when you are configuring the system or installing system-wide software — such as installing a new version of the Web server software, compiling and installing Perl for the entire system, or performing some similar task — you may use the superuser account. However, avoid using the root account or any superuser-equivalent account to do everyday tasks, such as sending e-mail, browsing the Web, running an IRC client to talk to friends or coworkers, transferring files via FTP, and so on.

Tip

Sometimes, new system administrators wonder why they can't Telnet to a system as the root user. The reason is that the /etc/securetty file specifies which tty device can be used for root logins. Typically, /etc/securetty lists tty[0-8] as allowed devices. Because Telnet access will use pseudo tty device ttyp[0-f], root cannot log in via Telnet. Keep /etc/securetty as is.

- Do not log in as root or an equivalent superuser from anywhere. The preferred method of performing administrative tasks is to log in as a normal user and then use the su command to become a superuser (such as root). This reduces chances of accidental damage to your system.

Tip

Run the su command with - as an argument so that it will make the shell a login shell, which in turn will make the shell read the shell startup files (such as .bashrc). This argument also makes su change the directory to the user's home directory.

- If you have a situation in which others need to have superuser access to perform their jobs, consider using sudo instead of giving everyone a superuser account. If others need to run some programs that require superuser access, you can specify these users in the /etc/sudoers file such that they will be able to run these programs without being a superuser. The sudo command allows a normal user to run certain commands (specified by the superuser) as a superuser. This is a good mechanism because it is less risky than giving someone full superuser access. The sudo command itself runs as a setuid root. This means that when sudo runs, it runs as a root user process, which allows it to run other programs that require superuser privileges. Red Hat Linux does not come with the sudo package, but you can get it from the `ftp://contrib.redhat.com/` site. Typically, accessing Red Hat's busy FTP servers is hard, so if you are having no luck with its servers, try the `http://www.courtesan.com/sudo/` site, the official sudo Web site, which has a great deal of information on sudo, including a list of FTP sites for sudo.

The main idea is to reduce superuser privileges whenever you can.

Restricting all access in an emergency or attack

In many cases, when a system administrator detects an attack or emergency (such as a disk problem), the first task is to disallow user logins until the problem has been resolved or the system has been taken offline. Sometimes, a bit of deliberation is required by the administrator before the system can be shut down. In such a case, disallowing new logins becomes important. To disallow new logins quickly, create a file called /etc/nologin with an appropriate message to let users know why you are blocking them and when the system is expected to come back online. The presence of this file disallows any normal user login. Because superusers are allowed to log in only from the console, be sure that you have physical console access to the system, or else you might accidentally log out of your current shell sessions and lock yourself out of the system.

Using Shadow Passwords

Only a handful of programs, including login, passwd, and so on, really need the encrypted password field in the /etc/passwd file. All the other programs just need user information, such as the username, UID, GID, and shell. Consequently, you can relocate the encrypted passwords from /etc/passwd to another file and change the programs that need access to encrypted passwords in a way that they can read this file. This file won't be world-readable, because the programs that will be allowed access will be run as setuid root programs. In other words, these programs will run as root user to read the new password file. A package called Shadow Utils does all of this for you.

Shadow password support is found in the Shadow Utils package, which is not installed by default. Once installed, this package provides utilities that enable you to convert your /etc/passwd file into a password-free file. The encrypted passwords will be relocated in /etc/shadow, which will be readable only by root and any program run as setuid root. This means that a bad guy who exploits weak programs to get access to /etc/passwd may still get it, but the file will not provide any password information. The shadow utility package provides other interesting features, too, such as password aging, account expiration, and locking features. The following section describes how to use shadow passwords on your system.

Installing the shadow utility package

Get the file shadow-utils-*(version-release-architecture)*.rpm (for instance, shadow-utils-980403-4.i386.rpm) from your Red Hat CD-ROM or the Red Hat FTP site. Install it using the rpm utility, as follows:

```
rpm -ivh shadow utility rpm file
```

After you install the package, you need to convert the existing /etc/passwd file into a shadow password-based /etc/passwd file.

Converting /etc/passwd and /etc/group to shadow format

The traditional /etc/passwd file has the following format:

```
username:passwd:UID:GID:full_name:directory:shell
```

To convert the /etc/passwd and /etc/group files to shadow /etc/passwd format, simply run

```
/usr/sbin/pwconv
```

After you convert /etc/passwd, it will have the following format:

```
username:x:UID:GID:full_name:directory:shell
```

The second field now has an x instead of the encrypted password. You also have another file called /etc/shadow, which has the following format:

```
username:passwd:last:may:must:warn:expire:disable:reserved
```

The encrypted password field (*passwd*) is now in this file. All the fields in the /etc/shadow file are described in Table 15-1.

Table 15-1 *Fields in the /etc/shadow File*

Fields	Description
username	The username
passwd	The encrypted character password
last	Date of last password change
may	Minimum number of days after which the current password may be changed
must	Maximum number of days after which the current password must be changed
warn	Number of days after which the user will be warned about the current password becoming expired
expire	Number of days after which the current password expires and the account is disabled
disable	Number of days since the account has expired

The new fields (everything but the *username* and *passwd*) can be used to provide the user accounting functionality, such as account expiration and password aging. The /usr/sbin/pwconv utility uses the PASS_MAX _DAYS (maximum number of days after which the current password must be changed), PASS_MIN_DAYS (minimum number of days after which the current password may be changed), and PASS_WARN_AGE (number of days after which the user will be warned about the current password becoming expired) values from /etc/login.defs file. Modify the /etc/login.defs file to set desirable values for these fields.

Managing user accounts

The shadow utility package installs replacements for utilities such as useradd, userdel, usermod, groupadd, groupdel, and groupmod, which typically are used to manage user accounts. You can run the following rpm command to find out what actually got installed when you installed this package:

```
rpm -q -l shadow-utils-version-release
```

Replace *version-release* with actual version and release information from your copy of the shadow utility package.

The new and increasingly popular linuxconf utility is also capable of working with shadow password systems. This dialog box becomes part of the user account creation process and allows you to specify information about password aging, account expiration, and so on. You can also change the default values for PASS_MAX_DAYS, PASS_MIN_DAYS, and PASS_WARN_AGE, which are stored in /etc/login.defs, using linuxconf.

Using Pluggable Authentication Modules (PAM)

You may wonder how programs such as chsh, chfn, ftp, imap, linuxconf, rlogin, rexec, rsh, su, login, and passwd suddenly understand the shadow password scheme and use the /etc/shadow password file for authentication. They can do so because Red Hat distributes these programs with shadow password capabilities. Actually, Red Hat ships these programs with a much grander scheme of authentication support called *Pluggable Authentication Modules (PAMs)*. These PAM-aware programs are capable of using not only the shadow password scheme but virtually any other authentication scheme that you care to implement to enhance your system security.

Traditionally, authentication schemes are built into programs that grant privileges to users. Programs such as login or passwd used to be built with the necessary code to handle authentication. Over time, this approach proved to be really nonscalable, because incorporating a new authentication scheme required that privilege-granting programs be recoded and recompiled. To relieve the privilege-granting software developer from writing secure authentication code, PAM was developed. Figure 15-1 shows how PAM works with privilege-granting applications.

When a privilege-granting application such as /bin/login is made into a PAM-aware application, it typically works in the manner shown in Figure 15-1 and described here:

1. First, a user invokes such an application to access the service it offers.

2. The PAM-aware application calls the underlying PAM library to perform the authentication.

3. The PAM library looks up an application-specific configuration file in the /etc/pam.d/ directory. This file tells PAM what type of authentication is required for this application.

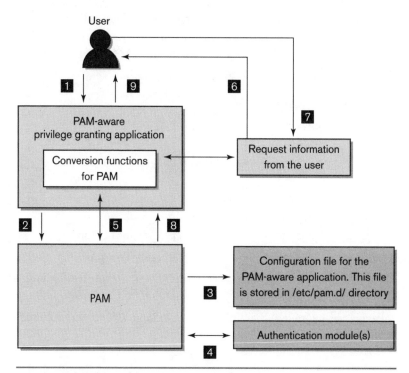

Figure 15-1 *How PAM-aware applications work*

4. The PAM library loads the required authentication module(s).

5. These modules can then make PAM communicate with the conversation functions available in the application.

6. The conversation functions can be used to request information from the user. For example, the user can be asked to enter a password or look into a retinal scanner.

7. The user responds to the request by providing requested information.

8. The PAM authentication modules supply the application with an authentication status message via the PAM library.

9. If the authentication process is successful, the application grants the requested privileges to the user or informs the user about the failure.

Think of PAM as a facility that takes the burden of authentication away from the applications and allows you to stack multiple authentication schemes for a single application. For example, the PAM configuration file for the rlogin application is shown in Listing 15-1.

Listing 15-1 *The /etc/pam.d/rlogin File*
```
auth        required /lib/security/pam_securetty.so
auth        sufficient /lib/security/pam_rhosts_auth.so
auth        required /lib/security/pam_pwdb.so shadow
nullok
auth        required /lib/security/pam_nologin.so
account     required /lib/security/pam_pwdb.so
password    required /lib/security/pam_cracklib.so
password    required /lib/security/pam_pwdb.so shadow
nullok \ use_authtok
session     required /lib/security/pam_pwdb.so
```

In this file, multiple authentication modules from /lib/security are used to authenticate the user.

Working with a PAM configuration file

Listing 15-1 shows what an application-specific PAM configuration file looks like. Lines starting with a leading # character and blank lines are ignored. A configuration line has the following fields:

```
module-type control-flag module-path module-args
```

Currently, four module types exist, which are described in Table 15-2

Table 15-2 *PAM Module Types*

Module Type	Description
auth	Does the actual authentication. Typically, an auth module requires a user to enter a password or provide some other proof to prove that she is who she claims to be.
account	Handles all the accounting aspects of an authentication request. Typically, an account module checks whether the user access meets all the access guidelines. For example, it can check whether the user is accessing the service from a secure host and during a specified time.

Module Type	Description
password	Handles things that need to be done before and after the user is given access to the requested service.
session	Used to handle session management tasks, such as refreshing session tokens.

The control flag is used to define how the PAM library will handle a module's response. Four control flags are currently allowed, which are described in Table 15-3.

Table 15-3 *PAM Module Control Flags*

Control Flag	Description
required	Specifies that the success of the module specified in the same line is a requirement. When a module returns a response indicating a failure, the authentication will definitely fail, but PAM will still continue with other modules (if any). This is done to ensure that the user cannot detect which part of the authentication process failed, because knowing that information might aid a potential attacker.
requisite	When this control flag is used, the authentication process aborts as soon as a failure response is received by the PAM library.
sufficient	When this control flag is used, the authentication process is considered complete if a success response is received. In other words, proceeding with other modules in the configuration file is unnecessary.
optional	This control flag is hardly used. It does not put any emphasis on the success or failure response of the module.

The module path is the path of a pluggable authentication module. Red Hat Linux stores all the PAM modules in the /lib/security directory. You can supply each module with optional arguments, as well.

Looking back at Listing 15-1, notice that the PAM library calls the pam_securetty.so module, which must return a response indicating success in order for the authentication to be successful. If the module's response indicates failure, PAM will still continue processing the other modules so that the user (who could be a potential attacker) is not aware of where the failure occurred. If the next module (pam_rhosts_auth.so) returns a success response, the authentication process is complete, because the control flag is set to sufficient. However, if the previous module (map_securetty.so) does not fail but this one fails, the authentication process will continue and the failure will not affect the final result. In the same fashion, the rest of the modules will be processed by the PAM library.

The order of execution exactly follows the way the modules appear in the configuration. However, each type of module (auth, account, password, and session) will be processed in a stack. In other words, for the example in Listing 15-1, all the auth modules will be stacked and processed in the order of appearance in the configuration file. The rest of the modules will be processed in a similar fashion.

Using PAM to fine-tune the authentication process

Now that you know so much about how PAM works, consider an example of how you can use PAM to fine-tune authentication processes for certain services. The very first step you should take is to read the documentation for all the available PAM authentication modules. All the available PAM modules are stored in the /lib/security directory, and you can find documentation on each module in the /usr/doc/pam-*X.xx* directory, where *X.xx* is your PAM version. Read the documentation for each module and determine which you want to use in building a more restrictive authentication scheme for your system. In this section I will show you how you can restrict login access to your server by time.

To restrict access to services by time, you need an accounting module called pam_time (/lib/security/pam_time.so). This module can be configured to deny access to (individual) users based on their name, the time of day, the day of the week, the service they are applying for, and the terminal from which they are making their request. Its actions are determined with the /etc/security/time.conf configuration file.

Because you want to control login access, you need to modify the /etc/pam.d/login PAM configuration file by adding the following line:

```
account    required   /lib/security/pam_time.so
```

Next, you need to devise an access policy for login service. In other words, you need to determine when you want users to be able to log in. This example assumes that you want to allow users to be able to log in after 6 a.m. and no later than 8 p.m. Now, you need to configure the /etc/

security/time.conf file. The configuration lines in this file have the following syntax:

```
services;ttys;users;times
```

You can use some special characters in each of the fields. Table 15-4 shows the meaning of the special characters that you can use.

Table 15-4 *Special Characters for Configuration Fields in /etc/security/time.conf*

Character	Meaning
!	NOT. For example, !login means "not login" or "except login."
|	OR. For example, kabir|ronak means "either kabir or ronak."
&	AND. For example, login&su means "both login and su."
*	Wildcard. For example, foo* means "everything that starts with foo."

Table 15-5 describes the fields in such a configuration line.

Table 15-5 *Fields of the /etc/security/time.conf File*

Field	Description
services	A list of services that are affected by the time restriction. For example, to control both login and su using a single rule, specify the service to be "login&su" in a configuration line.
ttys	A list of terminals that are affected by the time restriction. For example, to control only pseudoterminals and not the console terminals, specify "ttyp*!tty*," where ttyp* lists all the pseudoterminals used in remote login via services such as Telnet, and tty* lists all the console terminals.
users	A list of users that are affected by the time restriction. For example, to specify all the users, use the wildcard character * in a configuration line.
time	A list of times when the restrictions apply. You can specify time as a range in a 24-hour clock format. For example, to specify a range from 8 p.m. to 6 a.m., specify 2000–0600 (i.e., *HHMM* format, where *HH* is 00–23 and *MM* is 00–59). You can also specify days by using a two-character code, such as Mo (Monday), Tu (Tuesday), We (Wednesday), Th (Thursday), Fr (Friday), Sa (Saturday), and Su (Sunday). You can also use special codes, such as Wk for all weekdays, Wd for weekends, and Al for all seven days. For example, to restrict access to a service from 8 p.m. to 6 a.m. on a daily basis, specify a time range as !Al2000–0600.

For the ongoing example, you can create a time-based rule that prohibits login access from 8 p.m. to 6 a.m. for all users who access the system via remote means (such as Telnet), by adding the following line in the /etc/security/time.conf file:

```
login;ttyp*;*;!Al2000-0600
```

This line can be interpreted as follows:

```
If (requested service is login) and
   (access is made from a pseudo ttyp type device) and
   (current time is between 8PM to 6 AM) then

   Access to the requested service is not allowed.

Else
Access to the requested service is permitted.

End
```

If you want to allow a user called kabir access to the system at any time, but require all other users to follow the preceding rule, modify the rule as follows:

```
login;ttyp*;*!kabir;!Al2000-0600
```

This is just a single example of how PAM can be used to fine-tune your user authentication process. Again, read the module documentation and experiment with the settings to come up with the most suitable authentication scheme for your system.

Securing Services

Too often, a system's security is compromised by a bad guy because the system administrator did not take the time to weed out unnecessary services. Remember that the more programs you have on your system, the more ways a bad guy can break in. So, start the weeding-out process from the very beginning.

Removing unnecessary services during OS installation

Before you install Red Hat Linux on your computer, decide what you want to run on the system. Write down what services are needed to accomplish your goals. For example, if you are creating a Web server system, you are not likely to need the POP server, the gopher server, or the NNTP News server. Make a list of server software that you want to install. The Red Hat Linux installation program allows you to select individual packages before installation. Take the time to go through all the lists and select only the necessary packages. Sometimes, the installation program will install one or more packages that are prerequisites to the packages that you have selected. It will actually show you these prerequisite package names after you complete your package selection during the installation process. Write down the names of these packages.

After you install all the necessary packages and boot the system for the first time, you can either look at the installation log stored in /tmp or run the following rpm command to get the complete listing of all installed packages:

```
rpm —qa > /tmp/all.packages
```

Carefully go through the /tmp/all.packages file to detect any packages that you do not recall approving for installation. If the package does not show up in your prerequisite list, you may want to find out more about the package, by using the following command:

```
rpm —qi package_name
```

If the package seems unnecessary, remove it by using the following command:

```
rpm —e package_name
```

The rpm command checks whether the package_name is required by some other package. If it is, you get a warning message and the package is not removed unless you use the —e --force options. Carefully read what the warning says and decide accordingly. If the package is not a dependency for any other package, it is cleanly removed from your system.

I recommend not installing the following types of packages on a computer that will be used as a server on the Internet:

- Anything related to X-Windows and X-Windows itself.

- Any multimedia applications (except the real-audio/video server package if you plan to provide real-audio/video services).

- Any interpreter other than what is required. I personally use only Perl for scripting and therefore do not install other scripting languages.

- Any unnecessary server software, such as NFS, NIS, INN, POP2 or 3, or Samba, that you do not need to have.

- Any file editor that you do not use. I use only vi and therefore do not install a complex editor such as emacs. Of course, if you are an emacs kind of person, you would choose this beast over vi. I also do not install various newer vi clones.

- Any client program that you do not need. For example, do not install e-mail clients that you do not think will be used by you or your users.

As you can see, the theme is always the same — the less you install, the less you have to worry about.

Securing inetd-run services

The inetd daemon is called the Internet "super server" because it is used to provide many such popular Internet services as FTP, Telnet, POP2/3, and finger. The inetd daemon typically is started at some point during the multiuser boot process. At startup, the inetd daemon reads the /etc/inetd.conf configuration and listens for requests on all standard ports listed in /etc/services. When a request is received on a certain port, the inetd daemon starts the appropriate service to process the request. Listing 15-2 shows a typical /etc/inetd.conf file.

Listing 15-2 *An /etc/inetd.conf File*

```
#
# inetd.conf
# This file describes the services that will be available
# through the INETD TCP/IP super server.  To reconfigure
```

```
# the running INETD process, edit this file, then send
the
# INETD process a SIGHUP signal.
#
# Version: @(#)/etc/inetd.conf 3.10 05/27/93
#
# Authors: Original taken from BSD UNIX 4.3/TAHOE.
#          Fred N. van Kempen,
<waltje@uwalt.nl.mugnet.org>
#
# Modified for RHS Linux by Marc Ewing <marc@redhat.com>
#
# <service_name> <sock_type> <proto> <flags> <user> \
# <server_path> <args>
#
# Echo, discard, daytime, and chargen are used
# primarily for testing.
#
# To re-read this file after changes,
# just do a 'killall -HUP inetd'
#
#echo stream tcp nowait root internal
#echo dgram udp wait root internal
#discard stream tcp nowait root internal
#discard dgram udp wait root internal
#daytime stream tcp nowait root internal
#daytime dgram udp wait root internal
#chargen stream tcp nowait root internal
#chargen dgram udp wait root internal
#
# These are standard services.
#
ftp stream tcp nowait root /usr/sbin/tcpd in.ftpd -l -a
```

Continued

Listing 15-2 *Continued*

```
telnet stream tcp nowait root /usr/sbin/tcpd in.telnetd
gopher stream  tcp nowait  root    /usr/sbin/tcpd gn

# Do not uncomment smtp unless you *really* know what you
are doing.
# smtp is handled by the sendmail daemon now, not smtpd.
# It does NOT
# run from here, it is started at boot time from
/etc/rc.d/rc#.d.
#
#smtp stream  tcp  nowait  root    /usr/bin/smtpd smtpd
#nntp stream tcp nowait root /usr/sbin/tcpd in.nntpd
#
# Shell, login, exec and talk are BSD protocols.
#
shell stream tcp nowait root /usr/sbin/tcpd in.rshd
login stream tcp nowait root /usr/sbin/tcpd in.rlogind
exec stream tcp nowait root /usr/sbin/tcpd in.rexecd
talk dgram udp wait root /usr/sbin/tcpd in.talkd
ntalk dgram udp wait root /usr/sbin/tcpd in.ntalkd
#dtalk stream tcp waut nobody /usr/sbin/tcpd in.dtalkd
#
# Pop and imap mail services et al
#
pop-2 stream  tcp  nowait  root    /usr/sbin/tcpd ipop2d
pop-3 stream  tcp  nowait  root    /usr/sbin/tcpd ipop3d
imap  stream  tcp  nowait  root    /usr/sbin/tcpd imapd
#
# The Internet UUCP service.
#
#uucp stream tcp nowait uucp /usr/sbin/tcpd
/usr/lib/uucp/uucico -l
#
```

```
# Tftp service is provided primarily for booting.  Most
sites
# run this only on machines acting as "boot servers."
# Do not uncomment this unless you *need* it.
#
#tftp dgram udp wait root /usr/sbin/tcpd in.tftpd
#bootps dgram udp wait root /usr/sbin/tcpd bootpd
#
# Finger, systat, and netstat give out user information
# which may be valuable to potential "system crackers."
# Many sites choose to disable some or all of these
# services to improve security.
#
# cfinger is for GNU finger, which is currently not in
# use in RHS Linux
#
finger stream tcp nowait root /usr/sbin/tcpd in.fingerd
#cfinger stream tcp nowait root /usr/sbin/tcpd
in.cfingerd
#systat stream tcp nowait guest /usr/sbin/tcpd /bin/ps -
auwwx
#netstat stream tcp nowait guest /usr/sbin/tcpd
/bin/netstat -f inet
#
# Time service is used for clock synchronization.
#
time stream tcp nowait nobody /usr/sbin/tcpd in.timed
time dgram udp wait nobody /usr/sbin/tcpd in.timed
#
# Authentication
#
auth stream tcp nowait nobody /usr/sbin/in.identd
in.identd -l -e -o
```

Continued

Listing 15-2 *Continued*

```
linuxconf stream tcp wait root /bin/linuxconf linuxconf -
-http
#
# End of inetd.conf
```

As in many other UNIX configuration files, the lines starting with a # character are treated as comments and are ignored along with blank lines. Each of the configuration lines has the following format:

service_name sock_type proto flags user server_path args

The service_name field matches the service name specified in the /etc/services file. The following is an example:

```
finger stream tcp nowait root /usr/sbin/tcpd in.fingerd
```

The /etc/services file maps finger service to TCP port 79. When inetd gets a connection request on TCP port 79, it starts the /usr/sbin/tcpd service with the in.fingerd argument. The tcpd program, which is called a TCP wrapper, starts the in.fingerd finger server. The finger server responds to the request as it sees fit.

Removing unnecessary services from /etc/inetd.conf

The default /etc/inetd.conf is unlikely to be ideal for your needs. Go through this file and remove or comment out any service that you do not want to provide to anyone. For example, the preceding /etc/inetd.conf file, which was installed by default, enables FTP, Telnet, Gopher, remote shell (rsh), remote login (rlogin), remote exec (rexec), talk, ntalk, POP2, POP3, IMAP, finger, time (tcp), time (udp), auth (ident), and Web service for lin-uxconf. This is virtually like keeping the system wide open to attack. Any of the services that are available via inetd are open doors for potential attacks. On my Web server systems, I keep only the FTP, Telnet, and POP3 services, because these are used by the users. So, the /etc/inetd.conf on my Red Hat Linux server looks like this:

```
ftp     stream  tcp  nowait  root /usr/sbin/tcpd in.ftpd
-l -a
```

```
telnet  stream  tcp  nowait  root /usr/sbin/tcpd
in.telnetd
pop-3   stream  tcp  nowait  root /usr/sbin/tcpd ipop3d
```

Figure out what services you must keep and what you can live without. Do not forget to restart inetd services after modifying /etc/inetd.conf. You can use the killall −HUP inetd command to restart it.

Using the TCP wrapper to secure inetd run services

The configuration lines in /etc/inetd.conf indicate that the server_path part of each line is always /usr/sbin/tcpd and the actual server program is an argument to the tcpd program. For example,

```
pop-3   stream  tcp  nowait  root /usr/sbin/tcpd ipop3d
```

is functionally equivalent to having the following line:

```
pop-3   stream  tcp  nowait  root  /usr/sbin/ipop3d
```

When a POP3 request is received by inetd, the ipop3d server is started in both cases, but the first one is much more secure than the other, because the tcpd program is a TCP wrapper program that enhances security by providing the following services:

- **Logging service.** Logs information about a request by using the syslog facility.
- **Host-based access control.** Provides host-based access control by using pattern matching.
- **Host name and address verification service.** Detects spoofing of host names or addresses when a host is pretending to be some other host.

The TCP wrapper is sufficiently important that it comes as part of the default Red Hat Linux installation. Absolutely no reason exists for not wrapping each of your inetd services with the TCP wrapper.

Caution

By default, Red Hat Linux does not wrap the Web service for lin-uxconf using tcpd, because it appears to not work when wrapped with tcpd. This is a very good reason not to run a linux-conf Web service.

Restricting host access via the TCP wrapper As mentioned before, the TCP wrapper provides a great deal of flexibility in controlling access at an Internet host (or IP address) level. This flexibility can come in very handy for configuring a tight server system. This section discusses an example of a tightly controlled system that is based on a system I use on a daily basis.

First, decide on the goal of the example control configuration. Suppose that you want to create an Internet Web server system that allows only Telnet, FTP, POP3, and HTTP services. Because the Web service (HTTP) is typically a high-demand service, it is not run via inetd. Assume that the Web server is Apache and it is run as a standalone service. Thus, inetd will manage the rest of the service. Also, assume that you want to restrict Telnet, FTP, and POP3 access to only a single network whose network address is 206.171.50.0.

Listing 15-3 shows the /etc/inetd.conf file required for this example.

Listing 15-3 *The /etc/inetd.conf File*

```
ftp     stream  tcp  nowait  root /usr/sbin/tcpd in.ftpd
-l -a
telnet  stream  tcp  nowait  root /usr/sbin/tcpd
in.telnetd
pop-3   stream  tcp  nowait  root /usr/sbin/tcpd ipop3d
```

As you can see, all three services are wrapped with the tcpd wrapper. Now, you need to restrict access to these services via the /etc/hosts.allow and /etc/hosts.deny files. The /etc/hosts.allow file is used to specify which hosts are allowed access to inetd services, and the /etc/hosts.deny file is used to specify which hosts are not allowed access to inetd services. Both of these files use the same configuration format, shown here:

daemon list : client list [: shell command]

The daemon list is a list of one or more service process names. For instance, in.ftpd, in.telnetd, and ipop3d are daemon names for this example. The client list consists of one or more host names or IP addresses. You can use the wildcards shown in Table 15-6 in both daemon and client lists.

Table 15-6 *Wildcards for Daemon and Client Lists in /etc/hosts.[allow | deny] Files*

Wildcard	Meaning
ALL	Always matches.
LOCAL	Matches a local host name such as wormhole, but not `wormhole.nitec.com`.
UNKNOWN	Matches when the host name or IP address is unknown due to a problem.
KNOWN	Matches when a host or IP address is known.
PARANOID	Matches a host that does not match its IP address. This works only if the tcpd wrapper program is not built with the –DPARANOID option at compilation.

You can also use patterns such as the following:

- '.nitec.com' matches a host name such as `wormhole.nitec.com` or `picaso.nitec.com`. In other words, when a leading dot is used in a pattern, it can be matched from the right side of the host name.
- '206.171.50.' matches any hosts with addresses in the range of 206.171.50.0 to 206.171.50.255. In other words, when a trailing dot is used in a pattern, the matching is done from the left.
- '206.171.50.0/255.255.255.0' matches any hosts with addresses in the range of 206.171.50.0 to 206.171.50.255. The pattern is treated as a network/netmask definition.

Also, if you plan to use shell commands to perform some action, take advantage of the character expansions shown in Table 15-7.

Table 15-7 *Character Expansions for Shell Commands*

Character	Expanded Meaning
%a	The IP address of the client trying to access a service
%A	The IP address of the server
%c	Client information such as host name or IP address, or *user@host* or *user@ip_address*, etc.
%d	The name of the daemon or service
%h	The host name of the client trying to access a service
%H	The host name of the server

Continued

Table 15-7 *Continued*

Character	Expanded Meaning
%p	The process ID (PID) of the daemon or service
%s	Server information such as host name or IP address, or *user@host* or *user@ip_address*, etc.
%u	The client username, if known; otherwise, set to unknown
%%	The % character

Because the goal in this example is to disallow all the hosts except for the ones belonging to the 206.171.50.0 network, you can create a /etc/hosts.deny file, as shown in Listing 15-4.

Listing 15-4 *The /etc/hosts.deny File*

```
#
# hosts.deny   This file describes the names of the
# hosts that are not allowed to use the local INET
# services, as decided by the /usr/sbin/tcpd program.
#


# Deny all daemon access to all hosts.
#
ALL : ALL
```

The /etc/hosts.deny file is set up to deny all hosts. The single configuration line, ALL : ALL, tells the TCP wrapper (tcpd) to deny ALL daemon access to ALL hosts. If it is left as is and no /etc/hosts.allow file exists in the system, no host will be able to access any of the three inetd-run services (Telnet, FTP, and POP3). So, you must allow specific hosts, particularly the 206.171.50.0 network, to access these services in the /etc/hosts.allow file. This is done in Listing 15-5.

Listing 15-5 *The /etc/hosts.allow File*

```
#
# hosts.allow   This file describes the names of the
# hosts that are allowed to use the local INET
```

```
# services, as decided by the /usr/sbin/tcpd program.
#

# Deny all daemon access to all hosts.
#
ALL : 206.171.50.0/255.255.255.0
```

Here, the single configuration line, ALL : 206.171.50.0/255.255.255.0, states that the TCP wrapper (tcpd) should allow access to ALL daemons for the specified 206.171.50.0 network. In other words, all the hosts in the IP range of 206.171.50.0 to 206.171.50.255 should have access to the Telnet, FTP, and POP3 services.

That's all there is to configuring the TCP wrapper. Now, if you want to allow another network, 208.233.7.48/255.255.255.240, to access these services, the only change needed is in /etc/hosts.allow. Simply add this network in the client list as follows:

```
ALL : 206.171.50.0/255.255.255.0
208.233.7.48/255.255.255.240
```

As you can see, configuring tcpd using /etc/hosts.allow and /etc/hosts.deny is quite simple.

Using host and domain names in /etc/hosts.allow Suppose that you want to allow all hosts from the classifiedworks.com domain to access all the inetd services except for the msql.classifiedworks.com host. The /etc/hosts.deny file will have a single line, such as ALL: ALL, to deny all service to everyone not specified in /etc/hosts.allow. The /etc/hosts.allow file will have a line such as this:

```
ALL: .classifiedworks.com EXCEPT msql.classifiedworks.com
```

Blocking a service to a specific host This example demonstrates how to block the FTP service to a single host called reboot.nitec.com when all the other hosts in the nitec.com domain are allowed to access all the services. The /etc/hosts.deny file will have a single line, such as ALL: ALL, to deny all service to everyone not specified in

/etc/hosts.allow. The /etc/hosts.allow file will have lines such as the following:

```
in.ftpd: .nitec.com EXCEPT reboot.nitec.com
ALL EXCEPT in.ftpd: .nitec.com
```

The first line states that the in.ftpd daemon is allowed to service all the hosts in the `nitec.com` domain except `reboot.nitec.com`. The next line states that all daemons (that is, services) except the FTP service (in.ftpd) are allowed to service all the hosts in the `nitec.com` domain.

The TCP wrapper can also be configured using an extended host access control language that uses the following configuration syntax:

```
daemon list : client list : option : option : . . .
```

An *option* can be any of the keywords shown in Table 15-8.

Table 15-8 *Acceptable Keywords in Extended Host Access Control Language*

Keyword	Description
ALLOW *client list*	Used to permit access to one or more hosts. For example,
	ALL : .your-domain.com : ALLOW
	allows all the hosts in **your-domain.com** access to all the inetd-run services.
DENY *client list*	Used to restrict access to one or more hosts. For example,
	ALL: .bad-guy-domain.com : DENY
	denies all the hosts in **bad-guy-domain.com** access to all the inetd-run services.
SPAWN *shell command*	Used to execute a shell command. The command is run such that STDIN, STDOUT, and STDERR are directed to /dev/null. This makes sure the command does not interfere with the client software on the host trying to access a service. The character expansion discussed earlier applies before the command is called.
TWIST *shell command*	Used to execute a shell command. The command is run such that STDIN, STDOUT, and STDERR are directed to the client. The character expansion discussed earlier applies before the command is called. Use TWIST as the last option in the configuration line. I recommend using TWIST only for TCP-based services.
LINGER *seconds*	Used to make the kernel retry data delivery for a specified number of seconds.

Keyword	Description
RFC931 *seconds*	Used to look up user information on the client side when the client is running an RFC 931-complaint IDENT server. The specified seconds are used to time out in case the IDENT server is not responding. This works only for TCP-based services.
BANNERS *directory*	Used to display a text file to the client. The text file or banner is looked up in the specified directory. The filename must be the same as the daemon name. This works only for connection-oriented TCP-based services such as Telnet.
NICE *number*	Used to change daemon process priority. The higher the number, the lower the priority.
SETENV *name value*	Sets the *name=value* in the environment process of the daemon. This does not always work, because many daemon processes reset their environment when handling a request using a child process.
UMASK *mask*	Used to set the file permission policy in the same manner as the traditional umask shell command.
USER *username.group*	Used to specify the user and group of the daemon process.

Using a shell command in /etc/hosts.allow Suppose that you want to block Telnet service for a host called **spooky.badguy-domain.com**, but you also want to let the host know that you don't welcome it. In such a case, you can create an /etc/hosts.allow configuration file, as follows:

```
# Everyone but spooky is allowed Telnet access
In.telnetd: ALL EXCEPT spooky.badguy-domain.com


# spooky.badguy-domain.com is made clear that it is
# not welcome on this server.
in.telnetd: spooky.badguy-domain.com: twist /bin/echo \
You are not welcome here!
```

Or, if you want to get e-mail as soon as the spooky host tries to Telnet, you can send yourself a message using the /bin/mail program. In such a case, you need an /etc/hosts.allow configuration, such as the following:

```
# Everyone but spooky is allowed Telnet access
In.telnetd: ALL EXCEPT spooky.badguy-domain.com
```

```
# spooky.badguy-domain.com is made clear that it is
# not welcome on this server.
in.telnetd: spooky.badguy-domain.com: linger 5: twist
/bin/mail \
-s "%a (%c) tried to access %d (%p)" your@emailaddress <
/etc/badguy-came.txt
```

Here, the /bin/mail program is invoked when spooky tries to Telnet in. The mail program is called with the −s option to set the subject line as "%a (%c) tried to access %d (%p)," which expands to "*x.x.x.x* (spooky.badguy-domain.com) tried to access in.telnetd (*xyz*)," where *x.x.x.x* is the IP address of the host, and *xyz* is the PID of the daemon process.

Checking your TCP wrapper configuration Mistakes in /etc/inetd. conf can be very costly as far as security is concerned. Therefore, it pays to check the configuration by using a program such as tcpdchk. This program examines your /etc/inetd.conf configuration file and reports problems such as nonexistent path names, misconfigurations in the /etc/hosts.allow or /etc/hosts.deny files, invalid arguments, and so on. You can run the tcpdchk program as follows:

```
/usr/sbin/tcpdchk
```

You also can use the tpcdmatch utility to test your /etc/hosts.allow and /etc/hosts.deny configuration. For example, suppose that you have a line such as ALL: 206.171.50.48/255.255.255.240 in /etc/hosts.allow and a line such as ALL:ALL in /etc/hosts.deny. The previously mentioned configuration allows only hosts from the 206.171.50.48 network to access the inetd-run services. To find out what tcpd will do when a Telnet request from a host called blackhole.nitec.com (206.170.189.100) comes, run the following command:

```
/usr/sbin/tcpdmatch in.telnetd blackhole.nitec.com
```

The tcpdmatch program will apply the /etc/hosts.[allow, deny] configuration and tell you whether or not access is permitted. Here is what it shows when the preceding command is run:

```
client:    hostname blackhole.nitec.com
client:    address  206.170.189.100
```

```
server:    process   in.telnetd
matched:   /etc/hosts.deny line 10
access:    denied
```

This utility allows you to test your tcpd configuration quite thoroughly.

The TCP wrapper is a must if you are going to run inetd on your system. More information about tcpd and its configuration can be obtained by reading the tcpd (8), tcpdchk (8), tcpdmatch (8), hosts.allow (5), and hosts_options (5) man pages. You can also find the tcpd source at `http://www.cert.org/ftp/tools/tcp_wrappers/`.

Replacing the r commands with Secure Shell (ssh)

If you do not use the r* commands, including rlogin, rsh, rexec, and so on, consider removing them completely from your system. You can comment out the lines specific to r* commands in the /etc/inetd.conf file to ensure that the services these commands provide are no longer available.

If you use these services to access your system, consider replacing them with a secured solution called Secure Shell or ssh, which gives you all the benefits of the r* commands (and then some). For example, using ssh, you can log in to a remote system or execute a command on the remote system using a secured, encrypted connection. It provides extensive logging capabilities and works well with syslog. With ssh, you can also create secure remote X sessions. It can provide protection against IP and DNS spoofing, attacks based on the weaknesses in the X authentication protocol, and so on. You can get ready to run RPM packages for ssh from the following Web site: `http://www.replay.com/redhat/ssh.html`.

You need the base ssh package, the ssh client package, and the ssh server package. U.S. export control laws for encryption software may place some legal restriction on ssh, so make sure you read the documentation found in the preceding Web site.

Protecting Your Files and File System

One of the best way to ensure file and filesystem security is to provide least privileged access to them. If users can get by with read access only, then don't give users write or execute access just because you can. The section discusses a few such issues.

Mounting file systems as read-only

It is a good idea to mount certain file systems as read-only, when possible. For example, if you have to maintain in a separate partition a public FTP server on which the public files are stored, you can mount the partition as read-only. For example, suppose that the public files are stored in /dev/sda5 (a partition of a SCSI disk) and are automatically mounted on /public via the following line in the /etc/fstab file:

```
/dev/sda5  /public  ext2  defaults  1 2
```

The mount option for the partition is "defaults," which means the following:

- Mount the file system as read/write (rw)
- Allow set-UID or set-GID bits to take effect (suid)
- Interpret character/block devices on the file system (dev)
- Allow execution of programs (exec)
- Mount the file system when the system is booted or the mount command is run with the –a option (auto)
- Do not allow anyone but a superuser (UID = 0, GID = 0) to mount the file system (nouser)
- Use a synchronous I/O mode for the file system (async)

If you are certain that this partition doesn't need write permission, change the line as follows:

```
/dev/sda5 /public ext2 ro,suid,dev,exec,auto,nouser,async
1 2
```

If you further decide that you don't need to allow suid and exec support, remove them, as well, as follows:

```
/dev/sda5 /public ext2
ro,nosuid,dev,noexec,auto,nouser,async 1 2
```

Use the EXT2 file system's attributes wherever appropriate. The most useful one I've used is the immutable flag, which makes it possible to disallow even root to change some files. Check the chattr(1) and lsattr(1) man pages for details.

Taking advantage of ext2 file system

Linux ext2 file system has a few neat features that could come very hand in protecting your files and directories against human errors.. For example, use the chattr command to provide protection from accidental modification and deletion by even the root user. Here is how.

The ext2 file system used for Red Hat Linux provides some unique features. One of these features allows a file to be made immutable by even the root user. For example,

```
chattr +i filename
```

sets the i attribute of a file in an ext2 file system. When this attribute is set, the file cannot be modified, deleted, or renamed by anyone. No links can be added to point to this file, either. This attribute can be set or cleared only by the root user. So, you can use this attribute to protect against file accidents. When you need to clear the attribute, run

```
chattr -i filename
```

A few other interesting features of the ext2 system, such as the undelete attribute, are not yet implemented but will become available in a future ext2 file system version. If you start using the chattr command, you may notice that sometimes you can't modify or delete a file even though you have the permission to do so. This happens when you forget that you have previously set the immutable attribute of the file by using chattr; because this attribute does not show up in the ls output, it can be a bit confusing. To see which files have what ext2 attributes, use the lsattr program.

Unfortunately, what you know now about file and file system security possibly is known by informed hackers. Using tools such as chattr might make damaging your files or file systems a bit harder for hackers, but it won't make it impossible for them to do so. In fact, if the bad guy gets root level privileges, ext2 attributes provide only a simple hide-and-seek game. One major problem after a break is to determine whether you can trust your files. You might wonder whether the bad guy has installed a Trojan horse application or embedded a virus to infect new files and possibly provide access to other computers that you access. None of the methods discussed in this section handles this aspect of a security problem. The solution is to run a file integrity checker program, such as Tripwire.

Using Tripwire to ensure file integrity

Simply speaking, Tripwire is a file and directory integrity checker that creates a database of signatures for all files and directories and stores them in a single file. When Tripwire is run again, it computes new signatures for current files and directories and compares them with the original signatures stored in the database. If a discrepancy exists, the file or directory name is reported along with information about the discrepancy.

Thus, Tripwire can be a great tool for helping you determine which files were modified in a break-in. When setting up a new server system, many experienced system administrators do the following things:

1. Ensure that the new system is not attached to any network, to guarantee that no one has already installed a Trojan horse program, virus program, or something similar.

2. Run Tripwire to create a signature database of all the important system files, including all the system binaries and configuration files.

3. Write the database in a recordable CD-ROM. This ensures that an advanced hacker can't modify the Tripwire database to hide Trojan horses and modified files from the application. Administrators who have relatively few files to monitor often use a floppy disk to store the database. After writing the database to the floppy disk, the administrator write-protects the disk and, if the BIOS permits, configures the disk drive as a read-only device.

4. Set up a cron job to run Tripwire on a periodic basis (daily, weekly, or monthly) such that the application uses the CD-ROM version of the database.

Installing Tripwire The official Red Hat distribution (the boxed version) sold by Red Hat includes an Application CD-ROM that contains a version of Tripwire. This version of the software is suitable for a single-CPU, end-user setup. The software comes in two separate RPM packages — one contains the binary distribution and the other contains the source distribution. Unless you are interested in compiling your own copy, use the binary distribution. Normally, I compile security software if I can, but because Red Hat packages this software in its product, I have a certain degree of trust in its professionalism; therefore, the binary installation is presented here.

As usual, the binary installation is quite simple; run the rpm command as follows:

```
rpm -ivh tripwire_package.rpm
```

Replace *tripwire_package.rpm* with the RPM package appropriate for your system architecture. After you install Tripwire, run **rpm -ql tripwire_package.rpm** to find out where the files are installed. The default installation directory is /usr/local/bin/tw for Tripwire version 1.3.

The RPM package containing the binary distribution of Tripwire doesn't contain any man pages. However, the man pages are included in the source distribution, so install the source RPM distribution of Tripwire, which is also included in the Application CD-ROM shipped with Red Hat.

After you install the source distribution using rpm, extract the source in the /usr/src/redhat/SOURCES directory to an appropriate location to access the man pages. If you want to install the man pages, follow these steps:

1. Extract the source distribution tar file in a directory and change the directory to the man subdirectory.

2. Edit the Makefile in the man directory and add **MANDIR = /usr/man** in a line after the comment lines at the top of the Makefile

3. Run **make** to install the man pages into appropriate man page locations in your system.

After you complete these steps, you have access to the siggen (8), tripwire (8), and tw.config (5) man pages, which you should read before continuing with Tripwire any further.

Creating a Tripwire database The very first task to get Tripwire working is to create a database of signatures for all the files and directories you want it to compare against. To do that, you must specify the files and directory names in a configuration file called **tw.config**, which is also stored in the /usr/local/bin/tw directory. The RPM package version of the configuration file is custom-suited for Linux systems. Modify it after you have read the tw.config man pages and understand the syntax used. Listing 15-6 shows the tw.config I use on a Red Hat Web server system.

Listing 15-6 *An Example tw.config File*

```
# $Id: tw.conf.linux,v 1.1 1994/04/04 00:34:03 gkim Exp $
#
# last updated: 1998/04/17 genek
#
# tripwire.config for linux machines

#  First, root's "home"
/root                   R
/                       R


# critical boot resources
/boot                   R


# Critical directories and files
#               some exceptions are noted further down
/etc                    R
/etc/inetd.conf         R
/etc/rc.d               R
/etc/exports            R
/etc/mtab               L
/etc/motd               L
/etc/group              R       # changes should be
infrequent
/etc/passwd             L


# other popular filesystems
/usr                    R
/usr/local              R
```

```
/dev                    L-am
/usr/etc                R

# truncate home
=/home                  R

# var tree
=/var/spool             L
/var/log                L
/var/spool/cron         L
/var/spool/mqueue       L
/var/spool/mail         L
!/var/lock
!/var/tripwire

# GENE:  /sbin contains binaries critical when in single
user mode
/sbin                   R

# other critical directories
/usr/etc                R

# unusual directories
=/proc                  E
=/tmp
```

Because the syntax of such a configuration file is well documented in the tw.config manual page, the file syntax is not discussed here.

Before you create the database file, make absolutely sure that the files on your current system haven't been modified already by bad guys. The ideal time for creating this database is when your new system has not yet been connected to the Internet or any other network. After you are certain that your files are untouched, change the directory to /usr/local/bin/tw and run Tripwire as follows:

```
./tripwire —initialize
```

After you create the database, quickly move it to a read-only medium, such as a CD-ROM if possible. You can also print the entire database content so that you can verify information manually, if need be. After you create the database, you also need to protect the Tripwire files.

Protecting Tripwire itself

Bad guys can modify the Tripwire binary file (tripwire) or the configuration file (tw.config) to hide traces of their work. For this reason, run the **siggen** utility to create a set of signatures for these files. To generate a signature for the tripwire binary, run the following command from the /usr/local/bin/tw directory:

```
./siggen tripwire
```

You will see something like the following on the screen:

```
sig0: nullsig  : 0
sig1: md5      : 0f17oytjSfosJBXXCBZxuo
sig2: snefru   : 2UOlnsPiKYtb5K2DJ0Z06G
sig3: crc32    : 08arMS
sig4: crc16    : 000DFd
sig5: md4      : 2DDym8m3JGRry.Y5WuPzX4
sig6: md2      : 3N7KPOm:A5ynvixPGLCW.O
sig7: sha      : 4AZqq5nq16DM7D6pbaRtMk49wGX
sig8: haval    : 07QMyy6T4EERZw1pMyzZkw
sig9: nullsig  : 0
```

You can keep the signature in a file by redirecting it to that file. Print the signature, as well, and don't forget to generate a signature for the siggen utility itself. If you ever get suspicious about Tripwire not working right, run the siggen utility on each of these files and compare the signatures. If any of them do not match, don't trust these files — replace them with new copies and launch an investigation of how the discrepancy happened.

Running Tripwire to detect integrity problems

You can run Tripwire in two ways:

- In interactive mode; whenever Tripwire encounters a file or directory that has been added, deleted, or changed, it asks you whether or not to update the database.

■ As a cron job, by creating a small script such as the one shown in Listing 15-7.

Listing 15-7 *The tripwire.sh File*

```
#!/bin/sh
/usr/local/bin/tw/tripwire -q | /bin/mail -s "Security
report by Tripwire" your@email
```

The −q allows tripwire to run quietly and send a report via mail to your@email address. You can put a script like this in your /etc/cron.daily directory to run it on a daily basis. Any changes to your files will be reported to you every day.

Updating the Tripwire database To update the entire Tripwire database, run

```
./tripwire -update
```

Or, if you want to add a new directory and all the files and subdirectories underneath it, run

```
./tripwire -update  /some/dir
```

This same command works when updating an existing, modified directory or its files. If you want to add or update only a single file, use the following syntax:

```
./tripwire -update   newfile
```

Weighing speed against a higher level of security Tripwire employs multiple signature algorithms, such as the null signature, Message Digesting Algorithm (MD5) from RSA Data Security, Inc., a Secure Hash Function called Snefru from Xerox, a Cyclic Redundancy Check (CRC-32), CRC-16, MD4, MD2, a Secure Hash Algorithm (SHA), and Haval.

Performing all of these algorithms on each file on a large file system takes a great deal of CPU resources and a long time. To reduce load on the system or to speed up the checking process, you can tell Tripwire to ignore one or more of these algorithms. For example,

```
./tripwire −i   1
```

tells Tripwire to ignore the first algorithm, MD5. You can use the −i command-line option to ignore any algorithm as long as you know the corresponding number of the algorithm. The number-to-algorithm map is shown in Table 15-9.

Table 15-9 *Tripwire Algorithms*

−i Option	Signature Algorithm
−i 0	Null signature
−i 1	MD5
−i 2	Snefru
−i 3	CRC-32
−i 4	CRC-16
−i 5	MD4
−i 6	MD2
−i 7	SHA
−i 8	Haval
−i 9	Null signature (reserved for future)

To locate new or missing files without any signature integrity checking, run

```
./tripwire −i all
```

Playing Devil's Advocate

Many experienced administrators feel that just taking preventive measures and hoping that nothing bad will ever happen is purely wishful thinking. To get a real sense of security, they feel that a system should be put to real tests. In other words, why not attack your security infrastructure yourself before the bad guy does it? By posing as a potential attacker, you may be able to reveal potential vulnerabilities yourself before the unfriendly ones find out. Luckily, you do not have to work too hard to become a "bad guy" these days. Tools are available that can help you assume the role of a bad guy quite easily. This section discusses some of these commonly used tools.

Cracking your own passwords

Weak passwords typically are an easy target for attackers of all ages. After a bad guy manages to illegally acquire your /etc/passwd file (if you are not yet using shadow passwords), he or she will feed it to the password-cracking programs to reveal your secrets — the weak passwords. So, cracking your own passwords before hackers do can help you to eliminate weak passwords.

How passwords are cracked

The best way to understand the cryptic details of this cryptography is to use an example. If you create a new user on your system with a username bob and password umbrella, you will see a line in the /etc/passwd file that looks something like the following line:

```
bob:XoAlxlaiwepBs:Red Hat Linux User:/home/bob:/bin/bash
```

The line may not look quite the same, but the point is that you will have a line with bob's encrypted password. The encrypted password is a 13-character string created by a function called crypt() as follows:

```
Encrypted Password (XoAlxlaiwepBs) = crypt('umbrella',
salt)
```

The *salt* is a two-character string chosen from a set of [a–zA–Z0–9./]. This string is used to influence the encryption algorithm in one of 4,096 different ways. The *solt* value is stored in the encrypted password as the first two characters. For example, if XoAlxlaiwepBs is the encrypted password for umbrella, the *solt* value used is Xo. No known way exists of retrieving the original password from the encrypted version, because the encryption algorithm used is one-way only. However, if the encrypted password is known, then a program can be written to use the two-character *solt* value and encrypt a large dictionary of words with this *solt*. If the password happens to be a word in the dictionary, as it is in this example, it will be *solt*ed and a match will be found. In other words, when you know that the *solt* value for bob's password is Xo, you can use this *solt* to write a program to do the following:

```
Encrypted Password = crypt(each dictionary_word, Xo)
```

When this program chooses the word "umbrella," the encrypted password will be same as the one stored in /etc/passwd. Too bad, bob's password has just been cracked! Now the program knows which word (umbrella) was used to create the password. This is the simplified explanation of how cracking software works. However, bear in mind that today's cracking software is much more advanced, and as computer hardware becomes more and more powerful, cracking passwords becomes easier and faster.

Installing Crack to crack your own passwords

To crack your system's passwords, you need a password-cracking program. Crack is one such widely used, free software package. You can download an RPM package version of Crack from many of the Red Hat mirror sites that keep user-contributed software. One such site is `http://ftp.dig-ital.com/pub/linux/redhat/contrib/`.

You have to go into the directory corresponding to your system's architecture, such as i386 (x86 or Intel), sparc (Sun Microsystems), alpha (Digital Alpha), and so on, and download the crack-*X.xx-x.(architecture)*.rpm, where *X.xx-x* is a version number and *(architecture)* is your system's architecture. For example, for an x86 or Intel-based system, download crack-4.1f-1.i386.rpm. The version number may vary, because newer versions are uploaded over time.

After you upload the RPM package, install it as follows:

```
rpm -ivh crack_package_name.rpm
```

You then can find out what files got installed, by running the following command:

```
rpm -qi crack_package_name
```

Typically, Crack gets installed in /root/Crack-*X.xx*/ directory.

Running Crack

To run the Crack program from the installed directory, use the following command:

```
Crack /etc/passwd
```

Tip

If you use shadow passwords and want to run Crack, you need to use a support script called *shadmrg* (found in the Scripts directory) to merge the /etc/passwd and /etc/shadow files. The merged output typically is sent to STDOUT, so you have to point it to a file, which you can then use with Crack as the input password file.

Crack will start cracking your passwords. If you have a lot of users accounts in your password file, Crack might take a long time to complete the job. That's why Crack automatically runs in the background. You can also specify a few command-line options to Crack to control some of its behavior. Run Crack without any arguments to see a list of command-line options.

Getting Crack's output

After you run Crack, it creates output in two files: out.PID and out.*(host-name)*PID. For example, the output files could be out.5678 and out.picaso.nitec.com5699, where `picaso.nitec.com` is the name of the host running Crack. Listing 15-8 shows an example of a Crack output file.

Listing 15-8 *Example Crack Output File*
```
join: User apache (in /etc/passwd) has a locked
password:- !!
join: User uucp (in /etc/passwd) has a locked password:-
*
join: User operator (in /etc/passwd) has a locked
password:- *
join: User ftp (in /etc/passwd) has a locked password:- *
join: User bin (in /etc/passwd) has a locked password:- *
join: User daemon (in /etc/passwd) has a locked
password:- *
join: User adm (in /etc/passwd) has a locked password:- *
join: User lp (in /etc/passwd) has a locked password:- *
join: User sync (in /etc/passwd) has a locked password:-
*
```

Continued

Listing 15-8 *Continued*

```
join: User shutdown (in /etc/passwd) has a locked
password:- *
join: User halt (in /etc/passwd) has a locked password:-
*
join: User mail (in /etc/passwd) has a locked password:-
*
join: User nobody (in /etc/passwd) has a locked
password:- *
join: User news (in /etc/passwd) has a locked password:-
*
join: Guessed pikeb (/bin/tics in /etc/passwd) [book]
NssDRm.TU/EFc
```

The date stamp field that appears right after join: was removed to reduce line width. When Crack reports that a password is locked, it means that the password is set to *; in other words, the user account cannot be used to log in. The preceding last line is the most interesting one. It says that Crack has guessed the password (book) for user pikeb.

After you know which user passwords are crackable, lock out the account right away by using * as the password, and contact the user personally to discuss security. If that's not possible, notify the user to change the password immediately. If the user does not change the password in a given time frame, definitely lock out the account and advise your superiors on the matter.

Passwords are not the only weak points in a system. To find many other potential security holes, you need COPS.

Having COPS around

COPS is a set of tools that attempts to locate potential security holes in a system. Among other things, these tools focus on detecting potential security problems that can surface from file/directory/device permissions, passwords, init files in the /etc/rc.d directory, cron configuration, and anonymous FTP setup. Basically, the purpose of COPS is to detect potential security problems and warn you about them. It does not fix any of the problems that it detects.

Installing COPS

I have not yet seen an RPM-packaged version of COPS. So, you have to get a general COPS distribution from the following FTP site: `ftp://ftp.cert.org/pub/tools/cops/`.

Download the latest COPS distribution and uncompress and extract the files to an appropriate directory on your system.

The COPS distribution includes two versions of the same software. One version is written primarily in C, and the other is written primarily in Perl. You can run a version as long as you have either Perl or a C compiler, either of which is practically standard in Red Hat Linux. This discussion explains how to use the C version. If you are interested in running the Perl version of the software, read the bundled README files for the Perl version. You will also find the Perl version of the software in a perl subdirectory of your installation directory.

To configure the C version of COPS, do the following:

1. First, run the following script from the installation directory:

`./reconfig`

This adjusts a few paths for binaries, such as awk, in some scripts to match your system.

2. Next, modify the makefile in the docs directory to remove the –ms from the ROFFLAGS = –ms line. You don't need to do this if you have installed the –ms package for nroff. Then, run the following from the installation directory:

`./make all`

3. Edit the cops shell script and modify the following lines:

`SECURE=/usr/foobar`
`SECURE_USERS="foo@bar.edu"`

4. Change the first line so that the directory is the fully qualified directory name of your installation path. For example, if you installed COPS in the /usr/local/security/cops directory, then set SECURE to that directory. Set the second line to your e-mail address where the COPS output will be sent. If you do not want to receive the report in e-mail format, modify MMAIL=NO or change the line to be MMAIL=YES to receive the report via e-mail.

5. If you decide not to receive e-mailed reports, you can find the report files in the $SECURE/(short hostname) directory. For example, if your system's host name is `picaso.nitec.com`, and SECURE is set to /usr/local/security/cops, the report file will be stored in the /usr/local/security/cops/picaso/ directory. The report filename is created using the year_month_day format (for instance, 1999_Feb_25).

6. If you plan to use the Crack program as your password-cracking software, you can comment out the line (by inserting a # character in front of the line) that starts $SECURE/pass.chk. If you run an anonymous FTP site, you can modify the line that starts with $SECURE/ftp.chk to read $SECURE/ftp.chk –a.

Running COPS

Running COPS is quite simple; run it from the installation directory as follows:

```
./cops
```

Listing 15-9 shows an example COPS report.

Listing 15-9 *An Example COPS Report*

```
ATTENTION:
Security Report for Thu Jan 29 10:35:44 PST 1998
from host picaso.nitec.com


Warning!  /dev/fd0 is _World_ readable!
Warning!  /etc/security is _World_ readable!
Warning!  /etc/crontab is _World_ readable!


ATTENTION:
CRC Security Report for Thu Jan 29 10:34:39 PST 1998
from host picaso.nitec.com


replaced -rw-r--r-- root    root Jan 28 23:22:01 1998
/etc/passwd
```

```
removed  -r-------- root    root Dec 20 13:31:36 1998
/etc/shadow
```

COPS just finds the problems, it doesn't fix them. It is up to you to investigate and fix them. Run COPS on a regular basis by setting it up as a cron job so that you get regular reports on potential problems before they are exploited by the bad guys.

Back Up and Backtrack Everything

The most important security advice anyone can give you is to regularly back up all of your files. Here is what I recommend:

- Create a maintainable backup schedule for your system.
- Perform incremental backups on weekdays and schedule a full backup over the weekend. I prefer removable-media-based backup equipment, such as 8mm tape drives or DAT drives.
- Having a removable backup medium enables you to take the backup away from the location and store it in a secure offsite location.
- Periodically check that your backup mechanism is functioning as expected. Make sure you're able to restore files from randomly selected backup media.
- You may recycle backup media, but make sure you know the usage limits that the media manufacturer claims.
- Protecting your system involves more than simply keeping bad guys out. You want to protect your data from other sorts of disasters, as well, and good, periodic backups give you that protection.

Another type of "backup" you should get used to doing is backtracking your work as a system administrator. Document everything you do, especially work that you do as a superuser. This enables you to trace problems quicker. One of the things that I like to do when performing system administration is to keep a large history setting (a shell feature that remembers N number of your last commands) and periodically print the history in a file or on paper. You can also use the script command to record everything you do while using privileged accounts.

Get the Latest Security News

Being informed about what security problems are out there in the world helps you to keep a step ahead of the bad guys who might want to attack your systems. As soon as you know about a security issue that might affect your system, take immediate action before it is too late. You should subscribe to reputable security alert resources, available on the Internet. Here are two.

CERT

Computer Emergency Response Team (CERT) regularly issues advisories on computer security matters. Subscribe to its mailing list as soon as possible. Visit its Web site at `http://www.cert.org/` for details.

BUGTRAQ@NETSPACE.ORG

BUGTRAQ is another mailing list to which you can subscribe to access daily reports on security issues. Visit its Web site at `http://www.netspace.org/lsv-archive/bugtraq.html` for details.

Chapter 16

Network Security

Designing a Secure Network

As a network grows, implementing security as an afterthought becomes more difficult. Users grow accustomed to patterns of usage, poor choices become accepted handicaps, and the administrator must play political games to make changes. These are some of the reasons security of your network as a whole must be examined as you plan the topology.

Using private IP addresses

The simplest way to maintain security on a network is to ensure that hosts on your network cannot contact, nor be contacted by, the outside world. The easiest way to achieve this would be to never connect them to a public network such as the Internet. This security-through-isolation strategy is not an acceptable restraint in many situations. Using private IP addresses is an easy way of allowing your users to reach the Internet while holding off the bad guys from getting to the user machinesprivate.

RFC 1918 specifies blocks of IP addresses that may be used within a local TCP/IP network but may not traverse Internet routers. These groups of IP addresses are commonly called LAN IP addresses or private IP addresses. Because these IP addresses do not route across the Internet, you do not need to register to use them. By assigning an IP address from within this range, you effectively limit traffic to and from the computer to the local network. This is a quick and effective way of denying outside access to computers while allowing traffic to flow between your internal computers.

The blocks of private IP addresses are the following:

```
10.0.0.0     -   10.255.255.255
172.16.0.0   -   172.31.255.255
192.168.0.0  -   192.168.255.255
```

Remember that traffic coming from a private IP address is not able to traverse Internet routers, which means that any computer assigned a private IP address is unreachable by computers outside your network. However, this approach also has the effect of not allowing your users to talk to the outside world. IP masquerading is the solution for this.

Masquerading IP addresses

Private IP addresses are not routable in the Internet and therefore systems using private IP addresss can not reach the Internet. You can solve this problem by placing a IP masuqerading Red Hat Linux server. With IP masquerading in place, as a packet leaves a user computer, it has the "source address" of its own IP address. As the packet travels through the Red Hat server toward the outside world, it is transformed. The source address of the packet is changed to the address of the Red Hat server, which is a fully routable IP address. The Red Hat server also makes a note of which source address contacted which destination on the Internet. When the packet is sent to the Internet, it is fully capable of reaching its destination and getting a response.

This setup has one catch. Because the source address of the packet is set to the IP of the Red Hat server and not to the user machine behind the server, the response from the foreign computer is sent to the Red Hat server. Therefore, to complete the packet transmission, the Red Hat server has to search a table to see which machine this packet belongs to. It then sets the source address of the packet to the address of the private user computer and sends the packet to that computer. Voilà, a round trip across the Internet has been made from a machine with a private IP address. IP masquerading is also known as network address translation (NAT).

From the user's standpoint, the user has an Internet connection that appears to be fully routable. The security comes from the table that the

Red Hat server keeps of which user computers are talking to which foreign Internet sites. If some bad guy wants to gain access to one of your user computers, he will be unable to. The only IP address ever seen by the outside world is the address of the Red Hat server, and not all the addresses behind it. Even if the bad guy sends a packet to the Red Hat server, the server would have no way of knowing which user machine to forward it to.

By default, the Red Hat Linux kernel has IP masquerading support built in. However, if you have removed such support earlier or are using a kernel that does not have IP masquerading built in, you need to recompile the kernel, load a few modules, and set a packet-filtering rule to allow the address translation to occur. For IP masquerading to work, you need to enable IP forwarding service on the server. You can enable IP forwarding (for the default kernel shipped by Red Hat) by setting FORWARD_IPV4 to yes in the /etc/sysconfig/network file. This discussion assumes that you are using a kernel with IP masquerading and forwarding support built in, and that you have also installed the ipchains package on the Red Hat server.

To connect your internal network to the outside world, you need two network interfaces on the IP masquerading server. One interface will be used to connect to the internal network, and the other interface will be used to connect the server (and the internal network via IP masquerading) to the outside world. Because such a server has multiple interfaces, it is often called a *multihomed* server. You can assign a private IP address to the network card connected to the internal network. For example,

```
/sbin/ifconfig eth1 inet 192.168.1.1 netmask
255.255.255.0
```

This assumes that your network interface for the internal network is eth1 and that you will be running fewer than 253 user computers within your network. If you are in a situation where you will have more than 253 user computers, you may use a netmask of 255.255.0.0, which allows more than 65,000 user computers behind one Red Hat IP masquerade computer. If you exceed 253 user computers, set up a second IP masquerade computer and divide your network into two subnets.

By configuring your user computers with IP addresses starting at 192.168.1.2 and ending at 192.168.1.254, and by assigning them all a gateway of 192.168.1.1 and a subnet mask of 255.255.255.0, you should be able to ping the gateway (192.168.1.1) from each user computer.

At this point, all the user machines can talk to each other and to the Red Hat server, but you still can't reach the outside world from a client machine until you define a filter rule on the Red Hat server. After you enter the following commands, you should be able to browse and communicate from a user machine as if you were directly connected to the Internet:

```
/sbin/ipchains -A forward -j MASQ -s 192.168.0.0/24 -d
0.0.0.0/0
/sbin/ipchains -P forward DENY
```

The first command enables IP masquerading service for all IP packets that have a destination other than the 192.168.0.0 network. It forwards masqueraded IP packets originating from the 192.168.0.0 network to the default route to the network attached to the other interface. The second command sets the default forwarding policy to be deny for all packets not originating from the internal network. Put these commands into /etc/rc.d/rc.local so that IP masquerading will begin when you boot the Red Hat server.

What Is a Firewall?

Sometimes, you may not want the all-or-nothing approach achieved by using private IP addresses. You may want to give the general public access to browse Web sites on your Web server, but no other type of access. Or, you may have a policy restriction that limits employee use of the Internet to e-mail only. Both of these examples are situations in which a firewall would fit perfectly.

A *firewall* is a computer intended to enforce your policies about what type of traffic is allowed to pass from the public network to the private network. Most often, a firewall is placed between a private intranet and the Internet to allow traffic to pass that meets certain criteria while denying the rest. Firewalls can be very open, allowing nearly all traffic through, or they can be very restrictive, permitting very limited use. The firewall administrator controls all of this through configuration of rule sets.

It is wise to dedicate a computer solely to the task of being the firewall. If you are relying on your firewall to control access to your internal network, then make sure your firewall is as secure as possible. This machine will serve not only as a security checkpoint, but also as a gateway from a secured network to the rest of the world. The bad guys know that if they can control your firewall, they can gain access to your internal network. Because of this, you need to shut the windows and lock the doors. Some guidelines for basic firewall security are as follows:

- **Turn off any unneeded services.** To go one step further, consider disabling sendmail, finger, netstat, systat, bootp, and FTP.

- **Limit the number of people who have shell access to the firewall.** If you have only one or two user accounts, the bad guy has to get very lucky to find one of them.

- **Don't use the same password on the firewall as you do elsewhere.** Sometimes, people fall into the trap of using the same password for many different computers. Don't do that here! Otherwise, your network may topple like a line of dominos.

- **Make physical security a huge consideration.** Whereas you may find it acceptable to have your desktop machine sitting in an open office or cubicle, you should keep tighter tabs on the physical access people have to your firewall.

Firewalls come in all varieties. Some are software applications, while others are sold as hardware. Many cost in the tens of thousands of dollars, while others are free. Firewalls can usually be classified in one of two categories: packet-filtering firewalls or application-level firewalls.

Packet filters

Packet filters do nothing more than take each packet, test it against a set of rules, and either allow or deny the packet to reach the other network. Packet filters are fast, simple, and effective ways of deciding which traffic passes and which does not. Packet filters exist at the network level and do not concern themselves with the data contained within the packets.

Typically, a packet filter has the capability to examine the source IP address, destination IP address, source port number, destination port number, and protocol type. It can also distinguish between the separate network interfaces on your computer. This way, someone forging one of your IP addresses from the outside world can be blocked. Table 16-1 shows the strengths and weaknesses of packet filters.

Table 16-1 *Strengths and Weaknesses of Packet Filters*

Strengths	Weaknesses
Speed	Inability to log application data
Ease of administration	Inability to control access to specific applications

Because packet filters look at each packet individually, they don't see the "whole picture." For example, packet filters are unable to see which Web page you are looking at or to make sure you are not mailing all the company secrets to the competitors.

Using a basic packet-filtering firewall: ipchains

Red Hat Linux comes with a package called ipchains that enables you to create a packet-filtering firewall.

Tip

Those of you who have used ipfwadm to create packet-filtering firewalls on pre-6.0 Red Hat Linux systems will find that ipfwadm is no longer supported, because ipchains is an improved replacement for it.

Consider a real-world example of using ipchains to control access to an internal network. Assume that your network provider has given you the IP addresses 206.170.189.1 through 206.170.189.254. You have configured a multihomed Red Hat Linux server to be the firewall and have included two Ethernet interface cards, eth0 and eth1. You have given the outside Ethernet interface, eth0, IP address 206.170.189.1, and have given the inside Ethernet interface, eth1, IP address 206.170.189.2. Each of the computers in your internal network has been assigned an IP address starting at 20.170.189.3 and continuing up through the remaining 252 addresses. Each of the internal computers has its gateway set to the firewall computer with IP address 206.170.189.2.

First, you want to set a default filtering policy that denies all traffic to and from the firewall system. This will become the last rule in your set and is the natural way to enforce the security policy "All traffic not specifically allowed by the firewall is denied." You do this by issuing the following three commands:

```
/sbin/ipchains -P input DENY
/sbin/ipchains -P output DENY
/sbin/ipchains -P forward DENY
```

In order, this says that your default policy for incoming packets, outgoing packets, and packet forwarding is to deny anything that is not allowed by an ipchains filter rule.

Caution

Always administer your filter rules from the console of the firewall, not remotely. It becomes very easy to lock yourself out by using a deny rule that also excludes you. These rules become active the moment you press the Enter key. Also, if you flush your ipchains filter rules (using the –F command), you may find that the only rule still existing denies all traffic to or from your firewall. This situation has caused a few middle-of-the-night drives to the office for me. Be careful.

Next, you need the following rule:

```
/sbin/ipchains -A input -j DENY -i eth0 -s
206.170.189.0/24
```

This rule denies any packets that claim to be from your internal network but have been sent by a computer outside your firewall. In a normal situation, this should never happen, but bad guys have been known to place fake headers on packets to circumvent firewalls. This method of getting around the firewall is known as *packet spoofing*.

```
/sbin/ipchains -A input -j ACCEPT -i eth1
/sbin/ipchains -A output -j ACCEPT -i eth1
```

These two rules allow all traffic between the local network and the firewall. This allows any of your machines to talk to each other. They shouldn't have to bounce off the firewall, but it doesn't hurt to add the rules.

```
/sbin/ipchains -A input -j DENY -p icmp
```

This rule may cause some controversy among your users. By setting this rule, you deny all packets that are using the ICMP protocol, the protocol used by programs such as ping and traceroute. By denying this traffic, you can limit a popular denial-of-service attack called a *ping flood* in which a bad guy uses the ping program to send packets of an obscenely large size. A ping flood attack will not destroy any data but can be used to consume all of your bandwidth with the ping packets, thus giving no room for legitimate traffic. By disallowing ICMP traffic, you are also restricting your local network from using tools such as ping or traceroute to check the status of machines beyond the firewall. It is a tradeoff you will have to decide on.

```
/sbin/ipchains -A input -j ACCEPT -p tcp -d 206.170.189.3
smtp
```

This rule allows all traffic using the TCP protocol with a destination of 206.170.189.3 to travel to the SMTP port. In this example, 206.170.189.3 is your mail server, and you will allow any mail from the outside world to the mail server. You can also use the lines

```
/sbin/ipchains -A input -j ACCEPT -p tcp -d 206.170.189.5
www
/sbin/ipchains -A input -j ACCEPT -p tcp -d 206.170.189.9
domain
```

to allow access to your Web server (206.170.189.5) and your DNS server (206.170.189.6). This process can be continued ad infinitum for any number of hosts and services.

Using an application-level firewall

Situations will arise in which you need the ability to control your network at the application level rather than at the network level. You may need to restrict your users from sending e-mail to certain addresses, monitor the Web sites your users are hitting, or get a good idea of the average size of files users are sending through the firewall. When you want this type of information and control, you require an application-level firewall.

Application-level firewalls, sometimes called *application proxies* or *proxy servers*, work in a manner different from that of packet filters. Application-level firewalls work without a direct connection between the local and remote computers. They permit no traffic to pass from the inside to the outside. Instead, the local computer queries the firewall for the information it wants. The firewall then examines the request, makes the connection to the outside world, retrieves the information, and passes the information back to the client. As far as the outside world knows, all the requests for information are coming from the application firewall. With an application proxy, you need not worry about unwanted traffic getting into your network. It can't.

Because application-level firewalls are specific to the protocol they are passing, a separate application-level firewall is needed for each protocol, such as FTP, Telnet, and Web traffic. If you don't want your users to have the ability to view Web pages, you can just omit the Web proxy program from your suite of firewall programs. You can make rules based not only on which local IP addresses can see which external IP addresses, but also on the protocol they're communicating with.

Using the Squid Proxy Server

Squid is a proxy server that implements caching for the HTTP, FTP, and Gopher protocols. Squid has the capability to use access control lists (ACLs) to allow or deny access to locations. Because Squid is so configurable and robust, it takes some time to tailor it to your use, but you may find that it is easy to learn. Best of all, Squid can be configured in a way that your users never even know it is there.

Getting and installing Squid

As of this writing, Squid 2.2 is available only as a tar.gz file and not as an RPM. You can obtain the most current version from the FTP site at `ftp://squid.nlanr.net/pub`. Hopefully, by the time this book is published, a contributed RPM will exist. You can periodically check the contrib subdirectory of the Web site for an RPM version of the software.

This discussion assumes both that your proxy server has two network interfaces, one to the outside world and one to the internal network, and that you have turned off IP forwarding.

You can make Squid function on only one network interface, but I don't recommend it. This configuration doubles up traffic on your local network and can cause congestion. With the low price of network interface cards and hubs, it is well worth the investment, even for a relatively small network.

If you plan to use Squid to maintain a cache, you need to consider your hard drive and memory limitations. The nature of a Web cache is to have thousands of small files that you will need to serve out to clients both simultaneously and efficiently. The Squid authors recommend at least a 300MHz Pentium II CPU, 512MB RAM, and five ultrawide SCSI disks of 9GB each. I have heard of an entire Internet provider using nothing more than a few 486/66 processors with IDE drives. I suspect most people would be comfortable with something in between these two extremes. I recommend using at least a 100MHz Pentium CPU, 64MB RAM, and 6GB of SCSI disk. You may find you can get away with using slightly less.

After you obtain the tar.gz file, unpack it by using the following command:

```
gunzip -c squid-2.2.RELEASE-src.tar.gz |tar -xv
```

This unpacks the tar file into a directory called squid-2.2.RELEASE. Once inside that directory, run ./**configure** to check the capabilities of your computer and create the configuration files. When this completes, type **make** to begin compiling Squid into a usable product. If this completes without error, type **make install** to put the binary files into place.

Making Squid work for the first time

To create the swap directories, type the following:

```
/usr/bin/squid -z
```

Squid can run out of the box — with one exception. You need to change the configuration file /etc/squid/squid.conf before running it for the first time. The access control list for Squid defaults to denying all requests. You can change this behavior by editing the file /etc/squid/squid.conf and adding the line

```
acl local_net src 192.168.0.1/255.255.255.0
```

where 192.168.129.1 is an IP address in your local network, and 255.255.255.0 is the netmask of your internal network. You also need to add the line

```
http_access allow local_net
```

just before http_access deny all. This defines the group of IP addresses that is allowed to use the cache.

Type **squid &** to start Squid for the first time. You can verify it is working in several ways:

- Squid should show up in a **ps –x** listing.
- Running **client www.yahoo.com** should dump Web page text to your terminal.
- The files cache.log and store.log in the directory /var/log/squid should show Squid to be working.
- Running **squid –k check && echo "Squid is running"** tells you whether Squid is active.

Now, for the real test: If you configure the Web browser on a client machine to use the Squid proxy, you should see results. In Netscape Navigator 4.5, this can be achieved by selecting Edit ⇨ Preferences and then selecting Proxies from within the Advanced category. By selecting Manual Proxy Configuration and then clicking View, you can specify the IP address of the Squid server as the HTTP, FTP, and Gopher proxy server. The default proxy port is 3128, so unless you have changed it in the squid.conf file, place that number in the port field.

You should now be able to browse any Web site as if you had no proxy. You can double-check that Squid is working correctly by checking the log file /var/log/squid/access.log from the proxy server and making sure the Web site you were viewing is in there.

Tweaking Squid to fit your needs

Now that you have Squid up and running, you can customize it to fit your needs. At this point, it is not restricting your users from accessing any sites. You can define rules in your squid.conf file to set ACLs and allow or deny visitors according to these lists.

Adding the following line defines an ACL rule called BadWords that matches any URL containing the words foo or bar:

```
acl BadWords url_regex foo bar
```

This applies to `http://foo.deepwell.com/pictures` and `http://www.thekennedycompound.com/ourbar.jpg` because they both contain words that are members of BadWords.

Adding the following to squid.conf blocks your users from accessing any URLs that match this rule:

```
http_access deny BadWords
```

Caution

Almost every administrator using word-based ACLs has a story about not examining all the ways a word can be used. Realize that if you ban your users from accessing sites containing the word "sex," you are also banning them from accessing `www.buildersexchange.com` and any others that may fall into that category.

Because all aspects of how Squid functions are controlled within the squid.conf file, you can tune it to fit your needs.

By adding the line

```
cache_mem  16 MB
```

you allow Squid to use 16MB of memory to hold Web pages in memory. By trial and error, you may find you need a different amount.

Caution

The cache_mem is not the amount of memory Squid consumes; it only sets the maximum amount of memory Squid uses for holding Web pages, pictures, and so forth. The Squid documentation says you can expect Squid to consume up to three times this amount.

By using the line

```
emulate_httpd_log on
```

you arrange that the files in /var/log/squid are written in a form similar to the Web server log files. This allows you to use a Web statistics program, such as Analog or Webtrends, to analyze your logs and see where your users are going.

Some FTP servers require that an e-mail address be used when someone is logging in anonymously. By setting ftp_user to a valid e-mail address, as shown here, you give the server at the other end of an FTP session the data it wants to see:

```
ftp_user squid@deepwell.com
```

You may want to use the address of your proxy firewall administrator. This would give the foreign FTP administrator someone to contact in case of a problem.

If you type a URL and find that the page does not exist, that page likely won't exist any time in the near future. By setting negative_ttl to a desired number of minutes, as shown in the next example, you can control how long Squid remembers that a page was not found in an earlier attempt (called *negative caching*):

```
negative_ttl 2 minutes
```

This isn't always a good thing. The default is five minutes, but I suggest lessening this to two or possibly one minute, if not disabling it all together, because you want your proxy to be as transparent as possible. If a user is looking for a page she knows exists, you don't want the proxy to insert a delay (due to negative caching) before it actually becomes available to her.

```
cache_mgr proxy@deepwell.com
```

By setting this to your own e-mail address, you arrange to receive e-mail if Squid detects problem with cache.

```
cache_effective_user nobody
cache_effective_group nobody
```

These two lines are very important! If you are starting Squid while you are root, these two lines change the UID that Squid runs as to user "nobody." This will hopefully keep any bugs in the program from changing or deleting anything they shouldn't.

Ultimately, a tool such as Squid should be completely transparent to your users. This removes them from the complexity of administration and allows them to browse the Web as if there were no Web proxy server. Although the details of how to do that are not presented here, you may refer to the Squid Frequently Asked Questions at `http://squid.nlanr.net/Squid/FAQ/FAQ.html`. Section 17 details using Squid as a transparent proxy.

Also, if you find yourself managing a large list of "blacklisted" sites in the squid.conf file, consider using a program called a *redirector*. Large lists of ACL rules can begin to slow a heavily used Squid proxy. By using a redirector to do this same job, you can improve on the efficiency of allowing or denying URLs based on filter rules. You can get more information on Squirm, a full-featured redirector made to work with Squid, from `http://www.senet.com.au/squirm/`.

The cachemgr.cgi file comes in the Squid distribution. It is a CGI program that enables you to view statistics of your proxy as well as shut down and restart Squid. It requires only a few minutes of your time to install, but it gives you explicit detail about how your proxy is performing. If you'd like to tune your Web cache, this tool will help.

This section has only touched upon the basics of using Squid as a Web proxy firewall. Squid has many features above and beyond those discussed here. If you are interested in making Squid function beyond what is described here, visit the Squid Web page at `http://squid.nlanr.net/`.

Getting Help from SATAN

It always helps to be on the offensive with your network security. If you actively check the security of your computers on a regular basis, you will be aware of your weaknesses. Few things are as bad as walking in one morning to realize that an intruder has been in your system. SATAN is a tool that you can use to probe your computers, to look for possible weaknesses that hackers could exploit to get into your system.

SATAN, the Security Administrator Tool for Analyzing Networks, gained a lot of media attention at the time of its release. Back in 1995, when the tool was released, people went into a frenzy, expecting hackers to use it as a lock pick, thereby automating their work. But, hackers already had written and shared with one another many tools for getting into other systems, searching for known weaknesses, and removing their trail. However, the hackers weren't sharing with the good guys, who didn't have access to tools like this. Dan Farmer and Wietse Venema decided to write SATAN to even the odds for the good guys. By releasing tools such as SATAN to the public, they allowed everyone to have access to security tools. With such widespread access, administrators could discover problems and patch holes before someone with bad intent wandered in.

SATAN scans for known vulnerabilities and, when it is done, walks the user through HTML tutorials explaining how hackers exploit the problem, and how to patch it. The user interface is done through a Web browser, so anyone who is used to surfing the Web can operate it. SATAN was designed to be used on a UNIX computer, but you can probe any operating system.

Quoting from the documentation, SATAN tests for the following:

- NFS file systems exported to arbitrary hosts
- NFS file systems exported to unprivileged programs
- NFS file systems exported via the portmapper
- NIS password file access from arbitrary hosts
- Old (i.e., before 8.6.10) sendmail versions
- REXD access from arbitrary hosts
- X server access control disabled
- Arbitrary files accessible via TFTP
- Remote shell access from arbitrary hosts
- Writable anonymous FTP home directory

All of these are old and standard misconfigurations, so don't expect SATAN to tell you anything that a well-seasoned administrator wouldn't catch. But, it is much easier and cheaper to install and run the program than to explore the systems with a fine comb.

Installing SATAN

You can retrieve SATAN from any one of several sites. Remember, though, as with any security program, make sure you are downloading from a reputable site. My rule of thumb is that if a site isn't on the list of mirror sites, I don't trust it. You can find the list of mirror sites at `http://www.fish.com/~zen/satan/satan.html`.

Although you can get the satan-1.1.1.tar.gz file from the official SATAN site, doing so requires that you get additional patches from other sites. The cleanest way to compile and install SATAN is to download a source RPM version from `http://contrib.redhat.com/`. Assuming that you are running Red Hat on an *x*86 system, you need to get the satan-1.1.1.linux-3.i386.rpm package or a later version. After you download the RPM package, run the following command as root user:

```
rpm -ivh satan-1.1.1.linux-3.i386.rpm
```

By default, this installs the SATAN source distribution in the /root/satan directory. An automatic configuration and source compilation will be performed.

> **Tip**
>
> If you do not want to install and compile SATAN in /root/satan, use -- prefix *path* option in the preceding rpm command to install it in a different location.

The compilation process requires that you have the latest version of the GNU C compiler (gcc), glibc support, and C development libraries. You also need a Web browser installed on the system. Because the rpm program automatically compiles and installs SATAN, your next step is to start it.

Working with SATAN

Assuming that you have let rpm install SATAN in /root/satan, run it using the following command:

```
/root/satan/satan
```

If you run the preceding command from an xterm (that is, in X Windows), SATAN launches the Netscape Navigator browser (/usr/bin/netscape). If you do not have this Web browser and instead want to use the text-based Lynx browser, modify the /root/satan/config/paths.pl script such that the $MOSAIC variable is set to the fully qualified path name of the Lynx browser. Then, when you start SATAN, it will use the specified browser. This discussion assumes that you are using Netscape Navigator.

One other issue that you might have to tackle, depending on your Netscape Navigator version, is that when you click links from the SATAN main interface screen, they might not work. For example, when using Netscape Navigator 4 to access any of the links on the main page, the browser asks to download SATAN scripts. This is due to the fact that Navigator is unable to run the script, because of a misconfigured or missing MIME configuration. If you have this problem, do the following:

1. From Netscape Navigator's Edit menu, select the Preference option and click Applications.

2. Click New to associate the .pl extension to /usr/bin/perl (or wherever you keep the Perl interpreter).

3. In the dialog box that appears, type anything you want in the Description field (such as Perl Script); in the MIMEType field, enter **application/x-perl**; and in the Suffixes field, enter **.pl**.

4. Select Application to assign the handler for .pl files, and then enter the fully qualified path name of the Perl interpreter in the entry box.

5. Click OK to complete this process and close the Preference window as usual.

After you complete these steps, SATAN scripts will run as expected.

When you start SATAN, you may be surprised by its interface. Whereas most security tools have a very limited user interface, SATAN places a very high priority on user interaction. To jump right in to your first network security probe do the following:

1. Click the SATAN Target selection link from the main menu screen.

2. In the next screen, enter the name of the primary host or network at which you want to launch the probe.

3. Tell SATAN whether you want to also probe other hosts in the subnet, and set the level at which you want to probe. I suggest starting with one host on a light scan. From there, you will get the feel for SATAN, and you can then branch out into more powerful probes.

4. For a quick test, select a host on your own network. Select both the Scan the target host only option and the Light option to do a light scan.

5. Click Start the scan to start the probing.

6. After SATAN is finished probing a host (or network), click the View primary target results link to view the probe results. You will see the results of SATAN's probe in a new screen.

The light probe uses fping, nslookup, rpcinfo, and showmount to gather information about DNS, RPC services, and NFS. If the light probe does not detect problems, you should try the normal probe. In addition to the tasks in a light probe, the normal probe tries to determine information on UDP and TCP services, and finger service.

In the normal probe, if SATAN finds a problem with the trust configuration on your server, click the Trusted host(s) link in the results page to show more details of the problem.

Doing a more time-consuming, heavy scan might reveal more problems. As you can see, SATAN provides reasonably good documentation outlining problems SATAN encountered (or lack thereof). You can follow each vulnerability to see how you can make your systems more secure. After you master probing a single target host, try scanning all the hosts in a given subnet. You can also change SATAN's configuration by using the SATAN Configuration Management link from the home page. If you experience any problem while running SATAN, use the troubleshooting link to review commonly asked questions and answers.

Chapter 17

Customizing the Kernel

What Linux Kernel Do You Have?

Linux runs on many different hardware architectures, including *x*86 (Intel), Alpha, and Sparc, among others. However, because discussing kernel issues for all platforms in a single chapter is practically impossible, this chapter assumes that, like a majority of Red Hat Linux users, you have an *x*86-based (Intel) system. If you are running Red Hat Linux on a system based on the mighty Alpha processor, you can find useful kernel-related information at http://www.alphalinux.org/. Also, for all architectures (including *x*86), you can find useful information at http://www.kernel.org/.

To determine the version of your system's current kernel, run the following command:

```
rpm -q kernel kernel-headers kernel-ibcs \
kernel-pcmcia-cs kernel-source > /current-kernel-pkgs.txt
```

The current-kernel-pkgs.txt file has version information for the kernel-related packages. You also need to know the version numbers for mkinitrd (used to create initial ramdisk images), SysVinit (the init package), and the initscripts (the /etc/rc.d scripts) packages that often change with the new kernels.

You can run the following command to add version information for these packages to the current-kernel-pkgs.txt file:

```
rpm -q mkinitrd SysVinit initscripts > \
/current-kernel-pkgs.txt
```

By running the preceding rpm commands, you have placed version information for all the typical packages needed for a full kernel upgrade. Table 17-1 lists the names and RPM descriptions of these packages.

Table 17-1 *Typical Packages Needed for Kernel Upgrades*

Package	Description Found in the RPM
Kernel-2.*x.x.x–x*.i386.rpm	This package contains the Linux kernel that is used to boot and run your system. It contains few device drivers for specific hardware such as hard disk, video, keyboard, mouse, etc. Most hardware is instead supported by modules loaded after booting.
Kernel-headers-2.*x.x.x–x*.i386.rpm	These are the C header files for the Linux kernel, which define structures and constants that are needed to build most standard programs under Linux, as well as to rebuild the kernel.
Kernel-ibcs-2.*x.x.x–x*.i386.rpm	This package allows you to run programs in the iBCS2 (Intel Binary Compatibility Standard, version 2) and related executable formats.
kernel-pcmcia-cs-2.*x.x.x–x*.i386.rpm	Many laptop machines (and some others) support PCMCIA cards for expansion. Also known as "credit card adapters," PCMCIA cards are small cards for everything from SCSI support to modems. They are hot-swappable (they can be exchanged without rebooting the system) and quite convenient. This package contains support for numerous PCMCIA cards of all varieties and supplies a daemon that allows them to be hot-swapped.
kernel-source-2.*x.x.x–x*.i386.rpm	This is the source code for the Linux kernel. It is required to build most C programs, because they depend on constants defined in here. You can also build a custom kernel that is better-tuned to your particular hardware.
mkinitrd-x.x-x.src.rpm	Generic kernels can be built without drivers for any SCSI adapters that load the SCSI driver as a module. To solve the problem of allowing the kernel to read the module without being able to address the SCSI adapter, an initial ramdisk is used. That ramdisk is loaded by the operating system loader (such as LILO) and is available to the kernel as soon as it is loaded. That image is responsible for loading the proper SCSI adapter and allowing the kernel to mount the root file system. This program creates such a ramdisk image using information found in /etc/conf.modules.
SysVinit-*x.xx–x*.src.rpm	SysVinit is the first program started by the Linux kernel when the system boots, controlling the startup, running, and shutdown of all other programs.

Package	Description Found in the RPM
initscripts-*x.x.x–x*.src.rpm	This package contains the scripts used to boot a system, change run levels, and shut down the system cleanly. It also contains the scripts that activate and deactivate most network interfaces.

Now, you are ready to find out which kernel you are currently using to boot the system. One sure-fire way to do this is to take a look at your /etc/lilo.conf file. Here is an example /etc/lilo.conf file:

```
boot=/dev/hda
map=/boot/map
install=/boot/boot.b
prompt
timeout=50
image=/boot/vmlinuz-2.2.5-15
        label=linux
        root=/dev/hda1
        initrd=/boot/initrd-2.2.5-15.img
        read-only
```

Here the system with the above /etc/lilo.con file uses a single Linux kernel image (/boot/vmlinuz-2.2.5-15) labeled "linux," and the kernel is /boot/vmlinuz-2.2.5-15. If you have previously upgraded your Linux kernel, you might have multiple labels defined in your /etc/lilo.conf file. In such a case, you need to identify the kernel (image=/boot/vmlinux-2.*x.x.x*-*.x*) that you use to boot your system. Simply locate the LILO label you use to boot the system and find the corresponding image=/boot/vmlinux-2.*x.x.x*-.*x* line. Now that you have identified the kernel packages and the kernel you use, it's time to prepare for the upgrade.

Preparing for a Kernel Upgrade

The official FTP site for the Red Hat Linux updates is ftp://updates.redhat.com/. Accessing this busy site can be difficult, unless it's a very odd time, such as 3 a.m. or later. Your best choice is to locate a mirror site near you, by visiting http://www.redhat.com/mirrors.html.

After you locate a mirror site for the updated kernel RPM packages, connect to the site and compare the versions of the packages that you stored in the /current-kernel-pkgs.txt file earlier. Download the newer packages for the packages listed in the /current-kernel-pkgs file created earlier. If you do not see a newer package for one of the packages listed in the /current-kernel-pkgs.txt file, just ignore it, because a newer package is not yet available.

After you have the new packages for your kernel upgrade, you should create an emergency boot floppy, just in case something goes wrong with the kernel upgrade. Also, keeping a copy of the old kernel in a directory within the root partition is a good idea.

To create a standalone boot floppy, insert a formatted floppy disk into your floppy drive and run

```
mkbootdisk 2.x.x.x-x
```

replacing *2.x.xx-x.x* with your current kernel version that you identified earlier. Also, if you have multiple floppy drives and do not want to use the default floppy device (/dev/fd0), use the --device option to specify your floppy device of choice. For example,

```
mkbootdisk --device /dev/fd1 2.0.36-0.7
```

creates the emergency boot floppy on /dev/fd1 using kernel image version 2.0.36-0.7. After you create the boot disk, reboot your system using this floppy to ensure that the emergency boot disk actually works.

Installing the New Kernel

After you test the emergency boot disk, you are ready to install a new kernel. Using rpm, install all the packages you have downloaded. I typically download all the new packages to a new directory in a temporary space, such as /tmp/new-kernel-pkgs, and run the following:

```
rpm -ivh /tmp/new-kernel-pkgs/*.rpm
```

Tip

If you don't plan to compile the kernel ever, you may skip the kernel-headers-2.*x.xx-x*.i386.rpm and kernel-source-2.*x.xx-x*.i386.rpm packages, because they are needed only for compiling custom kernels.

After you upgrade the new kernel and its related packages, you need to create the initial ramdisk image file needed by the kernel to boot the system. The initial ramdisk image file allows a kernel to access modules such as disk drivers, which in turn are needed to access the rest of the modules residing on the root file system.

Creating the initial ramdisk

The mkinitrd command is used to create the initial ramdisk. Replacing *2.x.xx-x* with the version number of your new kernel, run the following command:

```
mkinitrd /boot/initrd-2.x.xx-x.img 2.x.xx-x
```

This creates the /boot/initrd-*2.x.xx-x*.img initial ramdisk image file. Using the ls utility, confirm that this file is really created in the /boot directory. After you create the initial ramdisk, you need to modify the /etc/lilo.conf file to configure LILO for the new kernel.

Configuring LILO

Configuring LILO is critical to your kernel installation, and you must not reboot the system until you have reconfigured LILO as discussed here. Using your favorite text editor, add a new configuration segment, such as the following, to your /etc/lilo.conf file:

```
image=/boot/vmlinuz-2.x.x.x-x
        label=new-linux
        root=/dev/hda1
        initrd=/boot/initrd-2.x.x.x-x.img
        read-only
        append="mem=128M"
```

Tip

Before you modify your /etc/lilo.conf file, you should make a copy of it just in case you need the old configuration back.

Replace *2.x.x.x-x* with the appropriate kernel version number for both the image= and initrd= lines. The label= line should be set to an arbitrary string of your choice. The root device should point to your root disk partition. For example, if your current root partition is /dv/sda1, make sure the root= line is set to that partition. If Linux does not recognize memory above 64MB, use the append= line to set the memory size to an appropriate limit. After you modify and save the /etc/lilo.conf file, run

```
/sbin/lilo
```

This makes LILO read the new configuration file and update the boot sector of the appropriate root partition. You can use the −v flag with the preceding command to make LILO be a bit more verbose. After you run LILO, you are ready to reboot the system.

Booting with the new kernel

Enter the **shutdown −r now** command to reboot your system as usual. At the LILO prompt, press the Tab key to see your choices. The labels you enter (in the label= lines) for your old and new kernels will appear onscreen. Enter the new label (in the preceding example, this label is new-linux) at the LILO prompt to boot the system with the new kernel.

The next step mostly depends on your facial expression after you have told LILO to start the new kernel. If you are smiling, your new kernel is up and running. If you are screaming or not smiling at all, do not panic — you still have the old kernel. If the system locks up, press Ctrl+Alt+Del or do a hard reboot. After you get the LILO prompt again, enter the label name for your old kernel. The system should reboot as usual. In such a case, check the steps you have already taken, especially regarding the /etc/lilo.conf configuration file. Make sure that you have the new configuration set up correctly. Rerun /sbin/lilo and try to boot the system with the new kernel. If the problem persists, you need to post the details of your problem (such as what is shown on the console when you attempt to boot the new kernel) to a comp.linux newsgroup specific to Linux. If your software license permits, you may also contact Red Hat for help.

In most cases, the new installation should go smoothly, without any incident. To make sure you are running the new kernel, run the following command:

```
uname -a
```

This displays the kernel version number along with other information. After your new kernel is up and running, create a new boot disk using the mkbookdisk command, as you did earlier in the preparation section of this installation.

Customizing the Kernel

The only way that you can customize a kernel to your liking is via custom compilation. To compile a kernel on your Red Hat Linux server system, you need to get the kernel header and source RPM packages. If the kernel you are trying to customize is not production grade, an RPM version might not be available. In such a case, you have to download the source in compressed tar format (.tar.gz). Check the official Red Hat Web site for availability of the kernel source and header RPM packages. If you can't find the RPM packages, download the .tar.gz distribution from the official http://www. kernel.com/ site (or any of its mirrors). This section assumes that you want to customize the latest 2.2.5 kernel and have downloaded the linux-2.2.5.tar.gz source distribution from the site just mentioned.

Installing Linux kernel source

Extract the linux-2.2.5.tar.gz distribution in /usr/src directory by entering the **tar xvzf linux-2.2.5.tar.gz** command. The source distribution will be stored in a subdirectory called linux-2.2.5 in /usr/src. The Linux kernel is traditionally stored in /usr/src/linux. Actually, /usr/src/linux is a symbolic link to the /usr/src/linux-*x.x.x* directory. Remove the symbolic link using **rm /usr/src/linux** and then create a new symbolic link using the following command:

```
ln -s /usr/src/linux-2.2.5  /usr/src/linux
```

The series of commands that you have to perform to arrive at this stage might look as follows:

```
cd /usr/src
tar xvzf linux-2.2.5.tar.gz
rm -f /usr/src/linux
ln -s linux-2.2.5 linux
```

Tip

When I extracted the source distribution in the /usr/src directory, it created a linux subdirectory, and therefore the symbolic link was unnecessary. However, if you plan to experiment with various kernels, I recommend that you keep a particular source distribution in the /usr/src/linux-*x.x.x* directory and always point a symbolic link (linux) to the kernel you are currently working on.

Although a freshly downloaded source distribution is not going to have any stale object files, it is wise to run the following command to clean up any such files just in case:

```
make mrproper
```

You are ready to configure (that is, customize) the kernel. You have multiple choices as to how you can customize the kernel.

Configuring the kernel the old-fashioned way

To configure the kernel the old-fashioned way, run the following command from the /usr/src/linux directory:

```
make config
```

This is the simplest way to configure a kernel; however, it might not be the most suitable for beginning kernel hackers. Here is an example session of how you can configure the Linux kernel using the above make command.

Code maturity-level options

In this section, you have to decide whether you want to be asked about features that are not yet ready for primetime. In other words, you are asked whether you want to be prompted for experimental features. You can choose to see (and perhaps use) these experimental features if you are configuring the kernel for a system on which experimentation or downtime and crashes are part of the fun and not a burden. The prompt appears as follows:

```
Prompt for development and/or incomplete code/drivers
(CONFIG_EXPERIMENTAL) [N/y/?]
```

The default answer is N, or no, which you can choose by pressing the Enter key. Also note that the default answer is always shown as a capital letter.

Processor type and features

In this section, you are asked about the processor family, the math coprocessor, multiprocessors, and other processor-specific questions. Here is the first question:

```
Processor family (386, 486/Cx486, 586/K5/5x86/6x86,
Pentium/K6/TSC, PPro/6x86MX) [PPro/6x86MX]
```

If the default processor architecture is incorrect, choose one of the listed ones. In my case, the default is wrong, so I entered "Pentium/K6/TSC" as the processor family.

```
defined CONFIG_M686
Math emulation (CONFIG_MATH_EMULATION) [N/y/?]
```

Unless you have a (really old) processor that does not have a math coprocessor built in, choose the default by pressing Enter.

```
MTRR (Memory Type Range Register) support (CONFIG_MTRR)
[N/y/?]
```

The preceding question is probably the first question that does not quite make sense to you (unless you are an expert in x86 CPU design). The default option often is the right one. Or, you can find out what Memory Type Range Register (MTRR) support actually means by entering **?** at the prompt. You will get a help screen, as shown here:

```
CONFIG_MTRR:

On Intel Pentium Pro and Pentium II systems the Memory
Type Range
Registers (MTRRs) may be used to control processor access
to memory
ranges. This is most useful when you have a video (VGA)
card on a
PCI or AGP bus. Enabling write-combining allows bus write
transfers
to be combined into a larger transfer before bursting
over the
PCI/AGP bus. This can increase performance of image write
operations
2.5 times or more. This option creates a /proc/mtrr file
which may
be used to manipulate your MTRRs. Typically the X server
should use
this. This should have a reasonably generic interface so
that
similar control registers on other processors can be
easily
supported.

Saying Y here also fixes a problem with buggy SMP BIOSes
which only
set the MTRRs for the boot CPU and not the secondary
CPUs. This can
lead to all sorts of problems.
```

You can safely say Y even if your machine doesn't have
MTRRs, you'll
just add about 3k to your kernel.

See Documentation/mtrr.txt for more information.

As you can see, this is quite helpful.

Symmetric multi-processing support (CONFIG_SMP) [Y/n/?]

If you have multiple processors on your system and want to turn on
symmetric multiprocessing support, choose the default, **Y**. I don't have a
motherboard with more than one processor on it, so I chose n to not have
SMP support.

Loadable module support

The Linux kernel uses an innovative method for keeping a low profile. It
uses features and drivers implemented as external modules. The modules
are dynamically loaded and unloaded on an as-needed basis. This allows
the kernel to require less memory and become increasingly hardware-
independent. The modules typically are loaded with a program called kerneld, which in turn uses a program called modprobe to manage available
modules. Modules can be device drivers, file systems, binary executable
formats, and so on. In this section, you are asked whether or not you want
module-related support. The first question is as follows:

Enable loadable module support (CONFIG_MODULES) [Y/n/?]

This really should not be a prompt, because you definitely want to have
loadable module support for almost all scenarios. So, the default, **Y**, is fine.

Set version information on all symbols for modules
(CONFIG_MODVERSIONS) [N/y/?]

When modules are compiled with version information, they can be
reused with newer kernels without needing to be recompiled from scratch.
However, the preferred method is to compile the modules along with the
new kernel to eliminate compatibility problems. Hence, the default option
to not include the version information is sufficient.

Kernel module loader (CONFIG_KMOD) [N/y/?]

As mentioned before, modules typically are loaded using the kerneld program. This prompt asks you whether you want to use a module loader inside the kernel itself and avoid using the kerneld daemon. Either way, modules will be loaded automatically, so this does not make much difference. The default answer **N** is fine.

General setup

In this section, you configure the general options.

```
Networking support (CONFIG_NET) [Y/n/?]
```

This is a dumb question, isn't it? Who would want to run Linux and not have networking support? Perhaps there are a few out there. The default is a must.

```
PCI support (CONFIG_PCI) [Y/n/?]
```

Unless you are on a really old *x*86 system with only an ISA bus, the default is fine. Note that on Sparc systems, you might not need PCI support if you have only sbus cards.

```
PCI access mode (BIOS, Direct, Any) [Any]
```

The default option allows the kernel to detect the PCI configuration using the direct method, and if that fails, it will get the PCI configuration from the system BIOS. So, the default is fine.

```
PCI quirks (CONFIG_PCI_QUIRKS) [Y/n/?]
```

This option is for motherboards with lousy BIOSs that fail to set up the PCI bus properly. If you don't have such a board, choose **n** for no. If you are unsure, you can keep the default.

```
MCA support (CONFIG_MCA) [N/y/?]
```

Unless you have an IBM PS/2 Micro Channel Architecture (MCA)-based system, the MCA support is not needed.

```
SGI Visual Workstation support (CONFIG_VISWS) [N/y/?]
```

If you are not using an SGI system, keep the defaults.

System V IPC (CONFIG_SYSVIPC) [Y/n/?]

Inter Process Communication (IPC) is needed by many programs, and therefore the default is a must.

BSD Process Accounting (CONFIG_BSD_PROCESS_ACCT) [N/y/?]

This allows a program to ask the kernel to dump information, such as a process owner's UID, creation time, memory stats, and other information about a process. This is not required; answer either way.

Sysctl support (CONFIG_SYSCTL) [Y/n/?]

This option allows dynamic changing of various kernel parameters in the /proc file system without a reboot or recompilation of the kernel. This is a must for all systems, so choose **Y**.

Kernel support for a.out binaries (CONFIG_BINFMT_AOUT) [Y/m/n/?]

The a.out format traditionally has been used to create executable and library programs; however, the new Executable and Linkable Format (ELF) has been in use for a while. You might want to keep the support in a module instead of making it part of the kernel. Hence, choose the **m** option for module.

Kernel support for ELF binaries (CONFIG_BINFMT_ELF) [Y/m/n/?]

The ELF support is a must; therefore, choose the default, **Y**.

Kernel support for MISC binaries (CONFIG_BINFMT_MISC) [Y/m/n/?]

If you plan on running Java applications, MS-DOS programs using interpreters or emulators, you might want to answer Y to have the miscellaneous binary support as a module.

Parallel port support (CONFIG_PARPORT) [N/y/m/?]

If you plan to connect a printer or other parallel port devices to your Linux system, enter **y** to add the support in the kernel or **m** to have the support available as a module.

```
Advanced Power Management BIOS support (CONFIG_APM) [N/y/?]
```

If you are not concerned about saving power, the default is fine.

Plug and Play support

In my personal experience, Plug and Play should really be called Plug and Pray (don't know who said it first). So, I urge you to not enable PNP in something so nice as Linux.

```
Plug and Play support (CONFIG_PNP) [N/y/?]
```

If you have a card that works only in PNP mode, you are likely to encounter problems, so be warned. The best thing to do is buy hardware that has an option to turn off PNP.

Block devices

In this section, you are asked about disk drives.

```
Normal PC floppy disk support (CONFIG_BLK_DEV_FD)
[Y/m/n/?]
```

Because most systems have floppy drives, select **Y**.

If you use IDE/EIDE hard disks, an IDE/ATAPI CD-ROM, tape drives, floppy drives, and so on, choose **yes** (or choose the module option) for all of the following questions:

```
Enhanced IDE/MFM/RLL disk/cdrom/tape/floppy support
(CONFIG_BLK_DEV_IDE) [Y/m/n/?]
Use old disk-only driver on primary interface
(CONFIG_BLK_DEV_HD_IDE) [N/y/?]
Include IDE/ATA-2 DISK support (CONFIG_BLK_DEV_IDEDISK)
[Y/m/n/?]
Include IDE/ATAPI CDROM support (CONFIG_BLK_DEV_IDECD)
[Y/m/n/?]
```

```
Include IDE/ATAPI TAPE support (CONFIG_BLK_DEV_IDETAPE)
[N/y/m/?]
Include IDE/ATAPI FLOPPY support
(CONFIG_BLK_DEV_IDEFLOPPY) [N/y/m/?]
```

```
SCSI emulation support (CONFIG_BLK_DEV_IDESCSI) [N/y/m/?]
```

SCSI emulation works only for IDE/ATAPI devices that do not have native driver support in Linux. You might want to consider a different drive to avoid emulation, which is not recommended.

The CMD-Technologies CMD640 IDE chip and the PC-Technologies RZ1000 IDE chip are common on many 486/P5 motherboards. If your system uses these chips, you need to choose **yes** for the following prompts (if you don't know, selecting **yes** isn't likely to cause any problem, either):

```
CMD640 chipset bugfix/support (CONFIG_BLK_DEV_CMD640)
[Y/n/?]
CMD640 enhanced support (CONFIG_BLK_DEV_CMD640_ENHANCED)
[N/y/?
RZ1000 chipset bugfix/support (CONFIG_BLK_DEV_RZ1000)
[Y/n/?] n
```

If you use IDE drives on a PCI system, keep the defaults for the following options:

```
Generic PCI IDE chipset support (CONFIG_BLK_DEV_IDEPCI)
[Y/n/?]
Generic PCI bus-master DMA support
(CONFIG_BLK_DEV_IDEDMA) [Y/n/?]
Boot off-board chipsets first support
(CONFIG_BLK_DEV_OFFBOARD) [N/y/?]
```

If your system is capable of using Direct Memory Access (DMA) for IDE drives, keep the default for the following question:

```
Use DMA by default when available (CONFIG_IDEDMA_AUTO)
[Y/n/?]
```

If you want to enable enhanced support for various IDE chipsets, choose **y** for the following question:

```
Other IDE chipset support (CONFIG_IDE_CHIPSETS) [N/y/?]
```

Additional block devices

For most cases, all the options found in this section are useless, so you can safely accept the default answers here:

```
Loopback device support (CONFIG_BLK_DEV_LOOP) [N/y/m/?] y
Network block device support (CONFIG_BLK_DEV_NBD)
[N/y/m/?]
Multiple devices driver support (CONFIG_BLK_DEV_MD)
[N/y/?]
RAM disk support (CONFIG_BLK_DEV_RAM) [N/y/m/?]
XT hard disk support (CONFIG_BLK_DEV_XD) [N/y/m/?]
Parallel port IDE device support (CONFIG_PARIDE)
[N/y/m/?]
```

Networking options

Networking is one of the most important sections. Here, you decide on various networking issues.

```
Packet socket (CONFIG_PACKET) [Y/m/n/?]
```

The Packet protocol is used by applications such as tcpdump, and therefore you should accept the default answer, **Y**.

```
Kernel/User netlink socket (CONFIG_NETLINK) [N/y/?]
```

If you want to use your system as a firewall or use the arpd daemon to maintain an internal ARP cache, select **y** here.

```
Network firewalls (CONFIG_FIREWALL) [N/y/?]
```

If you want to use your system as a packet-filtering firewall, set this to **y**.

```
Network aliasing (CONFIG_NET_ALIAS) [N/y/?] ?
```

If you have multiple network interfaces for your system, set this to **y**.

```
Socket Filtering (CONFIG_FILTER) [N/y/?] ?
```

This feature allows programs to attach filters to sockets and control how data goes through the socket. Unless you use such programs, the default answer, N, is fine.

```
Unix domain sockets (CONFIG_UNIX) [Y/m/n/?]
```

Sockets are the standard UNIX mechanism for establishing and accessing network connections. Therefore, the default answer, **Y**, is fine.

```
TCP/IP networking (CONFIG_INET) [Y/n/?]
```

The obvious answer is **Y** or yes.

```
IP: multicasting (CONFIG_IP_MULTICAST) [N/y/?]
```

IP multicasting typically is used to transfer large amounts of data, such as real-time, broadcast-quality video, using large bandwidth connections. Unless you have such needs, choosing the default should be fine.

```
IP: advanced router (CONFIG_IP_ADVANCED_ROUTER) [N/y/?]
```

If you intend to run your Linux box mostly as a router (that is, as a computer that forwards and redistributes network packets), choose **y**.

```
IP: kernel level autoconfiguration (CONFIG_IP_PNP)
[N/y/?]
```

This enables automatic configuration of IP addresses of devices and of the routing table during kernel boot, based on information supplied either at the kernel command line or by the BOOTP or RARP protocol.

```
IP: optimize as router not host (CONFIG_IP_ROUTER)
[N/y/?] ?
```

Some Linux network drivers use a technique called copy and checksum to optimize host performance. For a machine that acts as a router most of the time and forwards most packets to another host, using this technique results in a loss of performance. So if you plan on using your Linux system as a gateway or router, choose **y** or choose the default answer **N**.

```
IP: tunneling (CONFIG_NET_IPIP) [N/y/m/?]
```

Tunneling means encapsulating data of one protocol type within another protocol and sending it over a channel that understands the encapsulating protocol. This particular tunneling driver implements encapsulation of IP within IP, which sounds kind of pointless but can be useful if you want to make your (or some other) machine appear on a different network than it is physically connected to, or if you want to use mobile-IP facilities (allowing laptops to seamlessly move between networks without changing their IP addresses).

```
IP: GRE tunnels over IP (CONFIG_NET_IPGRE) [N/y/m/?] ?
```

GRE (Generic Routing Encapsulation) at this time allows encapsulating of IPv4 or IPv6 over existing IPv4 infrastructure.

```
IP: aliasing support (CONFIG_IP_ALIAS) [N/y/?]
```

If you want to attach multiple IP addresses to a single network interface, enter **y** here.

```
IP: TCP syncookie support (not enabled per default)
(CONFIG_SYN_COOKIES) [N/y/?]
```

Normal TCP/IP networking is open to an attack known as SYN flooding. This denial-of-service attack prevents legitimate remote users from being able to connect to your computer during an ongoing attack and requires very little work from the attacker, who can operate from anywhere on the Internet. SYN cookies provide protection against this type of attack. If you enter **y** here, the TCP/IP stack will use a cryptographic challenge protocol known as SYN cookies to enable legitimate users to continue to connect, even when your machine is under attack. Legitimate users don't need to change their TCP/IP software, but SYN cookies may prevent correct error reporting on clients when the server is really overloaded. If this happens frequently, then you should turn off SYN cookies. If you enter **y** here, note that SYN cookies aren't enabled by default; you can enable them by responding **y** to "/proc filesystem support" and "Sysctl support" below and executing the command

```
echo 1 >/proc/sys/net/ipv4/tcp_syncookies
```

at boot time after the proc file system has been mounted.

```
IP: Reverse ARP (CONFIG_INET_RARP) [N/y/m/?]
```

If you want your server to provide Reverse Address Resolution Protocol (RARP) service for other computers on your network, enter **y** or set this feature to be a module (enter **m**).

```
IP: Drop source routed frames (CONFIG_IP_NOSR) [Y/n/?] ?
```

Source routing is an IP protocol feature that allows the originating IP packet to contain full routing information for the destination IP address. This typically is the cause of many network security problems and should be avoided. The default option is recommended.

```
IP: Allow large windows (not recommended if <16Mb of
memory) (CONFIG_SKB_LARGE) [Y/n/?] ?
```

This option is useful only if you are dealing with 2MB/sec or above bandwidth and long-distance networks.

```
The IPX protocol (CONFIG_IPX) [N/y/m/?] ?
```

Unless you need support for Novell networking, the default answer is fine.

```
Appletalk DDP (CONFIG_ATALK) [N/y/m/?] ?
```

Unless you need AppleTalk networking support, the default answer is fine.

SCSI support

If you have SCSI disks, CD-ROM, tape drives, or other SCSI devices, this section enables you to configure support for such devices. Answer the following questions based on available SCSI hardware:

```
SCSI support (CONFIG_SCSI) [Y/m/n/?]
SCSI disk support (CONFIG_BLK_DEV_SD) [Y/m/n/?]
```

```
SCSI tape support (CONFIG_CHR_DEV_ST) [N/y/m/?]
SCSI CD-ROM support (CONFIG_BLK_DEV_SR) [N/y/m/?]
SCSI generic support (CONFIG_CHR_DEV_SG) [N/y/m/?]


Probe all LUNs on each SCSI device
(CONFIG_SCSI_MULTI_LUN) [Y/n/?]
```

Unless you have a SCSI device with multiple Logical Unit Numbers (LUNs), enter **n** for the preceding question.

```
Verbose SCSI error reporting (kernel size +=12K)
(CONFIG_SCSI_CONSTANTS) [Y/n/?]
```

The error messages regarding your SCSI hardware will be easier to understand if you enter **Y** here.

```
SCSI logging facility (CONFIG_SCSI_LOGGING) [N/y/?]
```

This turns on a logging facility that can be used to debug numerous SCSI-related problems. If you respond **y**, you have to enable logging by using the following command in /etc/rc.d/rc.local:

```
echo "scsi log token [level]" > /proc/scsi/scsi
```

Here, *token* can be error, scan, mlqueue, mlcomplete, llqueue, llcomplete, hlqueue, or hlcomplete. The *level* controls the verbosity of the log and can be any positive number, including 0.

The rest of the questions in the SCSI section are specific to SCSI host adapters. You should choose support for only the adapter(s) you have installed.

Network device support

In this section, you configure various network device features.

```
Network device support (CONFIG_NETDEVICES) [Y/n/?]
```

Because you are configuring the kernel for your server, respond **Y** to the preceding question.

```
ARCnet support (CONFIG_ARCNET) [N/y/m/?]
```

Unless you have ARCnet network interface cards, the default, **N**, is fine.

```
Dummy net driver support (CONFIG_DUMMY) [M/n/y/?] ?
```

This driver creates a dummy network interface device that can be used to fool a network client program. Keeping this as a module might come in handy; hence, the default, **M**, is recommended.

```
EQL (serial line load balancing) support (CONFIG_EQUALIZER)
[N/y/m/?]
```

This feature is not useful for most server configurations. The default answer is recommended.

```
Ethernet (10 or 100Mbit) (CONFIG_NET_ETHERNET) [Y/n/?]
```

If you are going to using your system on a Ethernet, choose the default answer **Y**.

Answers to the following questions depend on what types of network cards you have; therefore, respond accordingly:

```
3COM cards (CONFIG_NET_VENDOR_3COM) [N/y/?]
AMD LANCE and PCnet (AT1500 and NE2100) support
(CONFIG_LANCE) [N/y/m/?]
Western Digital/SMC cards (CONFIG_NET_VENDOR_SMC) [N/y/?]
Racal-Interlan (Micom) NI cards (CONFIG_NET_VENDOR_RACAL)
[N/y/?]
Other ISA cards (CONFIG_NET_ISA) [N/y/?]
EISA, VLB, PCI and on board controllers (CONFIG_NET_EISA)
[Y/n/?] ?
AMD PCnet32 (VLB and PCI) support (CONFIG_PCNET32)
[N/y/m/?]
Apricot Xen-II on board Ethernet (CONFIG_APRICOT)
[N/y/m/?
CS89x0 support (CONFIG_CS89x0) [N/y/m/?]
Generic DECchip & DIGITAL EtherWORKS PCI/EISA
(CONFIG_DE4X5) [N/y/m/?]
DECchip Tulip (dc21x4x) PCI support (CONFIG_DEC_ELCP)
[N/y/m/?]
```

```
Digi Intl. RightSwitch SE-X support (CONFIG_DGRS)
[N/y/m/?]
EtherExpressPro/100 support (CONFIG_EEXPRESS_PRO100)
[Y/m/n/?]
PCI NE2000 support (CONFIG_NE2K_PCI) [N/y/m/?]
TI ThunderLAN support (CONFIG_TLAN) [N/y/m/?]
VIA Rhine support (CONFIG_VIA_RHINE) [N/y/m/?]
Pocket and portable adaptors (CONFIG_NET_POCKET) [N/y/?]
FDDI driver support (CONFIG_FDDI) [N/y/?]
Frame relay DLCI support (CONFIG_DLCI) [N/y/m/?]
PPP (point-to-point) support (CONFIG_PPP) [N/y/m/?]
SLIP (serial line) support (CONFIG_SLIP) [N/y/m/?]
Wireless LAN (non-hamradio) (CONFIG_NET_RADIO) [N/y/?]
Token Ring driver support (CONFIG_TR) [N/y/?]
Comtrol Hostess SV-11 support (CONFIG_HOSTESS_SV11)
[N/m/?]
COSA/SRP sync serial boards support (CONFIG_COSA) [N/m/?]
Red Creek Hardware VPN (EXPERIMENTAL) (CONFIG_RCPCI)
[N/y/m/?]
WAN drivers (CONFIG_WAN_DRIVERS) [N/y/?]
LAPB over Ethernet driver (CONFIG_LAPBETHER) [N/y/m/?]
X.25 async driver (CONFIG_X25_ASY) [N/y/m/?]
```

Amateur radio, ISDN, and old CD-ROM support

Assuming you are not going to use Amateur Radio, ISDN, or old CD-ROM support, the default answers to the following questions are sufficient:

```
Amateur Radio support (CONFIG_HAMRADIO) [N/y/?]
ISDN support (CONFIG_ISDN) [N/y/m/?]
Support non-SCSI/IDE/ATAPI CDROM drives
(CONFIG_CD_NO_IDESCSI) [N/y/?]
```

Tip

If you plan to use an ISDN card to provide Internet connectivity for your system, get an ISDN router instead of an internal card. My personal experience with internal cards has made me come to this conclusion. I have tried a few name-brand ISDN cards that did not work very well. On top of the problems with dealing with yet another card (IRQ and I/O address resources are limited on a PC), the price difference between an internal card and an external ISDN router is not significant when you consider that dedicated ISDN itself is a fairly expensive service in most parts of the U.S.

Character devices

In this section, you are asked about terminal configuration.

```
Virtual terminal (CONFIG_VT) [Y/n/?]
```

This feature allows you to have virtual terminals. The default answer is required unless you are installing the kernel in an embedded Linux system.

```
Support for console on virtual terminal (CONFIG_VT_CONSOLE)
[Y/n/?]
```

This feature allows you to turn a virtual terminal into a system console. This is required for the same reason as the last answer.

```
Support for console on serial port
(CONFIG_SERIAL_CONSOLE) [N/y/?]
```

If you want to use your computer's serial port as the system console, select **y**.

```
Extended dumb serial driver options
(CONFIG_SERIAL_EXTENDED) [N/y/?]
```

Unless you enabled the serial port as the system console in the last question, keep the default here.

```
Unix98 PTY support (CONFIG_UNIX98_PTYS) [Y/n/?]
```

This feature provides support for the UNIX 98 pseudoterminal numbering convention, which is superior to the traditional Linux pseudoterminal number convention. You should keep the default.

If you keep the default, you are asked the following question, to set the maximum number of UNIX 98 PTYs that can be in use by the system:

```
Maximum number of Unix98 PTYs in use (0-2048)
(CONFIG_UNIX98_PTY_COUNT) [256]
```

For most cases, the default value should be sufficient.

```
Mouse Support (not serial mice) (CONFIG_MOUSE) [Y/n/?]
```

This feature allows you to use a mouse with terminals capable of using such a device. The default is recommended.

```
QIC-02 tape support (CONFIG_QIC02_TAPE) [N/y/m/?]
```

If you have QIC-02 tape, you can choose to add support for it here.

```
Watchdog Timer Support (CONFIG_WATCHDOG) [N/y/?]
```

If you want to create a watchdog timer such that it can reboot the system in case of a failure, answer **y** here. If you do enable this feature, you have to create a special device called /dev/watchdog (major,minor=130,10) by using the mknod program. Then, you can use a watchdog daemon program that will write to this special device every minute. If the kernel detects that the device has not been written to by the daemon for one minute, it will reboot the system.

```
/dev/nvram support (CONFIG_NVRAM) [N/y/m/?]
```

This feature allows you to create a special device /dev/nvram, which gives you read/write access to nonvolatile memory in the real time clock. Unless you know what you are doing, keep the default.

```
Enhanced Real Time Clock Support (CONFIG_RTC) [N/y/?]
```

This feature allows you to create a special device, /dev/rtc, which can be used to access the real-time clock in your system. Unless you know what you are doing, keep the default.

Video and joystick support

You likely do not have video capture hardware or joysticks on the system; therefore, you should accept the default answers for the following questions:

```
Video For Linux (CONFIG_VIDEO_DEV) [N/y/m/?]
Joystick support (CONFIG_JOYSTICK) [N/y/m/?]
```

Ftape, the floppy tape device driver

If you have a floppy controller-based tape drive, you need to choose to add support for it here:

```
Ftape (QIC-80/Travan) support (CONFIG_FTAPE) [N/y/m/?]
```

File systems

In this section, you configure the kernel for various file system-specific features.

```
Quota support (CONFIG_QUOTA) [N/y/?]
```

If you want to have disk quota support built into the kernel, enter **y** here.

```
Kernel automounter support (CONFIG_AUTOFS_FS) [Y/m/n/?]
```

If you want remote file systems, such as NFS file systems, to be automatically mounted and unmounted, choose to add direct or module-based support for the automounter.

Following are various vendor-specific file system support questions. Answer them according to your needs:

```
Amiga FFS filesystem support (CONFIG_AFFS_FS) [N/y/m/?]
Apple Macintosh filesystem support (experimental)
(CONFIG_HFS_FS) [N/y/m/?]
DOS FAT fs support (CONFIG_FAT_FS) [N/y/m/?]
ISO 9660 CDROM filesystem support (CONFIG_ISO9660_FS)
[Y/m/n/?]
Microsoft Joliet CDROM extensions (CONFIG_JOLIET) [N/y/?]
Minix fs support (CONFIG_MINIX_FS) [N/y/m/?]
```

```
NTFS filesystem support (read only) (CONFIG_NTFS_FS)
[N/y/m/?]
OS/2 HPFS filesystem support (read only) (CONFIG_HPFS_FS)
[N/y/m/?]
```

```
/proc filesystem support (CONFIG_PROC_FS) [Y/n/?]
```

The /proc file system is a must-have for any modern Linux system, and therefore the default answer is highly recommended for the preceding question.

```
/dev/pts filesystem for Unix98 PTYs (CONFIG_DEVPTS_FS)
[Y/n/?]
```

If you choose to add support for UNIX 98 pseudoterminals, you need to add /dev/pts file system support.

```
ROM filesystem support (CONFIG_ROMFS_FS) [N/y/m/?]
```

File systems of this type are not needed for most typical systems.

```
Second extended fs support (CONFIG_EXT2_FS) [Y/m/n/?]
```

Extended fs is the primary file system for Linux, and therefore the default answer is a must.

Choosing the default answers for the following questions should work for most systems:

```
System V and Coherent filesystem support (CONFIG_SYSV_FS)
[N/y/m/?]
UFS filesystem support (CONFIG_UFS_FS) [N/y/m/?]
```

Note that the UFS file system support is required if you choose to mount disk partitions created by other operating systems, such as Solaris *x*86 or BSD.

Network file systems

In this section, you can configure the kernel for advanced network file systems.

```
Coda filesystem support (advanced network fs)
(CONFIG_CODA_FS) [N/y/m/?]
```

The Coda file system is not yet popular enough, so I do not recommend adding it to the kernel; you might choose to add it as a module.

```
NFS filesystem support (CONFIG_NFS_FS) [Y/m/n/?]
```

If you plan to use NFS, use the default answer.

```
Emulate SUN NFS server (CONFIG_NFSD_SUN) [N/y/?] ?
```

Unless you want your Linux NFS server to behave like a Sun-based NFS server that allows NFS clients to access directories that are mount points on the local file system, leave the default as is.

```
SMB filesystem support (to mount WfW shares etc.)
(CONFIG_SMB_FS) [N/y/m/?]
```

If you want to mount Windows 9*x*/NT file systems on your Linux system as SMB file systems, enter **y** or set this feature to be a module (**m**).

```
NCP filesystem support (to mount NetWare volumes)
(CONFIG_NCP_FS) [N/y/m/?]
```

Unless you plan to mount NetWare volumes on your Linux system, keep the default answer.

Partition types

If you want to have support for disk partitions based on BSD, Macintosh, Solaris, and so on, answer the following questions accordingly:

```
BSD disklabel (BSD partition tables) support
(CONFIG_BSD_DISKLABEL) [N/y/?]
Macintosh partition map support (CONFIG_MAC_PARTITION)
[N/y/?]
SMD disklabel (Sun partition tables) support
(CONFIG_SMD_DISKLABEL) [N/y/?]
Solaris (x86) partition table support
(CONFIG_SOLARIS_X86_PARTITION) [N/y/?]
```

In most cases, the default answers are sufficient.

Console drivers

In this section, you will be able to configure console driver settings.

```
VGA text console (CONFIG_VGA_CONSOLE) [Y/n/?]
```

If you want to have a VGA text console, keep the default.

```
Video mode selection support (CONFIG_VIDEO_SELECT)
[N/y/?] ?
```

If you want to be able to specify text mode on kernel bootup, set this option or keep the default.

Sound

Assuming that you probably do not need to have a sound card in a server system, you can keep the default answer for the following question:

```
Sound card support (CONFIG_SOUND) [N/y/m/?]
```

Kernel hacking

The only option available in this section is support for the Magic SysRq key. If you enable support for this key by answering **y** to the following question, you will be able to press SysRq+Alt+PrintScreen to dump status information even when the system has crashed.

```
Magic SysRq key (CONFIG_MAGIC_SYSRQ) [N/y/?] ?
```

This is only useful for kernel developers. You should choose N here.

After you answer all of these questions, the configuration script will create a .config file in the /usr/src/linux directory. You might want to view the contents of this file to ensure that all the features are configured as you think they are.

Using make config to configure the kernel is quite a long process. It is also a bit cumbersome; however, it is quite appropriate if you happen to be configuring the kernel via a Telnet connection on a remote server. The line-based interface may not be elegant, but it works for virtually all scenarios and should be considered the default method of configuration when the following two methods are unusable.

Configuring the kernel using make menuconfig

One of the major problems with the make config-based configuration script is that if you make a mistake, you can't go back to fix it without starting over. Also, you can't review your choices unless you use a text editor to view the /usr/src/linux/.config file manually.

To remedy these shortcomings, the following command can be used:

```
make menuconfig
```

This runs a menu-driven configuration tool that is much more user-friendly than the make config script.

The user interface is quite simple and easy to navigate. However, the configuration questions are exactly the same. This configuration program also allows you to save and load configuration files. In other words, you can create multiple configuration files with different settings and use these configuration files to experiment with various features of the new kernel.

Although the make menuconfig script is quite friendly, it does impose some extra requirements on remote kernel configuration. For example, if you plan to configure and compile the kernel over a Telnet connection to a remote server, you have to make sure that the Telnet client program on your side is capable of good terminal emulation, which is required for a full-screen menu application. Also, make menuconfig is not the fanciest way to configure a kernel. That title goes to the make xconfig script.

Configuring the kernel using make xconfig

As you may have guessed from the script name, this method of kernel configuration requires the X Window System. Because I do not recommend installation of the X Window System on server systems, I can't recommend this method either. However, I must agree that on systems with X Windows, this is the preferred method of kernel configuration. Run the make xconfig script (wish −f scripts/kconfig.tk) from /usr/src/linux to start xconfig.

You can click any of the buttons to configure a particular section of the entire configuration. This is quite a user-friendly interface. Another advantage of this interface is that you can open multiple sections by clicking the appropriate buttons. For example, if you are configuring the Partitions Type section and want to confirm that you have enabled UFS file system support in the Filesystems section, simply click the buttons for these two sections and verify your selections.

Hopefully, you will be able to determine which method works well for your environment.

Compiling, installing, and booting the new kernel

To compile, and install and boot a new kernel do the following:

1. Run:

   ```
   make dep
   ```

   to make sure that all the dependencies within the source are set up correctly. This should return without error unless a problem exists with the kernel source code itself.

2. To compile and create a compressed Linux kernel, run the following command:

   ```
   make bzImage
   ```

3. If you have configured any part of the kernel as a module during configuration, run the following command to compile the modules:

   ```
   make modules
   ```

4. After you compile the modules, install them in the /lib/modules/2.2.5 directory by using the following command:

   ```
   make modules_install
   ```

5. Copy the new kernel to the /boot directory as follows:

   ```
   cp /usr/src/linux-2.2.5/arch/i386/boot/bzImage
   /boot/vmlinuz-2.2.5
   ```

6. Copy and rename the new System.map file to the /boot directory as follows:

   ```
   cp /usr/src/linux-2.2.5/System.map /boot/System.
   map-2.2.5
   ```

7. rm -f /boot/System.map

8. Create a new symbolic link called /boot/System.map as follows:

```
ln -s /boot/System.map-2.2.5 /boot/System.map
```

9. Next, create a new initial ramdisk as follows:

```
mkinitrd /boot/initrd-2.2.5.img 2.2.5
```

10. The final step before you boot the new kernel is to prepare LILO for the new kernel. See the earlier section, "Configuring LILO," for details on how you can create a new configuration segment in /etc/lilo.conf for the new kernel. After you modify the /etc/lilo.conf file and run /sbin/lilo, you can reboot the system and start using the new kernel

If everything goes well, you will have a fresh, new, custom-configured kernel running all of your favorite Linux applications.

Tip

Do not forget to make a new boot floppy by using the **mkboot-disk --device /dev/fd0 2.2.5** command.

Patching a Kernel

It is not uncommon to have a situation in which you need to patch an existing kernel to get something working the way you want. In such a case, you can simply patch the source and rebuild the kernel. You can patch the kernel source from the /usr/src directory by using the following command:

```
gzip -cd patchXX.gz | patch -p0
```

Caution

If multiple patches are available for a kernel, apply the patches in order. In other words, apply patch01.gz before you apply pach02.gz, and so on.

Alternatively, the script patch-kernel can be used to automate this process. Store the patch file(s) in the /usr/src directory and run the following from the /usr/src directory:

```
./linux/scripts/patch-kernel
```

After patching the kernel, follow the instructions for compiling and installing the new kernel, as discussed earlier.

Because the modern Linux kernel supports modules that can be automatically loaded and unloaded via the kerneld daemon, you might need to configure one or more parameters for these modules to work properly. You can use kernelcfg for such a job.

Using kernelcfg

All the module configuration information is stored in /etc/conf.modules. You can either modify this file manually or use the kernelcfg tool.

You can add, delete, or modify module configuration information using this interface. To understand how to configure a module, take a look at the /etc/conf.modules file, which is what the kernelcfg tool manages.

To add a new module configuration, click the Add button and select the module name from the drop-down menu. Click OK to continue. If the module requires any arguments, add them in the next screen.

After you add the arguments and click OK in the argument entry window, the new module configuration appears in the main window. You can also edit or delete an existing module configuration by using the appropriate buttons available on the interface. After you finish making changes, restart the kerneld daemon by clicking the Restart kerneld button.

Appendix A

Common Commands

General File and Directory Commands

This section reviews the file- and directory-specific commands that you are likely to use on a daily basis.

cat

Syntax:

```
cat  file  [>|>]  [destination file]
```

The cat command displays the contents of a file to stdout. It is often helpful to examine the contents of a file by using the cat command. The argument that you pass to cat is the file that you want to view. To view the contents of a file called myfile, run

```
cat myfile
```

cat can also merge existing multiple files into one:

```
cat name1 name2 name3 > allnames
```

This example combines the files name1, name2, and name3 to produce the final file allnames. The order of the merge is established by the order in which the files are entered at the command line.

Using cat, you can append a file to another existing file. For instance, if you had forgotten to add names4 in the previous command, you could still produce the same results by executing

```
cat names4 > allnames
```

to append names4 to allnames.

chmod

Syntax:

```
chmod [-R] permission-mode  file or directory
```

The chmod command is used to change the permission mode of a file or directory. The permission mode is specified as a three- or four-digit octal number. For example,

```
chmod 755  myscript.pl
```

changes the permission of myscript.pl script to 755 (rwxr-xr-x), which allows the file owner to read, write, and execute, and allows only read and execute privileges for everyone else. As another example,

```
chmod -R 744 public_html
```

changes the permissions of the public_html directory and all of its contents (files and subdirectories) to 744 (rwxr--r--), which is a typical permission setting for personal Web directories that are accessed using http://server/~username URLs under Apache server. The −R option tells chmod to recursively change permissions for all the files and directories under the named directory.

chown

Syntax:

```
chown [ -fhR ] Owner [ :Group ] { File . . . | Directory.
. . }
```

The chown command changes the owner of the file specified by the *File* parameter to the user specified by the *Owner* parameter. The value of the

Owner parameter can be a user ID or a login name found in the /etc/passwd file. Optionally, a group can also be specified. The value of the *Group* parameter can be a group ID or a group name found in the /etc/group file.

Only the root user can change the owner of a file. You can change the group of a file only if you are a root user or own the file. If you own the file but are not a root user, you can change the group only to a group of which you are a member. Table A-1 lists and describes the chown options.

Table A-1 *chown Options*

Option	Description
-f	Suppresses all error messages except usage messages.
-h	Changes the ownership of an encountered symbolic link but not that of the file or directory pointed to by the symbolic link.
-R	Descends directories recursively, changing the ownership for each file. When a symbolic link is encountered and the link points to a directory, the ownership of that directory is changed but the directory is not further traversed.

The following example changes the existing owner of the file to another user:

```
chown bert hisfile.txt
```

clear

Syntax:

```
clear
```

The clear command clears your terminal and returns the command-line prompt to the top of the screen. This command works properly only when an environment variable called TERM is set to an appropriate terminal type. Typically, the terminal type is vt100. If the clear command does not work, use your shell's set command to set the term. For example, to set TERM for a tcsh shell session, use

```
set TERM = vt100
```

cmp

Syntax:

```
cmp [-ls] file 1 file2
```

The cmp command compares the contents of two files. If no differences exist within the two files, cmp is silent, by default.

To demonstrate, file1.txt contains

```
this is file 1
the quick brown fox jumps over the lazy dog.
```

and file2.txt contains

```
this is file 2
the quick brown fox jumps over the lazy dog.
```

The only difference between the two files is the first line, last character. In one file, the character is 1, while the other file has 2:

```
cmp file1.txt file2.txt
file1.txt file2.txt differ: char 14, line 1
```

The results of cmp correctly identify character 14, line 1 as the unequal character between the two files. The −l option will print the byte number and the differing byte values for each of the files:

```
cmp −l file1.txt file2.txt
14 61 62
```

The results of the preceding example show that byte 14 is different between the two files, with the first file having an octal 61 and the second file having an octal 62 at that location.

Finally, the −s option will display nothing. The −s option only returns an exit status indicating the similarities between the files. A 0 (zero) is returned if the files are identical. A 1 is returned if the files are different. A number greater than 1is returned when an error has occurred.

cp

Syntax:

```
cp  [-R] source file or directory  file or directory
```

Use the cp command to make an exact copy of a file. The cp command requires at least two arguments. The first argument is the file you want to copy, and the second argument is the location or filename of the file. If the second argument is an existing directory, cp will copy the source file into the directory with the target file's name.

```
cp main.c main.c.bak
```

The preceding example will copy the existing file main.c and create a new file called main.c.bak in the same directory. These two documents will be identical, bit per bit.

cut

Syntax:

```
cut  [-cdf list]  file
```

The cut command extracts columns of data. The data can be in bytes, characters, or fields from each line in a file. For instance, a file called names contains information about a group of people. Each line contains data pertaining to one person:

```
Fast   Freddy:Sacramento:CA:111-111-1111
Joe    Smoe:Los Angeles:CA:222-222-2222
Drake Snake:San Francisco:CA:333-333-3333
Bill   Steal:New York:NY:444-444-4444
```

To list the names and telephone numbers of all the individuals in the file, the options –f and –d should suffice:

```
cut –f 1,4 –d : names

Fast   Freddy:111-111-1111
Joe    Some:222-222-2222
```

```
Drake Snake:333-333-3333
Bill  Steal:444-444-4444
```

The –f *list* option specifies the fields you elect to display. Each field is defined by the –d options. In the preceding example, –d : indicates that each field is separated by a colon. Using : as the field delimiter makes fields 1 and 4 the name and phone number fields.

To display the contents of a particular column, use the –c *list* option:

```
cut -c 1-5 names
Fast
Joe
Drake
Bill
```

The preceding example shows how to list columns 1 through 5 in the filename names and nothing else.

diff

Syntax:

```
diff [-iqb] file1 file2
```

The diff command is used to determine differences between files. By default, diff does not produce any output if the files are identical.

The diff command is different from the cmp command in the way the files are compared. Whereas diff reports differences between two files line by line, cmp reports differences between two files character by character. As a result, cmp is more useful than diff for comparing binary files. For text files, cmp is useful mainly when you want to know only whether two files are identical.

To illustrate the difference between considering changes character by character and considering them line by line, think of what happens if a single newline character is added to the beginning of a file. If that file is then compared with an otherwise identical file that lacks the newline at the beginning, diff will report that a blank line has been added to the file, whereas cmp will report that the two files differ in almost every character.

The normal output format consists of one or more hunks of differences; each hunk shows one area where the files differ. Normal format hunks look like this:

```
change-command
< from-file-line
< from-file-line. . .
---
> to-file-line
> to-file-line. . .
```

Three types of change commands exist. Each type consists of a line number or comma-separated range of lines in the first file, a single character indicating the kind of change to make, and a line number or comma-separated range of lines in the second file. All line numbers are the original line numbers in each file. The following are the types of change commands:

- **'lar'**. Add the lines in range r of the second file after line l of the first file. For example, '8a12,15' means append lines 12–15 of file 2 after line 8 of file 1; or, if changing file 2 into file 1, delete lines 12–15 of file 2.

- **'fct'**. Replace the lines in range f of the first file with lines in range t of the second file. This is like a combined add and delete, but more compact. For example, '5,7c8,10' means change lines 5–7 of file 1 to read as lines 8–10 of file 2; or, if changing file 2 into file 1, change lines 8–10 of file 2 to read as lines 5–7 of file 1.

- **'rdl'**. Delete the lines in range r from the first file; line l is where they would have appeared in the second file had they not been deleted. For example, '5,7d3' means delete lines 5–7 of file 1; or, if changing file 2 into file 1, append lines 5–7 of file 1 after line 3 of file 2.

For example, if a.txt contains

```
a
b
c
d
e
```

and b.txt contains

```
c
d
e
f
g
```

the diff command produces the following output:

```
1,2d0
< a
< b
5a4,5
> f
> g
```

The diff command produces output that shows how the files are different and what would need to be done for the files to be identical. First, notice how c is the first common character between the two files. The first line of output reads 1,2d0. This is interpreted as deleting lines 1 and 2 of the first file, lines a and b. Next, the third line reads 5a4,6. The letter a signifies append. If lines 4 through 6 of the second file are appended to line 5 of the first file, the files would be identical.

The diff command has some common options. The −i option ignores changes in case. diff considers upper- and lowercase characters as equivalent. The −q option gives a summary of information. Simply put, the −q option reports whether the files differ at all. For example:

```
diff -q a.txt b.txt
Files a.txt and b.txt differ
```

The −b option ignores changes in whitespace. The phrase "the foo" would be equivalent to "the foo" if the −b option is used.

du

Syntax:

```
du [-ask] filenames
```

The du command summarizes disk usage. If you specify a directory, du reports the disk usage for that directory and any directories it contains. If a filename or directory is not specified, du assumes the current directory. du −a breaks down the total and shows the size of each directory and file. The −s option displays the total. Another useful option is the −k option, which displays all file sizes in kilobytes. Here are some examples of the various options:

```
du -a
247      ./util-linux_2.9e-0.1.deb
130      ./libncurses4_4.2-2.deb
114      ./slang1_1.2.2-2.deb
492      .

du -s
492      .
```

emacs

The emacs program, a full-screen visual editor, is one of the best editors. It is known for its flexibility and power as well as for being a resource hog. The power of emacs is not easily obtained. It has a stiff learning curve that requires patience. Certain actions require as many as four sequential key combinations to perform them.

However, emacs can do just about anything. Aside from the basic editing features, emacs supports syntax highlighting, macros, editing multiple files simultaneously, spell checking, mail, FTP, and many other features.

When reading about emacs, you'll often see words such as meta-key and C-x. The meta key is the meta key on your keyboard (if you have one) or, most commonly, the Esc key. C-x is the syntax for Ctrl plus the X key. Any "C-" combination refers to the Ctrl key.

The two most important key combinations to a new emacs user are C-x C-c and C-h C-h. C-x C-c exits emacs. C-h C-h displays the online help, where you can follow the tutorial or get detailed information about a command. Table A-2 shows emacs's most commonly used commands.

Table A-2 *Common emacs Commands*

Commands	Effects
C-v	Move forward one screen
M-v	Move backward one screen
C-p	Move the cursor to the previous line
C-n	Move the cursor to the next line
C-f	Move the cursor right one position
C-b	Move the cursor left one position
M-f	Move forward a word
M-b	Move backward a word
C-a	Move to beginning of line
C-e	Move to end of line
M-a	Move back to beginning of sentence
M-e	Move forward to end of sentence
<Delete>	Delete the character just before the cursor
C-d	Delete the next character after the cursor
M-<Delete>	Kill the word immediately before the cursor
M-d	Kill the next word after the cursor
C-k	Kill from the cursor position to end of line
M-k	Kill to the end of the current sentence
C-x	Undo the previous command
C-x C-f	Open another file
C-x C-s	Save the current file
C-x C-w	Save the current file as another name
C-x s	Save all the buffers that have recently changed
C-x C-c	Exit emacs

fgrep

The fgrep command was designed to be a faster searching program (compared with grep). However, it can search only for exact characters, not for general specifications. The name fgrep stands for "fixed character grep." These days, computers and memory are fast enough that there is rarely a need for fgrep.

file

Syntax:

```
file filename
```

The file command determines the file's type. If the file is not a regular file, its file type is identified. The file types directory, FIFO, block special, and character special are identified as such. If the file is a regular file and the file is zero-length, it is identified as an empty file.

If the file appears to be a text file, file examines the first 512 bytes and tries to determine its programming language. If the file is an executable a.out, file also displays the version stamp, provided it is greater than 0.

find

Syntax:

```
find [path] [-type fdl] [-name pattern] [-atime [+-
]number of days] [-exec command {} \;] [-empty]
```

The find command finds files and directories. For example,

```
find .  -type d
```

The find command returns all the subdirectory names under the current directory. The –type option typically is set to d (for directory), f (for file), or l (for links).

The following command finds all the text files (ending with the .txt extension) in the current directory, including all of their subdirectories:

```
find .  -type f -name "*.txt"
```

The following command searches all the text files (ending with the .txt extension) in the current directory, including all of their subdirectories, for the keyword "magic" and returns their names (because –l is used with grep):

```
find .  -type f -name "*.txt" -exec grep -l 'magic' {} \;
```

The following command finds all the GIF files that have been accessed in the past 24 hours and displays their details using the ls −l command:

```
find . -name "*.gif" -atime -1 -exec ls -l {} \;
```

The following command displays all the empty files in the current directory hierarchy:

```
find . -type f -empty
```

grep

Syntax:

```
grep [-viw] pattern file(s)
```

The grep command allows you to search for one or more files for particular character patterns. Every line of each file that contains the pattern is displayed at the terminal. The grep command is useful when you have lots of files and want to find out which ones contain particular words or phrases.

Using the −v option, you can display the inverse of a pattern. Perhaps you want to select the lines in data.txt that *do not* contain the word "the":

```
grep −vw 'the' data.txt
```

If the −w option was not specified, then any word containing "the" would match, such as toge[the]r. The −w option specifies that the pattern must be a whole word. The −i option ignores the difference between upper- and lowercase letters when searching for the pattern.

head

Syntax:

```
head [-count | -n number] filename
```

The head command displays the first few lines of a file. By default, the first ten lines of a file are displayed. However, you can use the preceding options to specify a different number of lines. The following example illustrates how to view the first two lines of the text file doc.txt:

```
head —2 doc.txt
# Outline of future projects
# Last modified:   02/02/99
```

ln

Syntax:

```
ln [-s] sourcefile target
```

The ln command creates two types of links: hard and soft. A *link* can best be thought of as two names for the same file. After a link is created, it is indistinguishable from the original file. A file that has hard links to it will not be removed from the hard disk until all links are removed. Hard links are created without the —s option:

```
ln ./www ./public_html
```

However, a hard link does have limitations: it can link neither to another directory nor to a file on another file system. But, by using the —s option, you can create a soft link, which eliminates these restrictions:

```
ln —s /dev/fs02/jack/www /dev/fs01/foo/public_html
```

The preceding creates a soft link between the directory www on file system 2 and a newly created file public_html on file system 1.

locate

Syntax:

```
locate keyword
```

The locate command finds the path of a particular file or command. locate will find an exact or substring match. For example:

```
locate foo
/usr/lib/texmf/tex/latex/misc/footnpag.sty
/usr/share/automake/footer.am
/usr/share/games/fortunes/food
/usr/share/games/fortunes/food.dat
/usr/share/gimp/patterns/moonfoot.pat
```

The output that locate produces will contain the keyword "foo" in the absolute path or will not have any output at all.

ls

Syntax:

```
ls [-laRl] file or directory
```

The ls command allows you to list files (and subdirectories) in a directory. It is one of the most commonly used programs. When used with the −l option, the ls command displays only the file and directory names in the current directory. When the −l option is used, a long listing containing file/directory permission information, size, modification date, and so on is displayed. Using the −a option enables you to view all files and directories (including the ones that have a leading period in their names) within the current directory. The −R option allows the command to recursively display contents of the subdirectories (if any).

mkdir

Syntax:

```
mkdir directory . . .
```

To make a directory, use the mkdir command. Only two restrictions apply when choosing a directory name: filenames can be up to 255 characters long, and directory names can contain any character except /.

The following example creates three directories, all in the current directory, provided write permission is granted in the current directory:

```
mkdir dir1 dir2 dir3
```

mv

Syntax:

```
mv [-if]sourcefile targetfile
```

Use the mv command to move or rename directories and files. The command will perform a move or a rename, depending on whether or not the *targetfile* is an existing directory. To illustrate, suppose that you want to rename an existing directory currently called foo to the new name of foobar:

```
mv foo foobar
```

Because foobar does not already exist as a directory, foo will be renamed to foobar. If the following command is issued

```
mv doc.txt foobar
```

and foobar is an existing directory, a move will be performed. The file doc.txt will now reside in the directory foobar.

The −f option removes existing destination files and never prompts the user. The −i option prompts the user whether to overwrite each destination file that already exists. If the response does not begin with "y" or "Y," the file is skipped.

pico

Syntax:

```
pico [filename]
```

pico is a full-screen text editor that is very user-friendly and highly suitable for users who migrated from an MS Windows or DOS environment.

pwd

Syntax:

```
pwd
```

The pwd command prints the current working directory. The directories displayed will be the absolute path. None of the directories displayed will be hard or soft symbolic links.

rm

Syntax:

```
rm [-rif] directory/file
```

To remove a file or directory, use the rm command. Here are some examples:

```
rm doc.txt
rm ~/doc.txt
rm /tmp/foobar.txt
```

To remove multiple files with rm, you can use wildcards or type each file individually. For example,

```
rm doc1.txt doc2.txt doc3.txt
```

is equivalent to

```
rm doc[1-3].txt
```

rm is a powerful command that can cause chaos if used incorrectly. For instance, suppose that you have stored on your computer a thesis that you've worked hard on for the last six months. You decide to rm all of your docs, mistakenly thinking that you are in another directory from the one in which your thesis is stored. After finding out a backup file does not exist (and you are no longer in denial), you wonder whether you could have prevented this mistake somehow.

The rm command's –i option enables rm to be interactive. It tells rm to ask your permission before removing each file. For example, if you enter

```
rm –i *.doc
rm: remove thesis.doc (yes/no)? n
```

the –i option gives you a parachute, asking you whether to pull the cord (answer no, the default) or suffer the consequences (answer yes). The –f option is completely the opposite. The –f (force) option tells rm to remove all the files you specify regardless of the file permissions. Use the –f option only when you are 100-percent sure you are removing the correct file(s).

To remove a directory and all of the files and directories within it, use the −r option. rm −r will remove an entire subtree:

```
rm −r documents
```

If you are not sure of what you are doing, combine the −r option with the −i option:

```
rm −ri documents
```

The preceding example asks for your permission before removing each file and directory.

sort

Syntax:

```
sort [-rndu] [-o outfile] [infile/sortedfile]
```

The obvious task this command performs is to sort. However, sort also merges files. sort reads files that contain previously sorted data and merges them into one large sorted file.

To save the sorted results, use the −o option: sort −o sorted.txt a.txt will save the sorted a.txt file in sorted.txt. To use sort to merge existing sorted files into one file and save the output in sorted.txt, use the following:

```
sort -o sorted.txt a.txt b.txt c.txt
```

The −r option for this command reverses the sort order. Therefore, a file that contains the letters of the alphabet on a line will be sorted from z to a if the −r option is used.

The −d option sorts files based on dictionary order. sort considers only letters, numerals, and spaces and ignores other characters.

The −u option looks for identical lines and suppresses all but one. Therefore, sort produces only unique lines.

stat

Syntax:

```
stat file
```

This program displays various statistics on a file or directory. For example,

```
stat foo.txt
```

displays the following output:

```
 File: "foo.txt"
 Size: 4447232      Filetype: Regular File
 Mode: (0644/-rw-r--r--)  Uid: ( 0/root)  Gid: (0/root)
Device: 3,0   Inode: 16332     Links: 1
Access: Mon Mar  1 21:39:43 1999(00000.02:32:30)
Modify: Mon Mar  1 22:14:26 1999(00000.01:57:47)
Change: Mon Mar  1 22:14:26 1999(00000.01:57:47
```

As you can see, this output displays the file access, modification, change date, size, owner and group information, permission mode, and so on.

strings

Syntax:

```
strings filename
```

The strings command prints character sequences that are at least four characters long. This utility is used mainly to describe the contents of non-text files.

tail

Syntax:

```
tail [-count | -fr] filename
```

The tail command displays the end of a file. By default, tail displays the last 10 lines of a file. To display the last 50 lines of the file doc.txt, you would issue this command:

```
tail —50 doc.txt
```

The −r option displays the output in reverse order. By default, −r displays all the lines in the file, not just 10 lines. For instance, to display the entire contents of the file doc.txt in reverse order, use the following:

```
tail −r doc.txt
```

To display the last 10 lines of the file doc.txt in reverse order, use:

```
tail −10r doc.txt
```

The −f option is useful when you are monitoring a file. With this option, tail will wait for new data to be written to the file. As new data is added to the file, tail displays the data to the screen. To stop tail from monitoring a file, press Ctrl+C (the intr key), because the tail command will not stop on its own.

touch

Syntax:

```
touch file or directory
```

The touch command updates the timestamp of a file or directory. If the named file does not exist, it will be created as an empty file.

umask

See the section on setting default file permissions for users in Chapter 3.

uniq

Syntax:

```
uniq [-c] filename
```

The uniq command compares adjacent lines and displays only one unique line. When used with the −c option, uniq counts the number of occurrences. A file that has the contents

```
a
a
```

```
a
b
a
```

produces the following result when used with uniq:

```
uniq test.txt
a
b
a
```

Notice how the adjacent a's were removed but not all a's in the file. This is an important detail to remember when using uniq. If you want to find all the unique lines in a file called test.txt, you can run the following command:

```
sort  test.txt  | uniq
```

This command sorts the test.txt file and puts all the similar lines next to each other, allowing uniq to display only the unique lines. For example, suppose that you want to quickly find out how many unique visitors came to your Web site. You can run the following command:

```
awk '{print $1}' access.log | sort | uniq
```

This displays the unique IP addresses in a CLF log file, which is what Apache Web server uses.

vi

The vi program is a powerful, full-screen text editor that can almost certainly be found on all UNIX systems because of its size and capabilities. vi does not require much in the way of resources to utilize its features. In addition to the basic edit functions, vi can search and replace and concatenate files, it has its own macro language, and it provides several other additional features.

vi has two modes, which are important to learn and understand:

- **Input mode.** You can enter text in the document, and insert or append text.

■ **Command mode.** You can move within the document, merge lines, search, and so on. You can carry out all the functions of vi from command mode, except enter text. You can enter text only when in input mode.

A typical vi newbie assumes he is in input mode and begins typing in his document. He expects to see his newly inputted text, but instead sees his current document mangled because he was in command mode.

When vi is started, it is in command mode. You can go from command mode to input mode by using one of the following commands: [aAiIoOcCsSR]. To return to command mode, press the Esc key.

Table A-3 shows a summary of common vi commands and their effect when in command mode.

Table A-3 *Summary of Common vi Commands*

Command	Effect
Ctrl+D	Moves window down by half a screen.
Ctrl+U	Moves window up by half a screen.
Ctrl+F	Moves window forward by a screen.
Ctrl+B	Moves window back by a screen.
k or up arrow	Moves cursor up one line.
j or down arrow	Moves cursor down one line.
l or right arrow	Moves cursor right one character.
h or left arrow	Moves cursor left one character.
Return	Moves cursor to beginning of next line.
– (minus)	Moves cursor to beginning of previous line.
w	Moves cursor to beginning of next word.
b	Moves cursor to beginning of previous word.
^ or 0	Moves cursor to beginning of current line.
$	Moves cursor to end of current line.
A	Inserts text immediately after the cursor.
o	Opens a new line immediately after the current line.
O	Opens a new line immediately before the current line. Note that this is an uppercase letter O, not a zero.
x	Deletes character under the cursor.

Continued

Table A-3 *Continued*

Command	Effect
dw	Deletes a word (including space after it).
D or d	Deletes from the cursor until the end of the line.
d ^	(d caret) Deletes from the beginning of the line to the space or character to the left of the cursor.
dd	Deletes the current line.
U	Undoes last change. Note that two undos in a row will undo the undo (nothing changes).
:w	Writes out the changes for the current file and continues editing.
:q!	Quits vi without saving any changes.
:ZZ	Saves current file and exits vi.

wc

Syntax:

```
wc [-lwc] filename
```

The wc (word count) command counts lines, characters, and words. If the wc command is used without any options, the output displays all the statistics of the file. The example file test.txt contains the following text:

```
the quick brown fox jumps over the lazy dog
wc test.txt
        1        9       44 test.txt
```

The results indicate that the test.txt file has 1 line with 9 words containing 44 characters. To display only the number of lines, the –l option is used. The –w option displays only the number of words. The –c option displays only the total number of characters.

whatis

Syntax:

```
whatis keyword
```

The whatis command displays a one-line description for the keyword provided. The whatis command is identical to typing man −f. For instance, if you want to display the time, but you are not sure whether to use the time or date command, enter the following:

```
whatis time date
time            time (1)        - time a simple command
date            date (1)        - print the date and time
```

Looking at the results, you can see that the command you want is date. The time command actually measures how long a program or command takes to execute.

whereis

The whereis command locates source/binary and manual sections for specified files. The supplied names are first stripped of leading path name components and any (single) character file extension, such as .c, .h, and so forth.

```
whereis ls
ls: /bin/ls /usr/man/man1/ls.1.gz
```

The preceding example indicates the location of the command in question. ls is located in the /bin directory and its corresponding man pages are found at /usr/man/man1/ls.1.gz.

which

Syntax:

```
which command
```

The which command displays the path and any aliases of any valid executable command.

```
which df
/usr/bin/df
```

The preceding example shows that the df command is located in the /usr/bin directory. The which command also displays information about shell commands:

```
which setenv
setenv: shell built-in command.
```

File Compression and Archive-Specific Commands

The commands discussed in this section help you to compress, archive, and package files.

compress

Syntax:

```
compress [-v] file(s)
```

The compress command attempts to reduce the size of a file by using the adaptive Lempel-Ziv coding algorithm. Files that are compressed are replaced by a file with a .Z extension. Using any type of compression for files is significant, because having smaller file sizes increases the amount of available disk space. Also, transferring smaller files across networks reduces network congestion.

The –v (verbose) option displays the percentage of reduction for each file that was compressed and tells you the name of the new file. Here is a typical session using the command compress:

```
ls -alF inbox
-rw-------   1 username cscstd     194261 Feb 23 20:12
inbox
compress -v inbox
inbox: Compression: 37.20% -- replaced with inbox.Z

ls -alF inbox.Z
-rw-------   1 username cscstd     121983 Feb 23 20:12
inbox.Z
```

gunzip

Syntax:

```
gunzip [-v] file(s)
```

To decompress files to their original form, use the gunzip command. gunzip attempts to decompress files ending with the extensions: .gz, -gz, .z, -z, _z, .Z, or .tgz.

The –v option displays a verbose output when decompressing a file:

```
gunzip -v README.txt.gz
README.txt.gz:          65.0% -- replaced with
README.txt
```

gzip

Syntax:

```
gzip [-rv9] file(s)
```

The gzip command is another compression program. It is known for having one of the best compression ratios, but at a cost of being considerably slow. Files compressed with gzip are replaced by files with a .gz extension.

The –9 option yields the best compression, but at the sacrifice of speed. The –v option is the verbose option which lists the size, and compression ratios for each file. Also, the –r option recursively transverses each directory, compressing all the files along the way.

rpm

Syntax:

```
rpm -[ivhqladefUV] [--force] [--nodeps] [--oldpackage]
package list
```

rpm is the Red Hat Package Manager program. It allows you to manage RPM packages, making it very easy to install and uninstall software.

To install a new RPM package called precious-software-1.0.i386.rpm, run the following:

```
rpm -i precious-software-1.0.i386.rpm
```

You can make rpm become a bit more verbose by using −ivh instead of just the −i option. If you have already installed the package and for some reason want to install it again on top of the old installation, you need to use the —force option to force rpm.

If you are upgrading a software package, use the −U option. For example,

```
rpm -Uvh precious-software-2.0.i386.rpm
```

upgrades the previous version of the precious-software package to version 2.0. However, if you have already installed a newer version and want to go back to the previous version, rpm will detect it and display an error message saying that the installed version is newer than the one you are trying to install. In such a case, if you decide to proceed anyway, use the —old-package option with the −U option to force rpm to downgrade your software.

To find a list of all available packages installed on your system, run the following:

```
rpm -qa
```

To find out which package a program such as sendmail belongs to, run

```
rpm -q sendmail
```

which returns the RPM package name that was used to install sendmail. To find out which package a specific file such as /bin/tcsh belongs to, run

```
rpm -qf /bin/tcsh
```

which displays the package name of the named file. If you are interested in finding the documentation that came with a file, use the −d option along with the −qf options. To list all the files associated with a program or package such as sendmail, use the −l option, as shown here:

```
rpm -ql sendmail
```

To ensure that an installed package has not been modified in any way, use the −V option. For example, to verify that all installed packages are in the original state, run the following:

```
rpm -Va
```

This option becomes very useful if you discover that one or more packages may have been damaged by you or someone else.

To uninstall a package such as sendmail, run the following command:

```
rpm -e sendmail
```

If you find out that removing a package or program will break other programs, because they depend on it or its files, you have to decide whether you want to break these programs. If you decide to remove the package or the program anyway, use the —nodeps option with the −e option to force rpm to uninstall the package.

tar

Syntax:

```
tar [c] [x] [v] [z] [f filename]   file or directory names
```

The tar command allows you to archive multiple files and directories into a single TAR file. It also allows you to extract files and directories from such an archive file. For example,

```
tar cf source.tar *.c
```

creates a TAR file called source.tar, which will contain all the C source files (ending with extension .c) in the current directory.

The v option enables you to see which files are being archived:

```
tar cvf source.tar *.c
```

In the following example, all the files and subdirectories of the directory called important_dir are archived in a file called backup.tar.gz. Notice that this file is also being compressed because of the z option, and hence the resulting file should be given a .gz extension. Often, the .tar.gz extension is shortened to .tgz.

```
tar cvzf backup.tar.gz  important_dir
```

To extract an archive file, backup.tar, run the following command:

```
tar xf backup.tar
```

To extract a compressed tar file (such as backup.tgz or backup.tar.gz), run

```
tar xzf backup.tgz
```

uncompress

Syntax:

```
uncompress [-v] file(s)
```

When a file is compressed using the compress command, it no longer is in its original form. To retrieve a compressed file into its original form, use the uncompress command.

The uncompress command expects to find a file with a .Z extension, so the command line "uncompress inbox" is equivalent to "uncompress inbox.Z."

The –v option produces verbose output:

```
uncompress -v inbox.Z
inbox.Z:  -- replaced with inbox
```

unzip

Syntax:

```
unzip file(s)
```

The unzip command decompresses files with the .zip extension. These files can be compressed with the unzip command, Phil Katz's PKZIP, or any other PKZIP-compatible program.

uudecode

Syntax:

```
uudecode file
```

The uudecode command transforms an uuencoded file into its original form. uudecode creates the file by using the "target_name" specified by the uuencode command, which can also be identified on the first line of a uuencoded file.

To convert a uuencoded file from

```
uudecode a.out.txt
```

back into its original form, the executable file a.out is created from the text file a.out.txt.

uuencode

Syntax:

```
uuencode in_file target_name
```

The uuencode command translates a binary file into readable form, by converting the binary file into ASCII printable characters. One of the many uses of uuencode is to transmit a binary file through e-mail. A file that has been uuencoded appears as a large e-mail message. The recipient can then save the message and use the uudecode command to retrieve its binary form.

The *target_name* is the name of the binary file created when the uuencode utility is used.

The following example will uuencode the executable program a.out. The target name that uudecode creates will be called b.out. The uuencoded version of a.out will be saved in the file a.out.txt.

```
uuencode a.out b.out > a.out.txt
```

zip

Syntax:

```
zip [-ACDe9] file(s)
```

This compression utility compresses files in a PKZIP compatible format, enabling compatibility with systems such as VMS, MS-DOS, OS/2, Windows NT, Minix, Atari, Macintosh, Amiga, and Acorn RISC OS.

The zip command has an array of options that are toggled by its switches. This command can create self-extracting files, add comments to zip files, remove files from an archive, and password-protect the archive.

These are a few of the features supported by zip. For a more detailed description, see your local man page.

File System–Specific Commands

The commands in this section are used for administration of file systems.

dd

Syntax:

```
dd if=input file [conv=conversion type] of=output file
[obs=output block size]
```

This program allows you to convert file formats. For example,

```
dd if=/tmp/uppercase.txt   conv=lcase
of=/tmp/lowercase.txt
```

takes the /tmp/upppercase.txt file and writes a new file called /tmp/lowercase.txt, converting all the characters to lowercase (lcase). To do the reverse, you can use conv=ucase option. However, dd is most widely used to write a boot image file to a floppy disk that has a file system already created by mkfs. For example,

```
dd if=/some/boot.img   conv=lcase of=/dev/fd0 obs=16k
```

writes the /some/boot.image file to the first floppy disk (/dev/fd0) in 16K blocks.

df

Syntax:

```
df [-k] FileSystem | File
```

The df command summarizes the free disk space for the drives mounted on the system. Hard disk space is an important resource in a computer and should be monitored carefully. Mismanagement of hard disk space can cause a computer to crawl on its knees, and cause some unhappy users.

To view the disk space summary for the current file system, run

```
df .
```

The −k option displays the summary with 1024-blocks, instead.

edquota

To assign disk quotas per user, use the edquota command. For example, to allocate a disk quota for a user named kabir, run the following:

```
edquota -u kabir
```

This brings up the default text editor (such as vi or whatever is set in the $EDITOR environment variable) with contents similar to the following:

```
Quotas for user kabir:
/dev/sda5: blocks in use: 0, limits (soft = 0, hard = 0)
           inodes in use: 0, limits (soft = 0, hard = 0)
```

Here, the user kabir has so far used 0 blocks (in K) on disk partition /dev/sda5 (under usrquota control), and the limits (soft or hard) are not set yet. Similarly, this user has not yet owned any files (inodes), and no limit (soft or hard) has been set yet.

As you can see, you can simultaneously set limits for the amount of space (in blocks) a user can consume, and control how many files can be owned by the user. The soft limit specifies the maximum amount of disk space (blocks) or files (inodes) a user can have on the file system. The hard limit is the absolute amount of disk space (in blocks) or files (inodes) a user can have.

For example, suppose that you want to allow user kabir to have a soft limit of 1MB (1,024K) and a hard limit of 4MB (4,096K) for disk space. Also, suppose that you want to allow this user a soft limit of 128 files/directories (inodes) and a hard limit of 512 files/directories. You can set the quota limit using edquota –u kabir as follows:

```
Quotas for user kabir:
/dev/sda5: blocks in use: 0, limits (soft = 1024, hard =
4096)
         inodes in use: 0, limits (soft = 128, hard = 512)
```

After you save the configuration, the user no longer can exceed the hard limits. If the user tries to go over any of these two (disk space and inode count) limits, an error message will be displayed. For example, in the following, user kabir tries to create a new directory in /home, but the quota limit for this quota has been exceeded, so the error message is displayed:

```
[kabir@picaso /home]$ mkdir eat_space
mkdir: cannot make directory `eat_space': Disc quota
exceeded
```

If you have many users to assign quotas to, the preceding method could be quite time-consuming. To aid you with such a situation, the edquota program includes a –p *prototype user* option that allows you to copy the prototype user's disk quota configuration for others. For example, suppose that you want to use the quota configuration you just created for user kabir for three other users (sheila, jennifer, and mrfrog). You can run the following:

```
edquote -p kabir  -u sheila jennifer mrfrog
```

Now, all three of these users have the same quota configuration as kabir.

Placing groups under disk quota control is very similar. The edquota syntax for configuring a group quota requirements is as follows:

```
edquota -g group name
```

To enforce the soft limit for either user or group quotas, you need to configure the grace period by using the edquota –t command. When you run this command, your editor will display something similar to the following:

```
Time units may be: days, hours, minutes, or seconds
Grace period before enforcing soft limits for users:
/dev/sda5: block grace period: 0 days, file grace period:
0 days
```

You can specify the grace period in days, hours, minutes, or even seconds. For example, in the following, the grace period for the disk space limit (in blocks) is 7 days, and the grace period for the number of files (inodes) is only 5 hours:

```
Time units may be: days, hours, minutes, or seconds
Grace period before enforcing soft limits for users:
/dev/sda5: block grace period: 7 days, file grace period:
5 hours
```

fdformat

Syntax:

```
fdformat   floppy-device
```

The fdformat program does a low-level format on a floppy device. For example,

```
fdformat /dev/fd0H1440
```

formats the first floppy disk (/dev/fd0) using the high-density 1.44MB format.

fdisk

The fdisk program works with one disk at a time, and even though it provides a simple, inelegant user interface, it actually provides quite a bit more flexibility than the Disk Druid tool.

fdisk has a simple, command-prompt-oriented interface. It is also the default partitioning tool available after you have already installed Red Hat Linux. You can run fdisk from the command line by using the following syntax:

```
fdisk hard disk device
```

For example,

```
fdisk /dev/sda
```

tells fdisk that you want to work on the first SCSI disk's partitions. After you enter such a command, fdisk displays its command prompt, Command (m for help):, to which you can enter **m** to get a help screen such as the following:

```
Command action
   a   toggle a bootable flag
   b   edit bsd disklabel
   c   toggle the dos compatibility flag
   d   delete a partition
   l   list known partition types
   m   print this menu
   n   add a new partition
   o   create a new empty DOS partition table
   p   print the partition table
   q   quit without saving changes
   t   change a partition's system id
   u   change display/entry units
   v   verify the partition table
   w   write table to disk and exit
   x   extra functionality (experts only)
```

To view your existing partitions in the selected disk, enter **p**, which causes all of your current partitions to be displayed in a table format, such as the following:

```
Disk /dev/sda: 33 heads, 63 sectors, 1014 cylinders
Units = cylinders of 2079 * 512 bytes
```

Device Boot	Start	End	Blocks	Id	System
/dev/sda1	1	505	524916	83	Linux native
/dev/sda2	506	1014	529105+	5	Extended

```
/dev/sda5        506     886    396018   83  Linux native
/dev/sda6        887    1011    129906   82  Linux swap
```

As shown here, the /dev/sda disk has been divided into four partitions, where the first partition is /dev/sda1, which starts at block 1 and ends at block 505. Each block is 1,024 bytes, or 1K, so the first partition consists of 524,916 blocks, or 524,916K, or approximately 512MB.

To remove all existing partitions one by one, use the d command and enter the partition number you want to remove. After you remove one or more partitions, you can create new partitions as follows.

First, enter **n** to add a new partition:

```
Command (m for help): n
Command action
   e   extended
   p   primary partition (1-4)
```

As indicated, you get two choices: create either an extended partition or a primary partition. You need extended partitions only if you want to create more than four partitions. Because you only need /, /usr, /home, and a swap partition to get things going under Linux, you really don't need to create extended partitions. So, create a primary partition by entering **p** at the prompt. The next prompt asks you to select a partition number:

```
Partition number (1-4): 1
```

Enter **1** for the first partition, **2** for the second, and so on. The next prompt asks you to select the starting block number. The range shown in the parentheses is the total blocks available for partitioning. If this is the first partition, you can choose 1 as the starting block:

```
First cylinder (1-1014): 1
```

To create a 512MB partition, you can enter the size in bytes, kilobytes, or megabytes. Because a value in megabytes is easy to deal with, this example uses +512MB for the last cylinder:

```
Last cylinder or +size or +sizeM or +sizeK ([1]-1014):
+512M
```

To see whether the partition has been created as requested, use the p command to see the partition information:

```
Disk /dev/sda: 33 heads, 63 sectors, 1014 cylinders
Units = cylinders of 2079 * 512 bytes


  Device Boot    Start    End   Blocks   Id  System
/dev/sda1            1    505   524916   83  Linux native
```

As the last two lines show, the first partition has been created as requested, and the default partition type is Linux native; if you want to change this, use the t command to toggle a partition's system ID flag. For example, to toggle a partition's system ID flag to Linux swap, use the following commands:

```
Command (m for help): t
Partition number (1-4): 1
Hex code (type L to list codes): 82
Changed system type of partition 1 to 82 (Linux swap)


Command (m for help): p


Disk /dev/sda: 33 heads, 63 sectors, 1014 cylinders
Units = cylinders of 2079 * 512 bytes

  Device Boot    Start    End   Blocks   Id  System
/dev/sda1            1    505   524916   82  Linux
swap
```

First, the t command is entered to toggle the system ID of a partition. Then, the partition is selected and 82 is entered as the swap partition type. The L command can be used to list all the available partition types.

Note that if you use fdisk to create partitions, you must make a Linux native partition bootable. For example, to turn on /dev/sda1 as a bootable partition, the boot flag needs to be toggled, by entering the following:

```
Command (m for help): a
Partition number (1-6): 1
```

Using the p command displays the existing partition table:

```
Disk /dev/sda: 33 heads, 63 sectors, 1014 cylinders
Units = cylinders of 2079 * 512 bytes

   Device Boot   Start   End   Blocks   Id   System
/dev/sda1     *      1   505   524916   83   Linux native
/dev/sda2          506  1014   529105+  5    Extended
/dev/sda5          506   886   396018   83   Linux native
/dev/sda6          887  1011   29906    82   Linux swap
```

/dev/sda1 has "*" in the Boot column, showing that this partition is bootable.

mkfs

Syntax:

```
mkfs [-t fstype] [-cv] device-or-mount-point [blocks]
```

The mkfs command allows you to make a new file system. For example,

```
mkfs -t ext2  /dev/hda3
```

creates an ext2-type file system on the /dev/hda3 partition of the first IDE hard disk. The −c option enables you to instruct mkfs to check bad blocks before building the file system. The −v option produces verbose output.

mount

Syntax:

```
mount -a [-t fstype] [-o options] device  directory
```

The mount command mounts a file system. Typically, the mount options for commonly used file systems are stored in /etc/fstab. For example, if

```
/dev/hda6  /intranet  ext2  defaults 1 2
```

is found in /etc/fstab, you can mount the file system stored in partition /dev/hda6 as follows:

```
mount  /intranet
```

The same file system can also be mounted as follows:

```
mount  -t ext2 /dev/hda6 /intranet
```

The −t option is used to specify the file system type. To mount all the file systems specified in the /etc/fstab, use the −a option. For example, the following mounts all ext2 file systems:

```
mount  -a -t ext2
```

Commonly used arguments for −o option are ro (read-only) and rw (read/write). For example, the following mounts /dev/hda6 on /secured as a read-only file system:

```
mount  -t ext2 -o ro /dev/hda6 /secured
```

quota

To find out how much of your disk space a particular user is using, run the quota command as follows:

```
quota -u username
```

For example:

```
quota -u kabir
Disk quotas for user kabir (uid 500):
Filesystem blocks quota limit grace files quota limit
grace
/dev/sda5  0      1024 4096          1    128   512
```

You can run the same command to monitor disk usage of a group, as follows:

```
quota -g group
```

When you find users or groups that are over the limit, you can send them e-mail messages, so that disk usage is brought down to acceptable limits.

swapoff

Syntax:

```
swapoff -a
```

The swapoff command allows you to disable swap devices. The −a option allows you to disable all swap partitions specified in /etc/fstab.

swapon

Syntax:

```
swapon -a
```

The swapon command allows you to enable swap devices. The −a option allows you to enable all swap partitions specified in /etc/fstab.

umount

Syntax:

```
umount  -a [-t fstype]
```

The umount command unmounts a file system from the current system. For example,

```
umount  /cdrom
```

unmounts a file system whose mount point is /cdrom and the details of whose mount point are specified in /etc/fstab.

The −a option allows you to unmount all file systems (except for the proc file system) specified in the /etc/fstab file. You can also use the −t option to specify a particular file system type to unmount. For example,

```
umount  -a -t iso9660
```

unmounts all iso9660-type file systems, which are typically CD-ROMs.

DOS-Compatible Commands

If you need access to MS-DOS files from your Linux system, you need to install the Mtools package. Mtools is shipped with Red Hat as an RPM package, so installing it is quite simple. (Refer to the description of the rpm command in the previous section "File Compression and Archive-Specific Commands" for details on how to install an RPM package.)

Mtools is a collection of utilities that allows you to read, write, and move around MS-DOS files. It also supports Windows 9x–style long filenames, OS/2 Xdf disks, and 2m disks. This section covers the common utilities found in the Mtools package.

mcopy

Syntax:

```
mcopy [-tm] source-file-or-directory  destination-file-
or-directory
```

The mcopy utility is used to copy MS-DOS files to and from Linux. For example,

```
mcopy /tmp/readme.txt   b:
```

copies the readme.txt file from the /tmp directory to the b: drive. The −t option allows you to automatically translate carriage return/line feed pairs in MS-DOS text files into line feeds. The −m option allows you to preserve the file modification time.

mdel

Syntax:

```
mdel msdosfile
```

The mdel utility allows you to delete files on an MS-DOS file system.

mdir

Syntax:

```
mdir [-/] msdos-file-or-directory
```

The mdir utility allows you to view an MS-DOS directory. The –/ option allows you to view all the subdirectories, as well.

mformat

Syntax:

```
mformat [-t cylinders] [-h heads] [-s sectors]
```

The mformat utility allows you to format a floppy disk to hold a minimal MS-DOS file system. However, using an MS-DOS machine to format a disk is much easier than specifying cylinders, heads, sectors, and so on. My advice is to use an MS-DOS machine to do the job instead of using mformat.

mlabel

Syntax:

```
mlabel [-vcs] drive:[new label]
```

The mlabel utility displays the current volume label (if any) of the named drive and prompts for the new label if it is not entered after *drive*: in the command line. The –v option prints a hex dump of the boot sector of the named drive. The –c option clears the existing volume label. The –s option shows the existing label of the drive.

System Status–Specific Commands

The commands discussed in this section deal with status information on system resources.

dmesg

Syntax:

```
dmesg
```

The dmesg program prints the status messages displayed by the kernel during bootup.

free

Syntax:

```
free
```

The free program displays memory usage statistics. An example of output looks like this:

```
            total     used    free    shared  buffers  cached
Mem:        127776    124596  3180    30740   2904     107504
-/+ buffers/cache: 14188  113588
Swap:       129900    84      129816
```

shutdown

Syntax:

```
shutdown [-r] [-h] [-c] [-k]  [-t seconds] time [message]
```

The shutdown command allows a superuser or an ordinary user listed in the /etc/shutdown.allow file to shut down the system for a reboot or halt. To reboot the computer now, run the following command:

```
shutdown -r now
```

To halt the system after the shutdown, replace −r with −h. The −k option allows you to simulate a shutdown event without actually doing it. For example,

```
shutdown -r -k now System going down for maintenance
```

sends a fake shutdown message to all the users. The −t option allows you to specify a delay, in seconds, between the warning message and the actual shutdown event. In such a case, if you decide to abort the shutdown, use the −c option and run shutdown again to cancel it.

Note that you can use the *HH:MM* format to specify the time. For example,

```
shutdown -r 12:55
```

reboots the system at 12:55. You can also use +*minutes* to specify time. For example,

```
shutdown -r +5
```

starts the shutdown process five minutes after the warning message has been printed.

uname

Syntax:

```
uname [-m] [-n] [-r] [-s] [-v] [-a]
```

The uname command displays information about the current system. For example,

```
uname -a
```

displays a line such as the following:

```
Linux picaso.nitec.com 2.0.36 #1 Tue Oct 13 22:17:11 EDT
1998 i586 unknown
```

The −m option displays the system architecture (for instance, i586). The −n option displays the host name (for instance, picaso.nitec.com). The −r option displays the release version of the OS (for instance, 2.0.36). The −s option displays the OS name (for instance, Linux). The –v option displays the local build version of the OS (for instance, #1 Tue Oct 13 22:17:11 EDT 1998).

uptime

Syntax:

```
uptime
```

The uptime command displays the current time; how long the system has been up since the last reboot; how many users are connected to the server; and the system load in the last 1, 5, and 15 minutes.

User Administration Commands

The commands in this section pertain to user administration.

chfn

Run the chfn command to change a user's finger information. For example, the following enables you to change user jennifer's finger information, which is stored in the /etc/passwd file:

```
chfn jennifer
```

A user can change his or her own finger information by using this program, as well. A user can also create a .plan file in his or her home directory that will get appended to the information shown by the finger program.

chsh

Use the chsh command to change a user's shell. For example, the following enables you to change user brian's current shell:

```
chsh brian
```

If you specify any shell or program name that is not in /etc/shells, the user will not be able to log in. Note that a user can change his or her own shell using this command. An ordinary user does not need to specify the username as an argument, because the only shell he or she can change is his or her own.

groupadd

To create a new group, use the groupadd command. For example, the following adds a new group called mygroup in the /etc/group and in the /etc/gshadow file (if you are using shadow passwords):

```
groupadd mygroup
```

By default, the groupadd program creates the group with a GID above 499, because 0 through 499 are (sort of) reserved for system-level accounts such as root, bin, and mail. So if your /etc/group file has the last group GID set to 511, the new group you create with this program will have a GID of 512, and so on. If you want to set the GID of your new group specifically, use the −g *GID* option. Also, if you want to create a group with a GID in the 0 to 499 range, use the −r option with the −g *GID* option to force groupadd to create the new group as a system group. Note that if the group or GID you are trying to use with the program is already in use in /etc/group, you will get an error message.

groupmod

To modify an existing group name or GID, use the groupmod command. To rename a group, use the following syntax:

```
groupmod -n new group  current group
```

For example, the following renames the existing novices group to experts:

```
groupmod -n experts novices
```

To change the GID, use the −g *new GID* option. For example, the following changes the current GID of the troublemakers group to 666:

```
groupmod -g 666 troublemakers
```

groups

Syntax:

```
groups [username]
```

The groups command displays the list of group(s) the named user currently belongs to. If no *username* is specified, the current user's groups are displayed.

last

Syntax:

```
last [-number] [username]  [reboot]
```

The last command displays a list of users who have logged in since /var/log/wtmp was created. For example, the following command shows the number of times user julie has logged in since the last time /var/log/wtmp was created:

```
last julie
```

The following command shows only the last ten logins by julie:

```
last -10 julie
```

This command displays the number of times the system was rebooted since /var/log/wtmp file was created:

```
last reboot
```

passwd

Syntax:

```
passwd username
```

The passwd command allows you to change a user's password. Only a superuser can specify a username; everyone else must type passwd without any argument, which allows the user to change her own password. A superuser can change anyone's password using this program.

su

Syntax:

```
su  [-]  [username]
```

The su command can be used to change into another user. For example,

```
su john
```

allows you to be the user john.

The most common use of this command is to become root. For example, if you run this command without any username argument, it assumes that you want to be root and thus prompts you for the root password. If you enter the correct root password, su will run a shell using the root's UID (0) and GID (0). This effectively allows you to become the root user and perform administrative tasks. This command is very useful if you have only Telnet access to the server. You can Telnet into the server as a regular user and use it to become root to perform system administrative tasks. If you supply the –option, the new shell is marked as the login shell. After you become the root user, you can su to other users without entering any password.

useradd

To create a user account from your command line, you can run the useradd command. For example, to create a user called newuser, you can run this command as follows:

```
useradd newuser
```

This adds a new entry in /etc/passwd (and in /etc/shadow if you use shadow passwords) using system defaults. For example, when I run the preceding command on my Red Hat system, /etc/passwd shows a new line such as the following:

```
newuser:!!:506:506::/home/newuser:/bin/bash
```

If you remember the /etc/passwd fields from the earlier discussion, you will see that the password field (the second field) is set to !!. This means that this password is not set and newuser cannot log in yet. So, you need to create a password for this user by running the passwd command as follows:

```
passwd newuser
```

You are asked to enter the password twice, and after your password is accepted, it is encrypted and added to the user's entry in the /etc/passwd file.

The UID and the GID values will be automatically selected by useradd. Basically, it just increments the last UID in /etc/passwd by 1 and the last GID in /etc/group by 1 to create the UID and GID, respectively, for the new user. You can also manually set the UID and group using command line switches −u and −g respectively. The home directory is created in the default top-level home directory. Similarly, the login shell is selected from a system default. If you want to override a system default, you can specify a command-line option. To override the default home directory, use the −d *newdirectory* option (where *newdirectory* is the name of your directory). For example,

```
useradd newuser -d /www/newuser
```

The new user (newuser) will be created, and her home directory will be set to /www/newuser. Note that useradd will create only the final directory, not the entire path. For example, if you specify −d /some/new/dir/myuser as the option, useradd will create myuser only if /some/new/dir/ already exists.

When the new home directory is created, files contained in the /etc/skel directory are copied to the new home directory. These files are typically the dot configuration files for the default shell. For example, if the default shell is /bin/bash, you should have default versions of .bashrc, .bash_profile, and .bash_login in the /etc/skel directory so that the new user's home directory can be automatically set up with these files.

The useradd that comes with Red Hat Linux creates a private group for the user with the same name as the username. For example, if you run useradd kabir, then a new user named kabir will be created in the /etc/passwd file, and a new group called kabir will be created in the /etc/group file. This method allows the new user to be totally isolated from the rest of the users, and therefore ensures greater privacy for the user. Whenever the new user creates a new file, by virtue of this private group, the file is accessible only by the new user. The user has to change the file permissions explicitly to allow someone else to see the file.

However, if your user account philosophy clashes with this kind of private group idea, you can override it by using the −g *group* option (where *group* is the name of your group). For example,

```
useradd mjkabir -g users
```

makes useradd create the new user (mjkabir) with the default group set to the users.

If you want to make the new user a member of additional groups on your system, you can use the −G *comma-separated list of groups* option. For example,

```
useradd mjkabir -G wheel,admins
```

adds the new user (mjkabir) to the wheel and admins groups in the /etc/group file.

userdel

To delete an existing user, use the userdel command. For example, the following deletes the user called snake:

```
userdel snake
```

If you want to remove the user's home directory and all of its contents, use the −r option. Note that userdel will not delete the user if the user is currently logged in. Ask the user to log out by sending her a write message (write *username*), and if asking isn't an option, use the killall command to terminate all processes associated with the user, and then run the userdel command.

If you want to temporarily disable a user account, you can do one of the following:

- Use the usermod −s *new shell username* command to change the shell to /bin/false (make sure the new shell is listed in the /etc/shells file). This disallows the user from logging in to the system.

- If you are using the shadow passwords, use the usermod −e *MM/DD/YY username* command to cause the user account to expire.

If you want to disable all user account access temporarily, you can create a file called /etc/nologin with a message explaining why you are not allowing access. The login program will not allow any nonroot account to log in as long as this file is in place.

usermod

The usermod command is used to modify a user account. To change the home directory of an existing user, run the usermod command as follows:

```
usermod -d new home directory username
```

where *new home directory* and *username* are the correct values.

For example, if a user called keller has /home/keller as her home directory, and you want to move it to /home2/keller, you can run the usermod command as follows:

```
usermod -d /home2/keller keller
```

This sets the new directory as her home directory. However, if you want to move the contents of her home directory to the new location, use the −m option as follows:

```
usermod -d -m /home2/keller keller
```

To change the UID of a user, use the usermod command as follows:

```
usermod -u UID username
```

where *UID* and *username* are the correct values.

For example, the following changes the UID for user mrfrog to 500:

```
usermod -g 500 mrfrog
```

All the files and directories that are owned by the user within her home directory will automatically reflect the UID change. However, if the user owns files outside her own home directory, you will have to manually change the ownership using the chown command.

To change the default group for a user, use the usermod command as follows:

```
usermod -g group name or GID username
```

where *group name or GID* and *username* are the correct values.

For example, the following changes the default group for user mrfrog to 777:

```
usermod -g 777 myfrog
```

If you are using shadow passwords, you can change the expiration date of a user account using the usermod command as follows:

```
usermod -e MM/DD/YY username
```

where *MM/DD/YY* and *username* are the correct values.

For example, the following resets the account expiration date for user kabir to 12/31/99:

```
usermod -e 12/31/99 kabir
```

If you are using shadow passwords, you can change the expiration date of a user account using the usermod command as follows:

```
usermod -e MM/DD/YY username
```

where *MM/DD/YY* and *username* are the correct values.

For example, the following resets the account expiration date for user kabir to 12/31/99:

```
usermod -e 12/31/99 kabir
```

who

Syntax:

```
who
```

The who command displays information about the users who are currently logged in to a system. You can also use the w command for the same purpose.

whoami

Syntax:

```
whoami
```

This command displays your current username.

User Commands for Accessing Network Services

The commands discussed in this section enable you to access various network services.

finger

Syntax:

```
finger user@host
```

This program allows you to query a finger daemon at the named host. For example,

```
finger kabir@blackhole.integrationlogic.com
```

requests a finger connection to the finger daemon running on the `blackhole.integrationlogic.com` server. If the named host does not allow finger connections, this attempt will fail. On success, the finger request displays information about the named user. If the user has a .plan file in the home directory, this file also is displayed by most traditional finger daemons. Because finger has been used to cause security problems, most system administrators disable finger service outside their domains.

ftp

Syntax:

```
ftp ftp hostname or IP address
```

This is the default FTP client program. You can use this program to FTP to an FTP server. For example,

```
ftp  ftp.cdrom.com
```

opens an FTP connection to `ftp.cdrom.com` and prompts you to enter a username and password. If you know the username and password, you can log in to the FTP server and upload or download files. After you are at the FTP prompt, you can enter **help** or **?** to get help on FTP commands.

lynx

Syntax:

```
lynx [-dump] [-head] [URL]
```

lynx is the most popular interactive text-based Web browser. To run the browser, simply enter the desired URL as the command-line argument. For example,

```
lynx http://www.integrationlogic.com/
```

displays the top page of the site. lynx is a very handy program to have around. For example, to find out quickly what kind of Web server the site uses, without asking the Webmaster, run the following command:

```
lynx -head http://www.integrationlogic.com/
```

The preceding command displays the HTTP header the lynx browser receives from the Web server. An example of its output is shown here:

```
HTTP/1.1 302 Moved
Date: Tue, 02 Mar 1999 06:47:27 GMT
Server: Apache/1.3.3 (Unix)
Location: http://www.integrationlogic.com/index.shtml
Connection: close
Content-Type: text/html
```

This header shows that www.integrationlogic.com runs on the Apache 1.3.3 Web server on a UNIX platform. Note that not all Web sites will give out their Web server platform information, but most do. If you want to avoid the interactive mode, you can use the —dump option to dump the page on the screen (STDOUT). For example,

```
lynx -dump -head http://www.integrationlogic.com/
```

dumps the header to stdout. The —dump feature can be quite handy. For example,

```
lynx -dump -head http://webserver/new.gif > new.gif
```

allows you to save new.gif on the Web server host on a local file called new.gif.

The interactive mode allows you to browse a text-browser-friendly site in a reasonably nice manner.

mail

Syntax:

```
mail user@host [-s subject]  [< filename]
```

mail is the default SMTP mail client program. You can use this program to send or receive mail from your system. For example, if you run this program without any argument, it displays an & prompt and shows you the currently unread mail messages by listing them in a numeric list. To read a message, enter the index number, and the mail will be displayed. To learn more about mail, use the **?** command at the & prompt.

To send a message to a user called `kabir@integrationlogic.com` with the subject header "About your Red Hat book," run

```
mail  kabir@integrationlogic.com  -s "About your Red Hat
book"
```

You can then enter your mail message and press Ctrl+D to end the message. You can switch to your default text editor by entering ~v at the beginning of a line while you are in the compose mode.

If you have already prepared a mail message in a file, send it by using a command such as the following:

```
mail  kabir@nitec.com  -s "About your Red Hat book" <<
feedback.txt
```

This sends a message with the given subject line; the message consists of the contents of the feedback.txt file.

pine

Syntax:

```
pine
```

pine is a full-screen SMTP mail client that is quite user-friendly. If you typically use mail clients via Telnet, you should definitely try this program.

Because of its user-friendly interface, it is suitable for your Linux users who are not yet friends with Linux.

rlogin

Syntax:

```
rlogin [-l username] host
```

The rlogin command allows you to log in to a host remotely. For example, to log in to a host called `shell.myhost.com`, run

```
rlogin shell.myhost.com
```

Because rlogin is not considered safe, I recommend that you use it only in a closed LAN environment. The −l option allows you to specify a username to be used for authentication. If you want to log in to a host remotely without entering a password, create an .rhosts file in the user's home directory. Add the host name or IP address of the computer that you will use to issue the rlogin request. Again, because this is considered a security risk by many, I do not recommend wide use of rlogin.

talk

Syntax:

```
talk username tty
```

If you need to send a message to another user, e-mail works fine. But, if you need to communicate with another user in real time, similar to a telephone conversation, use the talk command.

To talk to another user who is logged in, use the following command:

```
talk ronak@csus.edu
```

The user who you request has to accept your talk request. After the user accepts your talk request, you can begin talking (typing) to each other. The talk program is terminated when either party executes Ctrl+C (the intr key).

telnet

Syntax:

```
telnet hostname or IP address [port]
```

This is the default Telnet client program. You can use this program to connect to a Telnet server. For example, the following opens a Telnet connection to the `shell.myportal.com` system if the named host runs a Telnet server:

```
telnet shell.myportal.com
```

After a connection is opened, you are prompted for your username and password. Upon successful login, you are allowed to access a local user account on the Telnet server.

wall

Syntax:

```
wall
```

The wall command allows you to send a text message to all users' terminals as long as they have not disabled write access to their tty via the mesg n command. After you type **wall**, you can enter a single- or multiline message and send it by pressing Ctrl+D.

Network Administrator's Commands

The commands discussed in this section enable you to gather information on network services and the network itself.

host

Syntax:

```
host [-a] host IP address
```

By default, the host program allows you to quickly check the IP address of a host. If you use the —a option, host returns various sorts of DNS information about the named host or IP address.

hostname

Syntax:

```
hostname
```

This program displays the host name of a system.

ifconfig

Syntax:

```
ifconfig [interface] [up | down] [netmask mask]
```

The ifconfig program allows you to configure a network interface. You can also see the state of an interface by using this program. For example, if you have previously configured your Red Hat Linux system for networking and have a preconfigured network interface device, eth0, you can run the following:

```
ifconfig eth0
```

You should see output similar to the following:

```
eth0 Link encap:Ethernet  HWaddr 00:C0:F6:98:37:37
inet addr:206.171.50.50  Bcast:206.171.50.63
Mask:255.255.255.240
UP BROADCAST RUNNING MULTICAST  MTU:1500  Metric:1
RX packets:9470 errors:0 dropped:0 overruns:0 frame:0
TX packets:7578 errors:0 dropped:0 overruns:0 carrier:0
collisions:0
Interrupt:5 Base address:0x340
```

Here, ifconfig reports that network interface device eth0 has an Internet address (inet addr) 206.171.50.50, a broadcast address (Bcast) 206.171.50.63, and network mask (255.255.255.240). The rest of the information shows how many packets this interface has received so far (RX packets), how many packets this interface has transmitted so far (TX packets), how many errors of different types have occurred so far, what interrupt address line is being used for this device, what I/O address base is being used, and so on.

You can run ifconfig without any arguments to get the full list of all network devices that are up.

You can use ifconfig to bring an interface up. For example, the following starts eth0 with IP address 206.171.50.50:

```
ifconfig eth0 206.171.50.50 netmask 255.255.255.240 \
broadcast 206.171.50.63
```

You can also quickly take down an interface by using the ifconfig command. For example, the following takes down the eth0 interface:

```
ifconfig eth0 down
```

netcfg

See the section on using netcfg to configure a network interface card in Chapter 7.

netstat

Syntax:

```
netstat [-r] [-a] [-c] [-i] [-n]
```

The netstat program displays the status of the network connections both to and from the local system. For example, the following displays all network connections on the local system:

```
netstat -a
```

To display the routing table, use the −r option. To display the network connection status on a continuous basis, use the −c option. To display information on all network interfaces, use the −i option. To display numeric IP addresses use the −n option.

nslookup

Syntax:

```
nslookup [-query=DNS record type] [hostname or IP] [name
server]
```

The nslookup command enables you to perform DNS queries. You can choose to query a DNS server in an interactive fashion, or just look up information immediately. For example,

```
nslookup -query=mx integrationlogic.com
```

immediately returns the MX records for the `integrationlogic.com` domain.

The following command does the same thing, but instead of using the default name server that is specified in the /etc/resolv.conf file, it uses `ns.nitec.com` as the name server:

```
nslookup -query=mx integrationlogic.com ns.nitec.com
```

You can also use −q instead of −query. For example, the following returns the IP address (Address record) for the named host name:

```
nslookup -q=a  www.formtrack.com
```

You can run nslookup in interactive mode, as well. Just run the command without any parameters, and you will see the nslookup prompt. At the nslookup prompt, you can enter ? to get help. If you plan to perform multiple DNS queries simultaneously, interactive mode can be very helpful. For example, to query the NS records for multiple domains, such as `ad-engine.com` and `classifiedworks.com`, simply enter the following command:

```
set query=ns
```

After you set the query type to ns, type **ad-engine.com** and wait for the reply; after you get the reply, try the next domain name; and so on. If you want to change the name server while at the nslookup prompt, use the server command. For example,

```
server ns.ad-engine.com
```

makes nslookup use `ns.ad-engine.com` as the name server. To quit interactive mode and return to your shell prompt, enter **exit** at the nslookup prompt.

ping

Syntax:

```
ping [-c count] [-s packet size] [-I interface]
```

This is one of the programs most widely used by network administrators. ping is used to check whether a remote computer is reachable via the TCP/IP protocol. Technically, this program sends an Internet Control Message Protocol (ICMP) echo request to the remote host. Because the response to an echo request is required by the protocol, the remote host is bound to send an echo response back. This allows the ping program to calculate the amount of time it takes to send a packet to a remote host. For example,

```
ping blackhole.nitec.com
```

sends ping messages to the blackhole.nitec.com host on a continuous basis. To stop the ping program, press Ctrl+C, which causes the program to display a set of statistics. Here is an example of output of the ping requests generated by the preceding command:

```
PING blackhole.nitec.com (209.63.178.15): 56 data bytes
64 bytes from 209.63.178.15: icmp_seq=0 ttl=53 time=141.5
ms
64 bytes from 209.63.178.15: icmp_seq=1 ttl=53 time=162.6
ms
64 bytes from 209.63.178.15: icmp_seq=2 ttl=53 time=121.4
ms
64 bytes from 209.63.178.15: icmp_seq=3 ttl=53 time=156.0
ms
64 bytes from 209.63.178.15: icmp_seq=4 ttl=53 time=126.4
ms
64 bytes from 209.63.178.15: icmp_seq=5 ttl=53 time=101.5
ms
64 bytes from 209.63.178.15: icmp_seq=6 ttl=53 time=98.7
ms
64 bytes from 209.63.178.15: icmp_seq=7 ttl=53 time=180.9
ms
```

```
64 bytes from 209.63.178.15: icmp_seq=8 ttl=53 time=126.2
ms
64 bytes from 209.63.178.15: icmp_seq=9 ttl=53 time=122.3
ms
64 bytes from 209.63.178.15: icmp_seq=10 ttl=53
time=127.1 ms

--- blackhole.nitec.com ping statistics ---
11 packets transmitted, 11 packets received, 0% packet
loss
round-trip min/avg/max = 98.7/133.1/180.9 ms
```

The preceding output shows 10 ping requests to the blackhole.nitec.com host. Because the program was interrupted after the 11th request, the statistics show that ping has transmitted 11 packets and has received all the packets, and therefore no packet loss has occurred. This is good, because packet loss is a sign of poor networking between the ping requester and the ping responder. The other interesting statistics are the round-trip minimum (min) time, the average (avg) time, and the maximum (max) time. The lower these numbers are, the better the routing is between the involved hosts. For example, if you ping a host internal to the same LAN, you should see the round-trip numbers in the one-millisecond range.

If you want ping to automatically stop after transmitting a number of packets, use the −c option. For example, the following sends ten ping requests to the named host:

```
ping -c 10 blackhole.nitec.com
```

By default, ping sends a 64-byte packet (56 data bytes + 8 header bytes). If you are also interested in controlling the size of the packet sent, use the −s option. For example,

```
ping -c 1024 -s 1016 reboot.nitec.com
```

sends a packet 1,024 (1016 + 8) bytes long to the remote host.

Caution

By sending large packets to a remote host running weak operating systems, you might cause the host to become very unusable to the user(s) on the remote host. This could be considered an attack and therefore is very likely to be illegal in most parts of the world. So, be very careful when you start experimenting with ping and someone else's computer.

route

Syntax:

```
route add -net network address netmask dev device
        route add -host hostname or IP dev device
        route add default gw hostname or IP
```

The route command enables you to control routing to and from your computer. To create a default route for your network, use the route command as follows:

```
route add -net network address netmask  device
```

For example, to create a default route for network 206.171.50.48 with a 255.255.255.240 netmask and eth0 as the interface, I can run the following:

```
route add -net 206.171.50.48 255.255.255.240 eth0
```

To set the default gateway, you can run the route command as follows:

```
route add  default gw gateway address device
```

For example, to set the default gateway address to 206.171.50.49, I can run the following command:

```
route add  default gw 206.171.50.49 eth0
```

You can verify that your network route and default gateway are properly set up in the routing table by using the following command:

```
route -n
```

Here is an example of output of the preceding command:

```
Kernel IP routing table

Destination    Gateway Genmask        Flags Metric Ref Use Iface

206.171.50.48 0.0.0.0 255.255.255.240 U     0      0   6   eth0

127.0.0.0      0.0.0.0 255.0.0.0       U     0      0   5   lo

0.0.0.0        206.171.50.49 0.0.0.0 UG     0      0   17  eth0
```

> **Tip**
>
> Make sure you have IP forwarding turned on in /etc/syscon-fig/network and also in the kernel to allow routing packets between two different network interfaces.

tcpdump

Syntax:

```
tcpdump expression
```

This is a great network debugging tool. For example, to trace all the packets between two hosts, `brat.nitec.com` and `reboot.nitec.com`, use the following command:

```
tcpdump host brat.nitec.com and reboot.nitec.com
```

This command makes tcpdump listen for packets between these two computers. If `reboot.nitec.com` starts sending ping requests to `brat.nitec.com`, the output may look something like the following:

```
tcpdump: listening on eth0
09:21:14.720000 reboot.nitec.com> brat.nitec.com: icmp:
echo request
09:21:14.720000 brat.nitec.com> reboot.nitec.com: icmp:
echo reply
09:21:15.720000 reboot.nitec.com> brat.nitec.com: icmp:
echo request
09:21:15.720000 brat.nitec.com> reboot.nitec.com: icmp:
echo reply
```

```
09:21:16.720000 reboot.nitec.com> brat.nitec.com: icmp:
echo request
09:21:16.720000 brat.nitec.com> reboot.nitec.com: icmp:
echo reply
09:21:17.730000 reboot.nitec.com> brat.nitec.com: icmp:
echo request
09:21:17.730000 brat.nitec.com> reboot.nitec.com: icmp:
echo reply
```

Suppose that you are having a problem connecting to an FTP server. You can use tcpdump on your LAN gateway system to see what is going on. For example,

```
tcpdump port ftp or ftp-data
```

displays the FTP-related packets that are originating and arriving to your network.

This allows you to debug a network problem at a low level. If you are experiencing a problem in using a service between two hosts, use tcpdump to identify the problem.

traceroute

Syntax:

```
traceroute host or IP address
```

This program allows you to locate network routing problems. traceroute displays the routes between two hosts by tricking the gateways between the hosts into responding to an ICMP TIME_EXCEEDED request. Here is an example of a traceroute from my local system to the blackhole.nitec.com host:

```
traceroute to blackhole.nitec.com (209.63.178.15), 30
hops max, 40 byte packets
 1 router (206.171.50.49)  4.137 ms  3.995 ms  4.738 ms
 2 PM3-001.v1.NET (206.171.48.10) 32.683 ms  33.295 ms
33.255 ms
```

```
 3 HQ-CS001.v1.NET (206.171.48.1) 42.263 ms   44.237 ms
36.784 ms
 4 ix.pxbi.net (206.13.15.97) 106.785 ms   63.585 ms
101.277 ms
 5 ix.pxbi.net (206.13.31.8) 86.283 ms   64.246 ms   69.749
ms
 6 ca.us.ixbm.net (165.87.22.10) 71.415 ms   72.319 ms
85.183 ms
 7 mae.elxi.net (198.32.136.128) 101.863 ms   80.257 ms
67.323 ms
 8 y.exli.net (207.173.113.146) 71.323 ms   104.685 ms
110.935 ms
 9 z.exli.net (207.173.113.217) 69.964 ms   137.858 ms
85.326 ms
10 z1.exli.net (207.173.112.251) 81.257 ms   107.575 ms
78.453 ms
11 209.210.249.50 (209.210.249.50) 90.701 ms   91.116 ms
109.491 ms
12 209.63.178.15 (209.63.178.15)  83.052 ms   76.604 ms
85.406 ms
```

Each line represents a hop; the more hops, the worse the route usually is. In other words, if you have only a few gateways between the source and the destination, then packets between these two hosts likely are going to be transferred at a reasonably fast pace. However, this won't be true all the time, because a single slow gateway can mess up the delivery time. Using traceroute, you can locate where your packets are going and where they are perhaps getting stuck. After you locate a problem point, contact the appropriate authorities to resolve the routing problem.

Process Management Commands

The commands discussed in this section are used to manage processes — running programs in your system.

bg

Syntax:

```
bg
```

This is a built-in shell command that is found in popular shells. The bg command allows you to put a suspended process into the background. For example, suppose that you run **du –a / | sort –rn > /tmp/du.sorted** to list all the files and directories in your system according to the disk usage (size) order and put the result in a file called /tmp/du.sorted. Depending on the number of files you have on your system, this can take a while. In such a case, you can simply suspend the command line using Ctrl+Z and type **bg** to send all the commands involved in the command line to the background, thus returning your shell prompt for other use.

Tip

If you want to run a command in the background from the start, simply append & to the end of the command line.

To find out what commands are running in the background, enter **jobs**, and you will see the list of background command lines. To bring a command from the background, use the fg command.

fg

Syntax:

```
fg [%job-number]
```

This is a built-in shell command that is found in popular shells. The fg command enables you to put a background process into the foreground. If you run this command without any argument, it brings forward the last command you put in the background. If you have multiple commands running in the background, you can use the jobs command to find the job number, and then supply this number as an argument for fg to bring the command to the foreground. For example, if jobs shows that you have two commands in the background, you can bring up the first command you put in the background by using the following:

```
fg %1
```

jobs

Syntax:

```
jobs
```

This is a built-in shell command that is found in popular shells. jobs enables you to view the list of processes running in the background or currently suspended.

Kill –signal PID

This command is used to send a signal to a process. Kill can be a built-in shell command for many popular shells, such as csh and tcsh. However, there is also an external kill program, which typically is found in the /bin directory. Both versions work the same way. To find out what signals you can send to processes via kill, you can run the following:

```
kill –l
```

You should see a list similar to the following:

```
 1) SIGHUP       2) SIGINT      3) SIGQUIT      4) SIGILL

 5) SIGTRAP      6) SIGIOT      7) SIGBUS       8) SIGFPE

 9) SIGKILL     10) SIGUSR1    11) SIGSEGV     12) SIGUSR2

13) SIGPIPE     14) SIGALRM    15) SIGTERM     17) SIGCHLD

18) SIGCONT     19) SIGSTOP    20) SIGTSTP     21) SIGTTIN

22) SIGTTOU     23) SIGURG     24) SIGXCPU     25) SIGXFSZ

26) SIGVTALRM   27) SIGPROF    28) SIGWINCH    29) SIGIO

30) SIGPWR
```

The preceding output is produced by the built-in kill command in the GNU Bourne-Again Shell (/bin/bash). Other shells or the /bin/kill command might print the output a bit differently. For example, /bin/kill –l produces the following output:

```
HUP INT QUIT ILL TRAP IOT UNUSED FPE KILL USR1 SEGV USR2
PIPE ALRM TERM STKFLT CHLD CONT STOP TSTP TTIN TTOU IO
XCPU XFSZ VTALRM PROF WINCH
```

For example, to send a SIGKILL (9) to a process with PID 1234, run

```
kill -KILL 1234
```

or you can also run

```
kill -9 1234
```

You can either use a signal's name (without the SIG prefix) or use its numeric value as the signal identifier as shown previously.

killall

This utility lets you kill a process by name. For example, if you have a process called signal_demo.pl and want to kill it without typing its PID, you can run

```
killall -KILL signal_demo.pl
```

When you do not provide a signal name, killall automatically sends the SIGTERM signal. However, be very careful when using killall, because it kills all instances of the named command. Sometimes, the convenience of not having to know the PID can go sour.

ps

This utility produces a report of all the processes in a system. For example, when I run ps from a login shell, it shows the following output:

```
PID   TTY STAT TIME COMMAND
31795 p7  S    0:00 -tcsh
31811 p7  R    0:00 ps
```

As you can see, ps provides a tabular report. Here, ps shows that I'm running two processes: the —tcsh shell, which really is the /bin/tcsh shell run as a login shell, and the ps process itself. Table A-1 explains the meaning of the common output fields for ps.

Table A-1 *Output Fields for ps*

Field	Explanation
USER or UID	Process owner's username.
PID	Process ID.
%CPU	CPU utilization of the process. Because the time base over which this is computed varies, it is possible for this to exceed 100 percent.
%MEM	Percentage of memory (in kilobytes) utilization of the process.
SIZE	Size (in kilobytes) of virtual memory used by the process.
RSS	Resident set size or size of real memory (in kilobytes) used by the process.
TTY	Terminal (tty) associated with the process. Usually, the tty name is shortened. For example, p7 is displayed for /dev/ttyp7.
STAT	State of the process. States of processes are represented by characters, such as R (running or ready to run), S (sleeping), I (idle), Z (zombie), D (disk wait), P (page wait), W (swapped out), N (lowered priority by nice), T (terminated), < (execution priority raised by superuser), and so on.
START	Process start time or date.
TIME	Total CPU time used by the process.
COMMAND	Command line being executed.
NI	The nice priority number.
PRI	Process priority number.
PPID	Process ID (PID) of the parent process.
WCHAN	Name of the kernel function where a process is sleeping. The name of the function is retrieved from the /boot/System.map file.
FLAGS	A numeric flag associated with the process.

The ps utility also accepts several command-line arguments. Table A-2 shows the commonly used options.

Table A-2 *Commonly Used ps options*

Options	Description
A	Show processes belonging to all users.
E	Show process environment variables after the command line being executed.
L	Show output in long format.
U	Show username and process start time.

Continued

Table A-2 *Continued*

Options	Description
W	Show output in wide format. Normally, output is truncated if it cannot fit in a line. Using this option, you can prevent truncation.
Txx	Show processes that are associated with xx tty device.
X	Show processes without controlling tty.

A few examples of using ps options are provided next.

To see all the processes you are running at any time, run the following:

```
ps u
```

An example of the output of the preceding command is shown here:

```
USER  PID %CPU %MEM  SIZE   RSS TTY STAT START TIME COMMAND
kabir  18  0.0  0.8  1556  1040 p5 S   08:41 0:00 -tcsh
kabir 135  0.0  0.8  1560  1040 p7 S   09:03 0:00 -tcsh
kabir 852 53.8  0.6  1604   788 p5 R   09:33 0:04 perl ./eatcpu.pl
kabir 855  0.0  0.3   848   484 p7 R   09:34 0:00 ps u
```

This shows all the processes that are running for a user called kabir. Notice that ps itself is listed in the output. The first two lines show that kabir is running two tcsh shell sessions. The third line is very interesting, because it shows that a Perl script called eatcpu.pl is utilizing approximately 53.8 percent of the CPU. The STAT flags indicate that the Perl script and the ps utility are the only running (or runnable) processes here. By looking at the TTY field, you can tell which process is attached to which tty.

In the next example, ps is told to display all the processes (excluding the one not associated with any controlling tty):

```
ps au
```

To find out what processes are owned by a particular user, run

```
ps au | grep username
```

where *username* is the name of the actual user.

For example, ps au | grep sheila will show all the interactive processes (processes associated with a tty) being run by a user called sheila. Typically, normal users are not allowed to run daemon processes or processes that are not associated with a tty. However, if you just want to find out whether any such processes exist for any user, run

```
ps aux
```

The x option tells ps to list processes that are detached from terminals. You can identify these processes by looking at the TTY field, which displays a ? character instead of a shortened name of a tty device such as p7 (/dev/ttyp7).

To find the PID of a process's parent, you can run

```
ps l PID
```

where *PID* is the PID of the process.

For example, if you want to find the parent of a process with PID 123, run **ps l 123**, and the parent's PID will be listed in the PPID field of the report.

To determine what initial environment variables are available to processes, run

```
ps e
```

The environment information is appended to the COMMAND field.

top

Using top, you can monitor process activity in real time. The top screen is automatically updated to provide a fresh look at the running state of the system. Here are the descriptions for the first five header lines displayed by top.

- **Line 1.** The uptime line, which shows the current time of the system, how long the system has been up since the last reboot, how many users are currently on the system, and three load average numbers. The load averages are the average numbers of processes ready to run during the last 1, 5, and 15 minutes.

- **Line 2.** The process statistics line that shows the total number of processes running at the time of the last top screen update. This line also shows the number of sleeping, running, zombie, and stopped processes.

- **Line 3.** Displays CPU statistics, which include percentage of CPU time used by the user, system, niced, and idle processes.

- **Line 4.** Provides memory statistics, which include total available memory, free memory, used memory, shared memory, and memory used for buffers.

- **Line 5.** Provides virtual memory or swap statistics, which include total available swap space, used swap space, free swap space, and cached swap space. The rest of the lines are similar to a ps-generated report.

Using top, you can identify which processes are using most of your resources, simply by looking at the few entries in the ps-like output. The process that consumes the second-most resources is the top utility itself! When you run top to monitor other processes, top takes some resources to run, but you still get a good idea about which process is consuming how much resources. To exit top, type 'q' at any time.

Task Automation Commands

The commands discussed in this section show you how to run unattended tasks.

at

The at utility allows you to queue a command for execution at a later time. For example, to run the disk usage summary generator utility called du at 8:40 p.m., you can run at as follows:

```
at 20:40
```

The at command displays a prompt such as at>, where you can enter the du command as follows:

```
at> du -a > /tmp/du.out
```

Here, the output of du is directed to a file. After you enter the command (the du command, in this example), at displays the prompt again. You can press Ctrl+D to exit. You will see a message similar to the one here:

```
at> <EOT>
warning: commands will be executed using /bin/sh
job 1 at 1999-12-06 20:40
```

This means that at has scheduled the du −a > /tmp/du.out job to be run by the at daemon (atd) at 8:40 p.m., 12/06/1999. You can use a wide variety of time formats to specify the time of execution. For example, instead of saying at 20:40, you can say at 8:40pm, as well. You can also specify the date along with the time. For example, 8:40pm feb 23, 10am + 5 days, 12:30pm tomorrow, midnight, and noon are all valid time specifications.

The scheduled job is run via the atd daemon process, which is started by init for run level 3 (multiuser mode). If you want to restrict use of the at facility, you can create an /etc/at.allow file and list all the users who are allowed to run it. Remember to enter a single username per line. Any user not listed in the allow file is refused access to the at facility. On the other hand, if you want to deny only a few users but allow the rest, you can create a similar file called /etc/at.deny. All usernames listed in this file are denied at access.

atq

This command is used to verify that your at job is in the job queue. When you run this command it shows the currently scheduled jobs in the queue. All the scheduled jobs are stored in the /var/spool/at directory.

atrm

To stop a scheduled at job, you can run the atrm command to remove a job. You need to know the job sequence number to remove a job with atrm. To find out what jobs you have scheduled, run the atq command. To delete any job, use atrm *job#*. For example, to remove job #1, run atrm 1.

crontab

The crontab command is used to to create and modify cron job settings. For example, if a user is allowed to run cron jobs, he can run crontab −e to create and edit cron job entries. A cron job specification has the following format:

```
minute(s) hour(s) day(s) month weekday username command
argument(s)
```

The first five time specification fields are discussed in Table A-3.

Table A-3 *Cron Time Specification Fields*

Fields	Description	Range
Minutes(s)	One or more minutes in an hour. You can specify a comma-separated list of minutes.	0–59
Hour(s)	One or more hours in a day. You can specify a comma-separated list of hours.	0–23, where 0 is midnight
Day(s)	One or more days in a month. You can specify a comma-separated list of days.	1–31
Month	One or more months in a year. You can specify a comma-separated list of months.	1–12
Weekday	One or more days in a week. You can specify a comma-separated list of days.	1–7, where 1 is Monday

For any of the fields shown in Table A-3, you can use * as a wildcard. The following is an example cron job specification:

```
01 * * * * root /some/script
```

This states that /some/script is to be run every first minute of every hour, every day, every month, and every weekday. The script will be run as the root user. To run this script every ten minutes, a cron job such as the following can be defined:

```
0,10,20,30,40,50 * * * * root /some/script
```

To run the same script but only once a month, a cron job can be scheduled as follows:

```
01 1 1 * * root /some/script
```

Here, the script will be run at 1:01 a.m. on the first day of every month.

The default cron job for the system is /etc/crontab, which includes a few interesting cron job entries, such as the following:

```
SHELL=/bin/bash
PATH=/sbin:/bin:/usr/sbin:/usr/bin
MAILTO=root

# run-parts
01 * * * * root run-parts /etc/cron.hourly
02 4 * * * root run-parts /etc/cron.daily
22 4 * * 0 root run-parts /etc/cron.weekly
42 4 1 * * root run-parts /etc/cron.monthly
```

These cron jobs are used to run the run-parts script located in the /usr/bin directory. This script is run every hour, every day, every week, and every month using the four cron job specifications in the preceding listing. It takes a directory name as an argument and runs all the scripts or programs located in that directory. For example, consider the first cron entry in the preceding listing. It states that the run-parts script should be run at the first minute of every hour. The script is fed the argument /etc/cron.hourly. Because the script runs all the files located in this directory, the entire process effectively works as if all the files in the /etc/cron.hourly directory had been set up as cron jobs. This trick allows you to put new files in the /etc/cron.hourly directory and automatically have it scheduled for an hourly run. Similarly, the other three cron entries allow you to run any program on a daily, weekly, or monthly basis simply by placing them in the /etc/cron.daily, /etc/cron.weekly, or /etc/cron.monthly directory, respectively. This makes it easy to create cron jobs for most everything without really having to configure a cron entry.

For example, suppose that you want to synchronize your system time with a remote time server on a daily basis. You decide to use the rdate utility to set the time via the Internet. The command to run is the following:

```
/usr/bin/rdate —s  time.server.host.tld
```

Because the default /etc/crontab contains a cron entry that allows you to schedule daily cron jobs simply by placing the script or program in the /etc/cron.daily directory, you can create a simple shell script such as the following and place it in the /etc/cron.daily directory:

```
#!/bin/sh
/usr/bin/rdate —s time.server.host.tld
```

Your job is done. Every day at 4:02 a.m., your script will run along with all the other scripts and programs in the /etc/cron.daily directory.

Productivity Commands

The commands discussed in this section help you to increase your productivity.

bc

Syntax:

```
bc
```

This is an interactive calculator that also implements a calculator-specific language. When you run bc without any arguments, it interprets your input as calculator programming statements. For example, to multiply 1024 by 4, simply enter **1024*4**, and the result is displayed. The current result can be reused by using the period character.

cal

Syntax:

```
cal [month] [year]
```

This nifty program displays a nicely formatted calendar for the month or year specified in the command line. If you do not specify anything as an argument, the calendar for the current month is displayed. To see the calendar for an entire year, enter the year in 1–9999 range.

ispell

Syntax:

```
ispell filename
```

The ispell program allows you to correct spelling mistakes in a text file in an interactive fashion. If you have a misspelling in the file, the program suggests a spelling and gives you options to replace it with a correctly spelled word. This is the spell checker for text files.

mesg

Syntax:

```
mesg [y | n]
```

The mesg program allows you to enable or disable public write access to your terminal. For example,

```
mesg y
```

enables write access to your terminal such that another user on the same system can use the write command to write text messages to you. The n option allows you to disable write access. If you do not want to be bothered by anyone at any time, add **mesg n** to your login script (.login) file.

write

Syntax:

```
write username tty
```

The write program allows you to write text messages to the named user if she has not disabled write access to her tty. For example, the following command enables you to type a text message onscreen:

```
write  shoeman
```

When you finish the message by pressing Ctrl+D, the message is displayed on user shoeman's terminal. If the user is logged in more than once, you have to specify the terminal name, as well. For example,

```
write  shoeman ttyp0
```

allows you to write to shoeman and display the message on terminal ttyp0. If someone has multiple terminals opened, run the w or who command to see which tty is the most suitable.

Shell Commands

This section describes some very basic shell commands.

alias

Syntax:

```
alias   name of the alias = command
```

This is a built-in shell command that is available in most popular shells. alias lets you create aliases for commands. For example,

```
alias dir  ls -l
```

creates an alias called dir for the ls –l command. To see the entire alias list, run alias without any argument.

history

Syntax:

```
history
```

This is a built-in shell command that is available in most popular shells. history displays a list of commands you have recently entered at the command line. The number of commands that history displays is limited by an environment variable called "history." For example, if you add **set history = 100** to your .login file, then whenever you log in, the history command remembers up to 100 command lines. The commands you see in the history can be easily rerun by entering their index number with a ! sign. For example, suppose the you see the following listings after you enter the history command:

```
1  10:25   vi irc-bot.h
2  10:25   vi irc-bot.c
3  10:26   which make
```

To run the vi irc-bot.c command again, simply enter **!2** in the command line.

set

Syntax:

```
set  var = value
```

This is a built-in shell command that is available in most popular shells. set allows you to set environment variables with specific values. For example,

```
set foo = bar
```

sets a new environment variable foo to have bar as the value. To see the list of all environment variables, run set by itself. To view the value of a specific environment variable, such as path, run the following:

```
echo $path
```

This shows you the value of the named environment variable. If you use this command quite often to set a few special environment variables, add it to .login or .profile or your shell's dot file so that the special environment variables are automatically set when you log in.

lpr

Syntax:

```
lpr [-i indentcols] [-P printer] [filename]
```

The lpr command sends a file to the print spool to be printed. If no filename is given, data from standard input is assumed.

The −i option gives you the option of starting the printing at a specific column. To specify a particular printer, you can use the −P printer option. The following example attempts to print the file main.c:

```
lpr main.c
```

lprm

Syntax:

```
lprm [-a] [jobid] [all]
```

The lprm command sends a request to lpd to remove an item from the print queue. The print jobs to be removed can be specified by the job ID or username, or they can include all items.

To remove all jobs in all print queues:

```
lprm -a all
```

To remove all jobs for the user kiwee on the printer p1:

```
lprm -Pp1 kiwee
```

Appendix B

Linux Resources

Usenet Newsgroups

The following Usenet newsgroups can be a great place to learn about advances in Linux, engage in Linux-specific discussions, and find answers to questions you might have.

The comp.os.linux hierarchy

Linux has its own hierarchy of Usenet newsgroups. These groups are strictly Linux-only. Before you post an article or a question in any of these newsgroups (or any Usenet newsgroup), make sure you know the charter of the group. In particular, when you are looking for answers to your questions or solutions to your problems, make sure that you have already read the available FAQs, man pages, and how-to documentation. If you post a question that has already been answered in a FAQ or a how-to document, chances are that some people who actively participate in that group might not take it kindly. Also, be careful when you post the same question in multiple groups (known as cross-posting) in the hope that you are increasing your chances of getting answers. As long as your post is relevant to the group, it is okay.

comp.os.linux.advocacy (unmoderated)

This newsgroup is intended for discussion of the benefits of Linux compared with other operating systems.

comp.os.linux.announce (moderated)

This newsgroup is intended for all Linux-specific announcements. You will find information on new Linux software, bug and security alerts, and user group information here.

comp.os.linux.answers (moderated)

Linux FAQs, how-to documents, readme files, and other informative sources are posted in this newsgroup. If you have a question on something, check this newsgroup before posting your question in any Linux newsgroup.

comp.os.linux.development.apps (unmoderated)

This newsgroup is intended for Linux developers who want to discuss development issues with others.

comp.os.linux.hardware (unmoderated)

This newsgroup is intended for hardware-specific discussions. If you have a question about a piece of hardware that you are trying to use with Linux, look for help here.

comp.os.linux.m68k (unmoderated)

This newsgroup is intended for Motorola 68K architecture-specific Linux discussion.

comp.os.linux.alpha (unmoderated)

This newsgroup is intended for Compaq/Digital Alpha architecture-specific discussion.

comp.os.linux.networking (unmoderated)

This newsgroup is intended for networking-related discussion.

comp.os.linux.x (unmoderated)

This newsgroup is intended for discussion relating to X Window System, version 11-compatible software, including servers, clients, libraries, and fonts, running under Linux.

comp.os.linux.development.system (unmoderated)

This newsgroup is intended for kernel hackers and module developers. You will find ongoing discussions on the development of the Linux operating system proper: kernel, device drivers, loadable modules, and so forth.

comp.os.linux.setup (unmoderated)

This newsgroup is intended for discussion on installation and system administration issues.

comp.os.linux.misc (unmoderated)

This is the bit-bucket for the comp.os.linux hierarchy. Any discussions not suitable for the other newsgroups in this hierarchy are discussed here.

Miscellaneous Linux newsgroups

The following newsgroups are considered not mainstream Linux newsgroups, because most of them are geographically oriented and typically used for local Linux-related announcements for Linux user group meetings and events:

- `alt.uu.comp.os.linux.questions`
- `alt.fan.linus-torvalds`
- `aus.computers.linux`
- `dc.org.linux-users`
- `de.alt.sources.linux.patches`
- `de.comp.os.linux.hardware`
- `de.comp.os.linux.misc`
- `de.comp.os.linux.networking`
- `de.comp.os.x`
- `ed.linux`
- `fido.linux-ger`
- `fj.os.linux`
- `fr.comp.os.linux`
- `han.sys.linux`
- `hannet.ml.linux.680x0`

- `it.comp.linux.pluto`
- `maus.os.linux`
- `maus.os.linux68k`
- `no.linux`
- `okinawa.os.linux`
- `tn.linux`
- `tw.bbs.comp.linux`
- `ucb.os.linux`
- `uiuc.sw.linux`
- `umich.linux`

Mailing Lists

Mailing lists provide a good way of getting information directly to your e-mail account. If you are interested in Linux news, announcements, and other discussions, mailing lists can be quite helpful. This is especially true of mailing lists that provide a digest option. Such mailing lists send a digest of all daily or weekly messages to your e-mail address.

General lists

The following Linux mailing lists are general in nature. They provide good general discussions of Linux news and helpful information for beginning Linux users.

Linux-announce

Subscribe to Linux-announce by sending e-mail to: `linux-announce-request@redhat.com` with the word "subscribe" in the subject line of the message.

linux-list

To subscribe, send e-mail to `linux-list-request@ssc.com` with the word "subscribe" in the body of your message.

linux-newbie

To subscribe, send e-mail to `majordomo@vger.rutgers.edu` with the words "subscribe linux-newbie" in the body of your message.

linuxusers

To subscribe, send e-mail to `majordomo@dmu.ac.uk` with the words "subscribe linuxusers" in the body of your message.

Security alert lists

The following mailing lists deal with Linux and computer security issues. I strongly recommend that you subscribe to the bugtraq mailing list immediately.

linux-security

This is a mailing list hosted by Red Hat Software, Inc. To subscribe, send e-mail to `linux-security-request@redhat.com` with the words "subscribe linux-security" in your subject line.

bugtraq

Although BugTraq is not specific to Linux, it is a great bug alert resource. To subscribe, send e-mail to `listserv@netspace.org` with the body of the message reading "SUBSCRIBE bugtraq *your-firstname your-lastname*."

Special lists

The following mailing lists deal with two issues: Linux as a server platform and Linux as a desktop platform.

SERVER-LINUX

To subscribe, send e-mail to `listserv@netspace.org` with the words "subscribe SERVER-LINUX" in your subject line.

WORKSTATION-LINUX

To subscribe, send e-mail to `listserv@netspace.org` with the words "subscribe WORKSTATION-LINUX" in your subject line.

Web Sites

Many Web sites provide Linux-oriented information. Here are few good ones.

General resources

The following Web sites are general in nature, and most of them act as portal sites:

- http://www.redhat.com
- http://www.linuxresources.com/
- http://linuxcentral.com/
- http://www.linuxcare.com/

Publications

The following Web sites are official Web sites for various Linux publications:

- http://www.linuxworld.com/
- http://www.linuxgazette.com/
- http://www.linuxjournal.com/

Software stores

The following Web sites offer commercial Linux software:

- http://www.linuxmall.com/
- http://www.cheapbytes.com
- http://www.lsl.com

Security resources

The following Web sites deal with computer security:

- http://www.cert.org
- http://www.rootshell.com/
- http://www.replay.com/redhat/

Index

source

Syntax:

```
source filename
```

This is a built-in shell command that is available in most popular shells. source lets you read and execute commands from the named file in the current shell environment.

unalias

Syntax:

```
unalias   name of the alias
```

This is a built-in shell command that is available in most popular shells. unalias lets you remove an alias for a command. For example,

```
unalias dir
```

removes an alias called dir. To remove all aliases, use * as the argument.

Printing–Specific Commands

This section discusses commands that help you to print from your Linux system.

lpq

Syntax:

```
lpq [-al] [-P printer]
```

The lpq command lists the status of the printers. If lpq is entered without any arguments, then information about the default printer is given.

The –P option specifies information about a particular printer. The –a option returns the status of all printers.

With the –l option, lpq reports the job identification number, username who requested the print job, originating host, rank in queue, job description, and the size of the job.